AN IDEOLOGICAL HISTORY
OF THE
COMMUNIST PARTY OF CHINA

(Volume 2)

www.royalcollins.com

An Ideological History of the Communist Party of China

(Volume 2)

Zheng Qian

Zheng Qian (Chief Editor)
Translated by Sun Li and Shelly Bryant

An Ideological History of the Communist Party of China, Volume 2

Zheng Qian
Translated by Sun Li and Shelly Bryant

First English Edition 2020
By Royal Collins Publishing Group Inc.
BKM ROYALCOLLINS PUBLISHERS PRIVATE LIMITED
www.royalcollins.com

Original Edition © Guangdong Education Publishing House, China
All rights reserved.

No part of this publication may be reproduced, stored in a retrieval system, or transmitted, in any form or by any means, electronic, mechanical, photocopying or otherwise, without the written permission from the publisher.

Copyright © Royal Collins Publishing Group Inc.
Groupe Publication Royal Collins Inc.
BKM ROYALCOLLINS PUBLISHERS PRIVATE LIMITED

Headquarters: 550-555 boul. René-Lévesque O Montréal (Québec) H2Z1B1 Canada
India office: 805 Hemkunt House, 8th Floor, Rajendra Place, New Delhi 110 008

ISBN: 978-1-4878-0391-9

We are grateful for the financial assistance of B&R Book Program in the publication of this book.

Contents

Chapter 1: Expansion and Preparation (1949–1978): The Circuitous Process of the Integration of Marxism into China and its Corresponding Rationale ... 3

    I. Four Stages in the Localization of Marxism in China over a Twenty-nine-year Span ... 4

    II: Challenges to Choosing Modes for Socialist Reform ... 11

    III. The Delayed Modernization of Marxism ... 16

    IV. Expansion and Preparation: The Features of the Localization of Marxism in China over a Twenty-nine-year Span ... 22

Chapter 2: Two Theories of the New Democracy ... 25

    I. The Shift from New Democratic Revolutionary Theory to New Democratic Socialization Theory ... 25

    II. Preliminary Exploration into Building a New Democratic Society ... 32

    III. Formation of the Theory of Building a New Democratic Nation ... 38

    IV. The Sum of the Theory of Building a New Democratic Nation: The Common Program ... 48

Chapter 3: The Development of New Democracy in the Implementation of the Common Program — 57

I. The Implementation of the Policy of a New Democratic Nation and the Recovery and Development of the National Economy — 58

II. The Party's Innovation in its Rural Policy in the Early Stages of New China — 63

III. Consolidation or Transition: Debating a Major Issue — 70

IV. Full Development of New Democratic Construction — 77

V. The Achievements of New Democratic Construction and Flaws in Ideological Recognition — 87

Chapter 4: New Thoughts on the Shift Toward Socialism and the Soviet Mode — 97

I. The Transition to Socialism Ahead of Schedule and its Causes — 97

II. Fundamental Features of the Overall Direction During the Transition — 112

III. Innovation in Marxist Theory During the Transition to Socialism — 121

Chapter 5: A Good Beginning for the Second Leap of the Localization of Marxism in China — 133

I. What is Socialism? — 134

II. Emancipating the Mind and Taking Our Own Way — 140

III. The Initiation of the New Conception on the Path of Socialist Construction as a Result of the Second Combination — 145

IV. The Eighth National Congress of the CPC and the Important Evolution of the Thought and Theory of Building the Ruling Party — 158

V. The Paradigm of the Localization of Marxism in China:
Theory of the Contradictions in a Socialist Society   164

Chapter 6: The Localization of Marxism in China Deviates from the Right Direction   173

I. The Deviation of the Rectification Movement from its
Original Intention   175

II. The Great Leap Forward: An Extremist Catching-up
Strategy   187

III. The People's Commune Movement Rushing into Transition 192

Chapter 7: Deepening the Understanding of Socialism in the Initial Rectification of the Left-leaning Errors   199

I. Reflection on the Nine-month Rectification of the
Left-leaning Errors   199

II. Investigation and Research into Rectifying the Ideological
Line   203

III. Specific Marxist Principles as the Guideline for Practice   208

IV. Democratization and the Localization of Marxism in China 220

Chapter 8: Two Trends of Development in Adjustment   229

I. Intra-Party Investigation and Research into Rectifying
the Line of Thought   230

II. Intra-Party Adjustment Toward a Deeper Understanding
of Socialism   235

III. The 7,000 People's Congress and Subsequent Adjustments 243

IV. Conflicting Patterns Resulting from Divergent Directions
of Economic and Political Development   253

Chapter 9: The Destiny of the Localization of Marxism in China During the Cultural Revolution — 261

  I. The Concept of Socialism at the Beginning of the Cultural Revolution — 262
  II. The Theory and Practice of Continuing the Revolution Under the Dictatorship of the Proletariat — 277
  III. The Theory of Continuing Revolution in Practice — 283
  IV. Resistance and Struggle: Relentless Exploration of the Localization of Marxism in China During the Cultural Revolution — 299

Chapter 10: The Great Ideological Liberation Movement and the Start of the Second Leap — 311

  I. Moving Forward Hesitantly — 313
  II. Discussion on the Criterion of Truth and the Preliminary Establishment of the Marxist Line of Thought — 321
  III. The New Starting Point of Socialism with Chinese Characteristics and the Beginning of the Second Historical Leap in the Localization of Marxism in China — 329

Notes — *341*

Index — *359*

AN IDEOLOGICAL HISTORY
OF THE
COMMUNIST PARTY OF CHINA

(Volume 2)

CHAPTER 1

Expansion and Preparation (1949–1978)

The Circuitous Process of the Integration of Marxism into China and its Corresponding Rationale

The Thirteenth National Congress of the Communist Party of China put forward the important viewpoint of the two historical leaps in the localization of Marxism in China, noting, "The combination of Marxism and China's practice has gone on for more than sixty years. In this process, there were two historic leaps. The first leap took place in the period of the new democratic revolution, and the second leap took place after the Third Plenary Session of the Eleventh Central Committee."[1] How should we summarize the course and characteristics of the localization of Marxism between these two leaps? Gong Yuzhi has drawn the reasonable conclusion that this was the "period of the extension of the first leap and the preparation (or brewing) of the second leap."[2]

I

Four Stages in the Localization of Marxism in China over a Twenty-nine-year Span

The localization of Marxism in China was a historical category that had different ideas, focuses, objectives, and applications in different historical periods. Its premise was to reveal the law of its development in an effort to examine the process and characteristics of its various stages. According to the various understandings of Marxism and socialism in different periods from 1949 to 1978, as well as the choice of mode and practice used at those times, the twenty-nine year process of localizing Marxism can be roughly divided into four stages.

The first stage was the period of implementing the New Democracy Program for the Founding of the People's Republic (1949–1952). In the first three years of the founding of New China, under the guidance of the new democratic theory produced by the first leap in the integration of Marxism into China, the Party fully implemented the New Democratic Outline of the Common Program of the Chinese People's Political Consultative Conference (or the Common Program). Economically, on the basis of giving priority to the development of the state-owned economy, starting from the very backward level of productivity at the time, the policy of giving consideration to both public and private interests, mutual assistance between urban and rural areas, and internal and external exchanges was implemented. Under the leadership of the state-owned economy, various economic components coexisted, plans coexisted with markets, and various forms of distribution and accumulation coexisted. At the same time, the implementation of the new democratic political and cultural program put productivity, production relations, superstructure, and economic foundations in a state of basic adaptation.

Based on the victorious new democratic revolution, with the goal of transitioning to socialism and based on the situation in colonial and semi-colonial areas, the full development of new democracy made the New Democratic Outline for the Founding of the People's Republic a prerequisite for the establishment of socialism in terms of politics, economy, and culture. Its distinct feature was to treat capitalism, the national bourgeoisie, the market economy, and the individual peasant economy correctly. Instead of generally eliminating capitalism, the state encouraged all private undertakings that were beneficial to the national economy and people's livelihoods to operate actively, while also implementing a mixed economy, permitting markets and plans, allowing state-owned, cooperative, and private economies, and coexisting with and making prosperous both the individual and cooperative economies. In these respects, it was very close to Lenin's new economic policy, his theory of the transitional period after 1921,[3] and Marx's theory of eastern society. As far as the ideological line of seeking truth from facts was concerned, it inherited and developed the essence of Marxism. Three years of economic recovery and social transformation saw miraculous achievements. While people marveled at these achievements, it was also important for them to pay great attention to the guidelines and system design that had led to such achievements. It was noted, "At the beginning of the formulation of the Common Program, people doubted whether we really wanted to implement it, but over the past three years we have really implemented it, and it has gained prestige among the people and all parties."[4]

Although only three years had passed since the implementation of the New Democratic Program for the Founding of the People's Republic, it was a brilliant chapter in the localization of Marxism in China. It greatly enriched the theory of underdeveloped countries' transition to socialism through particular paths. It had distinct Chinese characteristics both in form and in content. The Communist Party of China, led by Mao Zedong, consciously combined the basic principles of Marxism with the concrete situation in China and independently created a model different from the European revolutionary road.

The second stage was the period of imitating the Soviet model (1953–1956). After 1953, on the basis of the recovery of the national economy and according to the urgent needs of the changed domestic and international situation, the experience of the socialist construction of the Soviet Union, and the understanding of socialism at that time, an effort to realize the strategy of surpassing advanced countries, the Central Committee proposed the general line of that period. This general line included the gradual realization of the socialist industrialization of the country and the gradual transformation of agriculture, the handicraft industry, the capitalist industry, and commerce. In economic construction, the Party opted for a policy of giving priority to the development of heavy industry, while in social transformation, it chose to transform capitalist industry and commerce in the form of state capitalism and the policy of peaceful redemption. It also chose to transform agriculture and the individual handicraft industry through gradual transition. Under the guidance of this general line, the foundation of industrialization was preliminarily laid and a path of socialist transformation suited to China's national conditions was opened up, thus smoothly achieving the goal of socialism. This was another great victory for the Chinese Communist Party under Mao's leadership, and an important achievement for the integration of Marxism into China.

From the perspective of model selection, if the former three years were close to Lenin's new economic policy model, then the Stalin model was the basic foundation and standard after 1953. Mao many times later called this "generally learning from foreign experience,"[5] implementing a form similar to the Soviet model "fundamentally, though in the different details." In terms of economic construction, especially heavy industry, "almost everything is copied from the Soviet Union, with little creativity of its own" and "with little ingenuity or independence."[6] In terms of political and social transformation, in accordance with the Soviet model, it emphasized the elimination of individual production in capitalism, agriculture, and handicraft industries, the implementation of a single socialist public ownership, and the limitation of the scope and depth of the role of the commodity economy. This was in line with the then current notion that the general line of the transitional period was to solve the problem of ownership,[7] or in other words, to make private ownership "gradually illegal,"[8] "to make capitalism and small-scale production extinct,"[9] and so on. Its essence was to make socialist ownership of the means of production the sole economic basis of the Chinese nation and society.[10] Therefore, "the transitional period is inevitably a period of struggle between capitalism, which is dying, and communism, which is growing."[11] The understanding of Lenin's transitional theory reflected in the general line of the propaganda outline of the transitional period was actually Lenin's wartime Communist thought interpreted and developed by Stalin before 1920, rather than Lenin's new economic theory centered on the development of productive forces in his later years.[12] This was the common practice of some postwar socialist countries based on the traditional socialist concept prevailing in the international communist movement at that time. As far as China was concerned, its characteristic was often said to be the "Sinicization" of the Soviet model in a sense (at that time, the Soviet model was starting to become the object of reform), or the "Sinicization" of Marxism mediated through the Stalin model.

Because of the Party's profound grasp of the national conditions, rich experience, and great creativity in the period of the democratic revolution, although it mainly imitated the Soviet model during these four years, it had distinct Chinese characteristics in form, especially during the three major reforms. In political system construction, there were several unique, successful creations (such as the people's democratic dictatorship, people's Congress system, multi-party cooperation, political consultation system, etc.), which reflected the combination of the universal truth of Marxism with China's real situation.

The third stage was the period of reforming the Soviet model and exploring the path of self-construction (1956–1966). From 1956, with the tide of reform shifting in socialist countries all over the world, in view of the problems exposed by the Soviet model, Mao Zedong once again proposed to the entire Party the task of breaking through the Soviet model and realizing the integration of Marxism into China's context, similar to the first imitation and breakthrough of the Soviet model in the period of the democratic revolution at the beginning of China's comprehensive socialist construction. He pointed out that now that the Party had its own preliminary practice and the experience and lessons from the Soviet Union, it should put more emphasis on starting from China's national conditions and diligently "carry out a second combination and find the right way to carry out socialist revolution and construction in China."[13]

Marked by the convening of the Eighth National Congress of the Communist Party of China and the publication of important historical documents such as *On Ten Relations* and *On the Correct Handling of Contradictions Among the People*, China began the initial reform of the soviet model, making 1956 a peak in the integration of Marxism into China during the socialist period. The whole Party "learned from the Soviet Union" and emancipated the mind. It hoped to find a path of socialist construction with Chinese characteristics on the premise of eliminating the "intermediary" which relied entirely on the Soviet model. Mao Zedong later said on various occasions that the economic construction over the previous few years was mainly done as a means of learning from foreign experience. In 1956, in discussions on the ten major relations, Mao Zedong began to put forward China's own line of construction, with features of its own.[14]

Because of the great creative spirit and innovative ability of the Communist Party of China, around the time of the Eighth National Congress, the Party put forward some new and important ideas and policies in the development of the economy, politics, culture, and science, and the reform achieved preliminary results. It was true that, due to the limitations of the times, the preliminary reform could not touch upon some fundamental drawbacks of the traditional system, only making some micro, partial, or reparative adjustments within its basic framework. In other words, "the principles are the same as those of the Soviet Union, but the methods are different."[15]

The shaking of the authoritative status of the Soviet model provided space and power for emancipating the mind. However, for any reform to be successful, it was not enough to emancipate the mind. It also required other important conditions, such as mature conditions of understanding, correct methods of thinking, democracy inside and outside the Party, and the accumulation of necessary experience, including the lessons learnt from mistakes. It was precisely for the lack of these conditions that after 1957, although there was a strong desire to emancipate the mind, oppose dogmatism, and explore the way of self-construction, the result was often the absolutization of individual experience, or the replacement of other dogmas with individual dogma, while reverting to more traditional ideas. As a result, breakthroughs in the traditional mode led to serious mistakes in class struggle and economic construction in the socialist period, and the localization of Marxism in China tended to be dogmatic and empirical. From a formal point of view, bold experiments such as the Great Leap Forward and the People's Commune were indeed different from the traditional model,[16] but it was often much simpler to copy some of the classical writers' assumptions about the future society in the 19th century and wartime experience, or even to draw inspiration from ancient Chinese society to build the future one, essentially creating a more extreme traditional model.

From the end of 1958 to 1960, in the process of summing up experience and correcting Leftist mistakes, the Party deepened its understanding of the law of distribution based on work and the law of value, while emphasizing the importance of combining public ownership, the commodity economy, and planning for socialist construction. During the period of adjustment in the early 1960s, Mao Zedong once again proposed to the entire Party, "We must combine the universal truth of Marxism-Leninism with the concrete reality of China's socialist construction and with the concrete reality of the future world revolution, trying our best to understand the objective law of struggle systematically through practice. We should be prepared to suffer many failures and setbacks due to blindness, so as to gain experience and win the final victory."[17] The Central Committee called the whole Party to read carefully, review its studies, revitalize the style of investigation and research, sum up experience, and make comprehensive and profound adjustments. Through reflection on the Great Leap Forward and the People's Commune Movement that had occurred over the previous few years, the entire Party focused on the standards of productivity, adjusted industry, agriculture, and other industries, and adjusted political relations both inside and outside the Party. A large number of regulations concerning the formulation and implementation of many industries was represented by the Rural People's Commune Work Regulations (Amendment Draft) (referred to as the "60 Agricultural Articles"). The central front-line leaders supported "contracted farmland" and "contracted production to households." Mao's new understanding of this stage of socialist development was put forward. Liu Shaoqi's realistic estimation of the difficult situation and its causes, the socialist concept embodied in Deng Xiaoping's view of deciding on the form of production relations based on whether China was able to restore and develop production relatively quickly and whether the masses were willing to follow, Sun Yifang, Zhang Wentian, and others' views on the socialist commodity economy as a "planned commodity economy," and a series of other important ideas developed the understanding of socialism and involved some basic ideas and processes for China's future reform, marking another peak in the integration of Marxism into China during the period of socialism. Presumably, if these adjustments continued to deepen, the second leap of localization could occur ahead of schedule.

The adjustment began with the correction of the serious chaos caused by the Great Leap Forward and the People's Commune Movement in every aspect. Therefore, in the initial stage, more emphasis was placed on the restoration and return of the traditional system and order. The reform that was truly meaningful to the traditional system was still in its infancy. With the deepening of readjustment, some deep-seated problems related to the question of the essence of socialism emerged, and the integration of Marxism into China faced major choices, including whether to carry out theoretical innovation while promoting readjustment, breaking through the shackles of traditional concepts and achieving a second leap, or to use traditional concepts to measure new things and problems in readjustment, thereby negating the sprouting reform in the readjustments. At that time, the conditions for socialist reform throughout the world were not yet mature.[18] Some traditional ideas were still deeply shackling people's minds,[19] and several deep-rooted traditional ideas were not broken through. The theory and practice of adjustment were measured by these concepts and the assumptions of various 19th century classical writers about the future society, and the socialist reform was judged accordingly. As a result, some substantial reform measures and viewpoints were regarded as "revisionism," which challenged the orthodox status of Marxism. With such an urgent need to emancipate the mind, brainstorm, and explore innovation, democracy both inside and outside the Party tended to shrink because of the expansion of class struggle. It was under the influence of these factors that the deepening of the adjustment triggered a serious assessment of the state of class struggle. In this way, on the one hand, there was a gradual, in-depth adjustment and correction of the Leftist errors, to a certain extent, while on the other hand, there was a development of errors associated with expanding class struggle. The interaction of these two factors, together with the role of various international factors, made the development of the latter difficult to contain, which ultimately led to the Cultural Revolution.

The fourth stage was the period of the Cultural Revolution (1966–1976). Out of a serious assessment of the situation, the Cultural Revolution hoped to achieve "the rule of the whole world" through "the chaos of the whole world." The development mode of "grasping the revolution and promoting production" established by the Cultural Revolution was indeed different from the traditional mode, but it also completely deviated from the correct direction of socialist reform. The criticism of "capitalism," "revisionism," "capitalists," "material stimulus," "profit-oriented," "bonus-oriented," and "contracted production" in the movement, as well as the restrictions on the commodity economy, currency exchange, "bourgeois legal rights," and various other differences, all demonstrated a departure from modern society. The Leftist mistakes made during the ten years of the Cultural Revolution reached an extreme, which was a wrong response to the germination of some reforms in China in the 1950s and 1960s and to the reform trend in other socialist countries. Although it had obvious Chinese traits in form, in fact, it deviated from the concrete situation in China and the essence of Marxism, thus causing the localization of Marxism in China to go astray.

Over the previous ten years, the healthy forces within the Party had resisted and combated the unrest and ultra-Leftist trend of thought and adhered to the correct direction of the localization of Marxism in China even in a difficult environment. A series of principles and policies proposed in the two rectifications led by Zhou Enlai and Deng Xiaoping were important links in the extension of the localization of Marxism in China.

The Cultural Revolution pushed to the extreme those errors that did not conform to China's national conditions and were divorced from Marxism, thus clarifying and simplifying some long-standing, confusing problems, which in turn provided sufficient conditions for the final correction of these errors. "Without the lessons of the Cultural Revolution, it would be impossible to formulate ideological, political, and organizational lines and a series of policies since the Third Plenary Session of the Eleventh Central Committee [...] The Cultural Revolution has become our wealth"[20] and "the great classroom of the people of the whole country."[21]

In the two years after the end of the Cultural Revolution, an unprecedented ideological emancipation movement took the form of criticism of the "Two Whatevers" and discussion of the criterion of truth. The movement had completely shaken those traditional concepts that had long restrained people, broken through the shackles of dogmatism, and restored and established the ideological line of emancipation and seeking truth from facts advocated by Mao Zedong. The great ideological emancipation movement laid a solid foundation for realizing the second leap of the integration of Marxism into China and the successful socialist reform. All this was a sort of generous compensation for the arduous exploration of the past.

II

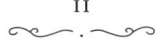

Challenges to Choosing Modes for Socialist Reform

The CPC had become a long-tested and creative Marxist Party, a leading collective that had successfully led the new democratic revolution through a circuitous path in the period of democratic revolution, and an unremitting use of Marxist theory to arm itself during the twenty-nine-year period after the founding of New China, emphasizing emancipation of the mind and seeking truth from facts. Why did the party that took Marxism as its responsibility in China fail to achieve its second leap during the twenty-nine years after the founding of New China? Among the many reasons, two seem to deserve special attention, namely, the delay of the modernization of the socialist model and the lag of the modernization of Marxism.

For the international communist movement and socialist countries, 1956 was the year when the traditional socialist model of the Soviet Union was reformed on a large scale. "Since 1956, the umbilical cord that united the Communists with the Soviet Union as their sole source of nutrition has been broken. The parties then began to formulate their own attitudes towards communist theory and practice."[22] In the communist movement, a "multi-center" situation emerged. "People are no longer talking about unique leadership. Instead, they are talking about progress made by taking different paths [...] The Soviet model cannot, and should not, be anything that must be followed."[23] From that time on, although socialist countries were greatly influenced by traditional models in general, they ultimately began the transition from one model to a multiplicity of models.

The shining halo over the traditional model disappeared, and the authority of the Marxist theoretical system interpreted by the Soviet Communist Party was weakened. While the ideological emancipation and theoretical activity were active, there was also, to a degree, a vacuum in the area of model. This not only relieved the constraints and pressures of the Communist Party and workers' parties in all countries to a certain extent, expanding the space for the nationalization of various forms of Marxism, but also meant the loss of standard answers that could be relied on and used for reference. Due to the differences of economic development level, historical and cultural traditions, and geographic conditions in different countries, there were necessarily great differences in the understanding and reform of the traditional (Stalinist) model.[24] In order to find their own path of development, while referring to the Soviet model, they also sought answers directly from the original works of Marx and Engels or drew inspiration from their own historical and cultural traditions and contemporary world civilization. Regardless of the vagaries of the reform at that time and its subsequent development, it was worth affirming that it independently sought its own road of socialist revolution and construction under the new historical conditions. Even in the 1950s and 1970s, the Soviet model, which was still in the mainstream, was different from the traditional model before 1956.

Over the next two decades, the reforms of the Soviet Union and other countries were repeatedly halted or hobbled. Although some achievements were made, owing to the constraints of traditional ideas, there were reforms in some areas, such as the ownership structure in a socialist society, the planned and market economy, highly centralized power, and eagerness to achieve success. The basic theoretical issues of class struggle and the transition to communism had not made substantial progress until the 1980s. Reform tended to be a repetitive revision of the periphery of the traditional system, satisfying itself with some improvement of the planned economy, but rarely touching on the core of the old model.

In 1956, China was facing a unique situation of dual transformation. First, the work center had changed from revolution to comprehensive socialist construction, and second, the construction mode had changed from duplicating tradition to exploring its own development path. This dual transformation made it more difficult to localize Marxism in China than it was in 1953, when "the climax of learning from the Soviet Union should be set up nationwide."[25] It called for a skeptical and reformative view of everything that was being built up in accordance with the Soviet model, emphasizing an independent model innovation. This not only provided the Party with a historical opportunity to emancipate minds and realize the second leap, but also increased the difficulty of mode selection and expanded the space for the influence of some historical and cultural traditions. Just as the first leap in realizing the localization of Marxism in China in the period of the democratic revolution was based on the core theory of putting forward the new democracy, the second leap in the period of socialism was measured by whether the Party could find the path of socialism with Chinese characteristics.

Under the guidance of the Eighth National Congress of the Communist Party of China, China's construction and reform saw new achievements after 1956, amending the drawbacks of the Stalinist model, making new progress in Mao Zedong Thought, and continuing to extend the localization of Marxism in China. However, due to the influence of dogmatism and empiricism, a tendency to revise the traditional model from another direction in order to be more "pure" and "radical" than before was also developing. In the 1960s, especially in the controversy over the international communist movement, the outline of a socialist model that was different from the Soviet model and not in line with China's national conditions and the trend of contemporary socialist reform gradually became clear. It included equating a single public ownership structure with a highly centralized and unified planned economy with socialism, taking the permission of the existence and development of private capital and private enterprises to a certain extent as the development of capitalism and viewing economic means such as valuing profit, price, market regulation, and material interests, narrowing the scope of planned regulation, and trading with capitalist countries in a certain range as capitalism and revisionism. During this time, it regarded class struggle as the main contradiction and motive force for the development of socialism. Efforts to break through the Soviet model lost sight of the correct path. Under this more extreme standard than the traditional model, when it was reasonable to constantly increase vigilance and worry about the restoration of capitalism, the idea of "taking class struggle as the main line" prevailed. In June 1966, Mao Zedong said that more than one hundred parties in the world had changed and did not believe in Marxism-Leninism any longer. This judgment was based on the fact that, to a considerable extent, the traditional or more extreme model was regarded as the criterion for judging the nature of a society being "socialist" or "capitalist," while the reform of it, some of which had indeed gone astray, was regarded as "revisionism." In the Cultural Revolution, this pattern was manifested in a more extreme form.

Looking at the political and economic development of China from 1956 to 1978, a kind of periodic "leftward" development is evident – correcting the left, redeveloping the left, and readjusting the left. This cycle was actually the external manifestation of the dilemma of mode selection, reflecting the difficulty of the transformation of the socialist mode from the traditional to the contemporary era, and also the difficulty of the second combination of Marxism with the real situation in China.

Socialist reform generally comes into being when socialism has developed to a considerable extent and contradicts the original model. The sharper the contradiction, the stronger the demand for reform, and the earlier it occurs. The reform of the Soviet Union took place nearly forty years after the October Revolution and nearly twenty years after the completion of the socialist transformation. Eastern European countries, especially those whose economic development level before the revolution was higher than that of old Russia, felt the restraint of the Soviet model from the beginning, and the contradiction became more prominent after the 1950s. "From 1955 to 1956, the consequences of the old and outdated management systems were obvious and considerable... These consequences have even reached catastrophic levels in some production sectors."[26] As both a reflection and result of this contradiction, the Soviet Union and Eastern European countries took the lead in the reform. That is to say, in terms of the conditions for reform, countries such as the Soviet Union and Eastern Europe were obviously more mature than China.

China entered the era of reform when it was just beginning to carry out comprehensive socialist construction in accordance with the Soviet model. Because socialist politics and the socialist economy were still underdeveloped, the drawbacks of the Soviet model were not obvious, and the contradictions caused were not as sharp as those in the Soviet Union and Eastern Europe. "We can only understand based on the conditions of our times and subjected to the extent these conditions have reached."[27] With the development of China at that time, although some preliminary reform ideas could be proposed, it was not enough to thoroughly understand the ongoing reform practice of the Soviet Union, Eastern Europe, and other countries. For example, when China had just established a highly centralized and unified planned economy, it should have provided the people with a deep understanding of its limitations, allowing those who had just gone through the three major transformative climaxes to attach importance to the necessary supplementary role of a certain number of individual economies in socialism and the positive role of market economy, and helping those who had just established ownership by all the people to rely on national strength. Understanding this deeply could not be equated with the direct management of enterprises by the state. Under the conditions of that time, it was not easy for those who had not experienced a stage of high development of the commodity economy to grasp some classical writers' knowledge of socialist commodity production from books and deeply understand the significance of vigorous development of the commodity economy into socialism. Although there were many insights in the Party at that time, they did not become the mainstream. It was against this background that dogmatism, empiricism, and traditional culture played an important role.

One of the important reasons the Party started from reforming the traditional model but then diverged to a more rigid path was that the conditions for socialist reform (i.e. modernization of the model) were not yet mature. The deeper reason lay in the lag of the modernization of Marxism.

III

The Delayed Modernization of Marxism

The integration of Marxism into China inherently encompassed the modernization of Marxism. Moreover, only by realizing the modernization of Marxism could the CPC scientifically realize the localization of Marxism in China. The so-called modernization of Marxism[28] involved combining Marxism with the development and characteristics of the current era. At the Sixth Plenary Session of the Sixth Central Committee of the Communist Party of China, Mao Zedong proposed the proposition and task of the "Sinicization" of Marxism, emphasizing national and regional characteristics, emphasizing a "flexible application based on Chinese characteristics," but not emphasizing the characteristics of the times, since this was still the age of imperialism, war, and revolution, as Lenin called it. This was another way of saying that that the times had not changed. As a result, "in the application and development of Marxism, the emphasis is on application, while in the nationalization and modernization of Marxism, the main focus is on nationalization."[29] After the founding of New China, great changes took place in the times and the theme of the times. The premise of the "Sinicization" of Marxism – that is, the problem of modernization – became prominent. Unlike the first leap, the second leap in the localization of Marxism in China could only be realized after the modernization of Marxism had been addressed. The vagaries of the socialist reforms in the 1950s and 1970s, and the direct reason why China failed to complete the second leap in the localization of Marxism, mainly lay in the dogmatization of Marxism, while the deeper reason lay in the failure to promote the modernization of Marxism in accordance with the changes of the times. The vagaries of mode transformation were only the external manifestation of the dilemma of theoretical development.

The traditional view held that Marxism itself was a complete scientific system and its development could only be carried out within its original framework, with only minor developments, revisions, and enrichment of some specific issues. This understanding reduced the level, scope, and degree of the development of Marxism and weakened the urgency and importance of the modernization of Marxism under the background of the new era. After the founding of New China, for some strategic considerations, the idea of the "Sinicization of Marxism" was replaced by the "concretization of Marxism in China." There was no substantive difference between the two propositions, so one might say that the important historical task of Sinicization of Marxism was only a matter of "concretization" or "concrete application" under the condition of a drastically changing era. The basic principle of meaning (or general principle) was a static, unchangeable, and fixed object. Its contemporary problems that kept pace with the times under the new historical conditions were often diluted. Against this sort of background, it was difficult to avoid dogmatism, promote the cause of the modernization of Marxism, and complete the second leap in the localization of Marxism in China.

Marxism is a multi-level theoretical system, which includes some basic theories at the highest level that offer long-term stability and have universal significance, as well as some principles and categories at the lower level that are concrete and less stable. This distinction is often only relative, because even some basic principles and methods have trouble keeping pace with the times. Some of the principles that were considered fundamental decades ago are only tangentially relevant today. For example, some of the basic principles that were once regarded as natural principles concerning capitalism, socialism, the planned economy, the characteristics of the times, the working class, and the bourgeoisie seem to have lost their universal explanatory power. Some of the philosophical and economic categories and principles once considered fundamental to Marxism have also been proved to be in need of development and supplement. The difficulty lies in how to develop Marxism in accordance with the needs of the development of the times, at and what levels, aspects, scope, and to what extent, so as to modernize it. How may one judge the truth of this development? In the Marxist theoretical system, "how many things can change while allowing the system to remain the same as its original premise?" Determining how far away and how many things are still organically connected with the original theory is often a difficult proposition.[30] It is thus necessary to rethink or revise Marxism so as to keep it in close contact with its environment, as well as to maintain knowledge or political connection with Marx's original doctrine or basic principles. "It is not always easy to coordinate the two needs."[31] Any bias may lead to dogmatism or nihilism. Therefore, people are increasingly inclined to accept Lukács' point of view as stated in *History and Class Consciousness*, published in 1919. He wrote, "Orthodoxy in Marxist issues refers only to methods. It is a scientific belief that dialectical Marxism is the correct research method, which can only be developed, expanded, and deepened in the direction laid down by its founders. Moreover, any attempt to overcome it or to 'improve' it has led and will only lead to superficiality, mediocrity, and eclecticism." In addition, Lenin's classical exposition remains worthy of great attention even today. He wrote, "For Russia, the era of debating the socialist program based on books has passed, and I am convinced that it is gone forever. Today we can only talk about socialism on the basis of experience."[32] These understandings emphasized that Marxism should develop and innovate on the basis of practice, keep pace with the times, help to expand the space for developing Marxism, and avoid restricting its development to minor and specific adjustments.

After the birth of Marxism, in the process of dissemination, practice, and development, great changes took place in its continuous inheritance and development. Vertically, Chinese scholars often divide this development into Marxist, Leninist, and Stalinist stages, and stages represented by proletarian leaders such as Mao Zedong and Deng Xiaoping. In the West, such divisions are too numerous to enumerate. For example, Mitchell Blowe, a major voice in Marxist sociology in the United States, divides the development of Marxism into three periods, namely, the classical Marxist era, the national socialist era, and the socialistic era. The third era of Marxism began in the mid-1970s.[33] Friedrich Jameson, a famous American postmodernist thinker, believes that different historical times will produce different forms of Marxism. He divides the development of Marxism into three stages: modernism, imperialism, and late capitalism.[34]

Horizontally, in the 20th century, besides the proletarian revolutionary leaders and Marxist theorists such as Lenin, Stalin, Mao Zedong, and Deng Xiaoping, who exerted tremendous influence all over the world, other leaders worthy of respect included Rosa Luxemburg, Lukács, Gramsci, and other leading figures of European Communism and Western Marxism for their contribution to the development of Marxism. For example, "Western Marxism," which appeared in the 1920s and reached its climax in the 1950s and 1960s, inherited and developed Marxism's critical approach to capitalism in contemporary developed capitalist society and broke through the shackles of Soviet dogmatism in the hope of revisiting, explaining, and developing Marxism on the basis of contemporary challenges. These theorists analyzed the new features and problems of capitalism on the basis of contemporary productivity and science and technology, predicted the characteristics of future society, and criticized the drawbacks and defects of the Soviet model. "It has been noted that although it differs from or conflicts with the traditional concepts and development of Marxism, and indeed contains some principled deviations from the basic contents of Marxism, it is still an indispensable aspect of the development of contemporary Marxism in the West, with a distinct sense of the times and reality."[35] As long as one avoids the attitudes of "us alone being revolutionary" or "us alone being Marxists" were avoided, it was possible to face up to the diversified situation in the development of Marxism. As Jameson emphasized, "We should not forget that today Marxism is not just one line of theory without diverse branches. In fact, there are all kinds of Marxist theoretical discourse."[36] This diversified situation represented the vitality of Marxism, embodied its quality of keeping pace with the times, and allowed it to develop and enrich itself in all aspects. It reflected the needs of the times in different aspects and to varying degrees, and it met the requirements of the modernization of Marxism.

After the Second World War, with the changes of the times and the rapid development of science, technology, and productivity, and with the reform of socialism from the traditional to the contemporary mode and from one mode to multiple modes, Marxism also faced a transformation from classic to contemporary theory, and its theme began to change from revolution and war to peace and construction. This was similar to what Lenin had observed in the early 20th century when he combined the classical Marxist theory produced in the era of free capitalism with the characteristics of the times to make it contemporary.

The modernization of Marxism can be roughly divided into two levels. The first is the development of some original theories of classical Marxist writers, including the change and development of their own understanding, along with the development of the times and practice, and on the basis of continuity. This can be called the development of basic theory. For example, in the 1980s and 1990s, classical Marxist writers greatly developed many of their ideas from the 1940s and 1950s. Lenin's understandings of socialism in the period of "wartime communism" and in the period of new economic policy were distinctly different. On the other hand, Marxists following Marx had different understandings,[37] explanations, and specific applications of classical theories set against different backgrounds, such as the characteristics of the times and the national conditions. This was attributed to more specific levels of development. Of the two, the former is obviously more fundamental. Without its modernization, the work of regionalization and nationalization would be impossible.

The era called for the modernization of Marxism, but it did not promptly prepare the corresponding conditions for it. The various vagaries in China's exploration in the 1950s and 1970s, as well as the stagnation and even failure of the reform of socialist countries, in fact, illustrated to a certain extent that at that time, the conditions for breaking through the severe bondage of dogmatism so that the conditions for socialism could shift from traditional to modern mode and Marxism could shift from classic to contemporary mode were not yet ripe. They also required the accumulation of practice, the exposure of contradictions, lessons learned from mistakes, and a leap in theory.

Mao Zedong was a great proletarian revolutionist and theorist with a strong sense of innovation. In the struggle against dogmatizing Marxism and sacrificing the experience of the Soviet Union, he led the entire Party to realize the first leap in the localization of Marxism in China. After the founding of New China, he still retained this creative spirit and called on the entire Party to develop Marxism on the basis of the earnest study of Marxism. "Marxism must move forward and develop with practice. It must not stagnate. If it stops or remains the same, it will no longer be living theory."[38] He also said, "The Communist Party and the ideological circles of any country should create new theories, write new works, and produce their own theorists to serve current politics. It is not possible to rely solely on our ancestors." However, due to the lack of mature conditions of the times, the excessive reliance on the experience of the war years, and the influence of Chinese cultural traditions, Mao actually confined this development to a certain extent in the process of realizing the "second combination," in that he did not touch the framework of some of the basic assumptions of socialism that classical writers had made in earlier times. That is to say, at a deeper level, it was still bound by some dogmatism and empiricism. This was quite a common phenomenon in the international communist movement at that time, though it took different forms in different places or times. Under such circumstances, it was impossible to realize the second leap in the localization of Marxism in China. Since the CPC still adhered to traditional views on a series of important issues, such as the essential characteristics of socialism, ownership by all the people, the planned economy, the commodity economy, and the times, there was no way to correct the reform of the

Soviet model, and the task of the second leap in the localization of Marxism in China could not be accomplished.

Since 1976, on the basis of summing up experience and lessons, Deng Xiaoping led the Party to raise the banner of emancipating the mind and seeking truth from facts, putting the task of modernizing Marxism sharply before the entire Party under the new historical conditions. "What changes have taken place in more than a hundred years after Marx's death and how to recognize and develop Marxism under the changing conditions have not been made clear."[39] He also noted, "Marx should not be expected to provide ready-made answers to the problems that would arise centuries after his death […] A true Marxist-Leninist must recognize, inherit, and develop Marxism-Leninism according to the present situation." Further, "the world situation is changing with each passing day, especially in the rapid development of modern science and technology. The progress in one year in modern times may be more than that over decades, centuries, or even longer in the old society. For this reason, anyone who does not inherit and develop Marxism with new ideas and viewpoints will not be a true Marxist."[40] In his speech at the Congress celebrating the 80th anniversary of the founding of the Communist Party of China on July 1, 2001, Jiang Zemin further pointed out, "Practice is the only criterion for testing truth. Under the guidance of the Party's basic theory, we should proceed from reality and consciously liberate our ideological understanding from the shackles of inappropriate concepts, practices, and systems, and liberate ourselves from wrong and dogmatic understandings of Marxism." It was under the guidance of this thought that the CPC realized the transformation of Marxism from classical to contemporary theory, and the socialist model from the traditional to the contemporary, thus realizing the second leap in the integration of Marxism into China.

IV

Expansion and Preparation: The Features of the Localization of Marxism in China over a Twenty-nine-year Span

From 1949 to 1978, the integration of Marxism into China went through a tortuous process between two leaps, with "extension" and "preparation" as their distinct features.

The extension was mainly evident in the extension and development of Mao Zedong Thought, the great theoretical achievement of the first leap. After the founding of New China, in the process of exploring China's own path to socialist construction, the first generation of the leading collective of the CPC Central Committee, represented by Mao Zedong, promptly put forward the task of integrating Marxism into China's reality for the second time, conducting various explorations and making significant strides and progress. As a result of various mistakes and failures, the second leap was not realized, but the theoretical achievement of the first leap, Mao Zedong Thought, continued to develop. This was reflected in the correct and relatively correct theoretical views, principles, and policies formed by the Party in the process of exploring China's own path to building socialism, and some correct and relatively correct practical experience accumulated.

The preparation during the leaps included not only the ideological and theoretical preparations mentioned above, but also their material basis. In the first twenty-nine years after the founding of New China, under the leadership of the Party, the country achieved unprecedented political unity, established a strong central government with effective control over organizations at all levels, even the most basic level, established an independent and relatively complete industrial system and national economic system, and achieved and consolidated the great unity of the people of all ethnic groups in the country. It built a highly prestigious Party armed with Mao Zedong Thought and strong capability in mobilization, which laid a strong material foundation for Reform and Opening Up. Over the previous three decades of exploration, both achievements and detours and both positive experiences and negative lessons prepared the necessary conditions for the second leap.

As mentioned earlier, in the 1950s and 1960s, the modernization of the socialist model and the modernization of Marxism throughout the world were still undergoing a tortuous process of exploration. Although the task of socialist reform had been put forward, the goal of reform was still unclear, the theory and method of reform lacked measures gained from positive and negative practice, and the conditions for substantive progress were not mature. This was evident in China's Cultural Revolution in the 1960s and 1970s, and in the criticism of the socialist market economy and the stagnation of its reform by the Soviet Union and Eastern European countries. With the rapid development of science, technology, the economy, and politics after the war, the task of modernizing Marxism became increasingly prominent, but dogmatism in the form of orthodoxy seriously hampered this development. The influence of this dogmatism was so profound and extensive that after the fierce movement of the Cultural Revolution, which was called "the all-round development of Marxism," China's new era began with a strong political discussion of issues as basic to philosophical common sense as "the criterion of truth." At the beginning of China's Reform and Opening Up, Deng Xiaoping suggested the strategy of "no debate," and it was also true that against this background of dogmatism continuing to have a very wide influence, endless debates would only delay the opportunity for reform.

At such a particular historical stage, many explorations in socialist countries had an obvious "trial and error" nature, using "trial and error" as a special form to make necessary preparations for reform. Regardless of the outcome, every attempt and practice accumulated experience and lessons, narrowing the scope of exploration for later generations, making knowledge close to truth, and making exploration close to success. At the beginning of the reform, people felt more painfully that they were unable to achieve it, rather than feeling how much they could do. It was with such rich accumulation and preparation of practice on both sides that the conditions for China's reform and for the second leap in the localization of Marxism in China grew ripe. At the beginning of the reform, the emergence of the situation and the relatively smooth development thereafter, as well as the proposition of Deng Xiaoping's series of important reform ideas, obviously benefited from the maturity of conditions and the adequate preparation.

In 1962, in summing up the experience of socialist construction in China, Mao Zedong once said that the important documents on the localization of

Marxism in China, such as "On New Democracy" in the period of the democratic revolution, "could only be produced at that time, which was impossible in the past, because without strong winds and waves, there would have been no two victories and two failures. By comparison, we haven't had enough experience, and we haven't fully understood the laws of the Chinese revolution."[41] The method put forward by Mao Zedong here was also suitable for the analysis and summary of the course of the localization of Marxism in China over the first 29 years after the founding of New China.

CHAPTER 2

Two Theories of the New Democracy

I

The Shift from New Democratic Revolutionary Theory to New Democratic Socialization Theory

1. Starting from the Common Program

On September 29, 1949, the First Plenary Session of the Chinese People's Political Consultative Conference unanimously adopted the Common Program as the basic program for the founding of the Chinese people's revolution. The Common Program embodied the CPC's basic conception of New China's state and regime, as well as its plan for the future development direction of the newly established nation. It was the product of the Communist Party of China's combination of the universal truth of Marxism with China's concrete situation, the result of the creative application of Marxism to that situation, and the crystallization of the first leap in the localization of Marxism in China.

The Common Program stipulated that:

"The People's Republic of China is a new democratic country, i.e. a people's democracy. It practices a people's democratic dictatorship led by the proletariat, based on the alliance of workers and peasants, uniting all democratic classes and nationalities in the country, opposing imperialism, feudalism, and bureaucratic capitalism, and striving for China's independence, democracy, peace, unity, and prosperity. The state power of the People's Republic of China belongs to the people. The organs of the people exercising state power are the people's congresses at all levels and the people's governments at all levels. The highest organ of state power is the National People's Congress. All organs of government at all levels shall practice democratic centralism."

"The People's Republic of China must abolish all the privileges of imperialist countries in China, confiscate bureaucratic capital, and systematically transform feudal and semi-feudal land ownership into peasant land ownership, protect the state's public property and the property of cooperatives, and protect the ranks of workers, peasants, and petty assets. The economic interests of the petty bourgeoisie and the national bourgeoisie and their private property will develop the new democratic people's economy and steadily transform the agricultural country into an industrial country.

"The fundamental policy of economic construction of the People's Republic of China is to achieve the goal of developing production and prospering the economy through the policy of giving consideration to both public and private interests and the interests of both the employer and the employee, providing mutual assistance between urban and rural areas, and facilitating internal and external exchanges, with proper labor division and all respective posts and positions."

The Common Program stipulated that the state-owned economy was a socialist economy and the leading force of the whole social economy, that the cooperative economy was a semi-socialist economy and the people's government should support its development and give preferential treatment to it, and that the people's government should encourage the initiative of private economic undertakings that were beneficial to the national economy and the people's livelihood. The economy of cooperation between state capital and private capital was the economy of state capitalism. Under necessary and possible conditions, private capital was encouraged to develop toward state capitalism.

Guided by the theory of a new democratic society, the Common Program was a new democratic nation building program. These basic provisions concerning the politics and economy of New China were one of the most important theoretical achievements of the CPC in the long-term democratic revolution, which combined the universal truth of Marxism with the reality of China and successfully realized the first leap in the localization of Marxism in accordance with China's specific national conditions. It developed the basic principles of Marxism in its understanding of a series of issues, such as the new democratic revolution and the new democratic society and its socialist orientation, the state and regime of new democratic countries, the implementation of regional national autonomy in a unitary country, the individual economy and the capitalist economy, and the petty bourgeoisie and the national bourgeoisie. It transcended the Soviet model and was a brilliant chapter in the localization of Marxism in China. The process of the formation and development of this theory constituted the process of integrating Marxism into China.

2. The Proposal of New Democratic Sociology

How to understand the bourgeois democratic revolution and the bourgeoisie of China, what kind of country should be built after the victory of the Chinese revolution, and the socialist future of the Chinese revolution were all fundamental issues of the Chinese socialist revolution and construction, as well as keys to realizing the integration of Marxism into China. The Party went through a tortuous process of exploring these issues. A relatively systematic and proper answer to this question began with a series of important works by Mao Zedong.

In *The Chinese Revolution and the Communist Party of China* and *On New Democracy*, Mao repeatedly stated that the bourgeois democratic revolution in China, which took place in the first half of the 20th century, was no longer the old general bourgeois democratic revolution, but a new special bourgeois democratic revolution, namely, the new democratic revolution. This kind of democratic revolution was different from the old bourgeois democratic revolution. It was led by a proletarian party and laid the foundation for socialism. The Chinese revolution was divided into two stages. Only through this revolution could Chinese society further develop into a socialist society. Mao's thoughts directly inherited the Marxist-Leninist exposition of bourgeois democratic revolutions in colonial and semi-colonial societies, which in his words were "based on Stalin's theory." For example, he offered thoughts on the nature of bourgeois democratic revolutions, on the mission of the proletariat in countries where the task of democratic revolution had not been fulfilled to take the democratic revolution as the first step in advancing the socialist revolution, on "the Chinese revolution as part of the world revolution" and as part of a "new socialist revolution," on continuing to struggle for the victory, rather than the discontinuation, of the socialist revolution after the victory of the democratic revolution, on the proletariat's duty to strive for the leadership to uphold the democratic revolution, and the like.

Proceeding from the actual situation in China, Mao and the CPC successfully applied the general principles of Marxism-Leninism concerning the bourgeois democratic revolution of the 20th century to the special historical conditions of the Chinese revolution, forming the theory and practice of the new democratic revolution with Chinese characteristics, thus realizing the first historic leap of the integration of Marxism into China. This was one of the theoretical peaks of the CPC's promotion of the localization of Marxism in the new democratic revolution.

It is noteworthy that in these two works, especially in *On New Democracy*, besides offering exposition and analysis of the new democratic revolution, Mao also gave a general theoretical and relatively complete description of the shape and nature of the new society established after the victory of the revolution, and clearly proposed the slogan of establishing a "new democratic republic." He pointed out that the goal and result of the new democratic revolution was to build a new democratic society. The economic characteristics of this society were to include "big banks, industries, and commerce owned by the state republic," "the state-owned economy of the new democratic republic under the leadership of the proletariat as the nature of socialism and the leading force of the whole national economy, though this republic will not confiscate the private property of capitalism. In fact, it does not prohibit the development of any capitalist production that is incapable of manipulating the livelihood of the people."[2]

The basic political characteristics of this new society were summed up in statements such as, "We shall never establish capitalism under the dictatorship of the Chinese bourgeoisie, but a new democratic society under the joint dictatorship of all revolutionary classes in China led by the Chinese proletariat."[3] The state system of the new democratic republic, i.e. the position of all social classes in the country and their political characteristics, "can only be a democratic republic under the leadership of the proletariat and the combined dictatorship of all anti-imperialist and anti-feudal people. This is the new democratic republic, that is, the republic of the new three democracies with three real revolutionary policies."[4] And, "on the one hand, this new democratic republic is different from the old democratic republic, while on the other, it is different from the Soviet-style socialist republic. It is a 'new democratic republic,' 'a joint dictatorship of all revolutionary classes,' a 'transitional form,' and an 'indispensable and necessary form.'"[5]

The future of this new society envisioned that "after the victory of the revolution, because the obstacles on the path of capitalist development will have been removed, the capitalist economy will develop to a considerable extent in Chinese society." Further, "this is the inevitable result of the victory of the democratic revolution in China with its underdeveloped economy [...] But this is only the result of one aspect of the Chinese revolution, not all of it. The total results of the Chinese revolution include on the one hand, development of capitalist factors, and on the other, development of socialist factors." The development of socialist factors would determine the final result of the bourgeois democratic revolution in China, avoid the future of capitalism, and realize the future of socialism.[6]

If Mao Zedong's theory on the new democratic revolution focused more on the concrete application of Marxist democratic revolution theory, then his exposition of the political, economic and cultural forms of the new democratic society in the future and his assumption of the new social form to be realized by the revolution were more based on the real situation in China and developed Marxist theory concerning the transition of underdeveloped countries into a socialist society.[7] Moreover, since the mid-1940s, in the writings of Mao and other Party leaders, the discussion of the new democratic society increased.

In April 1945, at the Seventh Congress of the Party, Mao made a political report entitled "On the United Government" on behalf of the Central Committee. As the War of Resistance Against Japanese Aggression was coming to a successful conclusion, the work of establishing a coalition government had been placed before the Party, and the Party had enjoyed more than a decade of successful practice in the revolutionary base areas. "On the Coalition Government" not only put more clearly and adequately the basic concepts contained in *On New Democracy* concerning the new democratism and socialism and how to treat capitalism in new democratic countries, but further concretized them too. Although some of the content of the report emphasizing the significance of the development of capitalism to the new democratic countries and the attitude of the new countries towards capitalism were deleted in the 1952 edition of *Selected Works of Mao Zedong*, the basic ideas contained in the full text remained intact.

Regarding the new state system, Mao pointed out that "after thoroughly defeating the Japanese aggressors, we advocate the establishment of a national system of a Democratic Alliance on the United Front based on the overwhelming majority of the people of the whole country and under the leadership of the working class," in other words, "the new democratic state system."[8] As for the relationship between new democracy and socialism, Mao offered a much quoted saying, "Only through democracy can we achieve socialism, which is the natural principle of Marxism."[9]

Compared with works such as *On New Democracy*, when discussing the characteristics of the new democratic society in this period, Mao and other Party leaders especially emphasized its connection with the productivity of a certain degree of development, that is to say, its material basis. On May 22, 1944, Mao attended a reception held by the Central Office in the auditorium of the Central Party School for factory directors and representatives of workers in the Shaanxi-Gansu-Ningxia Border Region. He said, "We don't know much about economic work, especially industry, but this determines everything, military work, politics, culture, thought, morality, and religion, as well as social change."[10] Three months later, Mao pointed out in a letter that "the foundation of a new democratic society is factories (social production, public and private) and cooperatives (including work teams). It is not a decentralized individual economy, such as family agriculture and handicraft industry, which is the foundation of a feudal, not a democratic, society (including old democracy, new democracy, and socialism), and is what distinguishes Marxism from populism. In short, the foundation of a new democratic society is machine, not handicraft industry. We haven't got the machines yet, so we haven't won yet. If we can never get machines, we can never win, and we will perish. The present countryside is a temporary base, which is not and cannot be the main foundation of China's democratic society. To shift from the agricultural to the industrial social basis is the task of our revolution."[11] Mao pointed out in his explanation of "On the United Government" at the Seventh National Congress of the CPC in 1945 that after the development of the new democracy and the transition to socialism, this would be the difference between the CPC and populism. This had a great influence in the Party. The report also developed the new democracy theory, which identified the need for the broad development of capitalism. The extensive development of capitalism was harmless and beneficial under the new democratic regime."[12] Mao's emphasis on the material basis of the new democratic society mirrored his emphasis on the determining role of Marxist productivity.

At that time, Mao believed that China, which was economically and culturally backward, must go through a considerable period of time to build a new democracy, vigorously develop its economy and culture, and improve its social productive forces. In the course of this development, the economic component of the socialist nature was increasing. Although the private capitalist economy had also developed to a certain extent, its proportion had been shrinking and was gradually incorporated into the scope of the national plan. Agriculture and other individual economies were gradually leading the way in mutual production and cooperation. When the goal of industrialization and agricultural collectivization was realized, great socialist steps would be taken to realize the transformation to a socialist society.

It was because it was rooted in scientific understanding of the material basis of the new democratic society that Mao was able to develop a scientific understanding of capitalism and the bourgeoisie in the new democratic country. He pointed out that it was not only progress, but also an inevitable process that would ultimately replace the oppression of foreign imperialism and domestic feudalism with some development of capitalism. It was beneficial not only to the bourgeoisie, but also to the proletariat. In fact, it was most beneficial to the proletariat. "China now has a surplus of foreign imperialism and a surplus domestic feudalism, not a surplus of domestic capitalism. On the contrary, our capitalism is too little."[13] He added, "Under the new democratic state system, in addition to the state's own economy, the individual economy of the working people and the cooperative economy, we must make it convenient for the private capitalist economy to develop within the scope of not being able to manipulate the livelihood of the people, so as to benefit the social development."[14] And "under the new democratic state system, we will adopt policies to regulate the interests between employees and employers [...] On the one hand, we should protect employees' interests." He also noted that "on the other hand, we should ensure the legitimate profits of state, private and cooperative enterprises under appropriate operation, and make both public and private enterprises, labor and management work together for the development of industrial production."[15]

II

Preliminary Exploration into Building a New Democratic Society

1. Planning for New China at the Conference in September 1948

With the victory in the war of liberation, the domestic political, military, and class forces underwent rapid, fundamental changes. The Communist Party of China became a decisive force in determining the future of China's development. The task of building a new country was more urgent for the CPC. Promoted by practice, the CPC's new democratic revolutionary theory developed and matured, and the CPC Central Committee could no longer be satisfied with the generalized description of the future new society. As Mao Zedong said, the development of the Chinese revolution in the two decades since Sun Yat-sen's death made great progress in the theory, program, and practice of the Party's new democracy, and it would see greater development in the future. According to the fundamental changes in the balance of power, the Party offered new reflections on the political and economic aspects of the country and further developed some of its previous ideas and strategies. This was particularly evident after the second half of 1948.

In September 1948, the Central Committee held a meeting of the Politburo in Xibaipo. In addition to reviewing and summarizing the process and experience of the War of Liberation, the conference also discussed the construction of New China "concretely and systematically,"[16] proposed the idea of "gradually shifting the focus of the Party's work from the countryside to the city,"[17] and put the task of preparing for the construction of New China on the agenda. It was at this meeting that the Central Committee more clearly and accurately drew up a blueprint for a new democratic society.

In his report, Mao expounded the class nature of the regime to be established, namely, the people's democratic dictatorship led by the proletariat, based on the alliance of workers and peasants and with the participation of bourgeois democrats.[18] Regarding the nature of the new democratic society, Mao revised the old saying that "new democracy" was "new capitalism," according to the practice of the anti-Japanese base areas. He pointed out that the term "new capitalism" was inappropriate, because it did not show that what played a decisive role in the social economy was the state-owned and public economies. It was led by the proletariat, so these economies were socialist in nature. Accordingly, he pointed out, "Our socio-economic name is still the new democracy."[19] At the conclusion of the meeting, he summarized the main contradictions in the new democratic society, saying, "Now it is clear that after the completion of the bourgeois democratic revolution, the main contradiction within China is the contradiction between the proletariat and the bourgeoisie, while the external contradiction is the contradiction with imperialism."[20]

In his speech at the meeting, Liu Shaoqi, on behalf of the Central Committee, discussed in detail the problem of how to build a new democratic economy. According to the spirit of "On the United Government," Liu Shaoqi pointed out that it was precisely because of the "small amount" of modern machinery industry in China that the socialist revolution could not be carried out immediately after the victory of the revolution. "The national economy as a whole is called the new democratic economy," which "contains the natural economy, small-scale production economy, capitalist economy, semi-socialist economy, state capitalist economy, and state-owned socialist economy," and "takes the state-owned socialist economy as its leading component."[21]

It is noteworthy that Liu Shaoqi not only pointed out the basic contradictions in the new democratic economy, but also discussed the specific ways to solve the contradictions incisively. He stated, "In the new democratic economy, the basic contradiction is the contradiction between capitalism and socialism […] The way of struggle is economic competition," which was to be long-term and run through all aspects as "peaceful competition." He also noted that "there is a question of who wins in the end," and "if we win the competition, the revolutionary shift can be made in a peaceful way." Therefore, although "we should not adopt socialist policy prematurely, we should not underestimate the contradiction between the proletarian working people and the bourgeoisie, but should see it clearly."[22] In such an economy, it was important to develop private capitalism that was beneficial to the national economy, while also paying attention to the struggle between private capitalism and the socialist economy. He demanded that the whole Party should have a clear mind, be good at managing the economy, and compete peacefully with the capitalist economy. Otherwise, "we will fail and the proletariat's leadership over the country will be overthrown."[23]

Mao expressed the same opinion as Liu Shaoqi at the meeting. In Liu Shaoqi's speech, he pointed out that the state power established after the revolution "is not a proletarian dictatorship but a worker-peasant dictatorship according to the level of political power and the nature of that political power. It is a worker-peasant dictatorship determined by the cooperation of the proletariat and the vast number of small producers" and "a new bourgeois democracy, a new democracy." He added, "There are socialist elements in the politics, economy, and culture of the new democracy, and they all have socialist characteristics."[24] When Liu said that "it is not necessary to adopt socialist policy too early," Mao interrupted, "When on earth will the official launch begin? Maybe it will be fifteen years after the national victory."[25] Speaking of the relationship between the proletariat and the bourgeoisie in the new democratic economy, Mao said, "There are two forms of struggle: competition and confiscation. Competition is needed now, while confiscation is not."[26] He also said, "Competition with capitalism alone will not solve the problem, and there is an issue of utilizing it to develop production."[27] It should be said that Liu and Mao were correct in their assertions on the new democratic economy and its basic contradictions, especially in their prediction and discussion of the "struggle mode."

2. Development of New Democratic Social Thought

Due to the development of practice and in-depth exploration during this period, the Party's theory of the new democratic society matured rapidly. In September 1948, in his article "On New Democracy's Economy and Cooperatives," Liu Shaoqi also discussed the social structure of a new democracy's economy, namely, the national economy, the cooperative economy, and the private capitalist economy. He stressed that since China was still a country with a great advantage in small production and an agricultural country, it was necessary to link tens of millions of independent, scattered small producers through a commercial relationship and with large industries. In the whole new democratic economic system, the cooperative economy should take an important position.[28] He also said, "Under the new democratic social system, there is still a considerable proportion of private capitalist economy in the national economy. This kind of economy will develop in the future, and the development of this kind of economy to a certain extent is necessary and beneficial, not terrible."[29] Liu Shaoqi's thoughts were obviously influenced by Lenin's idea of implementing the new economic policy, but his understanding of Chinese society and the Chinese revolution were added.[30]

On September 15, 1948, Zhang Wentian expressed basically the same views on the new democratic economic policy as at the September meeting in a report to the Central Committee of the Northeast Bureau in the Outline of the Basic Principles for the Economic Composition and Economic Construction of the Northeast (hereinafter referred to as the Outline). At that time, Northeast China was already the largest liberated area in the country, with the largest number of cities, the strongest industrial power in the liberated areas, and the greatest accumulated experience in large-scale economic construction. Therefore, the Outline elaborated five economic components of the new democratic economy in more detail than Liu Shaoqi's assumption, namely, the state-owned economy, cooperative economy, national capitalist economy, private capitalist economy, and small commodity economy. The Outline pointed out that the state-owned economy had occupied a large proportion of the total production in Northeast China and had grasped the lifeline of the social economy and took a leading position in the national economy. It noted, "The economy operated by the new democratic country under the leadership of the proletariat is already a socialist economy [...] This is the country's most precious property," and "its prospects for development are limitless."[31] As for the cooperative economy, it was "the cooperative economy under the new democratic state system led by the proletariat, the economy with a bureaucratic nature in varying degrees, and the most reliable and powerful assistant to the state-owned economy." As for the state capitalist economy, "it is the most conducive form for the development of the new democratic economy in the capitalist economy," and the Party should "consciously promote and organize it" so as to make it "a favorable direction in the development of private capitalism."[32] As for the private capitalist economy, because of the limited strength of the state-owned economy at that time, the underdeveloped cooperative economy, the war, the needs of the people in all aspects, and the development of free trade, "the existence of the private capitalist economy is inevitable and necessary to a certain extent [...] It must not be underestimated, nor should we adopt early measures to restrict the private capitalist economy that is still beneficial to the national economy and people's livelihood."[33] As for the small commodity economy, "this kind of economy is mainly the peasants' small commodity economy," and it "will also develop to the socialist side under the new democratic state system led by the proletariat." After a detailed analysis of various economic components, Zhang Wentian concluded, "Generally speaking, all five economic components mentioned above should be developed now, but in the process of development, we must implement a clear proletarian leadership line in our economic policy." This meant "taking the development of the state-owned economy as the main body, universally developing and closely relying on the mass's cooperative economy, helping and reforming the small commodity economy, allowing and encouraging the private capitalist economy that is beneficial to the national economy and people's livelihood, especially the national capitalist economy, preventing and opposing the speculative and destructive nature inherent in the capitalist economy of commodities, and forbidding and cracking down on all speculative operations harmful to the national economy and people's livelihood." It was "only by carrying out this line that we can develop the economy of the new democratic society smoothly and strengthen the socialist component of the new democratic economy."[34]

The Northeast Bureau report, drafted by Zhang Wentian, was highly valued and affirmed by the Party Central Committee. From October to December 1948, Liu Shaoqi revised the report. In his revision, he wrote that the contradiction between the proletariat and the bourgeoisie was the basic contradiction in the new democratic society, and that the struggle related to this contradiction, especially the long-term economic competition, "will determine the future development of the new democratic society."[35] He pointed out that the new democratic economy differed from the ordinary capitalist economy in its organizational and planned nature. "However, the organizational and planned nature of the national economy must be strictly limited to the necessary limits that may be possible and must be realized step by step […] We should not launch the entire, overly intense, or overly-large planned economy."[36] Therefore, "when we criticize and oppose the line of the petty bourgeoisie or bourgeoisie, we must resolutely and rigorously prevent any acute tendency of 'left-leaning adventurism,' that is, taking socialist steps prematurely and excessively in the national economy and mechanically implementing them beyond the actual possibility and necessity. The planned economy has deprived us of the support of small farmers. This is a very dangerous 'left-handed bias,' which we must strictly prevent."[37]

It is noteworthy that Liu Shaoqi here also put forward the idea of an "economic approach" for construction. He pointed out that the feudal system could be abolished by revolutionary means, i.e. administrative means, but it would be totally useless and dangerous to lead peasants and small producers economically. The proletariat must adopt economic methods acceptable to farmers and small producers in order to organize and lead farmers and small producers economically.[38]

After the September meeting, the Party's new democratic social thought developed rapidly in an all-round, in-depth way. On December 25, 1948, Liu offered a more systematic exposition of the nature of the new Chinese economy in his report to the North China Finance and Economic Commission. He said, "At present, the direction of the revolution is still imperialism, feudalism, and bureaucratic capitalism. Private capitalism is not the main goal of our struggle [...] Politically, we have formed a coalition government and are still absorbing the participation of the bourgeoisie." He went on, "When the revolution succeeds, capitalism is to develop. We need not be afraid of such limited development. But we can't do without restriction. It's terrible if we don't restrict it [...] Allowing the development of capitalism beneficial to the national economy and people's livelihood is a slogan for struggle." Further, "our policy is not to develop capitalism, but to restrict capitalism and make the transition to socialism."[39]

Liu noted, "Our regime is of a new democratic nature, and our economy is still a new democratic economy. Is the new democratic economy capitalist or socialist? Neither. It has both socialist and capitalist elements. This is a special historical form. Its characteristic is that the economy in the transitional period can transit to capitalism or socialism. This is an unsolved problem. The transitional nature cannot last for long, but it will be a considerable period of time."[40] He went on, "After we overthrow the Kuomintang, it is in the interests of the proletariat to keep the bourgeoisie for a period of time and develop it seriously within fifteen years."[41]

During this period, Mao Zedong's and Liu Shaoqi's related expositions developed the ideas presented in *On New Democracy* and "On the United Government" for the new society after the victory of the revolution, laying the groundwork for the Second Plenary Session of the Seventh Central Committee of the Party, which was soon to be held.

III

Formation of the Theory of Building a New Democratic Nation

1. Second Plenary Session of the Seventh Central Committee

In March 1949, the Second Plenary Session of the Seventh Central Committee was held. The conference, held on the eve of the victory of the new democratic revolution, was an important meeting to determine the basic principles and policies after the victory of the revolution. Mao Zedong's report at the meeting pointed out that "from now on, the period of spreading from the city to the countryside and the city leading the countryside has begun. The focus of the Party's work has shifted from the countryside to the city. The whole Party must make great effort to learn how to manage and build the city."[42]

Mao pointed out that the Party had carried out extensive economic construction work and that its economic policy had been implemented in practical work. "However, on the question of why we should adopt such an economic policy instead of adopting other economic policies, there are many confused ideas in the Party on theoretical and principled issues. How should this question be answered? We think it should be answered in the following way.

"China's industry and agriculture accounted for about 10% of the national economy, and agriculture and handicraft for about 90% of the national economy before the War of Resistance Against Japanese Aggression [...] This is the economic manifestation of the semi-colonial and semi-feudal nature of the old China, and the basic starting point of all problems in the period of the Chinese revolution and in a fairly long period after the victory of the revolution."[43] He also said that about 90% of China's backward, scattered individual agricultural and handicraft economies were "backward, which is not much different from ancient times, and we still have about 90% of our economic life lagging in ancient times [...] Anyone who neglects or despises this point will make the mistake of Leftist opportunism."[44] This was "the basic starting point of all problems in the period of the Chinese revolution and in the long period after the victory of the revolution. From this point of view, a series of strategic, tactical, and policy problems have arisen in our Party."[45]

From this point of view, he noted that "since China's economy is still in a backward state, it is necessary to make full use of the advantages of urban and rural capitalism for the development of the national economy for a long time after the victory of the revolution [...] In this period, the elements of urban and rural capitalism that are not harmful, but rather beneficial to the national economy should be allowed to exist and develop."[46] It was also a complete mistake to think that private capital should be strictly restricted or that it could be eliminated very quickly. This was the Leftist opportunist or adventurist perspective.[47] Mao added, "Regarding the recovery and development of production, we must make sure that the first is the production of state-owned industry, the second is the production of private industry, and the third is the production of handicraft industry."[48] Mao's classical expositions adhered to the most basic productivity standards of Marxism, criticized the idea of not proceeding from China's national conditions but seeking instead to enter socialism directly, and drew a clear line with those ideas which seemed to be "revolution" but were very close to populism.

Another important part of the Second Plenary Session of the Seventh Central Committee was the assertion of the basic contradictions in New China. In his report, Mao Zedong pointed out, "After the victory of the Chinese revolution throughout the country and the settlement of the land problem, there are still two basic contradictions in China. The first is the domestic contradiction between the working class and the bourgeoisie. The second is the contradiction between China and imperialist countries abroad."[49] This assertion pointed out two basic ideas that the Party needed to pay attention to in all its work, but it also raised several questions.

For example, when the People's Republic of China was founded, there was still a feudal land system in two-thirds of the country. That is to say, although the new democratic revolution had been victorious, its economic program had not yet been fully realized. So what were the main contradictions in China during the period from the founding of New China to the completion of the land reform in the new area?

For another example, the Party should not only make the best use of the advantages of urban and rural capitalism, but also allow the existence and development of urban and rural capitalist elements which were not harmful but beneficial to the national economy. It should also point out that the contradiction between the working class and the bourgeoisie was the "basic contradiction."

How was it to deal with the relationship between the two?

Another example was that Mao repeatedly emphasized in his report that all work in the city "revolves around the central task of production and construction and serves this central task." Then, how was this "central task" to be unified with the "basic contradictions"?

Such a situation could arise, as Hu Sheng noted, saying, "At that time it's still wavering. There's a bit of contradiction in thought."[50] On the one hand, it was a profound understanding of China's national conditions and the application of Marxist theory on productivity, but on the other, it was an understanding of Marxist socialist theory and a reference to the practical experience of the Soviet Union and Eastern European countries. Both factors exerted great influence on the CPC at that time. The emergence of the problem indicated not only the development of practice and the deepening of understanding, but also the difficulty of exploration.

After the Second Plenary Session of the Seventh Central Committee Meeting, the Party further explored a series of basic issues concerning the theory and policy of the new democracy.

In April 1949, in his report to the First National Congress of the Youth League for New Democracy of China, Ren Bishi said that in order to achieve complete economic independence in China, it was necessary not only strive to restore the damaged industries within three to five years, but also to plan to increase the proportion of industries in the national economy from about 10% to 30% within ten to fifteen years. Forty percent of them "lay a solid economic foundation for the future shift to socialism."[51] That May, Li Lisan, chairman of the All-China Federation of Trade Unions, pointed out in a speech that "China's main characteristic is that its economic development is too backward [...] Therefore, China cannot directly carry out the socialist revolution like Russia did at that time, nor can it begin to transit to socialism within several years of gaining victory in the revolution, like the new democratic countries in Eastern Europe." After the victory of the Chinese revolution, "it would be "necessary to go through quite a long period of new democratic construction to develop China's industry [...] Without the great development of industry, it is not only impossible to practice socialism, but also impossible for the Chinese nation to be truly and thoroughly independent of imperialism in its economy."[52]

More than three months later, on June 30, 1949, Mao Zedong published "On the People's Democratic Dictatorship," in commemoration of the 28th anniversary of the founding of the Communist Party of China, again expounding the above ideas. He said, "What are the people? In China, at the present stage, they are the working class, the peasant class, the urban petty bourgeoisie, and the national bourgeoisie. Under the leadership of the working class and the Communist Party, these classes are united to build their own country."[53] Further, "under these conditions, it is possible for China to move steadily from an agricultural to an industrial country and from a new democratic to a socialist and communist society under the leadership of the working class and the Communist Party."[54] He went on, "The foundation of the people's democratic dictatorship is the alliance of the working and peasant class and the urban petty bourgeoisie [...] To shift from new democracy to socialism, we mainly rely on the alliance of the two classes."[55] He added, "The national bourgeoisie is of great importance at this stage. [...] In order to cope with the oppression of imperialism and to improve the backward economic status, China must unite the national bourgeoisie and work together by utilizing all the factors of urban and rural capitalism that are beneficial to the national economy and people's livelihood rather than harmful to them. Our current policy is to control capitalism rather than eliminate it. But the national bourgeoisie cannot be the leader of the revolution, nor should it occupy a dominant position in state power."[56]

On the eve of the founding of New China, not only had the theory of the Party's new democratic revolution grown mature and complete, but the theory of the Party's new democratic nation-building and the theory of the new democratic society were also basically mature. The process of the development and maturity of the "two theories" of new democracy was the process of the development and maturity of the localization of Marxism in China.

2. A Model of Practicing New Democratic Sociology: Liu Shaoqi's "Tianjin Speech"

With the victory of the War of Liberation, many large and medium-sized cities were liberated. A large number of cadres who had been active in the backward countryside for a long time entered the cities and assumed the task of receiving and managing them. Because of the rapid victory and the lack of ideological and policy preparations for cadres, Leftist errors were quite common in the management of cities, which was very unfavorable to the implementation of the Party's principles and policies, the rapid resumption of urban production, and the stabilization of people's minds.

After the liberation of Tianjin in early 1949, social order recovered quickly, but production recovered slowly. Along with the damage caused by the war, the failure to deal with the public-private relations and labor-capital relations were important reasons for this situation. There was a general feeling of "wait and see" among capitalists. Bo Yibo recalled, "Workers and shop assistants mistakenly believe that we allow the division of stores and factories, as well as a liquidation struggle. Fifty-three liquidation struggles took place in Tianjin within one month of liberation. There are three fears in capitalists' minds. One is fear of liquidation, another is fear of the Communist Party's ignorance of workers' interests, and the final is fear that workers will not be able to control and produce after liberation." He went on, "Therefore, they take a passive wait-and-see attitude and even go to Hong Kong. According to Tianjin statistics, at that time, less than 30% of private enterprises started work."[57]

The Party organizations in Tianjin also lacked the means to implement the new policies on private capital. The seriousness of the problem also lay in the fact that the problems in Tianjin were quite common in the cities of the newly liberated areas. Whether these problems could be solved correctly and quickly in accordance with the spirit of the Second Plenary Session of the Seventh Central Committee depended on the stability and consolidation of the people's regime. According to the decision of the Central Committee, Liu Shaoqi traveled to Tianjin in April 1949, to solve the problem of restoring urban production as quickly as possible. After in-depth and extensive discussions and investigations, Liu delivered a series of important speeches in Tianjin. These speeches profoundly and vividly elucidated the spirit of the Second Plenary Session of the Seventh Central Committee, propagated the Party's thought on building a new democracy, affirmed the Party's national bourgeoisie policy, effectively corrected the Leftist errors in urban work at that time, and played a key role in stabilizing the situation and restoring and developing production.

Liu Shaoqi said in his speech that capitalists were not the object of struggle for the working class, but rather the object of solidarity. Current emphasis was on uniting the free bourgeoisie, not on struggle.[58] In view of the problems existing in Tianjin's work, he said that Chairman Mao had noted the importance of considering all aspects and taking care of all sides, including public-private relations, labor-capital relations, urban-rural relations, and internal-external relations. He likewise made mention of urban-rural relations, internal-external relations, and public-private relations, and both sides of labor relations. He quoted Mao's remarks in his conversation with representatives of the business community in Shanghai in the first half of 1949, which pointed out that when it came to revolution, the proletariat may be best, but in terms of production in cities, others should have a say.[59] He had previously stated, "Is the new democratic economy capitalist or socialist? Neither. It has both socialist and capitalist elements. This is a special historical form, which is characterized by the transitional economy and can transit to capitalism or socialism [...] The transitional nature can't last long, but it will require a rather long period of time."[60] Now he asked, "Why not abolish the bourgeoisie earlier? Because it is difficult to do so. What happens when it's eliminated? When it's eliminated, you'll have need to have it back."[61] Therefore, "after we overthrow the Kuomintang, it is beneficial for the proletariat to keep the bourgeoisie for a period of time and develop it seriously within fifteen years."[62]

Liu Shaoqi specifically analyzed the situation of capitalism in China at that time, noting, "The capitalist exploitation system cannot be completely abolished today [...] Today, workers suffer not from the development of capitalism, but also from the lack of development of capitalism. Under the current conditions in China, the development of the private capitalist economy is progressive and beneficial to the national economy, to China, and to workers. Exploitation under certain historical conditions is progressive."[63] He went on, "The exploitation of capitalism in our country today is not only innocent, but also meritorious. After the removal of feudal exploitation, capitalist exploitation was progressive. Today, there are not too many factories and too many exploited workers, but too few."[64] And "the contradictions between the working class and the bourgeoisie cannot be solved fundamentally today, but can only be alleviated by some means."[65]

Liu Shaoqi's Tianjin speech dispelled many fears among the cadres at that time and clarified some confused understandings. Although some points may have been overstated, for the most part, they correctly expounded the Party's policy toward the national bourgeoisie and concretely expounded the basic economic policy of the new democratic country. The most outstanding point was that it started from the standard of productivity, not from an abstract ideological standard or an abstract moral evaluation. After Liu Shaoqi's Tianjin speech, Tianjin's industrial and commercial production began to recover from May onward. In June and July, the main industrial production industries returned to pre-founding levels. The number of approved private businesses increased from 293 in April to 3800 in September, and the number of employees increased by nearly 20%. With the rapid recovery of industry and commerce as its symbol, Tianjin's economic construction witnessed a thriving scene. The Tianjin speech set an example for the whole Party to correctly handle a series of problems after taking over the city.

3. Guidelines for the Economic Construction of New China

In June 1949, in order to go to Moscow for talks with the leaders of the Central Committee of the Soviet Communist Party, and in accordance with the spirit of the Second Plenary Session of the Seventh Central Committee, and in hopes of exchanging views with other leading leaders of the Central Committee, Liu Shaoqi wrote an outline of a report entitled "Guidelines for the Economic Construction of New China." The Outline offered a more systematic, accurate, and standardized explanation of the economic components and their relations after the founding of New China and accordingly introduced the economic construction to be launched across the board. The outline ranked five economic components, the state-owned economy, the cooperative economy, the national capitalist economy, the private capitalist economy, the commodity economy, and the semi-natural economy. The nature of the five economic components was that the state-owned economy of the new democratic country under the leadership of the proletariat was a socialist economy, the cooperative economy was a socialist economy in varying degrees, and the state capitalist economy was very close to a socialist economy, the private capitalist economy, and the small businessmen. The product and semi-natural economies were the basis of the development trend of capitalism. According to the above analysis, the outline held that "in the present and the first period after the war, in order to cure the wounds of war and restore the destroyed and isolated economic life, generally speaking, the five economic components mentioned above should be encouraged and developed, except those speculative and manipulative operations and those harmful to the national economy and people's livelihood in the new democracy." Among them, "we must take the development of the state-owned economy as the main body."[66] Another important idea contained in the Outline was the analysis and identification of the basic contradictions within New China after the elimination of imperialist and feudal forces. The Outline reiterated the spirit of the Second Plenary Session of the Seventh Central Committee, stating, "This is the struggle between the factors and trends of socialism and capitalism, and between the proletariat and the bourgeoisie [...] This contradiction and struggle will determine whether China's future development will be transitional to a socialist or capitalist society."[67] The Outline held that the new democratic economy would be a transitional economy. "This transition will go through a long and arduous process of struggle, which is what Lenin said during the period of the new economic policy of the Soviet Union. It is a question of 'who will win over whom.'"[68]

The outline of the talks, written on the eve of the founding of New China, reflected the ever-maturing concept of nation-building, formed over twenty-nine years of democratic revolution. Compared with the previous discussions by the central leaders, it cleared up the main contradictions after the founding of New China, emphasized the struggle between socialism and capitalism and the proletariat and the bourgeoisie, and was more cautious about the development and utilization of capitalism, emphasizing its importance less than in "On the United Government" and *On New Democracy*. "Although the new democracy has been maintained, it seems that this time it is different from the discussion in 'On the United Government.'"[69] Moreover, the Outline equated the new democratic economy with Lenin's new economic policy and the new democratic period with Lenin's "transitional period," which was also different from works such as *On New Democracy*. This can be seen as a retreat from the standpoint of works such as "On the United Government," and could be understood as developing in step with the development of practice.

It was understandable that such a situation would occur. Simply speaking, absolute retrogression or absolute development seemed undesirable. First of all, on the cusp of the founding of New China, fundamental changes had taken place in the domestic political and military situation. The Communist Party of China and the revolutionary classes under its leadership had become the overwhelming forces. In such a situation, the understanding of the bourgeoisie, the new democratic revolution, and the new democratic society would surely have new developments in the new practice. It was to be expected that there were some different understandings. Second, in the process of restoring the national economy, the contradictions between the proletariat and the bourgeoisie and between the state-owned economy and the capitalist economy would gradually grow more prominent. It was much more complicated to deal with these contradictions correctly on the practical operation level than in a theoretical argument. Finally, with the development of large-scale economic work, the construction experience of the Soviet Union and the people's democratic countries in Eastern Europe were also becoming increasingly influential, and the influence of the Soviet Union's construction model was also gradually strengthened.

In the final analysis, in a new democratic country, the emergence of these issues involved how to deal with the relationship between socialism and capitalism and how to deal with the relationship between the proletariat and the national bourgeoisie. On this issue, the Party had gained experience in the revolutionary base areas during the Second Civil Revolutionary War and anti-Japanese democratic base areas during the Anti-Japanese War, bolstered with the experience of people's democratic countries in Eastern Europe after the Second World War. In theory, it encompassed Lenin's theory of new economic policy and the transitional theory, as well as Stalin's theory. But when victory came quickly, there was still a lack of comprehensive practice. When dealing with a large number of specific policies, the Party was faced with many unresolved contradictions. It was against this background that some inconsistencies and incompleteness in theory surfaced. For example, Liu Shaoqi contrasted the similarities and differences between China and the Soviet Union in terms of economy, politics and international aspects in his article "The Nature of New China's Economy and Economic Construction Guidelines," emphasizing the combination of the particularity of China's national conditions and the unity of the people's democratic state construction. He also pointed out that the experience of the Soviet Union could not be duplicated. For example, the Soviet Union did not implement state capitalism, but China did. He said, "Some people say that the Soviet Union did not implement this system, so we do not have to implement it." But "China's situation is different. Our conditions are better than those of the Soviet Union." The most important thing was that "our revolution has not yet opposed the bourgeoisie, and is to a certain extent united with the bourgeoisie, and we will do the same in the future."[70]

But there were also some aspects to be imitated. For example, after comparing the new democratic economic policy with Lenin's new economic policy, he pointed out, "Lenin asked, what is the new economic policy? The new economic policy is the cruel class struggle between the proletariat and the bourgeoisie. The new democratic economic policy is the policy of sharp class struggle between the proletariat and the bourgeoisie. It is also the final struggle. The later into the struggle, the more intense it will be. The more desperate the bourgeoisie is, the more rebellious and ruthless it will be. We must be vigilant."[71] Later practice proved that there was a comparable side and an incomparable side between the two. Both the new economic policy and the new democratic economic policy were based on the basic national conditions of backward countries and utilized capitalism to develop the economy. But how much, how long, and how to deal with the relationship between the proletariat and the bourgeoisie and between socialism and capitalism not only had different theoretical explanations, but were not easy to handle in practical work as well. Moreover, due to the different national conditions, there were considerable differences in the way countries dealt with it. This question was a test of whether the basic principles of Marxism could be combined with the specific conditions of each socialist country after the war.

Despite these circumstances, the Party's basic understanding of the new democratic society and the new democratic economy was still consistent. For example, although the basic contradictions were clearly defined, Mao Zedong and Liu Shaoqi still held positive attitudes toward the development of capitalism to a certain extent, especially emphasizing the use of "competition" to solve such basic contradictions. There was a cautious attitude toward the relationship between new democracy and socialism. For example, Party leaders at that time repeatedly stressed the long-term nature of the transition from a new democratic society to a socialist society.

IV

The Sum of the Theory of Building a New Democratic Nation: The Common Program

On October 1, 1949, the people's long-awaited new, independent, and unified democracy was finally born. The Common Program adopted by the Chinese People's Political Consultative Conference (CPPCC) served as the guiding principle and blueprint for the construction of New China. It stipulated the essence of the theory of the new democratic revolution and the new democratic society in the form of an interim constitution. It was for this reason that a distinctive feature of the Common Program was to show clearly what should be done and what could be done at the present stage, along with what should be done in the future and what could not be done at the present stage, so that it would remain silent for the time being and refrain from specifying a vision of the future society. This was a program of action that was truly based on China's reality and met the needs of the people. On this basis, Liu Shaoqi, on behalf of the CPC, solemnly declared at a plenary session of the CPPCC that the CPC fully complied with all the provisions of the Common Program and called on the people throughout the nation to strive for its complete realization.

1. Regarding State and Government

Regarding the state and political system, the Common Program stipulated that "The People's Republic of China, as a new democratic country, and specifically a people's democracy, will implement a people's democratic dictatorship led by the working class, based on the alliance of workers and peasants and uniting all democratic classes and ethnicities in the country [...] The state power of the People's Republic of China belongs to the people. The organs of the people exercising state power are the people's congresses at all levels and the people's governments at all levels. The highest organ of state power is the National People's Congress. All organs of government at all levels shall practice democratic centralism."

The provisions of the Common Program were continuously developed and finalized through long-term practice and exploration. Just before the outbreak of the War of Resistance Against Japanese Aggression, Mao pointed out, "There will be several stages of development in the democratic revolution, all under the democratic republic. From the bourgeoisie to the proletariat, this is a long process of struggle."[72] At the beginning of 1940, in *On New Democracy*, the Party clearly put forward the slogan of the new democratic republic, initially clarifying that the state of the new democratic republic was "the joint dictatorship of all revolutionary classes." In 1944, the CPC put forward the slogan of abolishing the one-party dictatorship of the Kuomintang and establishing a democratic coalition government. The Seventh National Congress of the CPC clearly proposed, "After thoroughly defeating the Japanese aggressors, we should establish a national system of Democratic Alliance on the United Front based on the overwhelming majority of the people of the entire country and under the leadership of the working class." On April 30, 1948, the Central Committee of the CPC issued the slogan "May Day Labor Day," which excluded the reactionary ruling group of the Kuomintang from the democratic coalition government according to the changes in the balance of forces. In 1949, "On the People's Democratic Dictatorship" further clarified, "Summarizing our experience, we should focus on several points. First is the people's democratic dictatorship led by the working class (through the Communist Party) based on the alliance of workers and peasants [...] next is that the foundation of the people's democratic dictatorship is the alliance of the working class, the peasant class, and the urban petty bourgeoisie, but mainly the alliance of the working and the peasant classes." Although the national bourgeoisie was still of great importance, its social and economic status determined that they "should not play a major role in state power."[73] Regarding New China's political system, i.e, the form of political power organization in the new democratic country, democratic centralism was adopted. The people's congresses at all levels decided on major principles and policies, elected the government, and did not separate the parliamentary system and legislative, administrative, and judicial powers, as in bourgeois countries.

In the latter part of the War of Liberation, when the political situation and the ratio of class forces changed dramatically, there were various doubts or fears among some cadres within the Party, some democratic parties, and non-party personages regarding whether to adhere to new democracy or return to the democratic dictatorship of workers and peasants during the Agrarian Revolutionary War, or to move directly to the dictatorship of the proletariat of the

Soviet Union. The formulation indicated that the Party had adhered to the theory of a people's democratic dictatorship formed and developed in the democratic revolution and put it into practice to establish a new state power. The people's democratic dictatorship excluded the reactionaries of the Kuomintang and was different from the coalition government, but it absorbed representatives of the national bourgeoisie and their political parties to participate in the government. The coalition had a broader class scope than the workers' and peasants' democratic dictatorship, which was an important characteristic that was different from it. However, the people's democratic dictatorship took the working class as its leadership, the worker-peasant alliance as its foundation, and socialism as its future, which was essentially the same as the workers' and peasants' democratic dictatorship. On this point, Liu Shaoqi offered a penetrating exposition in his written report to the Central Committee of the Soviet Communist Party when he visited the Soviet Union in July 1949, saying, "China's people's democratic dictatorship has something in common with Lenin's 'workers' and peasants' democratic dictatorship' proposed in the 1905–1907 revolution," but noted that it also had some differences, because it included representatives and factions of the free bourgeoisie. "The form of people's democratic dictatorship is the people's congress system. This is not a bourgeois parliamentary system, but is close to the Soviet system, though also different from the proletarian dictatorship of the Soviet system, because the representatives of the democratic bourgeoisie participate in the people's congress."[74] That August, he also said at the cadre meeting of the Northeast Bureau that "because we want to cooperate with the bourgeoisie for a considerable period of time, China cannot establish a proletarian dictatorship but a people's democratic dictatorship. If we do not want to pursue the dictatorship of the proletariat as seen in Eastern Europe, we should still pursue proletarianism. If we refer to Greece all the time, it will become dogmatism. Our problems should be decided based on the specific conditions of China."[75]

The CPC's conception of New China's state and regime was discussed at the plenary meeting of the Chinese People's Political Consultative Conference and reached a consensus, which was written into the Common Program. This new form of dictatorship was suitable for the development level and practical requirements of China's economy and politics at that time, and it was another great achievement in the integration of Marxism into China.

However, later development proved that the Party's understanding of the basic concepts of the people's democratic dictatorship, the workers' and peasants' democratic dictatorship, and the proletarian dictatorship was not very stable. After some later changes in the situation, when the development stage of the new democratic society was no longer mentioned, the boundaries between these concepts became blurred or were seen as directly equivalent.

2. On the Economic Composition and System of the New Democracy

The Common Program stipulated that the fundamental principle of economic construction in the People's Republic of China was to develop production and prosper the economy through the policy of giving consideration to both public and private interests and mutual assistance between urban and rural areas and in internal and external exchanges. The state should adopt various policies to enable various economic components to work properly under the leadership of the state-owned economy so as to promote the development of the entire social economy. The state-owned economy was a socialist economy and a leading force in the entire social economy. As a semi-socialist economy, the cooperative economy was an important part of the whole people's economy. It was necessary for the Party to encourage and assist the working people to develop cooperative undertakings on the basis of the principle of voluntariness. All private economic undertakings conducive to the national economy and people's livelihood should be encouraged to operate actively and their development aided, while under necessary and possible conditions, private capital should be encouraged to develop in the direction of state capitalism.

These economic principles were discussed many times in the writings of Mao Zedong and other Party leaders. For example, at the September 1948 meeting of the Politburo of the Central Committee, Mao Zedong focused on the socialist factors in the composition of New China's economy, pointing out, "What plays a decisive role in our social economy is the state-owned economy and the public economy. This country is led by the proletariat, so these economies are socialist in nature. The rural individual economy and the urban private economy are large in quantity, but they do not play a decisive role. Our state-owned economy and public economy are small in number, but they play a decisive role. The nature of socialism should be stated, but the whole national economy is still a new democratic economy, that is, the economic system under the leadership of the socialist economy."[76]

At the Second Plenary Session of the Seventh Central Committee of the CPC, Mao further clarified, "The state-owned economy is socialist in nature and the cooperative economy is semi-socialist in nature. In private capitalism, the individual economy, and the state capitalist economy with private cooperation, one of the major economic achievements of the People's Republic is that these constitute the economic form of new democracy. In the whole national economy, the state-owned economy is the leading component and plays a decisive role." Because "China's private capitalist industry occupies the second place in the modern industry, and it is a force that cannot be ignored," it was necessary to make full use of the enthusiasm of urban and rural private capitalism for the development of the national economy over a long period after the victory of the revolution. At the same time, it was important to adopt appropriate and flexible restrictive policies toward capitalism in several aspects. Mao highlighted that China's economy was still in a backward state and that the proportion of modern industry in the overall national economy was still very small, which was the most fundamental basis for the Party to formulate economic policies. "This is also the basic starting point for all problems in the period of the Chinese revolution and for a fairly long period after the victory of the revolution."[77]

The Common Program and the Party's basic economic policy for the new democratic society on which it was based would make full use of the productive forces of capitalist industry to gradually expand the proportion of modern industry in the overall national economy and rapidly restore and develop productive forces so as to realize the goal of turning to a socialist society by continuously developing and strengthening the socialist state-owned economy after the founding of the People's Republic of China. The transformation of doctrine laid a material and technological foundation and was of great significance.[78]

3. Multi-party Cooperation and Political Consultation System Led by the Communist Party of China

New China implemented a system of multi-party cooperation and political consultation under the leadership of the Communist Party of China, rather than a one-party system. The Common Program stipulated, "The Communist Party of China, the democratic parties, the people's organizations, and all localities shall be responsible for the implementation of the Common Program."

The People's Political Consultative Conference of the People's Republic of China, composed of representatives of districts, the People's Liberation Army, ethnic minorities, overseas Chinese, and other patriotic democrats, was the organizational form of the People's Democratic United Front. It was also pointed out that before the general election of the National People's Congress, the plenary session of the Political Consultative Conference should carry out the functions and powers of the National People's Congress and "exercise the roles and powers of the state."

In the long-term revolutionary struggle against imperialism and feudalism, the CPC established close cooperative relations with various democratic parties. Adhering to the people's democratic united front was a magic weapon for the Communist Party to successfully lead the new democratic revolution. After the victory of the new democratic revolution throughout the country, some people in the Communist Party believed that the revolution had succeeded and that the united front and democratic parties were "indispensable," while some people in the Democratic Party believed that the mission had been accomplished and wanted to end gloriously and without illness. In response to these understandings, before and after the Political Consultative Conference, Mao Zedong instructed the CPC to recognize the long-term legitimate existence of democratic parties and to create a "multi-party" political situation. Zhou Enlai also pointed out at the Political Association on September 22, 1949, that in order to build a new China, "we should unite all democratic classes, ethnicities, and overseas Chinese in our country to form such a great people's democratic united front [...] Such a united front should continue and be organized to promote its development." He added, "Since there are different classes in the new democratic era, there will be different parties."[79]

The system of multi-party cooperation and political consultation under the leadership of the Communist Party, as established in the Common Program, is the inheritance and development of Marxist political party and state theory. Marx and Engels had imagined that in the struggle of the proletariat to seize power, they should achieve unity and cooperation with other working class political parties and political parties striving for democracy, but they could not envision the political party relations after the realization of the dictatorship, of the proletariat because they had no practice of it. In the process of leading the Russian revolution, Lenin emphasized the need for the leadership of the Bolshevik Party, and at the same time considered inviting minorities such as the Mensheviks to participate in the new government, thus establishing a coalition government within the scope of the Soviet Union. However, due to the repeated non-cooperation of the other side, the idea of multi-party cooperation was not realized. The CPC's practice of building a country based on China's national conditions developed into a ruling system of multi-party cooperation on the basis of the united front of multi-party cooperation in the period of democratic revolution. This was the product of combining Marxism-Leninism with China's actual situation and a vivid embodiment of the localization of Marxism in China.

The system of multi-party cooperation and political consultation led by the CPC was different from the multi-party system in Western countries. It was a multi-party cooperation led by one party based on the Common Program. This kind of political system was suited to China's national conditions, and it demonstrated its unique political advantages and strong vitality, playing a key irreplaceable role in China's political and social life in the future.

4. A People's Republic with Multi-ethnic Unity

Another important contribution of the Common Program to the basic system of the country was to determine that China was a multi-ethnic unified people's republic, not a federal system of multi-ethnic republics.

Affected by the trend of national self-determination after the First World War and the Soviet Union, the CPC advocated national self-determination and the establishment of a "federation" in its previous program documents, including the proposal of the establishment of the "Federal Republic of China"[80] in the declaration of its Second National Congress in 1922. In the Constitution of the Seventh National Congress in 1945, the establishment of a "New Democratic Federal Republic of Free Union of All Ethnicities" was proposed.[81] The Declaration of the Chinese People's Liberation Army of October 10, 1947, also put forward the idea of "equal autonomy and free membership in the Federation of China" for all ethnic minorities in China.[82] This understanding continued until the 1949 Political Consultative Conference.

On the eve of the founding of New China, when drafting the Common Program, the Party's understanding changed greatly. Mao Zedong proposed that the Party should consider whether to pursue federalism or a unified republic with regional autonomy for ethnic minorities. On September 7, 1949, Zhou Enlai, in his report on political cooperation, proposed, "As regards the state system, another question is whether our country is a multi-ethnic federation… Please consider it." He said, "China is a multi-ethnic country, but its characteristics are that the Han nationality accounts for the largest majority of the population, and the ethnic minorities together are less than 10% of the national population. No matter how many people there are, all ethnic groups are equal […] The main question here is whether ethnic policy is aimed at or beyond autonomy. We advocate ethnic autonomy, but we must prevent imperialism from using ethnic issues to provoke the reunification of China. We should adopt such a policy to unite all ethnic groups into a large family and prevent imperialism from provoking division. Today, imperialism also wants to divide us from our own Tibet, Taiwan, and even Xinjiang. In this case, we hope that all ethnic groups will not listen to the imperialists' provocation. For this reason, the name of our country is the People's Republic of China, not a Federation."[83] According to such a new understanding, the CPPCC decided to establish a unified republic and implement ethnic autonomous regions instead of adopting a multi-ethnic federation system based on the characteristics of large minorities but small populations with large mixed and small cohabitation in China. The new name was the People's Republic of China, rather than naming it a federation.

The Common Program defined the implementation of regional autonomy for ethnic regions in a single nation, which was another important feature that distinguished New China from the Soviet model in the issue of nation-building. It was also a new achievement of the Chinese Communists in independently exploring the road to nation-building. It was a solution to China's ethnic and state system problems that applied the Marxist-Leninist ethnic theory. The determination of the system of regional ethnic autonomy would help maintain the unity of all ethnic groups and the unity of the state, forming a new type of equality, unity, and mutual assistance among all ethnic groups.

Ethnic relations played an important role in the early days of New China. The development of the latter half-century of New China demonstrated that this system design had far-reaching significance for the long-term stability of the country in a complex international environment.

When formulating the Common Program, because the revolutionary forces represented by the Communist Party were in an advantageous position politically and economically, the socialist factors greatly increased and the future of the transformation to socialism became clearer. Therefore, in discussing the general outline of the Common Program, there was a view that since new democracy was about to transit to socialism and communism, "the Outline should clearly define this future." In response to this understanding, Zhou Enlai, appointed by the Central Committee at the plenary meeting of the CPPCC on September 22, 1949, explained that the future of the transition to socialism was certain and beyond doubt, but it should be proved to the people of the nation through explanation, propaganda, and practice. "Only when the people of the entire country realize in their own practice that this is the only best future can they truly recognize it and be willing to fight for it wholeheartedly. So for the time being, we should not deny it, but should take it more seriously. And in the economic part of this program, it has been stipulated that we should ensure that we are heading for this future."[84]

The Common Program summarized the basic experience of China's new democratic revolution in the form of a fundamental law and laid out the strategies and directions for the construction of New China. It was the advanced stage of the development of the theory of the new democracy and the basic principle for the transition to the new stage. It contained all the minimum programs of the Communist Party of China, that is, the task of realizing the new democratic revolution and construction at the present stage, while linking up with the Party's future socialist program on the basic political principles, which was the Party's governing criteria for a considerable period of time.

The formulation and implementation of the Common Program was a model of the Party's adherence to Marxism and its foothold in China's actual situation, as well as a masterpiece of the Party's continuous promotion of the integration of Marxism into China through leadership of the new democratic revolution. It reflected the Party's profound grasp of the essence of Marxism on the cusp of its rise to power in the country, and it laid a fundamental prerequisite and institutional foundation for the development and progress of contemporary China.

CHAPTER 3

The Development of New Democracy in the Implementation of the Common Program

The founding of the People's Republic of China on October 1, 1949, opened a new chapter in the history of China, the CPC, and the localization of Marxism in China.

After the founding of the People's Republic of China, the Party led all the people of the nation to fully implement the New Democracy Program for the Founding of the People's Republic. While comprehensively restoring and developing industrial and agricultural production and various economic undertakings, it was also necessary to establish and develop the state-owned economy and ensure that it occupied a leading position in the national economy and to carry out in-depth land reform, vigorously suppress counter-revolutionaries, eliminate the remnants of the reactionaries of the Kuomintang, and clean up the remnants of the old society. There was a stable situation in China that had never existed before in history, and profound changes had taken place in China's social life.

The new democratic society was a transitional society, the intermediate stage of the transition from a semi-colonial and semi-feudal society to a socialist society. This basic understanding was established by the Party's long-term exploration during the period of the democratic revolution. The classic exposition of it was pointed out at the Second Plenary Session of the Seventh Central Committee, which pointed to the need to transform China from an agricultural country to an industrial one and from a new democratic society to a socialist one. Now with the Party in power and in the process of fully implementing the new democracy and building the country, the state-owned economy had firmly established its leading position in the whole national economy, but was still faced with many new problems, and the theory of the new democracy was similarly facing the task of development and enrichment. The question, then, was how it would develop and in what direction.

The Implementation of the Policy of a New Democratic Nation and the Recovery and Development of the National Economy

At the beginning of the founding of New China, the primary mission for the Party was to restore the economy and complete the unfinished task of democratic revolution. It should be noted that the completion of these basic tasks was carried out under the new democratic economic and political system, which in turn further promoted the consolidation and development of this system. That is to say, the period of economic recovery was that of building a new democratic society.

1. "It is Unlikely That We Will Practice Socialism Soon"

The construction of a new democratic economy aimed mainly to develop five economic components. In accordance with the spirit of the Second Plenary Session of the Seventh Central Committee, the Party persisted in relying wholeheartedly on the working class in its urban work, putting the restoration and development of the production of state-owned industries as a top priority, making it the dominant force in the dominant position in the national economy. At the same time, private capitalism and the development of the individual economy should be allowed to play an active role in the development of productive forces. At that time, although the Party's leaders and relevant policies and the Common Program had already stipulated principles, there was confusion and wavering among some cadres due to the contradictions inherent in the theory of the new democracy, especially those between the "basic" and central tasks, together with many new situations and problems in the actual work.

How should the Party understand and deal with the urban industrial and commercial bourgeoisie? Was it best to copy the experience of the Soviet Union and launch an attack on capitalism, or to adhere to the theory of the new democratic society in light of China's national conditions, affirming that in China, where productivity was very backward, capitalism was necessary for existence and development, and that the transition to socialism was only possible when productivity had developed to some extent? Faced with these and other conundrums both inside and outside the Party, the Central Committee attached great importance to guiding Party members and cadres to correctly understand and treat the position and role of the urban industrial and commercial bourgeoisie in the construction of the new democracy.

At that time, a strict distinction between feudal and capitalist exploitation and an affirmation of the important position and role of capitalism and the bourgeoisie in national life were the keys to correcting the Leftist mistakes in urban work. Liu Shaoqi's Tianjin speech in April 1949 played an important role in this regard. It is worth noting that in the early stages of the founding of New China, although some cadres only had some simple understanding of the national bourgeoisie, the understanding of the Central Committee was clear and firm. At the National United Front Conference held in April 1950, a senior cadre said in his speech, "The main target of today's struggle is the bourgeoisie." This erroneous statement attracted Zhou Enlai's attention. Zhou sent the transcript of the speech to Mao Zedong and Liu Shaoqi on April 12, and enclosed a letter stating that "this is a wrong and confused opinion. And the speaker is not the only one with such confused ideas."[1] On April 13, Zhou Enlai pointed out at the National United Front Conference that "today's central issue is not to overthrow the bourgeoisie, but to cooperate with them." He added that China's "state-owned economy is still very small, and the private economy that is beneficial to the national economy and people's livelihood has a certain positive role. It should be supported for its development" in order to "help the state-owned economy meet the needs of the people in many aspects." He went on to say that "socialism could not be "forced out" by coercion, and "the issue of encouraging the development of private enterprises is now on our agenda." If the public and private sectors were not taken into account, he said, it would be very difficult to realize the dual benefits of labor and capital.[2] In response to Zhou's reflections,

Mao Zedong declared, "Today's struggle is mainly against the remnants of imperialism and its watchdogs, the reactionaries of the Kuomintang, rather than the national bourgeoisie." For the national bourgeoisie, "the policy of unity and struggle will be adopted to achieve the goal of uniting the national bourgeoisie to jointly develop the national economy." In response to the statement that "the state-owned economy is developing indefinitely," Mao Zedong commented, "This is a long-term thing. At the present stage, it is impossible to develop indefinitely. Private capital must be used at the same time."[3]

In March and April 1950, the Central Committee held working meetings and Politburo meetings attended by leaders from various regions in preparation for the Third Plenary Session of the Seventh Central Committee. The meeting clearly pointed out that the principle of adjusting industry and commerce was to give consideration to both public and private interests and to benefit both labor and capital. It was necessary to correct the erroneous ideas and practices espoused by some cadres and to crush private industry and commerce. Mao Zedong said at the meeting, "Cooperation with the bourgeoisie is affirmative. If not, the Common Program would become a dead letter, politically disadvantageous, and economically disadvantaged. 'Taking a strategic view' has maintained private industry and commerce. First, production has been maintained, second, workers have been retained, and third, workers have gained some benefits. Of course, it also gives the bourgeoisie a certain profit. But comparatively speaking, the development of private industry and commerce is more beneficial to workers and the people than to capitalists."[4] He also said, "We are a big party and we should pay special attention to our strategy. Especially now that we have won, we should consolidate our victory and pay more attention to opposing the idea of Leftists and the practice of the Left."[5]

On May 25, Mao put forward at the Politburo meeting that private industry and commerce should be treated differently and equally. He explained that the so-called "different" treatment was the dominant position of the state-owned economy, which was progressive, and it was impossible to reverse these positions. However, on other issues, they should be treated equally and given overall consideration. He noted, "Today's capitalist industry and commerce are necessary and beneficial to society. It is reasonable for private industry and commerce to be under the wing of the government, because it adapts to the needs of the people and improves the lives of workers. Private industry and commerce will exist for a long time, and we will not be able to implement socialism soon."[6]

2. "Don't Go in All Directions"

In June 1950, the Third Plenary Session of the Seventh Central Committee of the Communist Party of China was held in Beijing. The central aim of the meeting was to determine the main tasks of the Party in the period of national economic recovery and to establish the various tasks that must be carried out and the strategic policies that should be adopted for this purpose. It was the most important meeting of the Central Committee in the early days of the founding of New China.

In view of the biases that appeared in the treatment of national industry and commerce at that time, and in order to make the work of the Party and the government prudent and steady, the Third Plenary Session of the Seventh Central Committee made clear that some opposition parties clung to the Leftist tendency of "carrying out socialism and annihilating capitalism ahead of schedule." In his speech at the meeting, Mao Zedong pointed out, "Some people think that we can eliminate capitalism and implement socialism at an early date. This idea is wrong and is not suitable for the situation of our country […] The national bourgeoisie will be wiped out in the future, but now it is necessary to unite them with us and not push them away. On the one hand, we should struggle against them, but on the other hand, we should unite them with us. We should explain this to cadres and prove by facts that it is right and necessary to unite the national bourgeoisie, democratic parties, democratic personages, and intellectuals."[7] The Party's policy towards the national bourgeoisie was still one of unity and struggle, with unity as the main principle, and aimed to control capitalism rather than to squeeze it out.

At the meeting, Mao Zedong put forward the famous strategic thought of "not going in all directions." He said that the Party's current general policy was to eliminate the remnants of the Kuomintang, secret agents, and bandits, overthrow the landlord class, liberate Taiwan and Tibet, and fight against imperialism to the end. In the land reform that was about to begin to overthrow the entire landlord class, the Party's enemies were numerous enough. Faced with such a complex struggle, the Party was presently in a tense relationship with the national bourgeoisie. Some workers, peasants, small handicraft workers, and intellectuals were not satisfied with the Party. In order to isolate and combat the current enemy, it was important to turn those among the people who were not satisfied with the Party into supporters. Faced with complex struggles and many difficulties, it was crucial not to create too many enemies. The Party needed to make concessions in one area, ease them, and concentrate its efforts on attacking the other. "In short, we should not go against all sides […] That is our policy, our strategy, and the line of the Third Plenary Session of the Central Committee."[8]

On June 23, in the closing speech of the First and Second Sessions of the CPPCC National Committee, Mao further stated that socialist transformation throughout the country, i.e. the nationalization of private industry and socialization of agriculture, was still in the distant future. He said, "Our country is steadily advancing through war and reform of the new democracy. In the future, when the economic and cultural undertakings of our country are greatly flourishing, we can enter the new era of socialism calmly and appropriately."[9]

At the plenary meeting, Chen Yun made a report on financial and economic issues, and made specific arrangements for the rational adjustment of industry and commerce. He pointed out that the five economic components should be taken into account as a whole, which would be good for the people. Only under comprehensive consideration and appropriate measures could the Party be bound together to develop the new democracy and enter socialism in the future. However, the status of the five economic components was different. They were under the leadership of the state-owned economy. In terms of adjusting public-private relations, it was necessary to organize the production and sale of private factories systematically through processing and ordering, while making private businesses profitable by properly adjusting prices and the division of labor in the acquisition of agricultural by-products.

The Third Plenary Session of the Seventh Central Committee was the first plenary session of the Central Committee convened by the CPC after the founding of New China. The strategic policy of "not going in all directions" put forward by the Party was based on the theory of the new democratic society and the Common Program, on the scientific analysis of the situation at that time, and on the class relations within the country and the united front. It was timely and clear in its criticism of the Leftist tendencies existing in the Party, opposing the notion that "we can eliminate capitalism and implement socialism at an early date." It played an important role in unifying the Party's ideology, uniting all social forces that could be united, striving for a fundamental improvement in the state's financial and economic situation, and prudently, actively, and fully carrying out the construction of the new democracy.

II

The Party's Innovation in its Rural Policy in the Early Stages of New China

1. Preserving and Developing the Rich Peasant Economy in the Land Reform of the New Area

The complete abolition of feudal and semi-feudal land ownership was an important part of the new democratic revolution and a basic condition for the recovery and development of the national economy. When the People's Republic of China was founded, land reform had not been carried out in the new liberated areas, and the feudal land system still existed in two-thirds of the country, which seriously restricted the development of productive forces. The complete abolition of this land system was a basic task at the beginning of the founding of New China. However, unlike the old land reform, which allowed the expropriation of surplus land for the rich peasants, the Central Committee formulated and implemented a series of new policies in the land reform of the new liberated areas in the light of the overall situation of implementing the New Democracy Program for the Founding of the People's Republic. Among them, the most important one was to preserve the rich peasant economy. The number of rich peasant households in the new liberated areas during the land reform accounted for about 3% of the total number of rural households, which did not occupy an important position in China's economy. But what policies the rich peasants adopted had a direct impact on other classes of peasants, especially the middle class peasants, and also on the national bourgeoisie, which was inextricably linked with the land. Therefore, when Mao discussed the land reform policy in the new area at the meeting of the Politburo in November 1949, he proposed that the land reform in the area south of the Yangtze River should treat the rich peasants with caution. In March

1950, Mao telephoned the central bureaus for advice on the policy toward the rich peasants, proposing that in the land reform movement in the new liberated areas, "not only the capitalist rich peasants but also the semi-feudal rich peasants should be settled, and then the situation of the semi-feudal rich peasants should be addressed in a few years." He pointed out that there were three reasons for this. First, the scale of the land reform was unprecedented, and there was a natural tendency toward a Leftist bias. If the Party only moved the landlords and not the rich peasants, it could isolate the landlords and protect the middle class peasants. Second, in the past, the land reform in the north was carried out during war. The atmosphere of war covered the atmosphere of land reform. Now, there was basically no war. The land reform was particularly prominent, and the shock to the society would be especially significant. Third, the united front between the CPC and the national bourgeoisie had now been formed politically, economically, and organizationally, and the national bourgeoisie was closely related to the land issue. For the sake of stabilizing the national bourgeoisie, it seemed appropriate to keep semi-feudal rich peasants at bay for the time being.[10]

When discussing the draft law on land reform at the Third Plenary Session of the Seventh Central Committee, according to the opinions put forward by some localities,[11] the relevant provisions were amended, replacing the original stipulation of the "land property of immovable rich peasants" with "protecting all land and property cultivated by self-employed and hired peasants from infringement," but only in some special areas. With the approval of the people's government at or above the provincial level, part or all of the leased land could be expropriated. This policy of the Central Committee was not only conducive to neutralizing the rich peasants politically, isolating the landlord class more, and reducing the resistance to land reform, but also conducive to encouraging the enthusiasm of middle class peasants to develop production, stabilizing the mood of the national bourgeoisie, and preventing Leftist deviations from occurring in the land reform.

In June 1950, at the First and Second Sessions of the CPPCC National Committee, Liu Shaoqi wrote the Report on Land Reform on behalf of the Central Committee. In the report, he further clarified his views on some basic rural issues. He said that the basic purpose of land reform was to focus on production. "It is not simply to relieve the poor peasants, but to liberate the rural productive forces from the constraints of the feudal land ownership of the landlord class, so as to develop agricultural production and open the way for industrialization in New China. Only when agricultural production can be greatly developed can industrialization in New China be realized and people's living standards be improved, and we can finally embark on socialist development, while farmers' poverty can finally be alleviated. Land reform can only partly solve the problem of peasants' poverty, but it cannot solve all the problems of peasants' poverty. The basic reason and purpose of land reform is to focus on production."[12] Every step of land reform had to be cared for and closely integrated with the development of rural production. It was precisely for this reason and purpose that the Central Committee proposed to preserve the rich peasant economy from destruction in the future land reform. Because the existence of the rich peasant economy and its development was to a certain extent beneficial to the development of the people's economy and to the broad masses of peasants, it was "necessary both politically and economically." According to his own understanding of the nature and tasks of the current revolution, Liu further explained, "The policy we have adopted to preserve the rich peasant economy is certainly not a temporary one, but a long-term one. That is to say, in the whole stage of the new democracy, the rich peasant economy should be preserved. Only when such conditions are ripe so that machine farming, collective farming, and socialist transformation in the countryside can be carried out in large quantities will the existence of a rich peasant economy become unnecessary, and this will be achieved in a fairly distant future."[13]

Beginning in the winter of 1950, an unprecedented scale of land reform was carried out in the new liberated areas, involving nearly 300 million agricultural people in a leading, systematic phased manner. Under the guidance of the new land reform law, not only were the vast number of poor and middle peasants allocated land and other means of production, which fundamentally changed the land ownership relationship in rural areas of China, but the economy of rich peasants and the land and other property of middle class peasants were also preserved, including that of rich and middle class peasants. With the successive completion of land reform in the new area, the farmers' enthusiasm for production was unprecedentedly high, agricultural production developed rapidly, and the farmers' income generally increased, which in turn provided a strong impetus for the recovery and development of the national economy.

The central government's decision on land reform in the new areas and Mao Zedong's and Liu Shaoqi's explanations of the Party's rich peasant policies came not only from the angle of class struggle, but also from the point of view of the backward situation of rural productive forces, starting from the rapid development of rural productive forces, that is, from the national conditions, independently exploring the road of China's construction and drawing up an important policy conducive to the development of productivity. Liu noted, "Marx and Lenin have talked about some basic viewpoints on land and peasants, but we should create new ways to deal with China's land and peasant problems and put forward concrete solutions based on China's actual situation. For example, the problem of the rich peasants used to expropriate the surplus land and property of the rich peasants and distribute it to the poor peasants and laborers [...] Today, the war has been won. To restore production and develop production, we must protect the rich peasant economy [...] This is a concrete analysis of the specific situation, which is the essence of Marxism."[14] This important policy in the land reform of the new area was a brilliant interpretation of productivity standards by the Communist Party of China at the beginning of its administration.

2. Arguments Arising from the Problem of Party Members Among the Rich Peasants in Northeast China

After the founding of New China, the production and living conditions of peasants in the old liberated areas of Northeast and North China, which had completed land reform earlier, generally saw significant improvement. On the basis of the recovery and development of agricultural production, many former poor peasants and hired peasant laborers gradually increased their economic income with better production conditions and labor skills and began to possess production and living conditions equivalent to those of the middle class peasants before the land reform. Individual peasants were developing toward the goal of having "three horses, one plough, and one cart" and "thirty *mu* of land and one cow" to become rich. The middle class peasants gradually became the majority and "central figure" of the rural class. In the ranks of Party members, there was also a phenomenon of employing people to work on their own.

It was a new problem for the Party to determine how they should look at the trend of the middle class peasant transformation and the emerging new rich peasants in the countryside. Not only was finding ready-made answers in the Marxist classics impossible, but so was finding a way to draw lessons from the experience of the Soviet Union. At that time, there were different understandings within the Party. Starting from some classical writers' comments and the Party's fundamental purpose, most people believed that Communists should not engage in exploitative acts, but should take the road of mutual assistance, cooperation, and common prosperity, and thus should restrict the newly emerged new rich peasants. Others believed that since the state policy allowed the existence of rich peasants, Party members among the new rich peasants should also be allowed to exist. Policies within and outside the Party had to be consistent, or it would affect the enthusiasm of peasants in developing production.

On January 22, 1950, the Central Organizational Department, in its draft Opinion to the Organizational Department of the Northeast Bureau, put forward its own views on issues such as whether Party members could employ workers or not and whether they could participate in work-changing organizations. It was noted that whether Party members employed workers or not was a matter over which they should have complete freedom. The Party should not impose compulsory measures, and their membership should not be suspended or dismissed if it was too strong at that time. If Party members were not allowed to exploit others, and if they were required to join the work-changing organizations and take the lead, some Party members would develop negative feelings toward production. Experience from all parts of the country had proven that if Party members did not employ workers, the masses would not dare to employ them, and if Party members were passive about production, the enthusiasm for production among the masses would never be aroused. Therefore, when educating peasant Party members, it was important not only to point out the advantages of organizing them, but also to clearly point out that "single-handedness" and "hiring workers" were permitted by the Party's policy. At the same time, cadres at all levels were to be told that on the basis of the individual economy in today's rural areas, a certain amount of development of rural capitalism was unavoidable. It was not a terrible thing for some Party members to develop into rich peasants. It was premature and therefore wrong for them to formulate ways to turn them into rich peasants.[15]

On January 23, Liu Shaoqi issued a letter from the Central Organizational Department in reply to the Northeast Bureau and talked with An Ziwen of the Central Organizational Department that evening. He said that after the land reform in Northeast China, the rural economy began to develop upwards. Farmers with three horses, a plough, and a cart were not rich peasants, but middle class peasants. This sort of relatively wealthy farmer with three horses, one plough, and one cart may and should grow to 80% of the population in a few years. "Now in the northeast, middle class peasants should be greatly developed." He believed that the mutual aid in Northeast China at that time was built on the basis of bankruptcy and a poor individual economy, which was a bad foundation. "In the future, the individual economy will be able to produce independently, so it is necessary to reduce the mutual aid of changing jobs." If farmers had three horses to develop their production, they could either change jobs or work alone. "Seventy percent of peasant households are now participating in mutual assistance in changing jobs, which will shrink in the future. This is a good phenomenon, proving that with economic development, farmers become more middle class peasants, and they can do it alone, which is also due to this phenomenon. Seventy percent of peasant households have three horses, so collective farming will be easier in the future. Therefore, we should not only publicize and explain the benefits of the shift team, but also allow them to work alone." In response to some people's opinions that mutual aid should be developed into collective farms as soon as possible, Liu Shaoqi believed that it was "impossible." "These are two different stages to prevent acute disease," he said. "From individual production to collective farms, this is a revolution in the mode of production, and collective farms without machinery and tools cannot be consolidated." As for the exploitation still existing in the new democratic countries, Liu Shaoqi's view was that "there must be exploitation now, and exploitation should also be welcomed. Workers are demanding that capitalists exploit, and they cannot live without exploitation. This year, a large number of refugees in regions inside Shanhaiguan went to the northeast, and the rich peasant regions outside Shanhaiguan exploited them, and they were grateful. Rich peasants employ many people and buy horses. Don't restrict them. Let them develop now without doing any harm [...] Let it develop to a certain extent, then limit it in the future." He added, "It's too early to limit doing it alone. It's good to be able to do it now. Nor can we regard the peasants who oppose single-handedness as collectivism, because they are still unable to do it alone, and are poor peasants who cannot do it alone [...] Hired workers, working alone, should be laissez-faire, so that farmers who have three horses and a pair of ploughs are in a very good situation. For those who do not allow hired workers to work alone, they should not be laissez-faire, and for those who interfere with those with three horses, they should not be laissez-faire."[16]

Liu Shaoqi's answer to the question of Party membership after the emergence and development of Party members into rich peasants showed his broad vision and profound understanding of the essence of the theory of new democracy. "It's too early," he said. "If there is exploitation, we can still be socialist. Saint-Simon was a capitalist, but he was also a socialist, though Utopian at that time. If there is a capitalist in the Northeast who wants to follow Saint-Simon's method, he may succeed, not collapse." He added, "Even if there are ten thousand rich peasant Party members in the Northeast in the future, it won't be terrible […] Therefore, the present peasant Party members can work alone. The Party regulations and laws allow Party members to work alone and employ people. It is a dogmatic idea that Party members should not be exploited […] But allowing them to do it alone is different from encouraging them to do it alone. We allow Party members to do it alone, but we don't encourage them to do it alone."[17]

The victory of the new democratic revolution and the completion of the land reform liberated the rural productive forces and improved the production and living conditions of most peasants relatively quickly. It was inevitable and unavoidable that there would be such phenomena as middle class farmers and hired workers in the countryside, because it was still "a society of private ownership at this time." The problem was how to recognize these phenomena. Was it to be based on the general exposition or Stalin's model of classical Marxist writers, or on China's national conditions and actual situation? Was it based on abstract ideological and moral standards, or on productivity standards? Liu Shaoqi started from the very backward level of productivity in rural areas and urged the development of production. Starting from all requirements and from the New Democracy Program for the Founding of the People's Republic, the Party opposed the over-generalized denial of all exploitation, just as it affirmed the exploitation of the national bourgeoisie within a certain limit and a certain period of time in cities. To affirm the trend of single-handedness, middle class farmers, and the exploitation of rich peasants to a certain extent in the countryside was not to deny the cooperative development there, but to link the cooperative development with the development of productivity to a certain extent. It was noted, "From individual production to collective farms – this is a revolution in the mode of production, and collective farms without machinery and tools cannot be consolidated." This view highlighted Marxism's most basic point of view –

the determination of productivity – but did not highlight the reaction of the superstructure and ideology. Under certain conditions, revolution could succeed in a country with backward productivity. However, in order to realize the new democratic nation-building program and prepare for the transition to socialism, it must have the corresponding material basis and productive conditions. Poverty could trigger revolution, but it could not be the basis of socialism. The Party's correct policy toward the rich peasants and other issues played a great role in preventing "acute diseases" in various aspects of social transformation at that time.

III

Consolidation or Transition: Debating a Major Issue

Since the new democratic theory was put forward, the entire Party had been very clear and firm about the future of the transition from new democracy to socialism. But how long would this transition take? It was generally believed that it would require quite a long time, mostly because China's productivity was sluggish. The direction of this conclusion was correct, but it was also abstract and general. Before the founding of New China, how long the transitional period would take was not an urgent issue, but later, after the beginning of the comprehensive construction of the new democracy, it became prominent. There were not only many pressing practical problems raised, but also some important theoretical issues that needed to be further clarified or developed. Faced with various important issues raised in theory and practice, the understanding within the Party was not consistent, which was of course understandable. At that time, the questions that had been unlikely to come up in the past, such as how long the stage of new democracy would last, when it would begin to make the transition to socialism, how capitalism could be allowed to develop in the new democratic country, and when it could begin to eliminate bourgeois exploitation, were placed before the Party after the full development of the new democracy. If the Tianjin speech and "rich peasant Party members" were mainly concerned with exploitation in the new democratic society, then how to view the beginning of the transition to socialism was closely related to them.

1. Problems Raised by the Development of Agricultural Cooperatives in Shanxi

In the spring of 1951, a controversy arose within the Party around the development of agricultural cooperatives in Shanxi Province. At that time, with the successive completion of land reform, there was a general trend of recovery and development in the rural economy, and some farmers reached the level of wealthy middle class peasants. By virtue of their advantages in capital, labor, and farm tools, a small number of wealthy middle class peasants developed into new rich peasants by purchasing land, hiring workers, and lending money at usurious rates. Some people with quicker economic growth regarded the set up of mutual aid groups after the land reform as "helping the poor," which led to the disintegration of such groups. At this time, some farmers began to sell land and fell into poverty, with lowered living standards. This was an unavoidable situation in the development of the new democratic economy. According to the understanding at that time, this was the spontaneous trend of the small-scale peasant economy, reflecting the new polarization in rural areas. Some cadres in the Party were quite worried about the spontaneous tendency of peasants, fearing that their new-found wealth would have an impact on the mutual aid groups, so they began to put forward the idea of "overpowering the spontaneous forces of peasants."

On April 17, 1951, in Shanxi Province, where land reform was completed earlier and mutual assistance and cooperation was carried out, the Provincial Party Committee wrote a report entitled "Raising the Mutual Assistance Group in Old Areas by One Step" to the Central Committee and the North China Bureau. "With the recovery and development of the rural economy, the peasants' spontaneous power has developed. It is not in the direction of modernization and collectivization, but in the direction of becoming rich peasants. This is the most fundamental reason why the mutual aid group has become scattered."[18] The report concluded that the development of mutual aid groups in old districts had reached a turning point that required them to improve in order to prevent them from retreating. Accordingly, the report proposed that new factors must be strengthened within the mutual aid group, namely, fostering and increasing the two new factors of "public accumulation" and "distribution according to work," in order to gradually overcome the spontaneous trend of farmers, completely reverse the trend of scattering, and guide the mutual aid group to a higher level. "For the foundation of private ownership, we should not consolidate it, but gradually shake it and weaken it until we deny it,"[19] the report said.

As for the report of the Shanxi Provincial Committee, the North China Bureau expressed different opinions. Liu Shaoqi also noted in April that it was not mature to take steps to shake private ownership. Without tractors and fertilizers, it was important not to rush into agricultural production cooperatives. On May 4, according to Liu Shaoqi's instructions and the opinions of several other provinces in North China, the North China Bureau approved the report of the Shanxi Provincial Committee and reported it to the Central Committee. The reply pointed out, "It is wrong and inconsistent with the Party's policies and the spirit of the Common Program in the period of the new democracy to gradually shake and weaken the basis of private ownership to the point of denying the basis of private ownership by accumulating provident funds and distributing them based on labor. During the period of the new democratic revolution, the revolutionary task can only shake the feudal private ownership, imperialist privileges in China, and bureaucratic capitalist private ownership. Generally, shaking private property is the task of the socialist revolution." At that time, "the main issue of improving and consolidating the mutual aid group concerns how to enrich the mutual aid group and production to meet the farmers' requirements for further development of production, instead of gradually shaking private ownership."[20]

Liu Shaoqi subsequently criticized the views of the Shanxi Provincial Party Committee several times in his speeches. On May 7, 1951, at the first national propaganda conference, he said that it was impossible for the Shanxi Provincial Committee to go directly toward socialization with a socialist cooperative. "If we believe in this theory, it is fantastic socialism, also known as fantastic agricultural socialism, which cannot be realized in practice [...] There are many ideas related to agricultural socialism in our Party, which should be corrected." He went on, "Because we can't build socialism by relying solely on the conditions of the countryside, the socialization of agriculture depends on industry [...] With the nationalization of industry and land, the peasants can become a collective." Further, he said, "if we call on peasants to organize cooperatives and think that this is socialism and mobilize mass movements, we will make major errors. That is fantastic agricultural socialism."[21]

On July 3, Liu Shaoqi wrote a comment on the report of the Shanxi Provincial Party Committee, "Raising Mutual Aid Organizations in Old Areas by One Step," and required that it be sent to the students of the School of Marxism, the members of the Central Committee, and the Central Bureau. The comment said, "In the economic development of the rural areas after the land reform, the spontaneous forces and class differentiation of farmers have begun to show. Some comrades in the Party have expressed their fear of such spontaneous forces and class division, and have tried to prevent or avoid them. They fantasize about using mutual labor groups and supply and marketing cooperatives to stop or avoid this trend […] This is a wrong, dangerous, and utopian idea of agricultural socialism. This document of the Shanxi Provincial Party Committee is an example of this idea."[22]

On the afternoon of July 5, Liu Shaoqi talked about his criticism of the Shanxi Provincial Committee in his lecture to the students of the School of Marxism. He said that the spontaneous power of the peasants could not be prevented. "It is impossible for the Shanxi Provincial Committee of the Communist Party of China to overcome it, prevent it, and avoid it […] Some people fear this spontaneous force and try to stop it. This is going to lead the wrong way […] It is an attempt to gradually shake and weaken the private property of the peasants in the mutual aid group until they deny it and move towards agricultural collectivization. This is impossible. It is reformism. It is right-leaning to go slowly and gradually to socialism. At the same time, destroying private property is a risk-taking tendency of the Left."[23]

Liu Shaoqi's opinions reflected a way of thinking on the issue of mutual assistance and cooperation in agriculture within the Party, which was that, according to the notion of building a new democratic country, the peasants' individual economy should be allowed to have a period of development over a considerable time after the land reform, and agricultural productivity should be developed to a certain extent, especially industrialization. It was possible to use certain industrial products to support agriculture, then take practical actions to start agricultural cooperation. That is to say, the development of the agricultural mutual aid and cooperation movement should be in accordance with the development level of productivity and meet the actual needs of farmers. It should not be divorced from the level of productivity and rush to eliminate individual private ownership of farmers.

When Mao Zedong saw the reports of the Shanxi Provincial Committee and the North China Bureau and Liu Shaoqi's comments, he clearly expressed his support for the views of the Shanxi Provincial Committee. He criticized the view that mutual aid groups could not grow into agricultural production cooperatives and that the private foundation should not be shaken at this stage. His basis for this idea was that since Western capitalism had a stage that focused on workshop handicraft industry in its development, that is, the stage of new productivity formed by unified management rather than steam-powered machinery, it was also feasible for Chinese cooperatives to rely on unified management to form new productivity and shake the private foundation. Mao Zedong's reasoning convinced Liu Shaoqi and others, and they withdrew their opinions, marking the end of the debate.

2. Resolution on Mutual Assistance Cooperatives in Agricultural Production

According to Mao Zedong's proposal, the Central Committee convened the First National Conference on Agricultural Mutual Assistance and Cooperation in September 1951, after which it drafted and formulated the Draft Resolution of the Central Committee of the Communist Party of China on Mutual Assistance and Cooperation in Agricultural Production (hereinafter referred to as the Resolution). During the drafting process, Mao listened to different opinions, affirmed the enthusiasm of farmers' mutual assistance and cooperation, and also affirmed the enthusiasm of the farmers' individual economy, noting that it was important to guard against both Rightist and Leftist tendencies. The revised Resolution was based on Mao's theoretical viewpoints, and also absorbed Liu Shaoqi's ideas of attaching importance to the farmers' individual economy and organizing work to meet the needs of production and development. The Resolution pointed out that farmers' enthusiasm for production on the basis of land reform was manifested in two aspects. The first was enthusiasm for the individual economy, and the other was enthusiasm for mutual labor assistance. Under the realistic economic conditions in rural areas, the farmers' individual economy would be large for a long period of time. The enthusiasm of farmers for the individual economy was inevitable, and the enthusiasm of farmers for the individual economy could not be ignored or frustrated. At the same time, in order to help peasants overcome the difficulties in individual household management and avoid polarization, and in order to develop production, build water conservancy projects, and resist natural disasters, agricultural machinery and other new technologies should be adopted to enable the country to obtain more food and industrial raw materials. It was important to advocate "organizing" and give full play to the mutual assistance of peasants' labor. The future of its development was agricultural collectivization. In accordance with the needs and possible conditions of production development, the Resolution proposed that farmers should be guided to take the road of mutual assistance and cooperation systematically by taking the policy of positive development and steady progress, and in accordance with the principles of voluntary mutual benefit, typical demonstration, and state assistance.

On October 17, Mao drafted a circular from the Central Committee on forwarding Gao Gang's report on mutual assistance and cooperation in rural areas of Northeast China. He believed that the principles put forward in Gao Gang's report were correct. The report held that, with the development of the majority of rural peasants and the spontaneous tendency of peasants, the main tendency to oppose and prevent them in guiding mutual assistance and cooperation was not to infringe on the interests of middle class peasants, but the spontaneous tendency of peasants, while the main concerns of peasants were not "fear of development" or "fear of large numbers." Rather, it called for rapid expansion of production. On December 15, in a circular written by Mao Zedong and issued by the Central Committee on the issue of the draft Resolution on Mutual Assistance and Cooperation in Agricultural Production, it was pointed out that this should be interpreted and implemented in all areas where land reform had been completed, and that the whole Party should "treat mutual assistance and cooperation in agriculture as a major task." In this spirit, the national agricultural mutual assistance and cooperation movement was soon launched nationwide, which became one of the bases for putting forward the general line of the transitional period in the second half of 1952.

Arguments about the development of agricultural production cooperatives in Shanxi Province were the continuation of the debate on the issue of rich peasants in Northeast China in 1950, and in fact later developed into the debate on agricultural cooperation in 1955. With the development of history, the problems and their significance reflected in these disputes became more profoundly manifested. It should be said that on the fundamental issue of guiding individual peasants to organize themselves to take the road of collectivization, there were no principled differences within the Party, and they all adhered to the New Democracy Outline for the Founding of the People's Republic and the spirit of the Second Plenary Session of the Seventh Central Committee. The difference lay in whether the old area mutual aid organizations should be promoted to semi-socialist agricultural cooperatives, that is, whether the rural areas after the land reform should immediately transition to socialism, at that time or in the future, and after a certain degree of productivity development or right away. Liu Shaoqi and the North China Bureau believed that the private foundation of the Mutual Assistance Group should not be shaken at present, and that the socialist steps should not be taken until the rural productive forces had developed to a certain extent. Mao Zedong and the Shanxi Provincial Committee believed that it was necessary to immediately raise the mutual aid groups in the old areas and establish semi-socialist agricultural production cooperatives.

Due to the limitations of the times and practice, both sides of the debate inevitably had some historical limitations. However, from the point of view of the importance of the issues being debated and the theoretical heights reached by the debates, its typical significance should not be ignored. For Liu Shaoqi and others, there were some shortcomings in their criticism of the Shanxi Provincial Party Committee, such as raising the "agricultural production mutual aid group to the collective farm of agricultural production" together with shaking, weakening, and even denying the basis of private ownership, which was generally seen as "wrong, dangerous, and utopian agricultural socialist thought." It did not indicate that, although China did not have the conditions for establishing high-level agricultural production cooperatives universally at that time, it did not exclude the possibility of finding specific forms of transitioning to high-level agricultural cooperatives. It overemphasized that the premise of cooperation was industrialization and modernization, and in fact copied the view that only mechanization could lead to cooperation in the Soviet model, and so on.[24] But for future practice, generally speaking, Liu Shaoqi and others were right. For example, he believed that the polarization of rural areas after the land reform was inevitable, which had a negative side, but was still conducive to promoting the development of productive forces under the conditions at that time. Because of China's backward economy, it was not possible to take steps to deny private ownership prematurely and hastily, but rather, it was important to continue to implement the new democratic policy, paying attention to the new historical conditions after the land reform. Next, it was important to oppose equalitarianism, consciously link the socialist transformation of agriculture with national industrialization, and so on. These problems adhered to the basic principles of Marxism, and there were some important innovations based on the actual situation in China. If the basic issues that fundamentally affected the socialist transformation and construction could be fully discussed within the Party at that time, many of the divergences that came later could have been avoided.

IV

Full Development of New Democratic Construction

From 1949 to 1952, the Central Committee also carried out a series of creative practices and reflections on the political construction of the new democracy during the period of the reform and comprehensive construction of the new democracy.

1. Democratization and Industrialization Cannot be Separated

At the beginning of the founding of the People's Republic of China, when the conditions for holding a general election of the People's Congress were not yet in place, the construction of democratic politics began with the creation and application of the semi-regime organizational form of people's congresses, with members gathered from all walks of life. At that time, the Central Committee attached great importance to the convening of people's congresses representing all sectors of society. In the first month after the founding of the Central People's Government, in discussion with the central bureaus and sub-bureaus, Mao approved the experience of convening people's congresses from all walks of life in Songjiang County, Shanghai, and cities in North China, and asked to "immediately notify all subordinates to follow these instructions." He pointed out that in order for such county-wide people's congresses to be held in more than one thousand counties and run well, "it will be very important for our Party to work with tens of thousands of people and for the majority of cadres inside and outside the Party to obtain education."[25]

According to the Common Program, in December 1949, the Central People's Government promulgated general rules for the organization of people's congresses representing all walks of life at the provincial, municipal, and county levels, stipulating that such people's congresses should be held promptly wherever conditions permitted. Through this form of organization, the leading organs of the Party and government at all levels could hear the voice of the masses, understand the demands of the masses, and obtain the assistance of the masses to solve difficulties and carry out the work. In 1950, the Third Plenary Session of the Seventh Central Committee of the CPC also emphasized the work of democratic political construction. It pointed out that the people's congresses should be serious enough to unite people from all walks of life to work together. All important work of the people's governments should be submitted to the people's congresses for discussion and decision.

In guiding and mobilizing the convening of the people's congress, Liu Shaoqi also put forward the idea that democratization could not be separated from industrialization. In his speech at the Third Beijing People's Congress in February 1952, he pointed out that the opening of the people's congress should be taken as an important political construction task and linked with the country's economic construction, especially industrialization construction. He pointed out clearly that "democratization and industrialization cannot be separated." He said, "Without the democratization of our country and the development of the new democratic regime, we cannot guarantee the development of the new democratic economy and the industrialization of our country. On the other hand, the development of the new democratic economy and the industrialization of the country should be greatly strengthened and the foundation of the new democratic regime consolidated. Therefore, our basic slogan is 'democratization and industrialization.'"[26] From such a perspective, it was possible to understand and emphasize the relationship between and characteristics of economic and political construction of the new democracy, reflecting the vision and ideals of the CPC. Although the understanding of this goal was still preliminary at that time, and although there were many detours in the process of realizing this goal later, the understanding and raising of questions at that time showed that the governing idea of the early period of the Party's rule was at the forefront of the times.

2. Adhering to the System of Multi-Party Cooperation and Political Consultation

In the process of building a democratic government, the Central Committee adhered to the system of multi-party cooperation and political consultation. At the beginning of the founding of the People's Republic of China, some people inside and outside the Party had only a vague understanding of the existence of a new democratic society, and their impatient and aggressive attitude toward bourgeois policies easily turned into a left-leaning bias toward democratic parties. Some cadres in the Party could not properly handle the relationship between democratic parties and non-party entities, and once adopted a policy of exclusion against them. At the First National United Front Work Conference held in March 1950, there was a view that democratic parties should not be elevated politically and expanded organizationally, or they would cause the CPC trouble. Some people even thought that the democratic parties were established to fight for democracy, and now that democracy existed, their tasks were completed, and that the democratic parties "were merely playing a role no bigger than a hair," and so on. In response to these erroneous tendencies, Mao Zedong pointed out in April that year that it was a social phenomenon, both inside and outside the Party, to pay little attention to democratic parties and non-party members. It should be made clear to all that in the long run and as a whole, democratic parties were necessary. The democratic parties were connected with the petty bourgeoisie and the bourgeoisie, and their representatives were needed in the regime. It was wrong to think that the democratic parties "were merely playing a role no bigger than a hair." Judging from the people connected to them, they were not "a hair," but "a lock of hair," not to be despised. They should instead be treated with equality and democracy.[27]

Zhou Enlai also pointed out in his report at the National United Front Work Conference that all democratic parties, no matter what their names were, were still political parties with certain representational power. "They originated in the soil of China." He criticized the view that the democratic parties would "give us trouble," saying, "The democratic parties play a very important role in the people's democratic united front." At present, the Party's people's democratic dictatorship was an alliance of four democratic classes. The democratic parties could develop and have a future. It was important to work together over a long period to build a new China and fulfill the tasks entrusted to that generation by history. He mentioned the bourgeoisie in particular, noting, "Today, the national bourgeoisie still has its historical task." It was important to communicate to the bourgeoisie to be confident that they not only had historical tasks to perform, but also had a bright future.[28]

The following January, Zhou Enlai emphasized in his speech at the reception held by the Central United Front Ministry that in the construction of New China at that time, the democratic parties were willing to do their part, and the CPC should help them enter socialism. Within the united front, the Party should deal with four relations, namely, class relations, party relations, national relations, and hierarchical relations. For the peasant class, bourgeoisie, and other petty bourgeoisie, it was necessary to educate them over a long time, "not only to build a new democratic society with us, but also to bring them into a socialist society." He also pointed out that the people's democratic dictatorship was the power of the people's democratic united front under the leadership of the Communist Party, and that more attention should be paid to the united front. He said, "Because of the long-term war conditions in the past, we formed a habit of issuing orders in the name of the Party, especially in the army. Now that we have entered a period of peace and established a national regime, we should change this habit […] Only by uniting the non-party masses can we do a good job." Greater attention was to be paid to the lower level organs, and more non-Party members were to have duties and powers. In the regimes below the county level, in addition to poor peasants and peasants, representatives of new and rich peasants, wealthy middle class peasants, handicraftsmen, and intellectuals were also to be included in the representative meetings.[29]

When the Central People's Government was established in 1949, non-communists accounted for a certain proportion of the members of the Central People's Government and the State Council, in accordance with the requirements of the Common Program. However, the policy of long-term cooperation between the CPC and democratic parties did not remain only at the central level, but also reflected the personnel composition of local people's governments at all levels. When examining and approving the list of chairmen of provincial people's governments, Mao Zedong believed that there were too many Communist Party members and that several representatives of the bourgeoisie should be added. On

March 8, 1951, the Central Committee issued a directive requiring the committees of people's governments at all levels to be equipped with an appropriate number of non-Party personages and to find suitable candidates among democratic parties, model workers and peasants, patriotic intellectuals, technical experts, and businessmen. Where the proportion of non-Party members in the committees of the people's governments at all levels was too small, the Party committees and the people's governments at higher levels were not to approve of or report it. This matter was to become one of the criteria for reviewing the work of the united front at all levels.

In accordance with the requirements of the Common Program and repeated emphasis by Mao Zedong and other central leaders, the long-term cooperation between the whole Party and non-party democrats was gradually clarified and consolidated. Government departments at all levels consciously and sincerely discussed and solved problems that had to be discussed and solved with non-Party personages, so that they had the right to hold positions and perform their duties conditionally. Implementing the new democracy program in the construction of the regime adapted the superstructure to the economic base and the level of productivity development, which was an important reason for the rapid recovery of the economy and the smooth progress of various social reform undertakings at that time.

3. Ethnic Minority and Religious Work in the Construction of the New Democracy

In all the undertakings carried out at that time, the Central Committee always attached great importance to the work of ethnic minorities. In view of the social and economic situation in ethnic minority areas, the central government formulated a "prudent and steady progress" reform policy that was different from that in Han areas. In June 1950, Mao stressed at the Third Plenary Session of the Seventh Central Committee that social reform in minority areas was an important matter and must be treated with caution. Without mass conditions, people's armed forces and cadres of ethnic minorities, it was important not to carry out any reform work with mass character. In the process of establishing a democratic coalition government in ethnic minority areas, Mao also proposed that a large number of people from ethnic minorities who could cooperate with the CPC should be recruited to participate in government work, and a large number of ethnic minority cadres should be trained in such cooperation. In June 1950, Zhou Enlai proposed that trade in minority areas should be subsidized and expended more in the future, so that minority compatriots could gain more benefits. It was a political task to train minority cadres, and governments of the autonomous regions should hold leading posts for ethnic minorities. The people's congresses of all ethnic groups and all walks of life should include representatives of various ethnic minorities, with larger proportions.[30]

Under the banner of the new democracy, it was also an important policy of the Central Committee in the early days of the founding of the People's Republic to unite religious circles to advance together. In May 1950, Zhou Enlai pointed out in several talks at a symposium on Christianity attended by religious figures and heads of relevant departments of the Central Committee and State Council that religious groups themselves should be independent and self-reliant. It was important to establish a self-governing, self-supporting, and self-teaching church. Patriotism and democracy were two conditions to distinguish whether a religious group was beneficial to New China. Those who believed in religion and those who did not believe in religion could cooperate politically, coexist, and respect each other. It was possible to cooperate on the basis of the Common Program. "We should unite and take care of all kinds of social forces so that everyone can find their own place and work together to build a new China. Only in this way can society be stabilized and move forward steadily."[31]

4. The Ideological and Cultural Education of the New Democracy

While carrying out various elements of economic construction and social reforms, the Central Committee had begun to propagate and educate the people with Marxism-Leninism and Mao Zedong Thought, making it the guiding ideology for mobilizing all social forces to jointly build a new China. At that time, the ideological and cultural education of the new democracy centered on Marxism and Mao Zedong Thought was carried out extensively and thoroughly, that is, nationally, through scientific, popular cultural, and ideological education.

The essence or innovation of this kind of education carried out by the Party lay in that it was the education in the new democracy guided by Marxism. In May 1951, Liu Shaoqi put forward at the first national propaganda conference that "educating the people on a nationwide and overall scale with Marxist ideological principles is one of the most basic political tasks of our Party." He said, "We must eliminate imperialism and feudalism and criticize all non-proletarian ideas, so as to establish the leadership of a Marxist-Leninist working class ideology." This was a prerequisite for strengthening the leadership of the working class politically and economically. It was important to criticize the ideological system of the bourgeoisie and the petty bourgeoisie, but not to eliminate it. What was the reason? Liu explained, "Because today we also allow the bourgeois economy to exist in our policy, and the petty bourgeoisie and the peasant class to exist in our economy. In fact, we not only allow them to exist, but also help them develop. Since we recognize their economic existence, we must recognize the existence and legitimacy of their ideas." But to allow a thing to exist was not to cease fighting against it. "If we don't refute it, we will have a problem of who wins over whom [...] So, although we cannot declare it illegal now, we must refute it and point out its mistakes. Only in this way can the ideological leadership of the working class be established, the political and economic victory of the working class be guaranteed, and the victory of Marxism-Leninism in China be guaranteed."[32] This ideological and cultural line, which was different from socialism and capitalism, was conducive to preventing and correcting erroneous tendencies of economic and political transcendence. It was also adapted to the needs of the economic foundation of the new democracy and the development of productivity.

5. Two Kinds of Contradictions in the New Democratic Society

After the founding of New China, many of the sharp class contradictions in society began to decrease gradually, while a large number of contradictions among the people in the new democratic society began to stand out. What were the characteristics of these new social contradictions and social relations, how would they develop, and how should they be dealt with? These new problems concerning the construction of New China attracted the attention of the Central Committee and some senior cadres. At that time, there were some different understandings within the Party. In May and June 1951, Liu Shaoqi wrote in his notes when he read the relevant articles, "When the working class state has been established, factories have been nationalized, and democratic reforms have been carried out, that is, when there is no class antagonism and exploitation within our state-owned factories, and the relationship between the factory management organs and the workers has changed, it will basically become a comrade relationship [...] There will be no class contradiction in the state-owned factories [...] State-owned factories will no longer deal with class contradictions and exploitative relations and problems arising from such contradictions and relations,"[33] but only with contradictions and relations between the working class and the people. This "is a contradiction that we should conscientiously adjust and deal with over a long period of time," and "such contradictions and relations should be dealt with in a comradely, conciliatory, and united way."[34] This constituted the basic internal contradiction of state-owned factories. "The contradiction between the management organs of state-owned factories and the masses of workers is the public-private contradiction within state-owned factories." From this point of view, he further discussed the contradictions in the new democratic society. "It can be seen that contradictions can be roughly divided into two categories: those that are fundamentally hostile and cannot be reconciled, and those that are fundamentally non-hostile and reconcilable. When we observe problems, we must distinguish the different nature of these two contradictions."[35] Starting from a specific problem and a special contradiction, Liu revealed the characteristics of the "contradictions among the people" with universality in the new society, emphasized the importance of distinguishing the two contradictions and correctly handling them, and reflected the keen observation and correct analysis of the new society and new problems by the top leaders of the Party, all of which was of pioneering significance.

Although this discussion was not fully carried out for various reasons at that time, later history showed that it was the forerunner of Mao Zedong's theory of correctly handling the two kinds of contradictions formally, which he comprehensively and systematically put forward in 1956, at the beginning of the Party's exploration of solving various social contradictions under socialist conditions during the Party's rule.

6. Three-year Preparation and Ten-year Planned Economic Construction

At the Third Plenary Session of the Seventh Central Committee of the Communist Party of China, the Central Committee had planned to resume production in three to five years, then carry out large-scale economic construction, but the Korean

War forced them to adjust the plan. In February 1951, Mao Zedong put forward the idea of a "three-year preparation and ten-year planned economic construction" at the enlarged meeting of the Politburo, in accordance with the situation that the Korean War had stabilized and all domestic work was progressing smoothly. The Central Committee believed that the Chinese people were confident that it would take three years to complete the task of economic recovery. Therefore, it was necessary to present the task of preparing for planned economic construction among the leading cadres of the Party and to make them understand that all the work being done at present aimed to prepare directly for the task of national industrialization.

In May and July of that year, entrusted with the task by Mao Zedong, Liu Shaoqi reported to the cadres attending the first national propaganda work conference and to the students of the first phase of the Marxist School, elaborating extensively on the important thought of the Central Committee regarding the "three-year preparation and ten-year planned economic construction." In addition to discussing the preparatory work of military, political, cultural, and economic aspects of the plan during the preparatory period, the report also addressed the position and significance of this strategic thought throughout the new democratic society in view of the Party's eagerness to transition to socialism (including the controversy with the Shanxi Provincial Committee). He said that after three years of preparation, the Party would have a ten-year economic construction plan. Ten years later, China would become a richer country than it was then. "Only then can we consider the question of proceeding toward socialism. We can't solve this problem yet. Now some people are talking about socialism. I said it was too early, by at least ten years […] Socialism cannot be built within ten years of construction. Ten years later, when we look at the situation, we can ask when socialism will be carried out. But the answer to this question now is that it depends on the actual situation. Ten years from now, we may take some considerable socialist steps, or we may not be able to take such steps at that time, but we will certainly have to wait for a few more years."[36]

He added, "The new democratic stage is both a transitional stage and a preparatory stage, i.e. preparing to enter socialism. Three years' preparation and ten years' construction are for the nationalization of industry. In a few years, at least fifteen years' time, the collectivization of agriculture will take place."[37]

And he noted "during the ten-year economic construction, all five economic components should be developed." Among these, the development of state-owned enterprises would be rapid, the proportion would increase, and its leading and control roles would become larger. The cooperative economy could develop rapidly, and its proportion and role would also increase. The private capitalist economy would increase in absolute numbers, but the proportion would not increase but decrease. The national capitalist economy would increase, while the individual economy would also increase and grow more organized.[38]

In October 1952, Zhou Enlai expressed similar ideas in his talks with some representatives of capitalists, saying "On the question of the future, I have said many times in the past that Chairman Mao's policy is to make steady progress, to recover in three years, and to develop in ten or twenty years." It was possible it would take ten or twenty years to develop the new democratic economy, so it was impossible to pin down the time in precise terms. "China's industrialization is a question of ten or twenty years. If you want to speed up, you need to move forward steadily."[39]

The elaboration of the thought of a "three-year preparation and ten-year planned economic construction" reflected the initial views of the Party's central leadership regarding when to start the transition to socialism. This strategic deployment of the Party demonstrated that from 1949 to 1952, the Party's basic assumption was that the People's Republic of China would be a new democratic country, which would develop from a new democratic society to a socialist society, and this would require a ten-year or longer transition period. This was consistent with the formulation in *On New Democracy* and the decisions of the Seventh National Congress.

From such a basic idea, in his keynote speech on behalf of the Central Committee at the First National Organizational Work Conference held by the Party Central Committee in March 1951, Liu Shaoqi put forward Eight Conditions for the Standard of Communist Party Members, in accordance with the Party's Constitution and the actual situation at that time. The second one was, "The ultimate goal of the Communist Party of China is to realize the Communist system in China. It is now struggling for the consolidation of the new democratic system and, in the future, for the transformation to socialism."[40] The statement that the Party was "struggling for the consolidation of the new democratic system" was in line with the understanding and deployment of the Central Committee at that time, but it was criticized shortly after the transition to socialism.

V

The Achievements of New Democratic Construction and Flaws in Ideological Recognition

In the first three years after the founding of New China, proceeding from its national conditions, the Central Committee combined Marxism with China's actual situation and creatively carried out the construction of a new democratic society in an all-round way on the basis of the victory of the new democratic revolution. Whether in New China's state system, political system, national economic composition, political structure, or its interactions, they did not copy the Soviet Union's socialist model, but indeed added a brilliant stroke in the process of the integration of Marxism into China.

1. Achievements in the Construction of the New Democracy

During these three years, under the guidance of the New Democracy Program for the Founding of the People's Republic, New China achieved extensive, profound, and significant historical changes. Politically, the people's democratic united front of the four class alliances was consolidated and developed, and the people's democratic dictatorship, led by the working class and based on the workers-peasants alliance, was constantly consolidated and strengthened. From the central government to the local government to the streets of the cities and towns in the countryside, a unified, efficient, and flexible system of government from top to bottom was firmly established. Economically, through the confiscation of bureaucratic capital and land reform campaigns, various new democratic reforms were carried out in depth, in an effort to break the shackles of feudal and semi-feudal production relations that restricted the development of productive forces. The socialist state-owned economy and cooperative economy were established, the national capitalist economy was encouraged and supported, and the private capitalist economy and individual economy that were beneficial to the national economy and people's livelihood were developed. The mixed economic structure of the five components created a good institutional space for the development and activation of the new Chinese economy. The unification of national financial and economic management greatly strengthened the state's control over economic operations and economic resources, which was absolutely necessary for the backward Eastern powers that had just ended the war and must quickly prepare for the initiation of industrialization. In terms of culture, it was necessary to reform the old cultural and educational undertakings systematically, establish a new ideology dominated by Marxism and Mao Zedong Thought, and form a common understanding of building a new democratic society throughout the nation.

Because of the combination of restoring the national economy with social reform and adjusting the interests of all classes and the comprehensive implementation of the policy of the division of labor and cooperation among various economic components under the leadership of the state-owned economy, the urban and rural economy was active and the socio-economic structure was significantly improved. Among the five economic components, the state-owned economy had given priority to growth. The cooperative economy, private capitalist economy, individual economy, and state capitalist economy had all been greatly developed, and the level of social productive forces had been greatly developed in a short period of time. During this period of economic recovery and development, the proportion of socialist economic components in the national economy gradually increased, and the socialist factors inherent in the new democratic economy continuously strengthened and expanded its scope.

In the profound transformation of economic and social relations, the national economy was fully restored and initially developed. With the rapid development of agricultural production and the rapid recovery of industrial production, a number of urgently needed industrial enterprises were planned. By the end of 1952, China's total grain output and industrial product output not only exceeded their 1949 levels, but also exceeded the highest historical level in 1936. Transportation, post, and telecommunications were rapidly restored, which promoted the exchange of goods and materials across the country. State revenue doubled and people's living standards were generally improved. These profound changes guaranteed that the entire country would gradually move toward the future of socialism along the track of the new democracy. It provided a good beginning for China's gradual transformation from an agricultural country to an industrial one.

The practice of the first three years after the founding of New China proved that under the historical conditions of a very low level of productivity and a very backward economic foundation, starting from the actual situation of productivity, that is, from China's national conditions, rather than from the experience and model of the Soviet Union, it was necessary to create conditions for the transition to socialism through the development of new democracy. This was the path to success.

At the beginning of the founding of the People's Republic of China, the construction of the new democracy was carried out in many ways, which further enriched the Party's understanding of the new democratic society formed in the period of the new democratic revolution, causing it to extend and develop under the new historical conditions. It embodied the characteristics of combining Marxism with the actual Chinese situation, accumulated new practical experience for promoting the development of social productive forces, and made necessary preparations for completing the great change from new democracy to socialism. The practice of these three years was a masterpiece of the successful realization of the localization of Marxism in China, which embodied the characteristics of the first historic leap of the localization of Marxism "extending" under the new historical conditions.

2. Internal Contradictions in the New Democratic Society

However, it should also be noted that in the construction and reform at the beginning of the founding of New China, due to the limitations of various historical conditions, the Party still had some obvious limitations and differences in its understanding of some important issues in the development stage of the new democracy. As Liu Shaoqi pointed out in his famous Speech at Chun Ou Zhai in July 1951, "Comrades are generally clear about our Party's future historical tasks. This is the transition from a new democratic society to a socialist society, and finally to a communist society. But I am afraid it is not clear how to move forward and what are the key issues in the process. There has not been much discussion within the Party. Many comrades think differently and have different opinions on many issues."[41] This limitation was mainly manifested in several different areas.

The question of the social nature of China after the founding of New China remained. The Second Plenary Session of the Seventh Central Committee of the Communist Party of China pointed out that the task of China after the victory of the new democratic revolution was to steadily "change from a new democratic country to a socialist country." The Common Program also proclaimed that the

People's Republic of China was a new democracy, i.e. a people's democratic country. These provisions reflected the historical process of the Chinese revolution and the social nature and development prospects of the early days of the founding of New China. However, in practice, the Party's understanding of the nature and characteristics of the new democratic society was not stable, and there were still differences in understanding. In some cases, the Party often equated the concept of the transition period of Marxist classical writers with that of the new democratic society, which was called the transition period.

The political transition period Marx mentioned in *Critique of the Gotha Program* referred to the transition from a capitalist society to the first stage of a communist society, that is, a socialist society. The object of analysis was the capitalist country with the highest level of productivity development at that time. In China, a look at the general and broad process of social development shows that it is certainly possible to define the social nature of the early period of the founding of New China with the concept of the transitional period and call this stage the transitional period to socialism, but this broad understanding is not conducive to highlighting the characteristics of the new democratic society, which were the characteristics that reflected the innovation and development of Marxism by the CPC and the new achievements in the localization of Marxism in China. In China, a new democratic society built on a very backward basis needed a relatively stable stage of development in order to provide a political and material basis for the transition to a socialist society. If there was no specific analysis of the actual social situation after the founding of New China and a proper estimate of the development level of China's social productive forces, it was difficult to grasp the particularity, arduousness, and long-term nature of the transition from new democracy to socialism, which was prone to the Leftist inclination to be overly eager to transition to socialism. Obviously, it was difficult for the theory of the transition period to accurately and comprehensively reflect the social nature of the early period of the founding of New China, which would not only have some influence on the correct understanding of the inevitability and necessity of the new democratic society, but also on the Party's formulation of strategic tasks at this stage and timely guidance for China's decision-making in moving to the socialist stage.

The Party offered many statements on the major contradictions (or basic contradictions) and major (central) tasks of the new democratic society. At the

Second Plenary Session of the Seventh Central Committee in March 1949, Mao expressed "the contradiction between the working class and the bourgeoisie and between China and the imperialist countries."[42] In June 1949, Liu also said in an outline of a report that there was "a struggle between the factors and trends of socialism and capitalism, that is, the struggle between the proletariat and the bourgeoisie" in the new democratic economy composed of five economic components, which was "the struggle against imperialism and feudalism." After that, there was a focus on the basic contradictions within New China.[43] It is evident that the contradictions between the proletariat and the bourgeoisie and between socialism and capitalism were identified as the main contradictions at the beginning of the founding of New China, which became the relatively consistent understanding among the central leadership at that time.

Corresponding closely to this was the understanding of the main tasks of the Party at that time. In his report to the Second Plenary Session of the Seventh Central Committee, Mao pointed out that the central task of the Party in the liberated areas was to mobilize all forces to restore and develop the cause of production, which was the focus of all work.[44] Liu Shaoqi also stressed in June 1949 that "the central task in the future is how to restore and develop China's economy."[45] It was the consensus of the Party's leadership at that time to regard economic construction and production development as the central task of the Party in the period of the new democracy. However, according to the cognitive framework that the main contradiction determined the central task, there arose a difficult problem to explain, which was the question of how to understand the relationship between the two, or how to understand the separation of the main contradiction and the central work. The emergence of this problem, on the one hand, reflected the gap between theory and practice after the rapid victory of the revolution, while on the other, it reflected the urgent need for traditional Marxist theory itself to keep pace with the times in the face of the reality of the people's democratic country after the war.

In fact, the main leaders of the Party at that time had discovered the problem and generated new thinking in connection with it. In the days leading up to the founding of New China, Liu Shaoqi offered new reflections on the main contradictions in the new democratic society. On July 4, 1949, he offered a new explanation of the main contradictions in his report to Stalin during his visit to the Soviet Union. He said that after the overthrow of the Kuomintang regime and the implementation of land reform, "the contradiction between the proletariat and the bourgeoisie in China will immediately become the main contradiction, and the struggle between workers and capitalists will immediately become the main struggle." In his view, this statement was incorrect. "Because if a regime opposes the bourgeoisie with its main firepower, it will be or will become a dictatorship of the proletariat. This will drive the national bourgeoisie, which can still cooperate with us, to the imperialist side. It will be a dangerous adventurist policy in China today." The report pointed out that "for a long period after the overthrow of the Kuomintang regime," the "main contradictions and struggles" remain "external contradictions and external struggles," i.e. contradictions and struggles with the three enemies and the remaining forces of the Kuomintang. The contradictions and struggles of all classes and parties within the people's democratic dictatorship, namely internal contradictions and struggles, "will gradually intensify in the future, but compared with external contradictions, for a relatively long period of time, it will retain a status of secondary obedience." The report also said that "from now, it will take a long time to nationalize the general national capital in China." It was estimated that it would take ten to fifteen years. During this period, the working class was to wage necessary and appropriate struggles against the bourgeoisie, but at the same time "it should also make necessary and appropriate compromises with the national bourgeoisie so as to concentrate its efforts on dealing with the external enemies and overcoming the backwardness of China."[46] Here, Liu's exposition of the main contradictions was obviously different from the provisions of the Second Plenary Session of the Seventh Central Committee of the Party. This should be regarded as the development and supplement of the Central Committee's original understanding according to the developing situation and tasks.

During the period after the founding of New China, Mao Zedong, Zhou Enlai, and other leaders recognized Liu's new understanding. In practice, they not only regarded the contradiction between the proletariat and the bourgeoisie as society's main contradiction, but also criticized the view that the national bourgeoisie had become the main object of struggle both inside and outside the Party. For example, Mao expressed the same idea at the Third Plenary Session of the Seventh Central Committee in 1950. In April 1950, Mao wrote these remarks in a transcript of his speech at the seminar of the Business Group of the United Front Work Conference. Mao commented in his speech notes that "today's targets of struggle are mainly the bourgeoisie [...] Today's targets of struggle are mainly the remnants of imperialist feudalism and its running dogs, the reactionaries of the Kuomintang, rather than the national bourgeoisie. There is struggle against the national bourgeoisie, but ultimately, it should be united, and the policy of both unity and struggle should be adopted to achieve the goal of uniting the national bourgeoisie to jointly develop the national economy." In his transcript, Mao commented on the restrictions and exclusions imposed on private industry and commerce, saying, "What should be restricted and excluded are those industries and commerce that are not conducive to the national economy and people's livelihood, namely speculative commerce, luxury goods, and superstitious goods, rather than legitimate industries and commerce that are conducive to the national economy and people's livelihood. These industries and commerce should be supported and developed when they are in difficulty [...] The state-owned economy is developing indefinitely." He added, "This is a long-term project. It is impossible to develop indefinitely at the present stage. Private capital must be used at the same time."[47]

In brief, in the first two or three years after the founding of New China, the central government's understanding on this issue was relatively clear and consistent. It emphasized the irreplaceable role of the private economy in the development of the national economy, emphasized the unity and utilization of the national bourgeoisie, and repeatedly criticized the view that the national bourgeoisie was the main object of struggle. The main contradictions set by the Second Plenary Session of the Seventh Central Committee were not overly emphasized. This different expression of the main contradictions and the separation of the main contradictions from the main tasks reflected that the Party's understanding of these issues was developing and changing at that time, as well as some uncertainties in this development. Later practice proved that the result of this development and change had returned to the understanding held by the Second Plenary Session of the Seventh Central Committee. The understanding of the main contradictions in the Second Plenary Session of the Seventh Central Committee after the founding of New China not only reflected the grasp of China's national conditions after the new democratic theory was put forward, but also reflected the provisions of classical writers on traditional socialist society. However, in the early days of the founding of New China, it was important to rely on the urgent need of the national bourgeoisie and other private economies to restore and develop the economy, which in turn weakened the Party's emphasis on major contradictions in a very realistic way. This contradictory phenomenon often appeared after the movement of the "Three Oppositions Campaign" and the "Five Oppositions Campaign."

In fact, since the founding of New China, when the Communist Party became the governing Party throughout the country, the political premise of taking economic construction as the center of all work was provided, and the fact that the economy was very backward made the task of restoring and developing production extremely urgent. At this time, taking the development of production as the central task and the contradiction between people's material and cultural needs and backward social production as the main contradiction seemed a correct choice. On the other hand, because many tasks left over from the democratic revolution (such as land reform) were yet to be completed, the contradiction between the people and the remnants of the three enemies also needed to be placed in a very important position. In such a special transitional period in which multiple tasks and contradictions coexisted, the main contradictions needed to reflect not only the unfinished reality of the new democratic revolution, but also the imminent economic task. Therefore, the main contradictions in this period had the characteristics of duality, crossover, and transition. This complex contradictory situation not only brought difficulties to the correct understanding of the main contradictions of the society and the central task of the Party at that time, but also implied a great opportunity for the integration of Marxism into China.

Owing to the domination of the traditional socialist concept and the restraint of the Soviet Union's understanding of the main contradictions in the transitional period, when determining the main contradictions in society at that time, the people still tended to proceed from the perspective of class contradictions, believing that the main conflicts in class contradictions were the main social contradictions under any circumstances. Thus, in understanding the main contradictions and the Party's central task, the Party continued to regard the contradictions between the working class and the bourgeoisie and between socialism and capitalism as the main contradictions in the new democratic society, but failed to connect them with the Party's guiding principles for the development of the economy at that time or to pay attention to the fact that they had not yet been solved through the many democratic revolutions advanced by the Party at that time. The major tasks completed (such as land reform) were all linked.

These factors led to several problems. First, the estimation of the period of existence for the new democratic society also showed a state of instability, growing shorter and shorter and shifting the original idea of building a new democratic society to a longer timeframe. Second, the understanding of the characteristics of the future socialist society was increasingly characterized by the Soviet model of a "big" and "pure" socialist society. Third, the understanding of the importance of utilizing capitalism to develop the economy tended to be indifferent under the condition of very backward productivity. Under this sort of background, during this period of time, when Leftist errors in dealing with the bourgeoisie and the individual economy appeared both inside and outside the Party, the Central Committee made a series of efforts to correct them, but failed to suppress them completely, so that when the situation changed, the tendency to eliminate the bourgeoisie and make the transition to socialism would return in a new form. This situation definitely affected the implementation of the Party's New Democracy National Founding Program and the process of the localization of Marxism in the early days after the founding of New China.

CHAPTER 4

New Thoughts on the Shift Toward Socialism and the Soviet Mode

After the founding of New China in 1949, the Second Plenary Session of the Seventh Central Committee of the Communist Party of China clearly stipulated the path and steps for development. That is to say, after the victory of the revolution throughout the country, one of the fundamental tasks of the Party was to steadily promote the two interconnected transformations, namely, the transformation from an agricultural to an industrial nation, and the shift from a new democratic to a socialist society. After the Second Plenary Session of the Seventh Central Committee, the Central Committee and Mao Zedong put forward some ideas concerning when and how these two transformations should begin. Later, with the development and change of the external situation, new thinking was carried out, and some new and important development ideas were advanced.

I

The Transition to Socialism Ahead of Schedule and its Causes

From the second half of 1952, the situation at home and abroad was advantageous to China's large-scale construction. Internationally, the War of Resistance Against

US Aggression and Aid to North Korea was basically stable, and peace talks had reached agreement on the major issues. The war that New China had been forced to carry out was expected to end soon. At home, large-scale land reform had been basically completed nationwide, and other social reforms had progressed smoothly. The work of restoring the national economy had been completed ahead of schedule, and remarkable achievements had been made in every aspect of the construction of the new democracy. The original idea of a "three-year and five-year recovery" had resulted in attaining and exceeding the expected target in the first three years, and the conditions for large-scale and planned economic construction had been met.

At this time, another important choice was before the Party. In accordance with the assumption of the "three-year preparation and ten-year planned economic construction," the Central Committee decided to implement the First Five-Year Plan for the development of the national economy from 1953, aiming to realize the transformation from an agricultural to an industrial country. At the same time, the transition to socialism began ahead of schedule. This was a significant new strategic change. It changed the original assumption that after a period of full development of the new democracy and certain economic conditions, it would shift to socialism, starting the transition to socialism in 1953 instead of in more than ten or twenty years. How did this change come about?

1. The External Requirements for the Early Transition

From the perspective of external requirements, the reasons for the early transition were as follows.

First, fundamentally, this transformation was determined by the nature of the Communist Party of China and should be included as part of the theme of the Chinese revolution. Achieving socialism in China had been the goal of the Communist Party of China since its founding. The ways and methods of realizing socialism had long been clear in the revolutionary program of the new democratic period. In semi-colonial, semi-feudal China, the realization of socialism had to be divided into two steps. The first step was to complete the anti-imperialist, anti-feudal new democratic revolution, while the second step was to transform the new democratic revolution into the socialist revolution. As for the timing and what form the revolution took to move to the socialist stage, the Party only generally pointed out that this was the inevitable trend of historical development and the conditions it needed. It was impossible to judge or estimate the specific timing and conditions of the transformation, because this needed to be determined through the practice of revolutionary development according to the specific circumstances.

Since late in the liberation war, especially after the founding of New China, an increasing number of leading comrades in the Central Committee discussed this issue in detail. The assumption at that time was that after the victory of the new democratic revolution, a new democratic country should first be established. After ten to fifteen years of new democratic economic construction, when industry had developed and the state-owned economy had grown, industrial nationalization and agricultural collectivization would be carried out to realize the transition from a new democracy to socialism. This was a "fairly long" historical process. For example, in September 1949, when Liu Shaoqi, on behalf of the Communist Party of China, explained why the Common Program did not include the future of socialism in China, he pointed out, "Taking serious socialist steps in China is still a long-term future proposition." During this meeting, when a representative asked Mao Zedong how long it would take to make the transition to socialism, he answered, "About twenty or thirty years." By 1952, at the end of the recovery period, due to the development of the situation and the accumulation of new experience, as well as the new understanding of the steps of socialist transformation, some important changes had taken place in the original idea. The Central Committee believed that the task of the gradual transition to socialism could then begin and was expected to be completed in fifteen years or more. In this way, the Party had put forward the general line in the transitional period and put new tasks and objectives before the entire Party and the people. Therefore, fundamentally speaking, the goal of struggle and the ideal pursued remain unchanged. Being ahead of schedule, the transformation was further accelerated.

Second, the Korean War put the task of giving priority to the development of heavy industry before the Party in a more urgent position. With the outbreak of the Korean War, China's international environment deteriorated rapidly and its national security was seriously threatened. China had to compete with the United States, the world's leading economic power, on the Korean battlefield. The backwardness of New China's economic strength and military equipment was exposed in the War of Resistance Against US Aggression and Aid to North Korea, making the CPC leaders eager to transform the extremely weak industrial base of

China, especially its heavy industry, and to narrow the gap with developed Western countries as soon as possible. This was one of the direct reasons for giving priority to the development of heavy industry to promote national industrialization.

On the threshold of the founding of New China and through the early stages of its founding, the Party generally held that China's economy was backward, its industrial base was weak, and its capital was scarce. Industrialization was to begin with giving priority to the development of agriculture and light industry with less investment and quick results, so as to accumulate funds for the development of heavy industry with large investment and a long construction cycle. Liu Shaoqi once conceived that such development should be done in "three steps." The first was to develop agriculture and light industry with the main force while establishing the necessary national defense industry, the second to vigorously develop heavy industry with the necessary foundation, and the third to greatly develop light industry and the mechanization of agricultural production on the basis of the established and developed heavy industry. He explained that only with the development of agriculture could industry be supplied with sufficient raw materials and grain and the market for the development of industry be expanded. Only with the development of light industry could a large number of industrial products be exchanged for raw materials and grain produced by farmers, and in this was accumulating capital for the continued development of industry. With the development of agriculture and light industry, the long-term low living standard of the people could be improved as quickly as possible, thus further uniting all the people politically. It would then be possible to concentrate the maximum funds and strength to build the foundation to develop heavy industry.[1] According to this sort of development idea, the role of the mixed economic structure was prominent.

In the first three years after the founding of New China, although the national economy had recovered and developed considerably, the backward situation of industry had not fundamentally improved. By 1952, the output of steel was only more than 1.3 million tons, and the output value of modern industry using machines accounted for about 28% of the total output value of industry and agriculture, and so on. Mao Zedong once said with emotion, "What can we build now? We can make tables and chairs, tea bowls and teapots, grow grain, grind flour and paper, but we can't build a car, an airplane, a tank, or a tractor."[2] The backward situation and severe international environment made the Party leaders realize that whether they could quickly change the extremely weak industrial base of China and catch up with the advanced industrial countries was a question that depended on safeguarding national security under the threat of a serious imperialist war and on the future and destiny of the country and nation. If, according to the original assumption, the new democratic mixed economy should be implemented for more than a decade or more, agriculture and light industry should be developed first, and heavy industry should be developed when funds had accumulated to a certain degree. Although industrialization could also be achieved, this was still a long way off, and it was not suitable for such an underdeveloped socialist nation as China bound by the conditions of the Cold War.

It was against this background that, once the task of restoring the national economy had been basically completed, the Central Committee lost no time in putting the task of industrialization centered on heavy industry on the agenda. In May 1952, when compiling the first Five-Year Plan, Li Fuchun, on behalf of the Finance and Economics Committee, proposed that the focus of economic construction should be on heavy industry in order to lay the foundation for China's industrialization, and that agriculture, light industry, and transportation should be developed around the center of heavy industry.[3] This was an important decision that gave priority to the development of heavy industry. Mao explained the origin and characteristics of this development strategy in a highly general way. He said that in order to guarantee the independence of the country, it was important to focus on heavy industry to strengthen national defense and advance towards socialism.[4] In this way, according to the new situation and tasks encountered after the founding of New China, the development strategy of agriculture, light industry, and heavy industry in the new democratic system had been changed in the past, but heavy industry had been developed first, then light industry and agriculture, and the realization of national industrialization as the main task of the country in the coming period had become a major strategy of the Party. This kind of catching-up development strategy, with industrialization as the center of an accelerated development, was the industrialization strategy generally chosen by most newly independent post-war developing countries, especially socialist countries. Particularly noteworthy was that the transformation of this development strategy had to have the corresponding institutional transformation as the basic guarantee. In China, this also meant that it was necessary to advance into socialism.

One of the biggest differences between industrialization and agriculture and light industry development was that a large amount of capital investment was needed and a huge capital gap would arise. This contradiction was highlighted by giving priority to the development of heavy industry. At that time, China's industrial base was weaker than that of the Soviet Union when the First Five-Year Plan was implemented, and the scattered and backward individual economy after the land reform could hardly meet cities' and industries' needs for the rapid growth of capital, food, and agricultural raw materials. Faced with this contradiction, the Party could neither take the start-up funds of industrialization through overseas expansion, as in the early capitalist countries, nor settle the huge payments necessary for the development of heavy industry from the decentralization of backward agriculture and light industry. It could only find other ways to achieve its goals. Whether or not there was sufficient knowledge at that time, and no matter how many components were based on realistic and ideological considerations, the realistic approach could only be to adopt a planned economic system through a highly centralized government, mainly through planning rather than the market, and to accumulate and allocate resources internally through a strong administrative force to meet the huge demand for various funds and resources in the early stage of industrialization. It was this urgent need for development that put the task of advancing the transition to socialism before the Party.

The recovery of industry and the start of a large number of new projects greatly increased the demand for commodity grain and other industrial raw materials. However, the ability of dispersed and vulnerable individual farmers to expand their production after the land reform was very limited, which was far from meeting the needs of large-scale industrial construction. At that time, the fact that simple and cooperative mutual aid groups and preliminary cooperation could significantly increase production made the Party believe that further cooperation could promote the development of productive forces more rapidly and meet industrialization's urgent need for agricultural products.

After three years of recovery, some new contradictions emerged and accumulated in China's social economy. In the countryside, the polarization between the rich and the poor after land reform had made it impossible for the Party to ignore the question of which direction the individual economy was heading. This not only concerned the stability and development of the vast rural areas, but also sharply raised several fundamental issues in the Party's ideology, including that of private or public ownership, socialism or capitalism, and the individual or collective economy.

Third, there was the movement of the "Three Oppositions Campaign" and the "Five Oppositions Campaign" and the return in the Second Plenary Session of the Seventh Central Committee to major domestic contradictions. Mao Zedong expressed his in-principle understanding of China's main contradictions since the founding of New China in his works on the united government. From the Central Working Conference in September 1948 to the Second Plenary Session of the Seventh Central Committee, this expression became clearer. He pointed to the contradiction between the proletariat and the bourgeoisie. But even at this time, the understanding of the main contradictions still lacked thoroughness and consistency. For example, Mao's statement of the basic contradictions (i.e. major contradictions) in his report to the Second Plenary Session of the Seventh Central Committee lacked logical consistency with the provisions of the central task. From that time, the central leaders offered new judgments about the main contradictions, which was to say that the understanding was repeated. They repeatedly criticized the view that the national bourgeoisie had been the main object of struggle, but there was still no clear consensus on this, and there was still a lack of firm, consistent understanding of the main contradictions. This contradiction and repetition in understanding was not entirely surprising. It reflected the Party's changes in its long-term and short-term goals, value pursuit and strategic considerations, consideration of recovery and the development of production, and its response to the new situation of class struggle. This inconsistent and unclear situation changed and developed due to changes in the understanding of the national bourgeoisie caused by the movement of the "Three Oppositions Campaign" and the "Five Oppositions Campaign."

Some changes in the understanding of the national bourgeoisie became important reasons driving the Central Committee's decision to make an early transition to socialism. At the beginning of the founding of New China, in accordance with the scientific understanding of the dual nature of the national bourgeoisie and the provisions of the Common Program for the protection of the legitimate operation and proper development of private industry and commerce, the Party always adhered to the principle of unity, utilization, and transformation, but the emphasis was on utilization. In the process of restoring the national economy, the lawless capitalists were not satisfied with obtaining general profits in normal ways. They tried to obtain high illegal profits by bribing state cadres, evading taxes, cutting corners, stealing state property and state economic information, and other illegal means (then referred to as the "five poisons"). In view of this serious situation, the Central Committee decided to launch a campaign against corruption, waste, and bureaucracy among Party staff and government organs ("Three Oppositions Campaign"), and a campaign against bribery, tax evasion, corner-cutting, and stealing state property and state economic information among private business people the ("Five Oppositions Campaign").

The vigorous "Three Oppositions Campaign" and "Five Oppositions Campaign" not only dealt illegal capitalists a strong blow, but also caused an ideological shock among Party members and cadres, which led to an important change in their understanding of the national bourgeoisie. In the process of exposing illegal capitalists' "five poisons" and criticizing bourgeois ideology, passionate feelings were inevitably aroused in some cadres and the masses. At the beginning of 1952, the journal *Learning*, edited by the Department of Theory of the Ministry of Publicity and Propaganda, published a series of articles that violated the Common Program and were in principle erroneous. These articles unilaterally denied that the bourgeoisie still had two sides at that stage. They held that the bourgeoisie had only a reactionary and decadent side, but no positive side, and they erased the position and role of the bourgeoisie in the new democratic stage. The article required the bourgeoisie as a class to accept the Marxist ideological system. Mao severely criticized the mistakes in the article, and the Ministry of Propaganda reviewed them. On March 27, 1952, Mao wrote in another directive, "In the period of the new democracy, that is, the period in which the bourgeoisie and the petty bourgeoisie are allowed to exist," and "in the period in which the bourgeoisie and the petty bourgeoisie are allowed to exist, the bourgeoisie and the petty bourgeoisie are not allowed to have their own positions and ideas. This idea is a divergence from Marxism and a childish and ridiculous thought," and it "should be corrected."[5] Here, Mao's understanding of the bourgeoisie and bourgeois ideology remained consistent with the position of the Party as stipulated in the Common Program, but was different from that expressed by the Second Plenary Session of the Seventh Central Committee. In other words, as of March, Mao put more emphasis on the position of the Common Program.

However, with the task of socialist industrialization being put forward, and especially with the development of the "Three Oppositions Campaign" and

"Five Oppositions Campaign," when the profit-seeking side of the bourgeoisie was more exposed and conflicted sharply with the values of the CPC, and as the contradictions between the anarchic impulse of the capitalist industrial and commercial economy and the highly concentrated planned economic system required by the industrialization of the country continued to develop, the struggle of restrictions and counter-restrictions between the working class, the state-owned economy, and the bourgeoisie became increasingly prominent. At this time, the attention of the central leadership swiftly turned to this increasingly prominent contradiction, which further increased the understanding of the negative role of the bourgeoisie and the capitalist economy, constantly clarifying the judgment that the contradiction between the working class and the bourgeoisie was the main contradiction in the transitional period. Three months later, at the end of the campaign, Mao Zedong's understanding of the bourgeoisie changed significantly. On June 6, 1952, he put forward in a decree that "after overthrowing the landlord class and the bureaucratic bourgeoisie, the main contradiction in China is the contradiction between the working class and the national bourgeoisie, so the national bourgeoisie should no longer be called the middle class."[6] To express the main contradictions in this way was in fact a return to the statement consistently made from the time of the September 1948 meeting of the Politburo until the Second Plenary Session of the Seventh Central Committee. It negated the view that the national bourgeoisie was the middle class and ended the Party's back-and-forth understanding on this basic issue. Three months later, Mao changed his assumption of gradual transformation from the new democracy to socialism and raised the issue of starting the transition to socialism.

While it was true that the contradiction between the negative factors of the private capitalist economy and national industrialization supported by the state-owned economy and centralized plan objectively required the transformation of the private economy to narrow its scope of activities, history later proved that during the period of large-scale economic production, the degree and speed of such transformation could have been steadier. After the transformation of the understanding of the national bourgeoisie in the "Three Oppositions Campaign" and the "Five Oppositions Campaign," the important ideas contained in the new democratic theory with Chinese characteristics had been weakened, and a great step had been taken toward the soviet model in Stalin's era.

Fourth, it was noted that when a country starts to build a planned economy, it needs to concentrate its limited resources and funds on key construction projects, while the private capitalist economy instinctively calls for the expansion of free production and free trade to develop itself, but it instinctively excludes the planned management of the economy. If the contradiction between planning management and free development were not prominent in the recovery period, it would be prominent after the First Five-Year Plan construction had been initiated. The only way to solve this contradiction was to speed up the transformation of the private economy and intensify the transformation so as to make it adapt to the planned economy.

Fifth, during the period of the First Five-Year Plan, China received a great deal of assistance from the Soviet Union and other socialist countries. All this tangible material equipment and funds bore the imprint of an invisible planned economy and corresponding economic system of public ownership, and thus could only be connected with China's public economy and economic system. This not only deepened the dependence of the private economy on the state-owned economy, but also highlighted the necessity of socialist transformation of the private economy.

2. Preferential Conditions for an Earlier Transition

Beginning the transition to socialism at an earlier stage had not only realistic objective requirements, but also certain favorable conditions at that time.

First, China had a relatively strong and rapidly developing socialist state-owned economy, which was not only an important force for the socialist transformation of the entire national economy, but also an important starting point for the transformation. After three years of recovery, the proportion of the public and private economy in the national economy had fundamentally changed. For example, among the total output value of national industry (excluding handicraft industry), state-owned industry rose from 34.2% in 1949 to 52.8% in 1952, cooperative operation and public-private joint industry accounted for 8.2%, and private industry decreased from 63.3% to 39%. At that time, most state-owned industries had advanced technology and a high rate of labor productivity with workers enjoying a strong sense of ownership, a stable life, various rights and welfare, and great enthusiasm for labor. In short, the socialist economy clearly displayed its superiority to other economic components. Such changes indicated that the dominant position of the socialist state-owned economy across the national economy had been greatly enhanced. It not only controlled the important industries and industrial sectors related to the national economy and people's livelihood, but also surpassed private industry in modern industry, which became the main material basis for China's gradual transition to socialism. China's industrialization could only depend on the development of the socialist state-owned economy.

Second, the Party employed many means of utilizing and restricting private industry and commerce, accumulating plentiful experience, which was actually the initial step of socialist transformation of the capitalist economy. During the recovery of the national economy, in the process of restricting and counter-restricting the capitalist economy and rationally adjusting industry and commerce, the state created a series of forms of state capitalism from low to high, such as processing and ordering, distribution and commission, wholesale purchase and guaranteed sale, and public-private joint ventures. These forms constituted not only the use and restriction of capitalist industry and commerce, but also the concrete steps to deepen their links with the socialist state-owned and planned economies, resulting in varying degrees of changes in their relations of production. In fact, their preliminary socialist transformation had begun in varying degrees, though they were not fully aware of it at first. Previously, the Party's understanding of the measures to achieve socialist transformation had been that, after a "fairly long" period of time, on the basis of industrial development and the growth of the state-owned economy, "serious socialist steps" were taken to nationalize capitalist industry and commerce and to, collectively and systematically, implement individual agriculture. In other words, when the conditions were met, nationalization would be announced at a certain time in the future, and capitalist private ownership would be abolished in one stroke. From 1952, through investigation, research, and summary of experience, the Central Committee realized that continuing to expand and improve various forms of state capitalism could be a specific way of enabling the gradual socialist transformation of capitalist industry and commerce. This understanding became another basic factor leading the Party to think that the general line of a gradual transition to socialism could be put forward at this time.

Third, after the basic completion of land reform throughout the country, the simple, cooperative agricultural mutual assistance and cooperation movement was carried out in rural areas, which preliminarily demonstrated the superiority of organizing individual farmers to increase agricultural production. In the process, the Party accumulated much experience in developing agricultural mutual assistance and cooperation. At that time, it was believed that these forms of mutual assistance and cooperation were not only an effective way to help poor peasants overcome difficulties and increase production, but also an appropriate way to prevent the spontaneous trend of rural capitalism and guide agriculture towards socialism. In the debate about Shanxi's cooperative transformation, the Party also formed a new understanding, stating that China's industrialization and agricultural mechanization would be a long process, and agricultural cooperative transformation could not wait for industrialization and mechanization. In the absence of large machines, smaller agricultural mutual aid and cooperation organizations generally relied on unified operation and cooperation, which could also increase production. This was a basic factor in the Party's view that the general line of gradual transition to socialism could be put forward.

Fourth, aside from ideological and other reasons, the influence of the international environment on the Central Committee's decision to give priority to the development of heavy industry and advance the transition to socialism cannot be overlooked. New China was born in an international environment of sharp confrontation between the world's capitalist and socialist camps. Therefore, after the founding of New China, China chose the "one-sided" diplomatic policy, becoming a member of the socialist camp. Imperialist countries, headed by the United States, threatened China's military assertion and kept its economy tightly locked down. They constantly set off a vicious wave of anti-China and anti-Communist sentiment. By contrast, the Soviet Union and other people's democratic countries gave China active assistance and support. At that time, the socialist camp was full of vigor for upward development, showing its superiority to capitalism. Since the birth of the first socialist country, after the comparison between the capitalist economic crisis in the 1920s and 1930s and the post-war recovery economy, the socialist development model with public ownership and a planned economy as the main body held great attraction for backward countries, allowing them to realize a catch-up strategy in a relatively short time.

3. Proposal of the General Line for the Transitional Period

In the context of this practice and understanding and with the interaction of various factors, by the second half of 1952, the Central Committee had begun to consider how to gradually make the transition to socialism in China. On September 24, 1952, when the "Three Oppositions Campaign" and the "Five Oppositions Campaign" were about to end, Mao raised the issue of the transition to socialism at the meeting of the Secretariat of the Central Committee. He said that China was now going to basically complete the transition to socialism in ten to fifteen years, rather than ten or twenty years. The Second Plenary Session of the Seventh Central Committee put forward restrictions and counter-restrictions, which had grown more abundant. In November, at the Central Committee meeting, he said that the bourgeoisie should be eliminated and that bourgeois industry and commerce should be eliminated. However, the elimination of the bourgeoisie would be done in stages, one of which involved eliminating it, and the other supporting it. Later, when he visited Hubei Province, he said, "What is the transitional period? The step of the transitional period is to move towards socialism." This kind of bridge-crossing was a transition of one year, two years, three years, or ten to fifteen years. Compared with the idea of the transition to socialism advocated by the Party in the early days of the founding of New China, Mao's idea had changed considerably.

In October 1952, Liu Shaoqi led a delegation of the Communist Party of China to participate in the Nineteenth National Congress of the Soviet Communist Party. He was entrusted by Mao to write to Stalin and seek his advice on the idea of the socialist transformation of agriculture, handicraft industry, and capitalist industry, and commerce by the Central Committee of the CPC and the gradual transition to socialism within ten to fifteen years. Stalin affirmed this assumption and said, "When we have the power, we should adopt a gradual transition to socialism. Your approach towards the Chinese bourgeoisie is correct."[7]

After Stalin's affirmation, the Central Committee further strengthened this new idea of the transition to socialism. In April 1953, Mao wrote in an outline that in ten to fifteen years or more, the country's industrialization and socialist transformation (agriculture, handicraft industry, capitalist industry, and commerce) would be basically completed. In mid-June, Mao formally put forward at the meeting of the Politburo that the general line and task of the Party in the transitional period should basically complete the industrialization of the country and socialist transformation of agriculture, handicraft industry, capitalist industry, and commerce in ten to fifteen years or more. This general line was a beacon that illuminated the Party's work.[8] In August, when reviewing a document, Mao made a relatively complete written statement on the general line of the transitional period for the first time, stating, "The time from the founding of the People's Republic of China to the basic completion of its socialist transformation is a transitional period. The general line and task of the Party in this transitional period is to basically realize the industrialization of the country and the socialist transformation of agriculture, handicraft industry, capitalist industry, and commerce over a fairly long period of time."

In order to meet the needs of education and propaganda, in December 1953, the Central Committee approved and transferred the "Struggle to Mobilize All Forces to Build Our Country into a Great Socialist Country" (hereinafter referred to as the Propaganda Outline) compiled by the Central Propaganda Department and revised by Mao Zedong. The Propaganda Outline finalized the overall formulation of the general line during the transitional period, noting, "From the founding of the People's Republic of China to the basic completion of socialist transformation is a transitional period. The general line and task of the Party in this transitional period is to gradually realize the socialist industrialization of the country and gradually realize the socialist transformation of agriculture, handicraft industry, capitalist industry, and commerce over a fairly long period of time. This general line is a beacon illuminating our work. If we depart from it, we will make right-leaning or left-leaning mistakes."[9]

The Party's general line in the transitional period marked the starting point of the transitional period from the founding of New China, which was a significant development and transformation of the Central Committee's theories on the nature of revolution, society, the new democratic society, and the transition to socialism since the Second Plenary Session of the Seventh Central Committee. Mao and other central leaders felt this great change and tried to explain it. In his study and in the Propaganda Outline, he added a note, saying, "When we say that what marks a change of revolutionary nature, meaning the basic end of the stage of the new democratic revolution and the beginning of the stage of the socialist revolution, is the change of political power, the demise of the Kuomintang's counter-revolutionary regime, and the establishment of the People's Republic of China, we do not mean that the great task of socialist transformation could have been carried out in all aspects of the country immediately after the founding of the People's Republic of China [...] At that time, the main contradiction in the countryside was the that between feudalism and democracy, not between capitalism and socialism, so it took two to three years to implement land reform in the countryside. At that time, on the one hand, we carried out democratic land reform in rural areas, while on the other, we immediately began to accept bureaucratic capitalist enterprises in the cities and turn them into socialist enterprises. At the same time, we started to establish socialist state-owned and cooperative businesses throughout the country, and in the past few years, we have implemented measures of state capitalism for private capitalist enterprises. All this shows the intricate image of our country in the first few years of the transition period." What Mao referred to as the "intricate image" here was probably meant to illustrate the changes in the understanding of major contradictions in the first three years after the founding of New China.

Zhou Enlai explained this problem in terms of the internal relationship between the two social forms. In September 1953, he clearly pointed out at the Enlarged Standing Committee of the CPPCC, "Collectively speaking, the period of the construction of new democracy in our country is that of the gradual transition to socialism, that is, the period of gradual increase in the proportion of socialist economic components in the national economy."[10] That is to say, China's new democratic society belonged to the socialist system and was a transitional society gradually becoming a socialist society. In this way, it was easier to see why the general line of the transitional period understood the transitional period as starting from the founding of New China.

II

Fundamental Features of the Overall Direction During the Transition

1. "Socialist Industrialization and the Three Transformations" and its Emphases

There were two basic characteristics of the general line in the transitional period. One was to be ahead of schedule, and the other was simultaneous development. Being ahead of schedule meant that the thinking current at the time had changed the idea that the transition to socialism from the construction of the new democracy would take a considerably long time after the great development of productivity, but that it would instead begin in 1953, significantly shortening the period of construction of the new democracy. Simultaneous development referred to "socialist industrialization and the three transformations" or "one main body [the socialist industrialization], two wings [three transformations]." The main body was to gradually realize socialist industrialization, and the "two wings" were to gradually realize the socialist transformation of agriculture, handicraft industry, capitalist industry, and commerce. The prominent feature of this general line was the simultaneous development of national industrialization and socialist transformation, that is, the simultaneous development of productive forces and the transformation of production relations, as well as the gradual transformation of the private ownership of the means of production, while giving priority to the development of heavy industry to achieve industrialization.

To systematically realize the task of socialist industrialization, the general line required the full development of socialist industry and the transformation of existing non-socialist industries into socialist industries, so that socialist industry could play a decisive role in the development of the national economy. With regard to the task of gradually realizing the socialist transformation of agriculture, handicraft industry, capitalist industry, and commerce, the general line stipulated that socialist ownership by the people and collective ownership of cooperative members should be expanded, that private ownership of farmers and handicraftsmen based on individual labor should be transformed into collective ownership of cooperative members, and that capitalist private ownership based on exploiting the surplus labor of the working class should be transformed into ownership by the people.

The general line of the transitional period developed the theory of classical Marxist writers on the transition to socialism. In the relevant theories of Marx and Engels, the transition from capitalism to socialism or communism was to be the transition from developed capitalist countries to socialism or communism. In these countries, the high development of productive forces was an integral part of the discussion. Therefore, in their theory of the transition period, there was no deliberate emphasis on the development of productive forces such as industrialization, but more emphasis on the revolutionary changes of the economic foundation and superstructure. Socialist practice in the 20th century went beyond the imagination of Marx and Engels, mostly coming into being in backward countries, which promoted the development of Marxist theory in the transitional period. In the practice of the Soviet Union's transition to socialism, because of its backward economy and culture, under Lenin's and Stalin's criteria for building socialism, alongside eliminating exploitation and realizing industrial nationalization and agricultural cooperation, the Soviet Union emphasized national industrialization. Because of their relatively backward productivity level, socialist countries that emerged after World War II mostly equated the realization of the transition to socialism with the realization of industrialization. In fact, this could be considered as the development of classical Marxist theory under contemporary conditions – an important achievement of the modernization of Marxism.

When putting forward the general line of the transitional period, the Central Committee drew lessons from the experience of the Soviet Union, took industrialization as the main task of the transition to socialism, and proposed that China should promote the development of socialism from the two aspects of productivity and production relations. Mao's passage succinctly summarized the essence and characteristics of this general line, which was to combine "the revolution of the social system from private ownership to public ownership" with "the revolution of technology from the handicraft industry to large-scale modern machine production."[11] This was different from Marx's transition theory and was a development of Marxist classical theory.

However, it should also be noted that the general line of the transitional period brought about considerable changes in the way, manner, time, and specific policies of the transition from the new democracy to socialism originally envisaged by the Central Committee. In connection with greatly shortening the period of the new democracy, Mao changed his understanding of its nature before and after the founding of New China, and the provisions of the Common Program on the nature of New China, as well as his understanding of the starting point of the transition. The general line of the transitional period changed the understanding and regulations of the transition period from a new democratic to a socialist society, replacing it with the notion of "from capitalism to socialism." Apparently, the social form before the founding of New China was not a "capitalist" society, but a semi-colonial and semi-feudal society, which was the starting point of the entire new democratic revolution and sociology. If it were "capitalism," the Chinese revolution would not be of a new democratic nature. This judgment ran counter to the understanding of all parties in the period of the democratic revolution, from the new democracy to the report of the Second Plenary Session of the Seventh Central Committee. In proposing the general line, Mao also criticized the three "wrong views" of establishing a new democratic social order, moving from a new democracy to socialism, and ensuring private property.[12] Regarding the time required to complete the transition, it was envisaged that there would be three five-year plans, plus three years for the recovery of the national economy – a total of eighteen years. It was shorter than previously suggested, but it would not be a problem if the plan were implemented effectively. This indicated that Mao was cautious in guiding the ideology at that time.

Although the general line was divided into the "main body" and "two wings," it juxtaposed the transformation of developing productive forces and realizing productive relations, emphasizing that although the main body was industrialization, in actual implementation and understanding, the transformation of productive relations was more emphasized in the issue of the relationship between productive forces and productive relations, highlighting the superstructure and production relations. The reaction of production relations did not regard the development of productive forces as the decisive factor for the realization of public ownership. Mao said in his two talks on mutual assistance and cooperation in agriculture in October 1953 that "the general line can also be said to solve the problem of ownership," and "the general line is to gradually change the relations of production," while "private ownership should gradually become illegal."[13] Later he even suggested, "Our aim is to exterminate capitalism, and to exterminate it throughout the earth."[14] In September 1953, Zhou Enlai said to the Forty-Ninth Standing Committee of the National Political Consultative Conference, "What is socialism? The most basic aspect of socialism is to complete the socialist transformation, that is, to abolish the private capitalist ownership of the means of production and return it to the state, which is to collectivize agriculture and handicraft industry."[15] In the study and Propaganda Outline on the Party's general line in the transitional period, it was also said that the reality of the Party's general line during this period was to make socialist ownership of the means of production the sole economic basis of the Chinese nation and society.[16] That is to say, between productivity and production relations, more emphasis was to be placed on production relations. It was precisely this that marked an important difference between the general line of the transitional period and the idea of building a new democratic transition to socialism.

In the process of agricultural development, the idea of industrialization first and collectivization later was modified. The original idea was to concentrate on the industrialization of the country and realize collectivization only when industry could provide a large volume of agricultural machinery, but now it was believed that under the condition of a lack of mechanization, cooperation could be achieved first, then mechanization. This was what Mao meant when he said, "We must cooperate before we can use big machines."[17]

In dealing with the principles and policies of capitalist industry and commerce, the Party changed the idea of using and restricting capitalist industry and commerce first, giving full play to its role in the national economy and people's livelihood, and when conditions were ripe, it would adopt nationalization laws and decrees to nationalize it. Instead, the Party now advanced the idea of using and restricting the capitalist economy, transforming it through different forms of national capitalism to ultimately lead it steadily onto the socialist track.

These changes in the general line of the transitional period demonstrated that the Party's understanding was gradually deepening with the development of practice. It was originally envisaged that after ten to fifteen years of new democratic construction, with a considerably solid economic and material foundation, China could smoothly enter a socialist society. Now it seemed that the socialist factors had been increasing since the founding of New China and would undoubtedly far exceed the development of private industry and commerce, increasingly strengthening its power and control. This demonstrated that the current period of new democracy construction was also a transitional period from new democracy to socialism, which was to say that the proportion of socialist economic components in the national economy was gradually increasing. It should also be noted that although this change had not changed the Party's strategic objectives and main tasks, it had a significant impact on the subsequent development of the understanding of the nature of society, the main contradictions in society, the non-public economy, and the transition to socialism. These changes not only conformed to the changes in the situation and the development of Marxist classical theory, but also extended China's existing experience based on the needs of reality and began to copy the Soviet model, abandoning some aspects of the original new democratic society that were more in line with China's national conditions.

2. The Soviet Union's Today is our Tomorrow

The general line of the transitional period was directly based on Lenin's theory of the transitional period. The proposal of the general line indicated that China had accepted the Soviet model to a considerable extent. As the first socialist country in the world, the experience of the Soviet Union's socialist construction provided a direct reference for China. As early as before the founding of New China, the Central Committee repeatedly proposed that the Soviet Union be the model from which to learn. In June 1949, Mao pointed out in *On the People's Democratic Dictatorship* that "the Communist Party of the Soviet Union is our best teacher, and we must learn from them" and "learn respectfully and honestly."[18] On September 3, 1949, at the Party's senior cadres meeting, Liu Shaoqi suggested that "we should learn from the Soviet Union in politics, organization, ideology, and technology, as well as in law, finance, economy, culture, and education." However, in the early days of the founding of New China, faced with the task of completing a large number of democratic revolutions, such as the comprehensive recovery of the economy and especially the land reform, the Party emphasized that "today's struggle is mainly against imperialism, feudalism, and the remnants of the reactionaries of its watchdog, the Kuomintang, rather than the national bourgeoisie."[19] Liu emphasized that "some people think capitalism can be eliminated early." He stated that the idea of immediately eliminating capitalism and practicing socialism was wrong and unsuitable for China's situation.[20] The emphasis was on carrying out the Common Program, launching the construction of the new democracy in an all round way, and so on. That is to say, more emphasis was to be placed on the implementation of the New Democracy Program for the Founding of the People's Republic, rather than on the transition to socialism. Although this idea was influenced by Lenin's "New Economic Policy," it was more a new democratic theory with Chinese characteristics that the CPC had explored and created in the long-term new democratic revolution. In this context, the Soviet Union's experience and model of learning was not prominent.

In the process of formulating, proposing, and implementing the general line of the transitional period, under the leadership of the Central Committee, a wave of learning from the socialist experience of the Soviet Union emerged. The Central Committee put the substance of this learning more specifically before the whole Party, regarding it as a key to the implementation of the general line.

In February 1953, Mao issued a call at the Fourth Session of the First CPPCC National Committee, saying, "We should set off a national wave of learning from the Soviet Union to build our country." He stressed that it was important to carry out the great Five-Year Plan construction, which was a daunting task, and the Party was inexperienced. Therefore, it was necessary to learn from the advanced experience of the Soviet Union. "We are now learning from the Soviet Union, learning extensively from the advanced experience of their various departments, inviting their consultants to come and sending our students overseas [...] In this regard, we should adopt a serious attitude and learn all their strengths. We should not only learn from the Marxist-Leninist concept, but also from their advanced science and technology. We should all learn with humility anything that is useful."[21]

On February 14, 1953, Liu Shaoqi pointed out in a speech, "We must work hard to learn from the Soviet Union, and we must regard modest learning and using the advanced experience of the Soviet Union as one of the conditions to promote our national construction."[22] On the same day, the *People's Daily* published an editorial, stating, "In order to realize the industrialization of our country, the first key task facing us is to learn from the Soviet Union [...] We should quickly and systematically learn throughout the nation from the movements in the Soviet Union." In December 1953, the Central Propaganda Department issued an outline for the general line of the transitional period, pointing out that "the path taken by the Soviet Union in the past is the model we are going to follow today." On September 15, 1954, Liu Shaoqi said in his Report on the Draft Constitution of the People's Republic of China, "The path we have taken is the path taken by the Soviet Union, for which we have no doubt. The Soviet Union's path is an inevitable one for human society in accordance with the law of historical development. It is impossible to avoid this path."[23] For a time, "the Soviet Union's today is our tomorrow" became a household slogan.

In the process of formulating and implementing the general line, in April 1953, the Central Committee issued the Directive on the Theoretical Education of Cadres from 1953 to 1954. In order to meet the needs of the entire Party in the period of economic construction, it was now stipulated that from July 1953 to December 1954, the senior and intermediate groups of Party cadres who studied theory should study from Chapter 9 to Chapter 12 of the *History of the Communist Party of China* and part of Lenin's and Stalin's works on socialist economic construction. This learning plan required all the main cadres of the Party to systematically understand the basic laws of the Soviet Union in realizing national industrialization, agricultural cooperation, and socialist construction, so as to make proper use of the experience of the Soviet Union in the course of China's economic construction in accordance with the specific conditions of China.[24] The Directive required the senior group to study twenty-six works of Lenin, Stalin, Kuybyshev, Molotov, and Malenkov in the course of studying *The History of the Communist Party of Soviet Union (Bolshevik)*. Among these were Lenin's *Economics and Politics in the Era of Proletarian Dictatorship*, *On the Unified Economic Plan*, *On the Food Tax*, and *On the Cooperative System*, Stalin's *On the Soviet Union's Economic Situation and the Party's Policy*, *Several Issues on the Soviet Union's Land Policy*, *Victory Breeds Pride*, and *The Summary of the First Five Year Plan*. These classical works, which laid the theoretical foundation of the Soviet model, had a profound and long-term impact on China's socialist construction.

For example, the tendency to emphasize the importance of productive relations rather than productivity in socialist transformation was a distinct feature of Stalin's model. When Stalin declared the building of socialism in 1936, his main basis was not the standards of productivity and the socialization of production, but the "promotion of socialism and extinction of capitalism" in production relations, and seeing the primacy of socialization of production replaced by the public ownership of the means of production. He said that to build socialism, "the most important thing is that capitalism be completely expelled from the industrial sphere of our country, and the socialist form of production becomes the system of exclusive domination in our industry." In agriculture, "the rich peasants have also been eliminated," forming an "all-inclusive system of collective farms and state-owned farms," where "the economic component of individual small peasants occupies a very small position." In brief, "the phenomenon of exploitation has been eradicated, and the socialist ownership of tools and means of production has been laid as the unshakable foundation of Soviet society." In terms of productivity, Stalin mentioned the achievements of industrial and agricultural production in the Soviet Union at that time, but he did not consciously link socialism with a certain level of productivity, which was quite far from what Marx and Lenin had envisaged. In connection with the three major reforms in China, the influence of Stalin's model was obvious.

In accordance with the requirements of the Central Committee, the Party greatly improved its consciousness in implementing the general line by systematically understanding the experience of the Soviet Union in building socialism and referring to the key relevant speeches made by Mao Zedong and other leading comrades of the Central Committee. The educational campaign deepened the Party's understanding of the significance and arduous complexity of socialist industrialization, the leading role of the working class in the workers' and peasants' alliances, and the significance of strengthening the Party's leadership. It also raised the awareness of various difficulties encountered in the process of industrialization, such as the insufficiency of industrial and agricultural products, the recognition of the necessity and importance of unified purchase and marketing, and the recognition of subordination to the national planning. The educational campaign had a great, far-reaching impact on the unification of ideas, the implementation of the general line, the launch of the First Five Year Plan and the future socialist construction of China, as well as on the establishment and popularization of the concept of the essence of socialism throughout the Party and the country.

Regarding China's transition from a new democracy to socialism, from the perspective of model selection, if the mixed economic model of the new democracy in the first three years of the founding of New China was close to Lenin's "New Economic Policy" in his later years, then since the general line of the transition period was put forward in 1953, the transition from the mixed economy of the new democracy to a single planned economy was largely based on Stalin's model. In order to build socialism in an Asian power such as China, it was necessary and inevitable to generally opt for the Soviet model under the conditions of that time. Practice proved that this was successful, but it inevitably brought some negative side effects with it. In the course of implementing the general line of the transitional period, the Party's extensive study of the theory and practice of the industrialization and collectivization of the Soviet Union led to the formation of an idea in people's minds that socialism was the Soviet model, and even that, in the Cold War environment where the two camps of socialism and capitalism were antagonistic, there was no other model except the Soviet one. This one-sidedness in understanding had a great impact on dogmatism in practice, and it was one of the important reasons for accelerating the transition to socialism, pursuing high-level public ownership, and weakening the role of the commodity economy and market at that time. The emergence of such a situation was inevitable under the current historical conditions, or it was at least a stage that could not be bypassed in the process of the localization of Marxism in China. Later, Mao pointed out that "copying foreign experience in the first eight years"[25] was "because we did not understand it and had no experience at all, and we had to follow, due to our lack of knowledge."[26] He noted, "Almost everything was copied from the Soviet Union, with little creativity" and there was a "lack of creativity and independence."[27] It can be said that in the course of China's transition to socialism and the beginning of socialist construction, the Party's exploration of the socialist path began from imitating the Soviet model. In 1956, when speaking with the delegation of the Communist Party to foreign countries, Mao said, "There is one direction and one idea: socialism, which forms the nation."[28] He did not realize that even the "idea of socialism" was not just the Soviet model, but that the national characteristics should be represented not only in the "form" but also in the "content."

However, overall, after 1953, the Party learned from the experience of socialist construction in the Soviet Union and adopted the policy of simultaneous socialist industrialization and transformation. It did a relatively good job of settling the issue that China, a large country with nearly a quarter of the world's population and a backward economy and culture, was gradually moving toward a new direction in theory and practice. The arduous task of socialist transition had developed Marxism to the point that it was able to deal with some important theoretical and practical issues. As a result, China entered a new period of planned economic construction and a full implementation of socialist transformation.

III

Innovation in Marxist Theory During the Transition to Socialism

In China, it was the process of the socialist transformation of agriculture, the handicraft industry, capitalist industry, and commerce that characterized the gradual transition from the new democracy to socialism. In the process of formulating and implementing the general line of the transitional period, the Party's innovation of the Soviet model was very important in demonstrating that it had settled more steadily the problem of the form of socialist transformation. This specific form of transition was not only influenced by the traditional socialist model, but also featured Chinese characteristics based on local conditions, which were region-specific and different from the Soviet model.

1. Gradually Leading Individual Agriculture and the Handicraft Industry on the Path of Collectivization through Mutual Assistance and Cooperation

An important aspect of the general line in the transitional period was to lead individual workers in agriculture and handicraft industries on the road of collectivization. According to the basic principles of Marxist cooperative agriculture and based on the nature of individual ownership of farmers and handicraftsmen, after the working class had taken state power, the individual farmers and handicraftsmen could not be deprived of their property by violence, but only through cooperation, "through demonstration and social assistance for this purpose," and "to turn their private production and ownership into those of cooperatives."[29] After the victory of the October Revolution, based on the assumption of classical Marxist writers and the fact that the Russian peasant commodity economy was as vast as an ocean, Lenin put forward in *On the Cooperative System* the plan of transforming agriculture through cooperatives with socialist principles and transforming peasants' individual ownership into the collective ownership of working people. He believed that cooperatives were the best form for combining individual with national interests, on the premise that farmers' individual interests were subject to national interests. After Lenin's death, Stalin led the Soviet people to start the process of agricultural collectivization on the basis of affirming Lenin's cooperative plan. Shortly after the beginning of agricultural collectivization, Stalin proposed to establish collective farms, emphasizing acceleration of their construction. Accordingly, the movement toward collectivization began immediately. When collectivization was accelerated, the Central Committee of the Communist Party of the Soviet Union (Bolshevik) decided that the main means of collectivizing farms was the combination of land use rights and agricultural labor with the public means of production, stipulating that the policy of restricting rich peasants should be modified into that of eliminating them. In the process of the overall collectivization movement, the practice of violating the principle of voluntariness and forcing peasants to join collective farms by administrative orders seriously damaged agricultural productivity. Agricultural collectivization in the Soviet Union provided food and raw materials for industrialization to a certain extent, but seriously damaged the alliance of workers and peasants, causing agriculture to stagnate for an extended period. The Marxist-Leninist theory of agricultural cooperation and the practice of agricultural collectivization in the Soviet Union exerted an important influence on the socialist transformation of China's agriculture and handicraft industry.

In China's rural areas, mutual assistance and cooperation was the initial means of the collectivization of agriculture. Mutual assistance and cooperation in rural areas in China, which originated from the practice of economic construction in the revolutionary bases, had a long history. During the Revolutionary War, Mao and others successfully led the mutual assistance and cooperation in agriculture, handicraft industry, and other fields in the bases, accumulating preliminary a certain measure of practical experience. It was the Party's consistent goal to gradually organize the decentralized individual agriculture and handicraft industries and implement mutual assistance and cooperation. On the eve of the founding of New China, Mao pointed out at the Second Plenary Session of the Seventh Central Committee, "With the state-owned economy alone and no cooperative economy, we cannot systematically lead the individual economy of the working people towards collectivization, nor can we develop from a new democratic society to a socialist one in the future, or consolidate the proletariat's leadership in the state power."[30] In the spring of 1951, Mao clearly supported the views of the Shanxi Provincial Committee when there were divergent opinions on whether mutual aid and cooperation within the Party in the old liberated areas should be immediately elevated from mutual aid groups to cooperatives. In September

1951, the Resolution of the Central Committee of the Communist Party of China on the Development of Mutual Assistance and Cooperation in Agricultural Production determined that, on the basis of temporary seasonal and perennial mutual assistance groups, the primary agricultural production cooperatives with land as shares should be developed, which steadily shifted to the advanced agricultural production cooperatives with public land ownership to realize the socialization of agriculture. In this way, through temporary and perennial mutual aid groups, and then into primary and senior cooperatives, the transition form of collectivization of individual agriculture was basically settled in the practice of economic recovery.

After the general line of the transitional period was proposed on the basis of summing up the long-term experience of leading agricultural mutual assistance and cooperation, Mao further proposed that agricultural mutual assistance and cooperation must be completed systematically through three forms, from low to high. This included calling on peasant organizations to form agricultural production mutual aid groups with some socialism beginning to sprout in a group of multiple households. On the basis of mutual aid groups, small primary agricultural production cooperatives with a semi-socialist nature characterized by land as shares and unified management were to be organized, while on the basis of primary cooperatives, large-scale advanced agricultural production cooperatives with a fully socialist nature were to be organized. Mao Zedong believed that there were three benefits to adopting the method of progressive progress from low- to high-level form. First, it steadily transformed the lifestyle of peasants so that they felt the sudden change of lifestyle less jarring. Second, it basically avoided the reduction of crop production over a period of time. Finally, it allowed for training of cadres. Mao also stressed that agricultural mutual assistance and cooperation must adhere to the principle of typical demonstration, voluntariness and mutual benefits, active leadership, and steady progress.

In December 1953, the Central Committee adopted the Resolution on the Development of Agricultural Production Cooperatives in accordance with the spirit of Mao's views on agricultural cooperatives. It suggested that the socialist transformation of agriculture should go through three steps – mutual aid groups, primary cooperatives, and senior cooperatives – pointing out that "the path from socialist sprouts to more socialist factors and to full socialist co-operative development is the one our Party has pointed to for the steady realization of the socialist transformation of agriculture." According to the understanding at that time, adopting this form of mutual aid and cooperation in agriculture was not only an effective way to help farmers overcome difficulties and increase production, but also an appropriate form for avoiding polarization and developing toward socialism.

After the comprehensive launch of the First Five Year Plan, in order to settle the outstanding contradiction between the rapid expansion of construction scale and the severe imbalance of grain supply and demand, China made a major decision that from the end of 1953, it would implement the policy of the unified purchase and marketing of grain, cotton, and other farm produce. As two major strategic measures for socialist transformation of the small-scale peasant economy, the movement of unified purchase and marketing and mutual assistance and cooperation fundamentally eliminated and replaced the position of private wholesalers in grain, cotton, oil, and other important materials, weakened the connection between peasants and the market, and strengthened the connection between the state-owned economy and peasants. This further led to the broad masses of farmers embarking on the path of cooperation and to the socialist transformation of capitalist industry and commerce. By the end of 1956, the entire country had achieved agricultural cooperation ahead of schedule, and the socialist transformation of the means of production in rural areas was basically completed.

Generally speaking, the target mode of realizing agricultural collectivization was mainly the mode of overall collectivization in the Soviet Union, which was a systematic transition to socialism through cooperation and collectivization. Because it exaggerated the reaction of production relations, believing that the improvement of the level of public ownership could always promote the development of productive forces, overcome the mentality of farmers' small private ownership, and solve the polarization that existed in the countryside at that time, the Party paid more attention to the advantages and strengths of collective management, with a serious lack of understanding of the enthusiasm and vitality of individual or family management of farmers, which was even regarded as a spontaneous tendency toward capitalism. Nevertheless, the Party's efforts to explore specific approaches in light of China's actual conditions should not be overlooked. Because of the Party and Mao's grasp of the rural situation and their rich experience in the long-term practice of mutual assistance and cooperation, they created specific approaches that were different from the Soviet

Union's overall collectivization in the socialist transformation of agriculture. For example, following the principles of voluntariness and mutual benefits, typical demonstration and state assistance, the Party created a transitional form from temporary and perennial mutual aid groups to semi-socialist primary societies, and then to high-level socialist societies. For the rich peasant economy, the Party did not confiscate and expel the rich peasant elements, but adopted the policy of moving from restriction to a phased elimination. These were just some of the practices, which admittedly were merely different in their specific modes of the transition to socialism. At that time, the Party's understanding of socialism was basically contained within the framework of the Soviet model during Stalin's time. Therefore, various contradictions were hidden in the success of the agricultural cooperative movement, which led to various complications in the development of agriculture and the rural areas.

The socialist transformation of individual handicraft industry was one of the three major tasks put forward by the general line in the transitional period. The guiding ideology of the socialist transformation of handicraft industry, like the socialist transformation of agriculture, was to transform the individual ownership of handicraft workers into collective ownership through cooperation. It mainly took three forms: supply and marketing cooperative groups, supply and marketing production cooperatives, and production cooperatives. It gradually organized a large number of scattered individual handicraftsmen to realize the socialist transformation from decentralization to centralization, and from a low to a high level.

2. Peaceful Redemption of the Bourgeoisie through State Capitalism

The socialist transformation of capitalist industry and commerce was also an important aspect of the general line in the transitional period. Compared with the socialist transformation of agriculture and handicraft industry, in terms of the socialist transformation of capitalist industry and commerce, the approaches created by the Party based on China's actual situation were more abundant, and the social achievements made by the localization of Marxism in China were more prominent.

Marx and Engels believed that after the proletariat seized power, it must use its political domination to deprive capitalists of all means of production, either by violence or by peaceful means, so that the means of production could be owned by the people. They believed that it would be the easiest for the proletariat if bourgeois property were completely nationalized through redemption.[31] Based on this understanding, after the victory of the October Revolution in Russia, Lenin conceived and tried to compromise with the capitalists who were willing to accept state capitalism and redeem them. However, it did not succeed because of the resistance of the Russian bourgeoisie.

While putting forward the general line of the transitional period, the Party and Mao creatively opened up a path for the socialist transformation of capitalist industry and commerce based on the actual situation in China. Based on the actual circumstances in China and the practice of cooperation with the national bourgeoisie during the period of the democratic revolution, the Party and the government summed up the experience of utilizing and restricting capitalist industry and commerce after the founding of New China, adopting the method of peaceful redemption and purchase through commissioned processing, planned ordering, exclusive purchase, commissioned distribution, public-private joint ventures, industry-wide public-private joint ventures, and a range of other forms, which effectively settled the issues of the principles, policies, and steps of the socialist transformation of capitalist industry and commerce, especially the successful redemption of the bourgeoisie.

In China, it was possible to realize the Marxist-Leninist ideal of peaceful redemption of the bourgeoisie. The Chinese national bourgeoisie had two sides in the periods of both the democratic revolution and socialism. In the course of socialist revolution, the Chinese national bourgeoisie had not only exploited the working class for profit, but also supported the Constitution, and it was willing to accept socialist transformation. As a result of the victory of the new democratic revolution, the people had taken over the powerful state machinery, the socialist state-owned economy had seized the economic lifeline of the country, the movement of agricultural cooperation was being carried out, and the alliance of workers and peasants had been consistently consolidated. Under such circumstances, the national bourgeoisie had to accept transformation.

Taking different forms of state capitalism to realize the peaceful redemption of private capitalism was the outstanding achievement of the CPC's localization of Marxism. Prior to 1953, in the process of restoring the national economy, primary state capitalism – mainly in the form of processing and ordering, unified purchase, and guaranteed sales – had developed considerably in private industry. After putting forward the general line of the transitional period, the Party entered a new stage of socialist transformation of capitalist industry and commerce. After investigation and study, the Party and the government determined the policy of actively and steadily bringing private factories that were required by the state and had the appropriate conditions for transformation onto the track of public-private joint ventures, then transforming the public-private joint venture into a socialist enterprise when the conditions were ripe. In this way, through the transformation of private industry and commerce by state capitalism, and the systematic and steady development of the primary to the advanced form of state capitalism, state capitalism became the main policy to promote the socialist transformation of capitalist industry and commerce. As Mao pointed out in 1953, state capitalism "is a capitalist economy under the management of the people's government, linked with the state-owned socialist economy in various forms and supervised by workers [...] It does not exist primarily for the profit of capitalists, but for the needs of the people and the country." He added, "This new state capitalist economy is of a great socialist nature and is beneficial to workers and the state."[32] That September, when speaking with representatives of democratic parties and business circles, Mao clearly pointed out that "state capitalism is the only way to transform capitalist industry and commerce and gradually complete the socialist transition."[33]

In the process of reforming capitalist industry and commerce, taking into account the legitimate profits that capitalists deserved, the Party and the government adopted a method of redemption for the means of production. On September 7, 1953, when Mao talked with representatives of democratic parties and business circles, he proposed the well-known principle of "dividing fertilizer by four horses."[34] According to this principle, while producing for the country, the working class also produced part of the profits for the capitalists to redeem the bourgeoisie. As a result of adopting a set of principles and policies for peaceful transformation, together with the positive cooperative role played by most of the progressives in the national bourgeoisie, the democratic parties, and the Federation of Industry and Commerce in the process of socialist transformation, China had successfully realized the peaceful redemption of the bourgeoisie envisaged by Marx and Lenin. In the course of the reform of the whole capitalist private ownership, productivity remained undestroyed, and in fact developed further.

In 1955, the labor productivity rate of workers in public-private joint industrial enterprises was about twice that of private industrial enterprises.

In the process of transforming capitalist industry and commerce, the Party and the government also combined the transformation of capitalist private ownership with that of capitalists and carried out the policy of unity, education, and transformation for the national bourgeoisie. While reforming capitalists, they were to be given the necessary working arrangements, the right to vote instead of being deprived of their political rights, and appropriate political arrangements for the representatives who contributed to the transformation. After the socialist transformation of capitalist industry and commerce, by 1956, capitalists were separated from the original possessors of the means of production. They were no longer the original exploiters and dominators, but the enterprise staff serving socialism under the leadership of the Party and the supervision of workers. Although capitalists still held a fixed annual interest rate of 5%, they had no connection with the original profits of enterprises. For most people, this was no longer their main income. Most moved from the position of the exploiting class to become laborers or state cadres who supported the leadership of the Party and the socialist system. This was a great victory for the Party and the government in carrying out the policy of the peaceful transformation of the national bourgeoisie.

In the process of the peaceful transformation of capitalist industry and commerce, the Party and the government creatively applied Marxism-Leninism to China's actual situation and successfully opened up a road to reform capitalism. Specific manifestations included, first, a series of transitional forms from a low to a high level, such as commissioned processing, planned ordering, unified purchase, commissioned distribution, public-private joint ventures, and industry-wide public-private joint ventures. These were adopted gradually, rather than suddenly changing the ownership of the bourgeoisie. Second, through the method of using state capitalism to redeem the bourgeoisie with financial compensations rather than without pay and by peaceful means rather than through violent deprivation, the national capitalist enterprises could be transformed into state capitalism and the successful redemption of the bourgeoisie could be realized. Third, it was important to maintain the political alliance with the national bourgeoisie, treat it as part of the contradiction among the people, and adopt the policy of unity and struggle to achieve the goal of eliminating the national bourgeoisie by gradually transforming the vast majority of the class into workers. After socialist transformation, China's united front continued to be consolidated and developed. The national bourgeoisie and the democratic parties, together with other workers, entered the socialist society and contributed to the construction of socialism. These experiences of peaceful transformation of capitalist enterprises enriched and developed the Marxist theory of scientific socialism.

In the socialist transformation of capitalist industry and commerce, the reason China succeeded in taking a path that conformed to its actual situation was that the Party had a profound understanding of China's national conditions and an accurate grasp of the characteristics of the national bourgeoisie. In the practice of the new democratic revolution and the establishment of New China, the Communist Party and the national bourgeoisie had a long history of cooperation. They had always given a pertinent evaluation of the special status and important influence of the Chinese national bourgeoisie, unlike the bourgeoisie in other countries. Even if the contradiction between the working class and the national bourgeoisie had become the main social contradiction and the struggle against restriction and counter-restriction had been carried out, the Party had turned to modern culture and the knowledge of modern enterprise technology management for the national bourgeoisie. Liu Shaoqi noted, "In the past and at present, this class has a great influence and role in our society,"[35] which allowed the Party to maintain a sober understanding. Based on this understanding, together with the Party's policy of utilizing, restricting, and reforming capitalist industry and commerce, as well as each step taken according to this policy, the Party had "studied the actual situation in all aspects and formulated each step in response to the urgent needs of the national economy and the people's livelihood." As a result, the socialist transformation of capitalist industry and commerce had "not only won the support of the broad masses, but capitalists cannot find any valid reason to reject or oppose it."[36] Here, the study of "the actual situation in all aspects" and "the urgent need of national economy and people's livelihood" was obviously an important link in the successful guidance of the socialist transformation of capitalist industry and commerce.

In brief, although the targeted model to be achieved in the transition and quickly achieved after a short period of time was basically the Soviet model, in terms of the specific ways and means of socialist transformation, the Party had its own creation in line with China's national conditions. But the central government soon discovered the limitations of the Soviet model and began to explore China's own construction path. Mao's "On Ten Relations" in 1956 was a landmark work in the Party's exploration of the path of building Chinese-style socialism and a precursor to building socialism with Chinese characteristics. Around the time of the Eighth National Congress in 1956, according to the basic principles of Marxism and the actual situation in China, the Party had worked on the main contradictions in a socialist society, the path of industrialization in China, the proportional relations among various departments of socialist modernization, the speed of construction, the Party's policy towards intellectuals, the Party's national policy and the united front policy, and the Party's policy of developing science and culture, promoting socialist democracy, and reforming the economic system, along with other major issues concerning the socialist modernization drive. The Party proposed a series of important, correct, or relatively correct principles and policies. In 1960, Mao Zedong stated in his Ten-Year Summary, "The first eight years were spent duplicating foreign experience. Since 1956, when the Ten Great Relations were proposed, we began to find our own line suitable for China and to reflect the objective economic laws of China." However, mainly due to the limitations of the times, this reform failed to touch the core of the traditional model of the Soviet Union, but was more of a modification within that system.

Practice proved that taking socialist public ownership as the sole economic basis of socialist society and taking a single socialist economic structure as the only correct way for China to reject the existence of multiple ownership economies was not in line with the basic national conditions of its backward economy. In the late period of socialist transformation, the formation of the single planned economy model in China had historical and realistic causes and played an important positive role. However, from the perspective of later development, this model and experience should not have been made absolute. In the late 1950s, the Great Leap Forward and the people's commune movement were too eager to achieve success. Their roots had actually existed in embryonic form during the three major reforms. The historical experience of socialist transformation in China indicated that the great practice of combining the basic principles of Marxism with the actual situation in China required the unremitting exploration and effort of the CPC, especially in the scientific treatment of the principle of universality and the accurate grasp of specific national conditions.

Although the Party's understanding of socialism was still immature in the mid-1950s, and there were some defects and deviations in the socialist transformation, in view of the overall situation of China's economic and social development at that time, it was inevitable and completely correct for the Party to lead hundreds of millions of people to take the socialist path against the international background of the two conflicting camps of socialism and capitalism, and that of the Cold War.

3. The Start of Socialist Industrialization

While carrying out socialist transformation, China implemented the First Five-Year Plan for the development of the national economy from 1953 to 1957. The economic construction tasks stipulated in the plan mainly depended on China's own strength, with the support of the Soviet Union and other friendly countries. By the end of 1957, great achievements had been made. Capital construction had progressed smoothly, and a large number of important projects had been completed. A number of industrial sectors, which were necessary for the industrialization of the country and had not been available in the past, had been built up from scratch and used to strengthen the foundation of basic industries, greatly strengthening industrial technology and greatly improving production levels. From 1953 to 1956, economic development was relatively fast, economic effects were relatively positive, and the proportion of important economic departments was relatively coordinated. The market was prosperous, and prices were stable. People's lives had improved significantly. Cultural, educational, scientific, and health undertakings had also made great progress. The completion of the First Five Year Plan and the great achievements it had made played an important role in the initial stage of industrialization in China and laid a preliminary foundation for the realization of socialist industrialization.

In the process of implementing the First Five-Year Plan, although China gave attention to learning from the experience of the Soviet Union's construction, it also paid attention to proceeding from its own internal situation, carrying out the consistent ideological approach of combining the general principles of Marxism with the practice of China's construction, while enriching and developing the scientific socialist theory of Marxism. First, it was important to concentrate efforts on the development of heavy industry, but not in isolation. Instead, overall plans and arrangements needed to be made to achieve a comprehensive balance among all sectors, so that the national economy could develop in a planned and proportionate manner. Second, it was important to emphasize the scale and speed of economic construction and correctly estimate the possibility of growth in China's subjective and objective forces according to its actual situation. Third, it was necessary to implement the policy of self-reliance as the main factor and foreign aid as the supplement. During the period of the First Five-Year Plan, China was greatly helped by the Soviet government. However, it adhered to and emphasized self-reliance and never relied on foreign aid to solve its problems. In 1956, the Central Committee further clarified the policy of establishing a complete and independent industrial system. This was of far-reaching significance in adhering to China's independent position through the dramatic changes of international relations. Fourth, the Party required that the relationship between accumulation and consumption be properly handled in the construction of the planned economy and that the development of production be properly combined with the improvement of the people's livelihood.

Under the leadership of Mao Zedong, who served as the core of the first generation of the central leadership, the establishment of New China and the basic socialist system was an important achievement of the integration of Marxism into China and a great historic change in Chinese society in the 20th century. Through this historic change, due to the influence of the Soviet Union and other socialist countries, as well as the level of understanding of socialism throughout the world at that time, the process of the localization of Marxism in this stage was realized through the Soviet model in Stalin's era, in combination with China's actual situation. Therefore, the socialist model formed after the completion of the three major reforms in China obviously bore the color of the Soviet model. This was unavoidable at that time. Although many problems left by the socialist transformation could be said to be a result of the deviation caused by the rush and roughness of the work, it was even more fundamentally due to the influence of the Soviet model. The Central Committee soon discovered these problems and began to adjust and reform the mode of socialist transformation, trying to find a practical way to build socialism.

CHAPTER 5

A Good Beginning for the Second Leap of the Localization of Marxism in China

It was only after a decade or even longer that it became much clearer that 1956 was a far-reaching turning point for both the CPC and the international communist movement. The significance of this turning point was that in that year, two major shifts took place domestically and internationally. Internationally, socialist countries had begun to reform Stalin's model, and socialism was facing a profound transformation from its traditional to its contemporary form. At this time, the main question for socialist countries was not whether to reform, but how to reform. By 1956, marked by the completion of the socialist transformation of private ownership of the means of production, the basic socialist system had been initially established in China, allowing it to enter the primary stage of socialism. One of the main tasks of the CPC was to shift from revolution to comprehensive construction. The other was to move from copying the Soviet model to reforming it – that is, to start exploring China's own path to building socialism. The intersection and overlap of the two not only provided a rare opportunity for China's construction and reform, but also greatly increased the difficulty of mode selection. For example, the methods, ways, and standards for building a socialist society and the socialist system basically copied the Stalinist model. That is to say, in 1956, the socialism China had just established needed to be reformed in many ways. However, compared with the Soviet Union, Eastern Europe, and other countries in the process of reform, this model had existed for only a short time in China, and there were many drawbacks. This undoubtedly increased the difficulty of understanding what needed to be done.

The starting point of China's socialist construction was far lower than the initial analysis of socialism by the founders of Marxism, and also lower than those of the Soviet Union, Eastern European nations, and other countries. In building socialism in a country like China, there was no ready-made answer to its needs to be found in basic Marxist theory and no successful experience in the world socialist movement that could be used as a reference. China had set the Stalinist model as a model for learning, but its dazzling aura faded in the era of reform that began in 1956. Pressure and frameworks were reduced, old dogmatism was shackled, and the space for exploration was expanded. Where was China's socialist path going? How was China's reform progressing? The first generation of Party leaders, represented by Mao Zedong, were vigorous in spirit and emancipated in mind. They were determined to continue to creatively develop Marxism on the basis of the first leap in the localization of Marxism in China and realize the second leap in that localization.

I

What is Socialism?

1. The Socialist Thought and Practice of Classical Marxist Writers

Socialism, as a kind of thought, theory, ideal, belief, practice, and movement, had a huge, far-reaching historical impact on human society. It demonstrated humankind's yearning for and pursuit of an ideal future society and triggered numerous social movements of various kinds, large and small, in modern times. Over the previous century, several generations of classical Marxist writers made various assumptions about socialism, which were inherited and different, universal and special. Under the guidance and influence of these ideas, Marxists and leaders of the left-wing movement in various times and countries put forward numerous ideas and programs. These schemes were different in the East and the West, in undeveloped and advanced countries, in countries with different historical and cultural traditions, and in different times, so that it was difficult for people to have a common, standard, generalized understanding of them. In the face of the history of scientific socialism over the span of a hundred years, the only possible conclusion was that it represented a social movement that adapted to the development of productive forces and the law of social development, while constantly improving the living conditions of human beings and striving for social equality and justice. Socialism, with its complex and rich history and real-world expression, profoundly influenced the socialist ideology of the CPC and its expectations and design of the socialist system.

In the 19th century, Marx and Engels founded historical materialism and the theory of surplus value, which secured the long-standing socialist thought "on the basis of reality" and established the theory of scientific socialism. They were convinced that in the process of realizing socialism and communism, no matter how many theories and ideals, propaganda, armed struggle, and selfless sacrifice were needed. This was part of "the history of nature," which must be based on a level of productivity development higher than that of capitalism. The realization of socialism inevitably depended on the proletarian revolution and the dictatorship of the proletariat. After the emergence of socialist society, it would undergo a process of development from immaturity to maturity, from stage to stage because of the differences in the degree of economic and social development. It would show different characteristics in different countries, times, and ethnic groups. In the future, society would take highly developed social productive forces as the material premise, with the means of production occupied by the entire society and the distribution of consumption materials based on work or even on demand. In this society, social production should be carried out in a planned and organized way. The state would gradually disappear, the members of society would enjoy free and comprehensive development, and so on.

In addition, Marx attached great importance to the exploration of the path to the development of Eastern society, pointing out that under certain conditions Asian society could leap over the "Caudine Forks" of the capitalist system and enter socialist society directly. Socialism should absorb "all the positive results created by the capitalist system." In his later years, Engels also linked the new features in the development of capitalism with this future society, putting forward some important ideas and pointing out that the development of capitalism should provide more sufficient material conditions for socialism and that the strategy of proletarian revolutionary struggle should adapt to changes in historical conditions.

Before and after the October Revolution, Lenin imagined that by relying on the power of the Soviet regime, he would suppress the resistance of capitalists and landlords and confiscate their means of production for the state of workers, expand the people's democracy, and quickly leap from the transitional period of the proletarian dictatorship to a socialist society. However, with practical development, Lenin realized that the backward nation of Russia, where small peasants accounted for the majority of the population and petty bourgeoisie forces were of unprecedented size, would inevitably go through a long and difficult process towards socialism, and Russia would enter the transitional period from capitalism to socialism for a long time. As a result, after seizing power, Lenin began to observe problems more from the angle of the continuous sharpening of class struggle in the revolutionary period, observe issues from the perspective of the development of productive forces, and more directly link the fate of socialism with the level of productive forces. He emphasized many times that after the Russian proletariat seized power, it was necessary to quickly shift its focus of work to economic construction and establish the material basis of socialism as early as possible, to draw lessons from and make use of the excellent achievements of capitalism, and to implement state capitalism under the control and guidance of the working class as an intermediate link for the transition to socialism. He also realized that some of the concepts of the envisioned future "socialist society" were often only abstractions. It could only become a reality through various imperfect, concrete attempts to establish this or that socialist country.[1] The difference between socialism in the Russian context and that envisaged by Marx and Engels made Lenin keenly aware that the era of debate on socialism based on book knowledge had passed and that everything should be based on practice from that time on. The methodological significance of Lenin's thought was that theory was necessary, but socialism in practice was even more fundamental. Theory must develop with the development of practice, and it must be tested by practice. Marxism must be constantly nationalized and modernized, which could only be achieved in practice. Such a socialist outlook was Lenin's precious spiritual legacy to future generations. However, for quite a long period, neither Lenin's successors nor his students had a profound understanding of his good intentions.

The attack of international imperialism and the rebellion of the domestic counter-revolutionary White Guard in 1918 disrupted the pace of socialist construction and transformation planned by Lenin and the Bolshevik Party, changing his understanding of socialism in the process. In order to meet the demands of war, the state began to implement the policy of "wartime communism." Although this policy played a great role in supporting the war, it soon caused national resistance and riots because it went beyond the actual historical stage. The convening of the Tenth National Congress of the Russian Communist Party (Bolshevik) in the spring of 1921 marked a historic shift from wartime communism to a new economic policy. The Report on Substituting the Collection System of Surplus Grain with Physical Tax and *On Food Tax* both reflected Lenin's ideological change in the early stage of the implementation of the new economic policy. Starting from the actual situation, he allowed free circulation of grain and free trade, pointing out that it had positive significance for realizing industrial and agricultural, urban and rural product exchange and consolidating the alliance between workers and peasants. By the time of Lenin's most important works in his later years, such as *On Cooperatives*, *On the Russian Revolution*, and *On Less but Better*, his socialist outlook made great progress. He began to break through the fetters of the traditional idea that socialism should eliminate commodity-monetary relations and control social production through the state plan, and that free trade was a form of capitalism, as well as other traditional thinking. For the first time, he brought the principle of the commodity economy into the socialist category and realized an important leap in the socialist concept. Lenin fully affirmed that a backward nation like Russia could create and develop a modern civilization and become a socialist society in ways that were different from Western European countries. The Bolshevik Party should thus strive to create the material basis for socialism on the basis of obtaining the political prerequisites necessary for the development of socialism. Lenin's socialist thought in his later years, based on the new development and new situation of Russian socialist practice and in the spirit of continuous exploration integrating revolution and flexibility, developed in his socialist theory and practice distinct Russian characteristics and a distinct Russian style, enriching and developing Marx and Engels' socialist thought.

After Lenin's death, Stalin gradually formed his own ideas of socialist construction in the process of leading the socialist revolution and construction of the Soviet Union. He adhered to the theory of building a country toward socialism, advocated giving priority to the development of heavy industry, and understood socialist industrialization as heavy industrialization. He also implemented the overall collectivization of agriculture, demanding that the form of ownership of the means of production in the entire rural area be changed as rapidly as possible, and that the Party should leap into socialism quickly so as to guarantee the commodity grain and industrial raw materials needed by the country. He put forward the argument that class struggle was becoming more acute and that all achievements in socialist construction were the result of class struggle. He changed Lenin's thought and path of the "New Economic Policy." After defeating the opposition within the Party, he launched a campaign of high-speed industrialization and the overall collectivization of agriculture, and carried out a great cleansing both inside and outside the Party. In the late 1930s and early 1940s, the "Stalin Model" was basically formed. Under the influence of various factors such as inexperience, strong enemies, the decisive speed of development, the need to rely on powerful administrative forces rather than economic leverage to promote rapid economic development, and Russian traditional culture, this model met the demands of rapid development in some major aspects and met the social development of the Soviet Union at that time. The inherent requirements of the exhibition laid the foundation for consolidating and developing the first socialist country and achieving the great victory of the patriotic war. This model, however, had many disadvantages, such as high centralization of power in politics, the economy, and culture, restriction of the commodity economy, elevation of hierarchical bureaucracy and personal worship, a dogmatic tendency toward Leftism in the socialist view, chauvinism of great powers in foreign relations, and so forth, which brought about serious consequences to socialist construction of the Soviet Union and even the whole international communist movement.

2. The Rise of the Great Wave of Socialist Reform

After the Second World War, socialism went beyond a single country and formed a socialist camp. As the first socialist country, the orthodoxy of the Soviet Union's historical status, its great achievements in economic construction in the 1920s and 1930s, its superpower status, and the needs of the international political struggle led many socialist countries to duplicate its construction model. Meanwhile, the Communist Party and the Workers' Party in various countries had shown a strong desire to take a national path, expressing their desire for a remedy to the drawbacks in the Soviet model, which resulted in the tendency toward the nationalization and regionalization of Marxism gradually becoming more noticeable. Even the Soviet Union, in view of its own historical experience and the new post-war situation, began to make limited amendments to the original model. Although Stalin's *Socialist Economic Problems of the Soviet Union*, published in 1952, failed to break through the traditional socialist model overall, his views on commodity production, the law of value, and the contradiction between productive relations and productive forces in a socialist society to correct some of this misunderstandings. Traditional understanding had developed the theory of scientific socialism and promoted the modernization of Marxism. After Stalin's death in 1953, on the basis of constantly reflecting on the gains and losses of the original model, the new leadership of the Communist Party of the Soviet Union had the potential to speed up the reform of the Stalin model, intensify the reform efforts, and put forward some reform measures that could be characterized as "breaking the ice." The preliminary reform opened the gates for the reform of the Soviet Union and contemporary socialism. From the early 1950s, other socialist countries similarly adjusted some aspects of the Soviet model according to their own national conditions.

The meeting of Twentieth National Congress of the Soviet Communist Party, held in February 1956, held a very important historical position in the history of socialist reform. The exposition and criticism of Stalin's cult of personality and its serious consequences brought some negative consequences, but more importantly, it brought about a new atmosphere of emancipation of the mind, independent thinking, and breaking through dogmatism, providing a new opportunity to transcend the Stalinist model. It made it possible for Communists and Marxists of all countries to re-evaluate the new situation and problems confronted by Marxism and the contemporary proletarian revolution, and to some extent to independently formulate the routes, guidelines, and policies suited to their own conditions and with their own characteristics. The Twentieth National Congress of the Soviet Communist Party adapted to the tide of reform in socialist countries at that time, promoted the process of the nationalization and modernization of Marxism, and thus pushed the movement of Marxism and international communism into a new stage of development, despite its obvious one-sidedness. Another point to be noted was the fact that, after Stalin's death, the leadership of the Communist Party of the Soviet Union began to reform the Stalinist model to a certain extent, which tended to accelerate its development after 1956. It was, therefore, inappropriate to generalize the Soviet model after 1953, because it would deny the reform of Stalin's successors and the existence of two "Soviet models," with the year 1953 as the dividing line, though they had much in common.

From a direct point of view, these ideas and practices in socialist reform in the 1950s were based on the new historical conditions and the actual situation of various countries, trying to break through Stalin's socialist model and answer the questions "what is socialism" and "how do we build socialism" under new historical conditions. At a deeper level, it included the development of Marxism under the new situation, that is, the promotion of the modernization of Marxism, according to the characteristics of the times and the specific national conditions of various countries that had undergone tremendous changes. This was not only a breakthrough in Stalin's model, but also a breakthrough in some important concepts of traditional socialist theory. A failure to break through some traditional socialist concepts would lead to an inability to break through the Soviet model. In this sense, the era of socialist reform was also the era of Marxist modernization. The 1950s were an important critical point for the modernization of Marxism. Communist regimes all over the world were shouldering the arduous burden of promoting the modernization of Marxism under the new historical conditions, combined with their own actual situations.

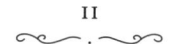

II

Emancipating the Mind and Taking Our Own Way

1. Eliminating Superstition and Opposing Dogmatism

The Communist Party of China was deeply influenced by Lenin and Stalin's thought in many areas. To a considerable extent, it can be said that the understanding and acceptance of the basic principles of Marxism by the CPC was mainly realized through the intermediary and bridge of the Soviet Union Communist Party during Stalin's period. As mentioned earlier, shortly after the founding of New China, the CPC gradually revised and restored the Soviet model because of the restrictions of ideology and the international pattern and the urgent need to restore the national economy, because the Soviet model itself met the requirements of extensive development in the early stage of industrialization in underdeveloped countries after the war, and because of the submission to the Soviet socialist model at that time. Some ideas and plans for a new democratic society presented in *On New Democracy, On the Coalition Government*, and the Common Program had been abandoned. The Soviet Union's model was comprehensively studied and introduced in the political, economic, cultural, and military fields. At that time, it possessed a certain sense of historical inevitability and played an important role in building a strong industrial, national defense, and scientific foundation in a short period of time.

With the basic completion of the socialist transformation of the private ownership of the means of production, the socialist economic system featuring public ownership of the means of production and distribution according to work and the basic socialist political system featuring the system of the people's congress were finally established. At the same time, the drawbacks of the planned economic system with a strong Soviet imprint began to emerge gradually, and the newly established planned economic system was actually in need of adjustment and reform. From 1953 to 1956, in the process of comprehensively learning and introducing the Soviet model, Mao Zedong, known for his opposition to dogmatism in the period of the democratic revolution, was not unaware of the drawbacks of this model. He even felt "depressed" over this and criticized the phenomenon of simply duplicating the Soviet model.

At this time, the Twentieth National Congress of the Soviet Communist Party unveiled Stalin's cover, pierced the halo of Stalin's socialist model, and broke the long-standing superstition surrounding the Soviet experience. At that time, there was a sense of liberation among the leaders of the CPC. Mao repeatedly affirmed Khrushchev's criticism of Stalin, saying that it "broke the deification and uncovered the lid. It is a kind of liberation and a 'war of liberation so that everyone dares to speak up and starts to think more.'"[2] He also said that the Twentieth National Congress of the Soviet Communist Party showed that "the Soviet Union, the Soviet Communist Party, and Stalin were not all right, which broke the superstition" and "was conducive to opposing dogmatism."[3] He believed that socialist construction did not necessarily follow the Soviet Union's set of formulas. The Party could put forward policies and principles suited to China's specific conditions. "Successful experience is successful in this country, but it may lead to failure in another, if it is duplicated exactly without taking into account that country's own situation." Further, "this is an important international experience."[4] He pointed out that the Polish-Hungarian incident was the result of blindly copying the Soviet model, which demonstrated that the problem facing the ruling parties of all countries was how to integrate the universal truth of the October Revolution with their own actual situation. For the CPC, it was important to stop thinking that everything the Soviet Union had done was absolute truth, and instead to consider China's problems more seriously. At the Second Plenary Session of the Eighth Central Committee of the Communist Party of China, he pointed out, "Are there any differences between China and the Soviet Union in their socialism? Yes, there are." After enumerating many differences between the two countries, he criticized some comrades for "not having dialectics or analysis… but merely looking at the problem from one side, believing that everything in the Soviet Union is good and blindly copying things that should not be brought in. The things that have not been properly copied and are not suitable for our country must be changed."[5]

At the same time, other members of the leading group of the Central Committee put forward many similar ideas. Liu Shaoqi said, "We have new experience on some issues in socialism. We should emphasize summing up our own experience and solving our problems with our own experience. We should not copy others' experiences." He said that those who could think independently would not fall, while those who only copied blindly would make mistakes, though many experiences of the Soviet Union were clearly worth studying.[6] He also severely criticized the dogmatism of learning from the Soviet Union in the field of education. During the Eighth National Congress, Zhou Enlai said in his meeting with the delegation of the foreign party that Stalin's views had overwhelmed everything in the past, but now the idol had been overthrown, as the Chinese said, and the superstition broken. After that, "the ideas of the Communist Parties of all countries have been activated and are no longer dulled." Overthrowing the cult of personality and "liberating everyone's mind are a great progress for all parties."[7] This was the ideological emancipation of the Communist Party. He also reminded the whole Party that in learning from the experience of the Soviet Union, it was necessary to "think independently, avoid blind obedience, and not believe in superstition."[8] Deng Xiaoping pointed out that "the universal truth of Marxism should be combined with the concrete situation in our country, which is a universal truth in itself. It includes two aspects. One is universal truth, the other, combining with the reality of our country. We have always believed that it is impossible to leave aside either of these [...] We must study the characteristics of our country and properly transfer foreign things, without which universal truth cannot be realized."[9] At the end of 1956, the *People's Daily* published the article "Re-examining the Historical Experience of the Proletarian Dictatorship," following the criticism of dogmatism in the article "Historical Experience of the Proletarian Dictatorship," which clearly pointed out, "All the experiences of the Soviet Union, including the basic experience, are combined with certain national characteristics. None of them should be blindly copied by other countries." The idea of "going our own way" aroused wide resonance and echoes both inside and outside the Party, becoming the consensus of the entire Party.

2. Proposal of the "Second Combination" Task

On April 5, 1956, the *People's Daily* published the editorial article "Historical Experience of the Proletarian Dictatorship," which was reviewed and revised by Mao Zedong and discussed by the enlarged meeting of the Politburo. It clearly pointed out that it was necessary to draw useful lessons from Stalin's mistakes in evaluating Stalin from the perspective of history. In discussing this article in the Politburo, Mao emphasized that, with regard to the Twentieth National Congress of the Soviet Communist Party, the important question was what lessons could be learned from it, and what was important was to combine the basic principles of Marxism-Leninism with the specific reality of the Chinese revolution and construction. During the period of the democratic revolution, the CPC succeeded in realizing this combination and won the victory of China's new democratic revolution after suffering great losses. This was the period of socialist revolution and construction, making it essential to make a second combination to learn how to build socialism in China during this time. Mao had begun thinking about this several years earlier. Now that Khrushchev had lifted the lid, the Party could consider how to act in accordance with China's situation in all aspects and eliminate its previous superstitions. In fact, in the past, the Party had not been totally superstitious, and it had its own originality. Now, he said, it should do its best to discover the concrete road for building socialism in China."[10] Here, Mao proposed a far-reaching historical task to the whole Party, that is, to realize the "second integration" of Marxism into the actual Chinese situation in the period of the new democratic revolution on the basis of the successful "first integration" during the initial stage of building socialism. "The second combination" included two basic meanings. One was to affirm that under socialist historical conditions, Chinese Communists still needed to adhere to the correct direction of combining Marxism with the Chinese situation. The other was to point out that adapting to the new situation and tasks meant the Party could no longer be satisfied with the results of the first combination, but instead must achieve a new and greater combination on the basis of the past and in accordance with the new historical conditions.

Mao Zedong's speech "On the Ten Relations" in April 1956 marked the beginning of the CPC's exploration of China's own path to building socialism. "On the Ten Relations" was an encapsulation of the wisdom of the first generation of leading collectives of the Central Committee, represented by Mao Zedong, on the basis of extensive, in-depth investigation and research, discussed by the leading collectives of the Central Committee many times then summarized by Mao Zedong. This report defined the basic principle and guiding ideology for how to build socialism, namely, by "striving to turn negative factors into positive ones as far as possible," and "mobilizing all positive factors, both inside and outside the Party, at home and abroad, and through direct and indirect positive factors, so as to build a strong socialism in China."[11] The ten major issues discussed in the report (i.e. the ten relations) were raised by summing up China's experience and studying China's construction and development, and by studying the experience of the Soviet Union. At the beginning, the report clearly pointed out, "It is particularly noteworthy that the Soviet Union has recently exposed some of its shortcomings and mistakes in the process of building socialism. They have gone through many detours, yet you still want to go the same way? In the past, in view of their experience and lessons, we have taken fewer detours. Now, of course, we should take warning from them."[12] It goes on, "What we want to learn is what belongs to the universal truth, and learning must be combined with the reality of China. Copying every word of anyone, including Marx, would be impossible. Our theory is the combination of the universal truth of Marxism-Leninism and the concrete practice of the Chinese revolution."[13] This clarified the fundamental guiding ideology that building socialism must follow its own path in accordance with its own national conditions and stressed the importance of building socialism on the basis of its own national conditions, breaking the long-standing superstition of the Soviet experience, and actually denying the uniqueness of the Soviet model and emphasizing the social construction of all countries. The pluralistic orientation of doctrine had formed a distinct idea of "taking one's own way."

As mentioned earlier, before and after 1956, China actually faced two fundamental turning points. One was from the establishment of the socialist system to the beginning of the comprehensive socialist construction, that is, during the shift of the focus of work. The other was from Stalin's traditional model to the contemporary socialist reform model and the exploration of a suitable model different from the Soviet one, allowing China to build socialism in its own national context. The two turning points occurred at the same time and interacted with each other. On the one hand, they provided favorable conditions for the "second combination," while on the other, they increased the difficulty of the combination. This required, in particular, the opposition to dogmatism and empiricism, development of Marxism on the premise of adhering to its basic principles, and the promotion of the localization of Marxism in China under the new historical conditions.

The proposition of the task of "the second combination" demonstrated that the localization of Marxism was not a task that could be accomplished all at one shot, but a process of continuous development. It was not a successful or correct process that could be done once and for all, but through a series of twists and turns and arduous exploration. It also proved once again that it was historically far-sighted for the CPC to advance and emphasize this great historical task in a timely manner.

III

The Initiation of the New Conception on the Path of Socialist Construction as a Result of the Second Combination

From 1956 to the first half of 1957, under the guidance of the second integration of Marxism into the Chinese context, the Central Committee put forward many new policies and concepts full of a creative spirit and pioneering consciousness, ranging across the economy, politics, and culture. Under the new historical conditions of its times, it promoted the historical process of the localization of Marxism.

1. A Correct Grasp of the Main Contradictions in a Socialist Society

With the early completion of the socialist transformation, Mao Zedong and other central leaders began to pay more attention to and study the main tasks and contradictions of socialist society. At the National Party Congress held in August 1955, Mao raised the issue of the shift in the Party's work center. He said that the Party had entered a period in which it was now engaged and to which it devoted much thought and study. The Party was delving into a historical period of socialist industrialization, socialist transformation, modern national defense, and atomic energy. Based on a correct understanding of the great changes that had occurred since the founding of New China, the Eighth National Congress clearly defined the transformation of the main domestic contradictions after the completion of the socialist transformation and determined the strategic objectives of socialist construction.

The Eighth Political Reports and Resolutions pointed out that after the decisive victory of the socialist transformation, the main contradiction in China would be that between the people's demands for the establishment of advanced industrial countries and the reality of backward agricultural countries, and between the people's need for rapid economic and cultural development and the current situation in which the economy and culture could not meet the needs of the people. In essence, this was a contradiction between the advanced socialist system and the backward social productive forces. This conclusion was not only a correct summary of China's political situation, but also a new understanding of China's national conditions. It was the basis for the Party to determine its correct line after the establishment of the socialist system in China. The report's formulation of the essence of the main contradictions in China was not exactly accurate in theory as it failed to fully point out that socialist production relations had been established and that they were compatible with the development of productivity. Meanwhile, they were far from being perfect, and these imperfect aspects contradicted the development of productivity. However, the point of this formulation was to highlight the basic national condition that the development of productive forces in China was still very backward. It emphasized that the main task of the state was to protect and develop productive forces under the new production relations, and that the entire Party should concentrate its efforts on developing productive forces so as to develop China as soon as possible, once the socialist transformation of the private ownership of the means of production had been basically completed. The land had changed from a backward agricultural country to an advanced industrial country. This was the most important theoretical contribution of the Eighth National Congress, the basis and core of the Eighth National Congress line, and the consensus within the Party at that time. Although Mao disagreed with this statement at the time, he recognized the main contradiction. Shortly after, he expressed this idea again in "On the Correct Handling of the Contradictions among the People." He said, "Our fundamental task has changed from liberating the productive forces to protecting and developing them under the new relations of production," and it was necessary to "unite the people of all ethnicities throughout the country to wage a new war – to fight against nature, develop our economy, and develop our culture," and "consolidate our new system and build our new country."

2. Moving Beyond the Soviet Model in Economic Construction

According to the correct judgment of the main contradictions in a socialist society, the Eighth National Congress determined the strategic objectives and conceptions of socialist construction in two steps. The first step was to complete the preliminary industrialization through three five-year plans, and the second was to approach or catch up with the most developed capitalist countries in the world in a matter of decades. The new Constitution of the Eighth National Congress pointed out that the Party's task was to develop the national economy in a planned way, to industrialize the country as quickly as possible, and to carry out technological transformation of the national economy systematically, "so that China will have a strong modern industry, modern agriculture, modern transportation, and modern national defense."[14]

It was important to adhere to the principle of economic construction, which combined conservatism with rash progress and made steady progress through a comprehensive balance. As early as the days leading up to the Eighth National Congress in 1956, Zhou Enlai and Liu Shaoqi pointed out in 1956 that the development of production and all other undertakings must be on a sound, reliable basis, and that while opposing conservatism, it was also important to oppose the tendency toward rash and aggressive development. Guided by the spirit of Mao's *On Ten Relations*, the Eighth National Congress continued to adhere to the policy of economic construction, which was both anti-conservative and anti-aggressive, steadily advancing in overall balance. In his report to the General Assembly, Zhou Enlai emphasized the importance of combining key construction with comprehensive arrangements in accordance with the financial and economic tensions during the First Five-Year Plan period, so as to enable all sectors of the national economy to develop proportionally, increase reserve forces, improve the material reserve system, and properly handle the relationship between economy and finance. These incisive summaries reflected the Party's correct understanding and prudent attitude toward the law of economic development at the beginning of its comprehensive socialist construction. The Second Plenary Session of the Eighth Central Committee of the Communist Party of China adopted Zhou Enlai's policy of "guaranteeing key points and appropriately downsizing" in 1957, and correctly worked out the 1957 construction plan, thus ensuring that the economic work that year was among the best since the founding of New China. To put forward such a socialist economic construction policy was not simply to repeat the experience of China during the First Five-Year Plan period or of other countries, but to make a strategic decision under the guidance of Marxism and in combination with China's national and economic conditions.

The idea of industrialization with Chinese characteristics was proposed. In response to the tendency of the Soviet Union and some Eastern European countries to unilaterally emphasize the development of heavy industry and seriously neglect agriculture and light industry and the adverse effects of these errors on China, Mao pointed out that the development of more agriculture and light industry "will make heavy industry develop more and faster, and because it guarantees the needs of people's lives, its development will be steadier."[5] The Eighth National Congress further confirmed this policy. In 1957, Mao explicitly raised the question of China's industrialization road in his article "On Correctly Handling Contradictions Among the People." He pointed out that the issue of the path to industrialization "mainly refers to the development relationship between heavy industry, light industry, and agriculture. China's economic construction is centered on heavy industry, which must be affirmed. But at the same time, full attention must be paid to the development of agriculture and light industry." He also pointed out, "China is a large agricultural country, with a rural population accounting for more than 80% of the national population. To develop industry, we must develop agriculture at the same time. Only when industry has raw materials and markets can we accumulate more funds for the establishment of a strong heavy industry."[16] In addition, he pointed to the importance of actively developing coastal industries so as to accumulate strength to support inland industries and reduce the proportion of defense expenditures. He further proposed to establish an independent and complete industrial system as the main symbol of industrialization. Zhou Enlai further explained industrialization based on Mao's view, saying, "Our industrialization means that we should have an independent and complete industrial system." What he meant by establishing a basically complete industrial system in China was that the country could produce sufficient major raw materials and do it independently. China would make not only general machines, but also heavy, sophisticated machines and new defensive weapons, such as atomic bombs, missiles, and long-range aircraft for use in national defense, and also create the corresponding chemical, power, transportation, and light industry, as well as agriculture and so on.[17] All these thoughts enriched and developed Marxist industrialization theory.

3. A Preliminary Idea for Reforming the Economic System

During the period of the First Five-Year Plan, China established a highly centralized economic management system in accordance with the Soviet model. This system, which played a prominent role in the early stage of industrialization in backward countries, had obvious disadvantages. The Soviet Union had clearly pointed out this point in its rethinking of the Stalinist model at that time, and the Party was keenly aware of it in its preliminary practice. When Mao and other central leaders summed up China's construction experience, they repeatedly proposed changes to the highly centralized economic management system. From the Eighth National Congress of the Party in 1956 to the Third Plenary Session of the Eighth Central Committee of the Party in 1957, the Party made an initial attempt to reform the economic management system, mainly manifested in several areas.

1) *Decentralization of power from central to local authorities.* Mao Zedong raised the issue of the relationship between the central government and the local

government in his *On Ten Relations*. He said, "What we should pay attention to at present is that, on the premise of consolidating the unified leadership of the Central Committee, we should expand the powers of some places, give them more independence and let them do more […] China is so large, its population so huge, and its situation so complicated. It has two initiatives, the central and local, which is much better than having only one. We can't concentrate everything on the central government, like the Soviet Union does. This would lead many places to death or to the loss of mobility."[18]

Accordingly, Zhou Enlai focused on this issue at the National Institutional Conference held from May to August 1956. He pointed out that the most centralized power was equal to no power, and the decentralization of power between the central and local governments aimed to give full play to local initiatives. He proposed expanding local power in planning, finance, enterprise, undertakings, capital construction, and the establishment. The Eighth National Congress pointed out that in order to correctly adjust the relationship between the central and local governments, it was necessary to improve the state administrative system, divide the scope of management of enterprises, undertakings, plans, and finances, and appropriately expand the administrative authority of local governments in accordance with the principles of unified leadership, hierarchical management, local adaptation, and adaptation to actual circumstances.

2) *Expanding the power of enterprises.* As "On Ten Relations" notes, "It is not appropriate to concentrate everything in the central, provincial, or municipal areas without giving factories some power, room for maneuvering, and benefits. The interests of the central government, provinces, municipalities and factories should be appropriately divided. We have little experience, but we still need to study it […] Every production unit must have the sort of independence associated with unity in order to develop more vigorously." After this, Mao said in several speeches that enterprises should have "autonomy" and become open and legal "semi-independent kingdoms," and factories should likewise have autonomy, which would be better for nationwide industrialization.

3) *Three main bodies and three supplements.* In view of the increasingly single ownership and economic management structure, Chen Yun suggested at the Eighth National Congress the idea of "building a socialist economy beneficial to the people" and "three main bodies and three supplements." In terms of industrial

and commercial operation, state operation and collective operation were the main bodies of industry and commerce, and a certain number of individual operations were the supplements of the state and collective operation. Planned production was the main body of industrial and agricultural production, and free production within the scope of state planning permission according to market changes was the supplement of planned production. The national market formed the main body. The free market led by the state, within a certain range, was a complement to the national market."[19] Zhou also said, "The mainstream is socialism, allowing small freedom. In this way, we can help the development of socialism. Maybe industry, agriculture, commerce, academia, and the military, with the exception of soldiers, can enjoy a little freedom and engage in a little private enterprise in all walks of life. Culture can also be slightly privatized."[20] Mao Zedong, Liu Shaoqi, and Zhou Enlai also called this policy of "both eliminating and developing capitalism" the "new economic policy."

4) *A planned, diversified, flexible socialist economy*. At the end of 1956, Mao's notion of allowing the opening of underground factories to simultaneously eradicate and promote capitalism actually represented the ideas of many people in the leading group of the Central Committee of the Communist Party. When Liu Shaoqi visited the south in the spring of 1957, he gave full play to Mao's thought. He said at the meeting of the Party members and cadres in Shanghai that the socialist economy was characterized by the planned economy. "But the actual social and economic activities include various trades and professions, in all aspects, numbering in the thousands, tens of thousands, and hundreds of thousands. It is impossible for the state to plan so many thousands, tens of thousands, and hundreds of thousands of activities. As a result, we can only plan some kinds, which makes social and economic life plain and rigid." In order to make the socialist economy "planned, diversified, and flexible, it is necessary to make use of the free market."[21] Later, he said, "In studying the socialist economy, we should pay special attention to the problem of making the socialist economy not only planned, but also diversified and flexible." The lessons of the Soviet Union in this respect deserved attention. It was only planned in its socialism, paying attention to the planned economy. It was rigid and lacked diversity and flexibility. "We must be more diverse and flexible than the capitalist economy. If our economy is not as flexible and diverse as the capitalist economy, but only rigid and planned, what

are the advantages of socialism? We must make the diversity and flexibility of the socialist economy surpass capitalism and make our people's economic life richer, more convenient, and flexible."[22]

Although these important ideas were soon interrupted by the expansion of the Anti-Rightist movement, they broke through the highly centralized planned economy model of the Soviet Union at a certain level and surpassed the understanding of traditional socialism to a certain extent. In fact, to a certain extent, they touched on the relationship between socialism and capitalism, and on the planned economy and the market economy. It was an extremely important theoretical issue.

4. Thoughts on Building Socialist Democratic Politics

1) *Initial proposal of the idea of multi-party cooperation and the political consultation system under the leadership of the CPC in the socialist period.* In 1956, according to the specific conditions in China, the Central Committee summed up the experience and lessons of the period of the democratic revolution, learned from the experience and lessons of the international communist movement, and clearly put forward that the CPC, as the core of leadership, should establish socialist mutual assistance and cooperation with all democratic parties. In April 1956, Mao Zedong first proposed the idea of "Two Long Lives" when he listened to the reports from the relevant departments of the State Council. He said, "Long live the Communist Party and the democratic parties. They can look to us. We're also a democracy."[23] In "On Ten Relations," he said, "Is it good to have one party or several parties? For now, I'm afraid, it's good to have one. It worked in the past, and will do so in the future, providing long-term coexistence and mutual supervision […] We should unite with all the democrats who have expressed their views in good faith." He added, "We should continue to mobilize their enthusiasm." This was beneficial to the Party, the people, and socialism.[24] In September, when revising the political report of the Eighth National Congress, he pointed out that "the state form of proletarian dictatorship, the one-party system, or the multi-party system under the leadership of the revolutionary Party of the working class" existed because different countries had different political and economic conditions. And, "such differences exist in any ethnic group, and in some ethnic groups there may even be more."[25] In "On the Correct Handling

of Contradictions Among the People," Mao stated his plan to implement the policy of "long-term coexistence and mutual supervision" as an important issue to correctly handle contradictions among the people. In Mao's view, whether there was a one-party system or a multi-party system, it should be combined with the actual situation in China and should not merely be duplicated. At the Eighth National Congress, Liu Shaoqi stressed that China should adhere to the principle of "long-term coexistence and democratic supervision" to properly handle the relationship between the CPC and democratic parties and democratic entities, while also continuing to strengthen and consolidate the People's Democratic United Front. Deng Xiaoping also pointed out that in the country's political life, it was important to give full play to the role of the democratic parties, so that they could play a greater role in all aspects of the nation's affairs. In this way, the Party clung to the sentiment, "long live both the Communist Party and the democratic parties," and initially established the democratic political structure of the multi-party cooperation system under the leadership of the CPC. This was a socialist democratic model different from that of the Soviet Union.

2) *Proposing the idea of expanding socialist democracy and strengthening the construction of the socialist legal system.* In July 1956, Zhou Enlai said, "Now our people's democratic dictatorship should be a situation in which the dictatorship continues and democracy should be expanded," and "this is more essential [...] To solve this problem, we must think of some approaches within our national system."[26] In response, Liu Shaoqi pointed out at the Eighth National Congress that it was necessary to strengthen the supervision of the National People's Congress and its Standing Committee over government organs at the central level and local people's congresses at all levels over local government organs. The Party should further expand democratic life and carry out the struggle against bureaucracy. At the same time, it also recognized that the realization of socialist democratic systems required the institutionalization and legalization of democracy. The Eighth National Congress Political Report clearly pointed out that one of the urgent tasks in the current state work was to systematically formulate relatively complete laws and improve the legal system. Dong Biwu pointed out at the Eighth National Congress that to act in accordance with the law meant to abide by the law, which was "one of the main ways to eliminate the phenomenon of neglect and non-compliance with national laws."[27] After outlining the incomplete nature of the legal system in China, he pointed out that

the Party should gradually complete the legal system, enact a series of laws as early as possible, including criminal law, civil law, procedural law, labor law, and land use law, and accelerate the implementation of a lawyer and notarization system. These understandings and requirements reflected the Party's great concern for political democracy around the time of the Eighth National Congress and the orientation of government management toward institutionalization and legalization.

5. Attaching Importance to Intellectuals and Scientific and Technological Problems, and Adhering to the "Two Hundreds" Policy

Because of the special national conditions that existed in socialist revolution and construction in backward countries, the question of how to treat intellectuals correctly had always been a prominent problem. In China, because the revolutionary base areas had long been far away from cities in the rural areas, the main body of the revolutionary ranks was made up of farmers. How to deal with intellectuals was similarly a prominent problem. With the completion of the socialist transformation and the full development of socialist construction, and in view of the advent of the world's new scientific and technological revolution, the importance of intellectuals and science and technology had become increasingly prominent. However, at that time, some cadres in the Party lacked awareness of the importance of intellectuals and had divergent views on their class attributes, or even serious sectarianism that led them to disrespect intellectuals. At that time, after investigation, the United Front Department of the Central Committee summed up the problems of intellectuals as "six lacks," pointing to the lack of estimation, trust, proper arrangement, proper use, fair treatment, and adequate help. In order to change this situation rapidly, when reporting to Mao Zedong on the issue of intellectuals on November 22, 1955, Zhou Enlai stated his intention to discuss the issue of intellectuals at the meeting of the National Committee of the CPPCC. The next day, Mao convened a meeting of all the members of the Central Secretariat and the heads of relevant departments of the Central Committee. He decided to adopt Zhou's opinions and convene a meeting to comprehensively address the problem of intellectuals. In January 1956, the Central Committee convened a conference on intellectuals. Zhou emphasized the importance of science, technology, and intellectuals in his report on intellectuals. He pointed out that in the era of socialism, it was more necessary than ever to improve production technology, develop science, and make full use of scientific knowledge. Science and technology were "decisive factors affecting our national defense, economy, and culture."[28] At this meeting, the Central Committee called for "a march toward modern science." It was impossible to develop and utilize science without the participation and effort of intellectuals. In his speech at the meeting, Mao pointed out that in order to carry out a technological and cultural revolution, it was important to transform all sorts of foolishness and ignorance. Simply relying on the old regime of important figures without input from intellectuals would not work.

On the basis of fully affirming the change and progress of the intellectuals' political position after the founding of New China, the conference on intellectuals made a new judgment on their class attributes. Zhou declared in his report that the vast majority of China's intellectuals had become state functionaries, served socialism, and become part of the working class. In February, the Central Committee's Directive on Intellectuals also pointed out that "fundamental changes" had taken place before China's intellectuals would be fully accepted. Most of them either actively supported the CPC and socialism politically or had at least taken the stand of supporting them. The basic team of intellectuals had become staff members serving socialism and a part of the working people. It was noted, "In the cause of building socialism, a coalition of workers, peasants, and intellectuals has been formed."[29] Based on this understanding, the Central Committee particularly emphasized that intellectuals should be given full political trust and proper arrangements for their work in order to enable them to play an important role in the cause of socialist construction. This greatly enhanced the intellectuals' sense of class belonging and mobilized their enthusiasm to participate in socialist construction.

At the conference on intellectuals, Zhou also emphasized the great role of science and technology in socialist construction. He said that in the socialist era, it was more necessary than ever to improve production technology, develop science, and make full use of scientific knowledge. In view of the extremely backward situation of science and technology in China and the reality of the rapid progress of science and technology in the world, on behalf of the Central Committee, he put forward the call "to march toward science," hoping to develop and improve China's scientific and technological strength as far as possible, so as to catch up with the advanced world in a short time. After the meeting, the

Central Committee actively began to formulate a long-term and medium-term plans for the development of science and technology, in order to promote the development of various construction undertakings. In March 1956, the State Council set up the Scientific Planning Committee. Under the leadership of Zhou Enlai, Chen Yi, Li Fuchun, and Nie Rongzhen, more than six hundred scientists were brought together. Nearly a hundred Soviet experts were invited for repeated demonstrations over a period of months, and the Outline of the Vision Plan for Scientific and Technological Development (Draft) from 1956 to 1967 was compiled. Four emergency measures were formulated in 1956 for some particularly important links that were relatively weak in China."[30] Under the guidance of the Central Propaganda Department, the Ministry of Philosophy and Social Sciences of the Chinese Academy of Sciences also organized a group of experts to prepare a twelve-year plan for the development of philosophy and the social sciences.

In view of the drawbacks of the cultural system of the Soviet Union, the Party put forward the fundamental policy of "letting a hundred flowers bloom and a hundred schools of thought contend" for the prosperity and development of culture and science and technology. In the first few years after the founding of New China, under the background of fully accepting the experience of the Soviet Union, the field of science and culture was influenced by the brutal style and dogmatism of Soviet academic criticism, and the phenomena of advocating a school, suppressing a school, and placing political labels on it were more serious in some academic fields. In response to these circumstances, Mao Zedong asked the Ministry of Propaganda and China to study the dogmatic attitude toward Soviet scientific schools in scientific and academic research. In late April 1956, in discussing Mao Zedong's report "On Ten Relations", the Enlarged Meeting of the Politburo proposed that political and ideological issues should be distinguished from those of an academic, artistic, or technical nature. In order to develop culture and science, it was important to carry out the slogans of "letting a a hundred flowers bloom and a hundred schools of thought contend" earlier mentioned by Mao. The "Two Hundreds" policy advocated that different artistic forms and styles could develop freely and different scientific schools could argue freely, and it opposed the use of administrative force to enforce a specific style or school. The premise of implementing the "Two Hundreds" policy was that it could not be unconstitutional. Implementing the "Two Hundreds" policy would not weaken but strengthen the leading position of Marxism in ideological circles.

In March 1957, Mao further pointed out at the national propaganda conference that "letting a hundred flowers bloom and a hundred schools of thought contend is a basic and long-term policy, not a temporary one,"[31] which demonstrated his firm determination to implement the "Two Hundreds" policy. He even suggested that the guiding ideology of the Party, Marxism, could also be questioned and criticized. If Marxism was afraid of criticism, then it was right that it fail under criticism, because such a flimsy form of Marxism was useless. This understanding and guiding ideology provided an open, relaxed, democratic atmosphere for intellectuals to put their tools to work.

6. The Correct Handling of Ethnic Relations

Around the time of the Eighth National Congress, the CPC made various explorations in order to correctly handle ethnic relations. In April 1956, the Central Committee issued instructions on the inspection of the implementation of ethnic policies. When Mao discussed the relationship between Han and minority nationalities in "On Ten Relations", he said, "Our policy is relatively stable and has been approved by minority nationalities. We focus on opposing Han chauvinism. Local nationalism should also be opposed, but that is generally not the focus."[32] On December 26, the Central Committee issued the Directive on Further Inspection of the Work of the United Front and the Implementation of Ethnic Policies, requesting that all localities earnestly carry out the inspection of the implementation of ethnic policies and not end it too hastily. The following year, Mao emphasized again in "On Correctly Handling the Contradictions Among the People" that "the relationship between the Han ethnic group and the minority ethnic groups must be well executed. The key to this problem is to overcome Han chauvinism. Among ethnic minorities with local tribalism, that tribalism should be overcome at the same time. Neither Han tribalism nor local tribalism is conducive to the unity of the people of all ethnicities, which is a contradiction among the people that should be overcome."[33] The inspection began in mid-1956 and ended at the end of July 1957. It lasted more than a year, and made the cadres and people generally receive the education of the Party's national policy. It had a long history of the correct implementation of the national policy and the healthy development of various undertakings in minority areas, especially the continuous strengthening of national unity. The Eighth National Congress also attached great importance to ethnic issues in socialist construction. Liu Shaoqi pointed out in his political report that "correctly handling minority issues is an important task in our national work. We must intensify our efforts to help ethnic minorities make economic and cultural progress so that they can play an active role in our socialist construction."[34] The report also pointed out that, in order for minorities to develop into modern ethnicities, apart from carrying out social reforms, the fundamental key was to develop modern industry in their areas. It was important to continue to build new industrial bases in some minority areas and organize large-scale modern industries and transportation industries. It was necessary to pay attention to helping ethnic minorities form their own working classes and train their own scientific and technological cadres and enterprise management cadres. In order to adapt to the development of the situation and carry out the Eight Routes, the United Front Department of the Central Committee of the Communist Party of China drew up the Draft National Ethnic Work Plan (1956-1967), which outlined the blueprint for economic and cultural construction in minority areas. Preliminary achievements were made in socialist construction in ethnic minority areas, and fundamental changes took place in the social outlook.

IV

The Eighth National Congress of the CPC and the Important Evolution of the Thought and Theory of Building the Ruling Party

After the basic completion of the socialist transformation, the Party's own situation and historical position also underwent important changes. The ruling position of the Party was greatly consolidated, the scale of Party members and organizations was greatly developed, and the Party faced the task and goal of building socialism across the board. This brought a new issue to bear on the Party's construction and forced the Party to face a new historical test. Around the time of the Eighth National Congress, great attention was given to strengthening the construction of the ruling party, which was a historic topic, and the exploration of the theory of the construction of the ruling party had an important historical position in the history of the Party's construction. It made outstanding contributions to the historical process of promoting the localization of Marxism in China.

1) *The core force leading the cause of socialist construction.* The Eighth National Congress emphasized that the CPC was the core force leading the cause of socialist construction, and socialist construction needed to adhere to the leadership of the Party. The general outline of the Party Constitution of the Eighth National Congress stipulated, "The Party is the supreme organization of the working class, and it must strive to play its correct leading and core role in all aspects of national life."[35] The political report of the Eighth National Congress pointed out that the Party could and should play a leading role in all its work in ideology, politics, principles, and policies.[36] That is to say, the leadership of the Party was not an all-in-one structure. The leadership of the Party was to be embodied in ideology, politics, and policies. The Party should realize its political program through its own members and organizations. The Eighth National Congress planned to give full play to the correct leadership role of the Party and put it into the Party Constitution and other important political documents, marking the deepening of the Party's understanding of the leadership provided by the ruling party and the development of Marxist party ideology. In order to ensure the correct leadership of the Party, the Eighth National Congress carefully analyzed the situation of the Party and the state, putting forward new ideas to strengthen the construction of the ruling party according to the changes of the situation and tasks.

2) *Adhering to the Party's collective leadership, improving democratic centralism, strengthening the construction of a supervision system inside and outside the Party, developing democracy within the Party, and opposing the worship of individuals.* In view of the historical lessons on Party building learned by the Communist Party of the Soviet Union and other socialist countries and the shortcomings of the Party in its work, the Eighth National Congress emphasized adhering to the principle of the collective leadership of the Party, improving the democratic centralism of the Party, strengthening the supervision of Party organizations and Party members (including intra- and extra-Party supervision), developing intra-Party democracy, and opposing cults of personality. In his political report, Liu Shaoqi emphasized the principle of the collective leadership of the Party and the expansion of democracy within the Party. He said that all decisions on major issues should be thoroughly discussed, allowing unrestrained disputes among different views, so as to comprehensively reflect the opinions of the masses inside and outside the Party and all aspects of the development of objective things, resolutely accept reasonable objections or reasonable parts of objections, and put forward proposals

in accordance with normal procedures. No comrade who opposed it could adopt an exclusive attitude. Deng Xiaoping elaborated on strengthening supervision inside and outside the Party in his Report on Revising the Constitution of the Party. He said that the Party needed to carry out intra-Party supervision and receive supervision from the people and non-Party personages. The key to intra-Party supervision and extra-Party supervision was to develop the democratic life of the Party and the state and carry forward the fine traditions of the CPC.

In order to further strengthen and improve the CPC's leadership, the Eighth National Congress made some relevant provisions in the Party and state system. The General Assembly pointed out that when Party members had the right to give full play to their creativity in their work and hold different opinions on Party resolutions, they also had the right to reserve and present their opinions to the leading organs of the Party, in addition to unconditionally implementing them. If the lower organizations of the Party believed that the resolutions of the higher organizations did not conform to the actual conditions of their respective regions and departments, they should go to the higher organization and request a change. The Eighth National Congress stressed that the Party and the state should strengthen their supervision work, promptly detect and correct all kinds of bureaucracy, and deal with all kinds of speech and actions that violated law and discipline. The Supervisory Committee should not confine itself to the acceptance of cases, but also actively examine Party members' compliance with the Party Constitution, Party discipline, Communist morality, and state laws and decrees. The Eighth Congress also pointed out that the regular convening and full play of the Party's congresses at all levels was one of the basic requirements of the Party's democratic centralism. The Party congresses at and above the county level were changed into permanent ones, and annual meetings were held to make it easier for Party committees at all levels to gather the opinions of the broad masses and make the congresses the highest decision-making and supervisory organs.

In his report on Revising the Party Constitution at the Eighth National Congress, Deng Xiaoping also focused on preventing deified leaders and opposing personal worship. He pointed out that the situation in the Soviet Union demonstrated how serious the consequences of deifying individuals could be, that cults of personality were a social phenomenon with a long history and would not be reflected in the Party's and society's life, that the Party should firmly oppose the act of highlighting individuals and extolling their merits and virtues, and that it should adhere to collective leadership and individual responsibility. In combining the system, it was important to fully implement the democratic principles and the mass line. The new Party Constitution also added the clause "when the Central Committee deems it necessary, one honorary chairman of the Central Committee may be established" to prepare for the abolition of the existing system of lifelong leadership, which was a very meaningful idea for the reform of the Party and the state leadership system. In addition, following Mao's many proposals, the Eighth National Congress Party Constitution did not mention Mao Zedong Thought in the Party's guiding ideology. The Eighth National Congress set a precedent against individual worship at its Party Congress.

3) *Adhering to the mass line and firmly opposing bureaucracy.* At the preparatory meeting for the Eighth National Congress, Mao Zedong pointed out that "this Congress should continue to carry forward the fine tradition of our Party in terms of ideology and style of work, effectively reverse subjectivism and sectarianism, and in addition, oppose bureaucracy."[37] The Eighth National Congress took the implementation of the Party's mass line as a historical task that the ruling party must focus on. In his report on the Party Constitution, Deng Xiaoping profoundly and systematically expounded the important point that the mass line was the fundamental line of the Party in light of the new situation and tasks faced by the ruling party. He pointed out that the CPC was born, developed, strengthened, and matured in close contact with the people and through joint struggle. If it correctly implemented the mass line, the cause of the Party would succeed. If not, the cause of the Party and the people would suffer losses. Because the CPC had become a ruling party, the danger of divorcing itself from the masses and its potential for harm had greatly increased. The existence of bureaucracy showed that the Party's mass line had not been fully implemented in the CPC. It was important to constantly fight against these bureaucratic phenomena that were divorced from the masses. Moreover, it was necessary to see that bureaucracy was a legacy of the long-term rule of the exploiting class throughout human history and had a far-reaching impact on social and political life. Therefore, it was also a long-term struggle to implement the mass line and overcome bureaucracy. Deng also stressed that one of the signs distinguishing the CPC from any other political party was that it served the people wholeheartedly and kept close contact with

the masses. The advanced nature of the CPC was "its wholehearted service of the people and the fact that it reflects the interests and will of the people and strives to help the people organize and fight for their own interests and will."[38]

4) *Safeguarding and consolidating the unity of the ruling party*. Deng Xiaoping pointed out in his report on the revision of the Party Constitution that the unity of the CPC was one of the most important issues in party-building. The unity and solidarity of the Party was the life and strength of the CPC. It was the sacred duty of every Party member to constantly safeguard and consolidate the unity of the Party. This was not only in the interest of the Party, but also the interest of the people throughout the country. When talking about the principles for Party members who had made mistakes, he pointed out that every comrade may have shortcomings or errors. Every comrade needed help from others, and the unity of the Party was precisely for the development of such comradely mutual assistance. The shortcomings or errors of Party members should be distinguished from each other and different approaches should be adopted. It was important to lay stress on analyzing the essence and root causes of errors from facts rather than on organizational sanctions, so as to cause losses to the Party's strength. On the other hand, taking a sheltered and palliative attitude towards comrades who had made mistakes, rather than giving them proper punishment and not to carrying out ideological struggle, was a liberal tendency that must be firmly opposed. In order to maintain the unity and solidarity of the Party on the basis of Marxism-Leninism, it was important to greatly develop criticism and self-criticism within the Party. The new Party Constitution also listed "safeguarding the unity of the Party and consolidating the unity of the Party" as obligations of all Party members.

5) *Setting higher standards for the members of the ruling party*. Improving the standard of Party members was an important political task of the CPC. Deng Xiaoping pointed out that the victory of the Party's cause, the aggravation of the Party's responsibility to the people, and the growth of the Party's prestige among the people all required the Party to set higher standards for its members. In order to improve the standard of Party members, the Party Constitution of the Eighth National Congress made some new provisions on the conditions of Party members. The Party Constitution first required that Party members must be those who engage in labor without exploiting the work of others. The Party Constitution also added many new items to the obligations of Party members,

giving attention to protecting and expanding the democratic rights of Party members while adding new items to their democratic rights. In addition, Deng Xiaoping also pointed out that if the Party put forward strict requirements to every ordinary Party member, it needed to put forward stricter requirements to Party cadres, who had a higher responsibility than ordinary Party members. They should first learn to never leave the masses, never be complacent or afraid of difficulties, to accept criticism from the bottom up, to constantly improve their work, and to set an example and patiently educate the staff under their leadership.

On the basis of summing up the experience and lessons of party-building in the period of democratic and socialist revolution, the Eighth National Congress advocated the construction of the ruling party, proposed many new ideas, guidelines, and concepts in the theory and practice of the construction of the ruling party, and preliminarily formed a more comprehensive and systematic theory of the construction of the ruling party. After that, the construction of the ruling party pointed the way. This was the enrichment and development of Mao Zedong's party-building thought, and the premise and guarantee for promoting the localization of Marxism. Such ideological understanding was not only a result of the Party's initial experience in the construction of the Party under the ruling conditions over the previous seven years, but was also due to some prominent problems in the construction of socialist political parties exposed in the international communist movement after the Twentieth National Congress of the Soviet Communist Party. It was on this basis that the Eighth National Congress deepened its understanding of the construction of the ruling party.

At the same time, it was also evident that the Eighth National Congress had some historical limitations in the theory of party-building. For example, around the time of the Eighth National Congress, central leaders attached great importance to the criticism of bureaucracy, but they mainly understood the problem from the perspective of the legacy of the old society, mainly positioning bureaucracy as a style or moral issue, while paying insufficient attention to the problems within the system. If the Party could not go deep into such a high level of understanding, the struggle against bureaucracy could not achieve the desired goal. Moreover, if the Eighth National Congress failed to raise the awareness of strengthening intra-Party democracy to a strategic level, the idea of building the rule of law would also be weak. In addition, many theories and ideas had not formed specific operational methods and policies. Because of this, some important ideas, theories, and policies put forward by the Eighth National Congress often failed to be implemented in practice.

V

The Paradigm of the Localization of Marxism in China: Theory of the Contradictions in a Socialist Society

1. Classic Marxist Writers' Thoughts on Contradictions in a Socialist Society

Regarding the contradictions in a socialist society, Marx and Engels did not have direct experience because of historical limitations. Therefore, they did not create a fantasy of divorcing themselves from objective reality in solving the contradictions between production relations and productive forces or between the superstructure and the economic foundation in the stage of socialist and communist society, though they also pointed out that there were still "three big differences" (between workers and peasants, between urban and rural areas, and between brain and body). These differences were also contradictory in nature, but they did not clearly and systematically raise those contradictions in the context of a socialist society.

In 1920, when commenting on Bukharin's *Transitional Economics*, Lenin pointed out how best to observe and study this problem, saying, "Confrontation and contradiction are not the same thing at all. Under socialism, confrontation will disappear and contradictions will still exist."[39] This point of view affirmed that there was another kind of contradiction in socialist society which was quite different from the previous class contradiction, that is, a non-antagonistic contradiction. It also distinguished the two different categories of "antagonism" and "contradiction" philosophically, which was a development in Marx and Engels' socialist theory. But Lenin did not have time to make a detailed, in-depth study and analysis of the contradictions in a socialist society.

For a long time, Stalin did not recognize the contradictions in socialist society. He only talked about the "perfect fit" of productive relations and productivity and the "harmony" of politics and morality. In 1938, Stalin wrote in *Dialectical Materialism and Historical Materialism* that under the socialist system, "production relations are perfectly suited to the conditions of productive forces, because the sociality of the production process is consolidated by the public ownership of the means of production," and "the socialist national economy of the Soviet Union is the end of production relations." For example, the public ownership of the means of production fit perfectly with the sociality of the production process, so there was no economic crisis or destruction of productivity in the Soviet Union.[40] With the development of socialist construction practice, Stalin began to recognize the contradiction between productive relations and productive forces under the socialist system in 1952, in his book *The Socialist Economic Problems of the Soviet Union*. He said, "'Perfect fit' is a phrase that cannot be understood in absolute sense… It should be understood that under the socialist system, there is usually no conflict between productive relations and productive forces, and that society may make backward productive relations suit the nature of productive forces in a timely manner [...] Even under the socialist system, there will be backward inert forces, which do not grasp the necessity of changing productive relations, but this force, of course, is not difficult to overcome and will not bring matters to the point of conflict."[41] In a word, the contradiction in a socialist society was gradually recognized by classical Marxist writers, and it was also a problem that was preparing for a major breakthrough.

2. The Party Leaders' Understanding of the Contradictions in a Socialist Society after the Founding of New China.

At the beginning of the founding of the People's Republic of China, the leaders of the Party had some important points to consider, and formulated key understandings about the contradictions under socialist conditions. In the first half of 1951, Liu Shaoqi wrote *On Public and Private State-owned Factories*.

"When the state led by the working class has been established, factories have been nationalized and democratic reforms have been carried out," as mentioned in the article *Contradictions*, "there will be no class antagonism and exploitation within our state-owned factories, and the relationship between factory management organs and workers will fundamentally become a comradely relationship [...] There is no class contradiction in the state-owned factories, but are there other contradictions?" After giving an affirmative reply, he pointed out that the basic contradiction in the state-owned factories was "the contradiction between the management organs of the state-owned factories and the workers, that is, the public-private contradiction in state-owned factories. This contradiction is totally different from class confrontation in capitalist factories. It is a contradiction that is fundamentally non-hostile, reconcilable, and solvable."[42] At that time, Li Lisan, Deng Zihui, and other leading comrades also expounded these ideas.

The Twentieth National Congress of the Soviet Communist Party and the tremendous shock it sent through the international communist movement further caused Mao Zedong to realize that there were still various contradictions under the socialist system. Whether it was possible to correctly distinguish and deal with contradictions among the people and between the Party and the enemy was related to the success or failure of socialist construction and the survival of the people's regime. The Communist Party of China began to think deeply and study the contradictions in socialist society. "On Ten Relations" was Mao Zedong's key work in the discussion of the contradictions in a socialist society from the perspective of China's national conditions, drawing lessons from the Soviet Union. He pointed out that the Ten Relations in socialist construction were all contradictions. The world was made up of contradictions, and there was no world without contradiction. The Party's task was to deal with these contradictions correctly.[43] These ten problems already contained the idea that contradictions in a socialist society could be divided into two categories. In fact, they put forward two methods for dealing with contradictions of different natures, which was that the contradictions between the enemy and the Party should be distinguished, and the contradictions among the people should distinguish between right and wrong. "On Ten Relations" held an important historical position in the emergence and development of the two kinds of contradiction theories of the Communist Party of China, and it can be regarded as an important achievement in the development of the socialist social contradiction theory.

In April and December 1956, in accordance with the spirit of the enlarged meeting of the Politburo, the editorial department of the *People's Daily* wrote two articles, "Historical Experience of the Proletarian Dictatorship" and "Historical Experience of the Proletarian Dictatorship Again." Beginning with a summary of the historical experience of the international proletarian dictatorship, for the first time they explicitly stated that socialist society still existed. Regarding contradiction, this paper criticized the metaphysical view of denying contradiction, put forward the concept of "contradiction of two different natures," and pointed out that the contradiction between productive relations and productive forces and between the economic base and the superstructure were the basic contradictions applicable to all societies. On December 4, 1956, Mao Zedong also addressed two kinds of contradictions, especially among the people, in a letter. He wrote, "Society is always full of contradictions." This was true even in socialist and communist societies, but the nature of their contradictions was different from those of class societies. Both contradictions needed to be exposed and addressed. There were two ways to expose and address these problems. One was between the enemy (that is to say, the spy saboteurs) and oneself, and the other was within the people (including within the Party and between the Party and the people). The former was the method of repression, while the latter was the method of persuasion, that is, the method of criticism. Class contradictions within China had basically been resolved (though they had not been completely resolved yet, as reflected in ideology, and would still exist for a long time). In addition, there would be a small number of agents who would exist for a long time, and all the people should unite. But the Party's internal problems would continue to emerge. The way to solve them was to start from unity and achieve unity through criticism and self-criticism."[44]

In the autumn and winter of 1956, in the face of the "disturbances" in some parts of the country, Mao pointed out that it was important to take a positive attitude toward the disturbances, some of which were due to the existence of bureaucracy and subjectivism in the leadership, making mistakes in politics or economics, and some of which were not wrong in policy, but in working methods, being too rigid. Another factor was the existence of counter-revolutionaries and bad elements.[45] In the final analysis, it was the reflection of the contradictions between the enemy and the self and the contradictions among the people in the socialist society, in which the contradictions among the people were manifested in large quantities. Mao emphasized that all contradictions among the people and within the Party should be solved by rectification, criticism, and self-criticism rather than by force.[46] He also pointed out in particular that during the revolutionary period, people concentrated their efforts on class struggle and that contradictions among the people were not prominent. The remaining part of class struggle in the period of construction was largely manifested in the struggle among the people. China's experience in this matter was insufficient, and it was worth studying carefully. It was a science.[47] This demonstrated that correctly understanding and dealing with various contradictions in China's socialist society had become a major issue for the Central Committee to focus on during this period.

3. On the Correct Handling of Contradictions among the People

In February 1957, at the eleventh meeting of the Supreme Council of the State, Mao Zedong made a speech entitled "How to Handle Contradictions Among the People," in which he systematically clarified the two types of contradictions in socialist society and how to correctly address contradictions among the people. After sorting out, revising, and supplementing these thoughts, the speech absorbed Liu Shaoqi's and Zhou Enlai's ideas on this issue and was published in June of the same year under the title of "On The Correct Handling of Contradictions Among the People." In this work of great theoretical and practical significance, Mao thoroughly studied and explained the contradictions in socialist society, formulating a systematic and original theoretical system. This was the continuation and development of the Eight Routes of the Communist Party of China, which concentrated on the theoretical height of the localization of Marxism in China at this stage and the achievements of the localization of Marxism in the years before and after 1956.

Mao observed the contradictions of socialist society from the perspective of the law of the unity of opposites, which was the fundamental law of the universe that existed everywhere in nature, human society, and people's thoughts. He pointed out, "In socialist society, the basic contradiction is still the contradiction between productive relations and productivity and between the superstructure and the economic foundation. However, these contradictions in socialist society are fundamentally different in nature and circumstances from those in the productive relations and productive forces of the old society and between the superstructure and the economic base." This contradiction was fundamentally different from those in the old society, as "the contradictions in the capitalist society are manifested in fierce confrontation and conflict, and in fierce class struggle. Such contradictions cannot be resolved by the capitalist system itself, but only through socialist revolution. Contradictions in a socialist society are another matter. On the contrary, they are not antagonistic contradictions. They can be resolved continuously through the socialist system itself." Mao believed that socialist relations of production had been established, and they were compatible with the development of productive forces. However, they were still far from perfect, and these imperfect aspects contradicted the development of productive forces. In addition to the compatible and contradictory situation of production relations and the development of productive forces, there were also compatible and contradictory situations of the superstructure and economic foundation. After solving these contradictions, there would be "new contradictions, which need to be solved by the people."[48] This was the first time in the history of Marxist development that a systematic theory of the basic contradictions of socialism had been established, which raised the understanding of the law of socialist social development to a new theoretical level.

On this basis, "On the Correct Handling of Contradictions Among the People" created new theories and concepts of two kinds of contradictions in a socialist society, clearly putting forward the idea that the correct handling of contradictions among the people should be the theme of national political life. Mao pointed out that there were two kinds of social contradictions in socialist society, namely, the contradiction between the enemy and oneself and the contradiction among the people. The contradiction between the enemy and oneself was antagonistic. Contradictions among the people could be divided into two situations: the working people and the exploited class and within the exploited class. The former was non-confrontational, while the latter had both an antagonistic and a non-antagonistic side.

Under socialist conditions, there were many contradictions among the people. It was important to correctly distinguish and deal with the contradictions between oneself and the enemy and the contradictions among the people, which were of a different nature. To resolve the contradictions among the people, it was necessary to adopt democratic methods, "unity-criticism-unity" methods, and self-education methods. It was necessary to prevent the intensification of contradictions among the people, prevent the transformation of contradictions among the people into contradictions between the Party and the enemy, and promote the transformation of contradictions between the Party and the enemy into contradictions among the people. He also pointed out that the correct handling of contradictions among the people should be the theme of the political life of the country, and that "all positive factors inside and outside the Party, at home and abroad should be mobilized to create a political situation characterized by centralism, democracy, discipline, freedom, unity of will, personal ease of mind, and liveliness." According to the historical experience of the united front, especially the positive performance of the national bourgeoisie and the democratic parties in the socialist transformation, Mao suggested that "the contradiction between the working class and the national bourgeoisie belongs to the contradiction among the people [...] The class struggle between the working class and the national bourgeoisie generally belongs to the class struggle within the people." This laid a new theoretical foundation for upholding and developing the people's democratic united front under socialist conditions. This was the great theoretical and practical creation of Mao Zedong and the Communist Party of China and the product of the combination of the basic principles of Marxism and the concrete reality of China.

Admittedly, due to the limitations of the times, there were still some imperfections in the theory of correctly handling contradictions among the people. Nevertheless, the establishment of the theory of social contradictions in socialism was a concentrated reflection of the combination of Marxism and the actual situation of China after it entered the socialist stage. It was a major breakthrough of the Communist Party of China in the theory of Marxism and traditional socialism, and it greatly promoted the historical process of the localization of Marxism.

In the year 1956, under the guidance of Marxism and on the basis of earnestly summarizing the experience and lessons of the international communist movement, the CPC made significant explorations into many aspects of administering the country and government with the spirit of innovation, advancing with the times and putting forward many new ideas and concepts that were different from the traditional socialist model. These ideological understandings made a great breakthrough in the theoretical framework of traditional socialism, offering rich new content and distinct national characteristics, and having the distinct flavor of a localized Marxism. They were an important milestone in the integration of Marxism into China after the beginning of the stage of comprehensively building socialism, and they marked a brilliant chapter in the history of the Party's ideological development. This chapter was also an important milestone in the history of Mao Zedong Thought. The all-round exploration of China's socialist construction in the period before and after the Eighth National Congress was the historical starting point of the second great revolution led by the Communist Party of China.

However, due to the limitations of history and the times, the localization of Marxism in China during this period could not be freed from various constraints. Some of these ideas and theories were imperfect, some had certain theoretical defects and internal contradictions, some were correct but had not yet gained general consensus and had not risen to the level of a guiding ideology of the whole Party, and some were often more manifested in the ideological and theoretical level but lacking specific operable policies and methods. The limitations and theoretical deficiencies of these times were the deep-seated reasons for the failure to realize the "second leap" in the localization of Marxism in the 1950s and 1960s.

CHAPTER 6

The Localization of Marxism in China Deviates from the Right Direction

Around the time of the Eighth National Congress, on the basis of a correct understanding of the national conditions and a summary of the experience gained and the lessons learned from the Soviet Union, great achievements were made in China's newly launched comprehensive socialist construction and in the understanding of China's socialist construction by the first generation of leadership in the CPC. However, regrettably and incomprehensibly, only half a year later, this positive momentum of development was interrupted by the anti-Rightist struggle, causing the localization of Marxism to go astray.

At the beginning of the overall socialist construction, whether China was aware of it and no matter how aware it was, it was necessary to face several fundamental issues of vital importance, including what socialism was, the main contradictions of socialism, and how to carry out socialist construction. The first was a seemingly superficial issue for many socialist countries. The second was not a big one for many countries, because according to classical Marxist writers' theory and their respective methods and historical traditions of seizing power, they were reluctant to acknowledge that there were still contradictions in socialist countries, let alone regard class contradictions as the main conflict existing within socialism. In those countries, many mistakes were made in the expansion of class struggle, but in theory, they did not regard class struggle as the main contradiction in a socialist society. Even in a country with a long tradition of fierce class struggle, such as China, there was little controversy about the understanding of the main contradictions in the assumptions made by the Eighth National Congress and before. It was for this reason that, during the Cultural Revolution, "revisionism within the Party" was repeatedly criticized and mistaken notions of the main contradictions were put forward at the Eighth National Congress, while the establishment of class struggle as the main contradiction as a major development of Marxism was praised. The third issue was based on the previous two, but focused more on practice and operation. In the orthodox Stalinist model, the socialist economy was a highly centralized planned economy dominated by administrative power, while market forces were small. On the surface, this model was in line with Marxist assumptions at that time. Because it greatly weakened the role of the law of value, this economic form, under the influence of administrative power and subjective will, was easy to launch and arrange at a rate beyond the conventional pace of development, which was especially suitable for a costly catching-up strategy. This development strategy gradually became the object of socialist reform in the 1950s. In this way, when China began to build socialism overall, it had to face a major choice, determining whether to basically follow the traditional model or the reform model. In the years around 1956, the understanding of the Central Committee and Mao Zedong was quite consistent on the issue of the need to reform the traditional model, but on the question of what and how to change, because some deep contradictions had not yet been revealed, there were no differences of understanding within the central leadership.

After the anti-Rightist struggle in 1957, Mao and the Central Committee gradually deviated from the correct understanding of socialism gained around the time of the Eighth National Congress and gradually deviated from Marxism in their understanding of the law of socialist development. Serious deviations occurred in their understanding of the main contradictions in socialist society, which led to the failure of the expansion of class struggle. In terms of the scale and speed of economic construction, the Party made the left-leaning mistake of trying to hurry success and rushing forward blindly, replacing the correct principles and policies of the Eight Major Routes with the so-called "three red flags." The Party's exploration of China's socialist path suffered major setbacks, and the localization of Marxism in China deviated from the correct path. During the previous nine months, from the end of 1958 to the first half of 1959, the Central Committee under Mao's leadership immediately began to correct the Leftist mistakes that had been discovered and made some important progress. However, due to the limitations of rectifying the Leftism that existed, serious deviations occurred after the Lushan Conference.

I

The Deviation of the Rectification Movement from its Original Intention

1. The Origin of the Rectification Movement

From the second half of 1956, with the upsurge of the international communist movement, some tensions emerged in China's economic and political life. There were dozens of strikes across the country, involving more than 10,000 people. In the countryside, there were incidents of withdrawal from the community and dozens of student strikes. At the beginning of these incidents, Mao and the Central Committee maintained a relatively sober understanding. Mao believed that the main reason for the minor disturbances was the existence of bureaucracy and subjectivism in the leadership, which led to mistakes in political or economic policies, and that some of the methods of work were incorrect or too rigid. He held that, "now there are some people who seem to have won the world, have no worries, and can run rampant. The masses oppose this kind of people, throwing stones at them, which I think is appropriate and should be appreciated. Sometimes, only fighting can solve the problem. When students and workers go to the streets or things like that occur, our comrades need to perform our work well." He also suggested, "In the future, if we are amending the Constitution, I advocate adding an item about the freedom to strike and allow workers to strike. This will be conducive to resolving the contradictions between the state, factory directors, and the masses.'" He earnestly warned the cadres and Party members, "We must be vigilant not to foster a bureaucratic style, nor to form an aristocratic class divorced from the people. Whoever enacts bureaucracy, fails to solve the problems of the masses, scolds the masses and oppresses them, or remains unchanged will be dismissed by the masses, and for good reason. I say it's good to dismiss him, and it should be done."² Therefore, the first choice to settle the disturbances caused by a small minority was to overcome bureaucracy and expand democracy. Based on this understanding, the Central Committee decided to carry out a rectification movement throughout the Party in hopes of overcoming some of its own problems and allowing the Party to adapt to the requirements of the new task of comprehensively building socialism.

The task of the Party's rectification movement was advocated by the Eighth National Congress. In the opening speech of the Eighth National Congress, Mao Zedong pointed out in connection with the Yan'an Rectification Movement that there were still subjectivism, bureaucracy, and sectarianism among many Party members, which were not conducive to intra-Party unity and unity between the Party and the people. It was important to vigorously remedy these serious weaknesses to carry out the great construction work facing the Party at that time, and to do it well. At the Second Plenary Session of the Eighth Central Committee held in November 1956, taking the events in Poland and Hungary as a warning, it was emphasized that while taking into account national construction and people's livelihood, the Party must guard against the particularization of cadres and isolation from the masses. It was decided that the rectification movement of the Party should be carried out in 1957, but that now was the time to let it brew and prepare. The Central Committee pointed out that rectification was an effective method throughout the history of the CPC. In the future, all matters within the people and within the Party were to be settled through rectification, criticism, and self-criticism, rather than by force. In this way, the Party could unite the people throughout the country and mobilize all the positive factors of 600 million people to build socialism.

On March 8, 1957, Mao once again mentioned in a talk that the Party should carry out the rectification movement. He said that the Central Committee would hold a meeting and issue an instruction to prepare that year and start work the following. "Rectification focuses on subjectivism, particularly dogmatism; on sectarianism, which always intends to take dominance and holds that 600 million people are too many and a little less is good; and on rampant bureaucracy. There has been no rectification for many years."³ On March 12, in his speech at the National Propaganda Conference, Mao devoted himself to rectification of an additional issue. He said, "China's reform and construction depends on our leadership. If we rectify our style of work, we will be more proactive in our work and more competent in doing our work better."⁴ He clearly declared that the rectification movement should first be carried out within the Party, with the voluntary participation of those outside the Party. It aimed to criticize subjectivism (including dogmatism), sectarianism, and bureaucracy to overcome mistakes, creating an environment and forming the habit of independent criticism. Rectification, as it was applied in Yan'an, involved studying documents, criticizing mistakes, making small democracies, making small advances, curing diseases and saving people, and opposing the method of killing many people with one stick.⁵

Mao Zedong's "On the Correct Handling of Contradictions Among the People" and his speech at the National Conference on Propaganda Work aroused strong repercussions both inside and outside the Party. The Central Committee continuously issued circulars requiring Party committees at all levels to take practical measures to strengthen the relationship between the Party and the people. In the Directive on the Communication of the National Propaganda Conference, issued by the Central Committee on March 16, it was pointed out that "at present, there are some abnormal conditions in the relationship between the Party and intellectuals. The reason for this abnormal situation is that there are two kinds of anti-Marxist-Leninist ideas in the Party, namely dogmatism and right-leaning opportunism. Dogmatism treats intellectuals, ideological issues, and the study of Marxism in a crude rather than a persuasive way, a reproachful rather than rational way, and a coercive rather than voluntary way." It added, "Right opportunism, on the other hand, negates everything about our past work, sees only shortcomings, and fails to see achievements, thus losing confidence and describing the great cause of revolution and construction as a dark mass." Therefore, it was essential to "oppose these two wrong ideas both inside and outside the Party." In response to the workers' strikes, students' strikes, and mass marches, the Central Committee issued Instructions on Strikes and Notices on Studying Several Important Issues Concerning the Working Class. According to the Central Committee, "The first reason for such incidents is that our work has not been done well, especially because of the bureaucracy of the leadership." The fundamental way to prevent such incidents was to adjust the existing problems in the internal relations of socialist society at any time, "first of all, to overcome bureaucracy."

At the same time, Mao and other major leaders of the Central Committee inspected all parts of the country separately and directly expounded to the cadres inside and outside the Party the idea of correctly handling contradictions among the people, which was actually the ideological mobilization of the rectification movement. In March, Mao pointed out in his speech to the cadres' congresses in Shandong and Shanghai the necessity of carrying forward the tradition of arduous struggle of the Party through rectification, which was expected to make considerable progress for the Party. Regarding the policy of "letting a hundred flowers bloom and a hundred schools of thought contend," Mao Zedong emphasized that this was not only the basic policy for the development of science and literature, but also the basic policy for dealing with contradictions among the people under the new historical conditions. "With the current policy, literature, art, science, and technology will flourish, the Party will always remain vigorous, the cause of the people will flourish, and China will become a great power and make the people friendly."[6] With regard to the shift in the focus of the Party's work, he said, "When the class struggle is basically over, what is our task? To turn to construction, lead all of society, lead 600 million people, fight against nature, make China prosperous, and allow it to become an industrial country." He pointed out that in the 20th century, revolution took place in the first half of the century and construction took place in the second half. From that point to the middle of the 21st century, it would take 100 years to build China well.[7]

Liu Shaoqi explained in an internal conversation what rectification was about, saying that it was to check whether the Party regarded contradictions among the people as those between it and the enemy, and vice versa. Had the Party pursued sectarianism without considering the interests of 600 million people? That was what rectification was concerned with.[8] He especially emphasized the significance of opposing bureaucracy. Contradictions among the people were manifested in those between the people and the leadership, more precisely, in those between the people and the bureaucracy of the leadership. "If the leading organs do not impose bureaucracy, the problem can be solved and the contradiction eased." He also pointed out that in some places, some hierarchical systems emerged, which was a feudal system and should be abolished.[9]

2. From Rectification to the Anti-Rightist Movement

On April 27, 1957, the Party Central Committee issued the Directive on the Rectification Movement (hereinafter referred to as the Directive). The Directive stated that as the Party had been in the ruling position throughout the country and won the support of the masses, many comrades were likely to turn to a simple administrative order to address problems, and some of those who were wavering were likely to be contaminated by the remnants of the old social style, forming a concept of privilege, or even oppressing the masses with force. Therefore, it was necessary to carry out a general and in-depth rectification campaign against bureaucracy, sectarianism, and subjectivism throughout the Party. The Directive stipulated that the guiding ideology of the rectification movement was the two reports generated by Mao Zedong on behalf of the Central Committee at the Enlarged Supreme State Conference in February and at the Propaganda Work Conference held by the Central Committee in March. The theme of the rectification movement was to correctly handle contradictions among the people. The Directive stated, "The transmission of these two reports has aroused heated discussion. As far as our Party is concerned, this is actually the beginning of the rectification movement." The rectification movement was meant to be a serious and gentle ideological movement, a proper criticism and self-criticism movement, and more focused on individual talks or small-group talks. Generally speaking, the Party did not aim to hold critical meetings or struggle meetings in the form of symposiums and group meetings. Mao later pointed out that the goal the Party hoped to achieve through rectification was to create a political situation characterized by centralization, democracy, discipline, freedom, unity of will, individual ease of mind, and liveliness.[10] On April 30, while speaking with leaders of various democratic parties and representatives of non-Party democrats, Mao said that he had been trying to rectify the situation for several years, but could not find the opportunity. Now he had found it. An atmosphere of criticism had been built up and should continue. At this time, it was more natural to upgrade the rectification movement. The general theme of rectification was to deal with contradictions among the people and oppose subjectivism, sectarianism, and bureaucracy. He hoped that through the criticism of people from all walks of life, the Party's style of work would really be improved. He also envisaged that the contradictions between the Party and the democratic parties and the Party and the intellectuals in practical work would be properly resolved through further improvement of some of the specific leadership systems of the Party.

On May 1, the *People's Daily* issued the rectification directive of the Central Committee, and the rectification of the whole Party began. After the rectification movement was launched, people from all walks of life made extensive and concentrated criticisms of the Party's work in various symposiums and newspapers. In this process, in addition to a large number of critical opinions on the manifestations and harms of bureaucracy, sectarianism, and subjectivism in the Party's work style, there were also some opinions concerning the fundamental evaluation of the major issues of leadership within the Party, the socialist system, the political movements since the founding of New China, and the internal and external policies of the Party. From mid- and late May to early June, some doubts about and denials of the Party leadership and the socialist system emerged in newspapers and magazines, which aroused the vigilance of the Central Committee and Mao Zedong. In particular, after the Party changed from not encouraging "major contending" and "big criticism" to advocating them and supporting the big-character posters, the political tension and instability throughout the country were artificially intensified. Although the Central Committee and Mao Zedong affirmed a large number of positive criticisms, they overreacted to the opinions concerning major political issues and some indignant talk that was not calm and lacked ideological preparation. Later, they overestimated the situation of class struggle at home and abroad, which promptly transformed the rectification movement into an anti-Rightist struggle. The Central Committee believed that this was a rampant attack by Rightists on the Party and socialism, and that only by repelling the attack by the Rightists could the rectification movement be carried out smoothly. The contradictions between the Party and the people and the Rightists were confrontational, irreconcilable, and viewed as life-and-death contradictions between the enemy and the Party, and the fight against the Rightists was seen as a sharp struggle to defend socialism. "If we do not win this battle, socialism will not be built, much like the dangers seen in Hungary."[11] According to this guiding ideology, the theme of the movement shifted from correctly handling contradictions among the people to fighting against the enemy, from rectification within the Party to fighting against the Rightists, and from harmony to "a large-scale ideological and political war."[12] The anti-Rightist struggle followed the mode of a struggle of a mass political movement and did not carefully control the rapid development of the struggle, resulting in a serious expansion of the struggle. What was more serious was that the leaders of the Party, especially Mao Zedong, changed the correct analysis of the main social contradictions, class, and class struggle in China at the Eighth National Congress and gradually formed the theory of the expansion of class struggle. Mao pointed out, "The significance of criticizing the bourgeois right this time should not be underestimated. This is a great socialist revolution on the political and ideological fronts. The socialist revolution in 1956 focused solely on the economic front (in terms of ownership of means of production) is not enough and is not consolidated. The Hungarian Incident is proof of that. There must also be a thorough socialist revolution on the political and ideological fronts."[13]

The original intention of the rectification movement in 1957 was to generate a beneficial exploration and practice in which the Central Committee and Mao Zedong might comprehensively strengthen and improve the Party's construction, guided by the correct handling of contradictions among the people and the shift of the focus in the Party's work. These were the inheritance and development of the Eight Major Routes and the new efforts to explore China's own socialist path. However, due to the limitations of history and practice, the rectification movement, originally based on good intentions, soon deviated from the correct direction. Broadly speaking, the problem of bureaucracy was a phenomenon with a long history, which was born alongside the modern country. As long as there was management (state, administrative, enterprise, etc.) and hierarchical obedience, its existence was unavoidable. Modern management, politics, and sociology often used the "system of hierarchy" to explain its causes, manifestations, and characteristics. Bureaucracy was not, first of all, a matter of morality or style, but more a legacy of the "old society" and system. At that time, socialist countries implemented a highly centralized planning system, weakened the law of value and the role of economic leverage, carried out economic construction through a strict top-down administrative mobilization system, and emphasized that the modernization process should be dominated by high-intensity administrative forces. This would only reinforce the top-down hierarchical obedience, thus providing institutional resources and space for the growth of bureaucracy. In the process of implementing a catching-up and surpassing strategy, at a certain stage of socialist development, this phenomenon was inevitable. Lenin had been keenly aware of this problem in the early practice of socialism and pointed out its harm to socialism. He rightly noted that bureaucracy should be restricted and eliminated by expanding the broad participation of the masses in state administration, i.e., making everyone a "bureaucrat" so that no one was a bureaucrat. During the socialist reform in the mid-1950s, Yugoslavia and leaders of some other Eastern European countries raised this issue. However, these understandings were still preliminary and remained far from a point where consensus could be reached on such issues in these young socialist countries. To understand and solve this problem, the only path was to develop Marxism with the times and solve it scientifically in the process of advancing the modernization of Marxism. Obviously, in the rectification movement of 1957, the understanding of bureaucracy had not yet reached the level of system reform, and it was more regarded as a moral or style problem, a legacy of the old society, or even a class struggle problem. Rectification was definitely important, but it was more important to solve the problems of the system, and it was not advisable for the rectification to adopt the methods of the "four big issues" – big contending, big criticism, big debate, and big character posters – to intensify contradictions and destabilize society.

On the one hand, they were eager to do a good job in Party building, but on the other, they were misguided because of the limitations of the times. They noted new problems under the new situation and tried to solve them appropriately, but at the same time, they used inappropriate means and methods. They tried to settle various social contradictions, but also further intensified contradictions by expanding the problem. The negative consequences of this deviation were serious. It not only seriously damaged China's political and economic development, but also seriously interfered with the second leap of the localization of Marxism in theory.

3. Deviation of the Anti-Rightist Movement and Understanding of the Major Contradictions of Socialism

The serious expansion of the anti-Rightist movement resulted in serious long-term consequences. The rectification movement, originally conceived with the theme of correctly handling contradictions among the people, ended with the serious confusion of two types of contradictions. It was hoped that the rectification movement would lead to a lively political situation, but as a result, democratic life inside and outside the Party was hit hard. Some effective attempts made in economic life were either criticized or abandoned, such as some beneficial explorations in agricultural cooperatives suitable for the productive forces at that time and various new ideas related to the reopening of the private economy. The anti-reckless advance on the speed of economic development was criticized as being close to Rightism. In terms of political thought and cultural life, the implementation of the two major principles of socialist democracy and construction of the legal system, the two policies of "letting a hundred flowers bloom and a hundred schools of thought contend" and "long-term coexistence and mutual supervision" were greatly undermined.

But the most severe consequence of the great expansion of the anti-Rightist movement lay in the fact that through the Third Plenary Session of the Eighth Central Committee and the Second Session of the Eighth National Congress, the diagnosis of the eight major social contradictions in China changed. After the war, with the emergence of the socialist camp and the development of the international communist movement, how to recognize and deal with the conflicts and major contradictions in a socialist society was increasingly prominent among the concerns facing the ruling party of a socialist country. On the basis of correctly pointing out the new main contradictions, the Eighth National Congress of the Communist Party of China noted that the main task of the state was to "protect and develop the productive forces" under the new production relations, and the entire Party should concentrate its efforts on developing productive forces. This was the most important theoretical contribution of the Eighth National Congress, and it became the consensus of the whole Party.

However, the expression of the major contradictions by the Eighth National Congress was still inaccurate, and there were still some limitations in dealing with class and class struggle. When the Eighth National Congress was convened, the socialist transformation had been basically completed and the transitional period was basically over. However, the Eighth National Congress failed to accurately specify what the end of the transitional period would entail or when it should come, instead estimating that the transitional period would last a long time. The Eighth Political Report no longer interpreted the transitional period as "from the founding of the People's Republic of China to the basic completion of socialist transformation," but as "from the founding of the People's Republic of China to the realization of industrialization," and it extended the limit of the transitional period to the end of the Third Five Year Plan, that is, 1967. Subjectively prolonging the transitional period was likely to lead to an exaggeration of the contradictions and struggles between the working class and the bourgeoisie and the socialist and the capitalist paths, because based on the original understanding of the transitional period, this period was full of class struggle. This provided a theoretical basis for the transformation of the understanding of the main contradictions of socialism and the expansion of class struggle.

Mao was aware of the flaws in the theoretical expression of the Eighth National Congress Resolution, and he also put forward some critical opinions. However, he was confined to the statement of "verbal illness," and did not oppose the basic spirit of the Eighth National Congress on major contradictions. With the change of the domestic and international situation, Mao had shown some vacillation and doubt about this judgment from time to time, but through most of the year after the Eighth National Congress, his understanding of the main domestic contradictions was basically correct. In his speech at the Second Plenary Session of the Eighth Central Committee in November 1956, Mao affirmed that "class contradictions in China have been basically solved."[14] In his letter to Huang Yanpei in December of the same year, he once again affirmed that "class contradictions within our country have basically been solved."[15] In his writing and propaganda on contradictions among the people at the beginning of 1957, he also emphasized the view that "class struggle is basically over."

Shortly after the Eighth National Congress, several important events in Poland and Hungary occurred one after another. On the one hand, Mao and the Central Committee followed the exploratory ideas of the Twentieth National Congress of the Soviet Communist Party, further advancing the theory of correctly handling the two kinds of contradictions in socialist society and trying to avoid such events in China. On the other hand, Mao believed that the occurrence of the Bosnia-Hungary Incident was due to the failure of class struggle. He further emphasized the role of class struggle in a socialist society and shifted the focus of criticism from dogmatism to revisionism. On the basis of this contradictory understanding, shortly after the rectification movement was launched, Mao made a serious and disconnected estimate of the domestic class struggle situation, thus launching an anti-Rightist struggle. An important consequence of the expansion of the anti-Rightist struggle was that the Third Plenary Session of the Eighth Central Committee changed the correct judgment made at the First Session of the Eighth National Congress on the class situation and the main contradictions in China, turning to the view that at present, "the contradictions between the proletariat and the bourgeoisie and between the socialist and the capitalist paths are undoubtedly the main contradictions in our society."[16]

The Second Session of the Eighth National Congress, held in May 1958, further promoted the development of the theory of expanding class struggle. The meeting asserted, "The experience of the rectification movement and the struggle against the right once again proves that the struggle between the proletariat and the bourgeoisie and between the paths of socialism and capitalism have always been the main contradictions within our country throughout the transitional period, that is, until the socialist society was built."[17] The deviation from the Eight Routes on the major contradictions in socialist society had a profound, long-term impact on the process of socialist construction in China. It had become the basic cause for undermining socialist democracy, damaging the construction of the ruling party, launching frequent political campaigns, and intensifying class struggle. It had also led various errors to emerge in the following twenty years.

However, it should also be noted that the major amendments to the main contradictions made at the Third Plenary Session of the Eighth Central Committee and the Second Session of the Eighth National Congress were still preliminary, that is to say, they were far from reaching the level of "taking class struggle as the guiding principle," as happened after the Tenth Plenary Session of the Eighth Central Congress. Here, the most obvious sign was that on the one hand, the Eight Major Routes were revised to establish class struggle as the main contradiction, but at the same time, the Central Committee and Mao emphasized that a climax of production and construction should be set off, that is, "it is necessary to make a great leap forward on the production front," or "surpass Britain and catch up with the United States," and so on. That is to say, the main contradiction was not the same as the main task, which was similar to the relationship between the main contradiction (then called basic contradiction) and the work of the Central Committee during the period after the Second Plenary Session of the Seventh Central Committee in 1949. At the Nanning Conference held in January 1958, Mao suggested the idea of "continuous revolution." He believed that in 1956, the socialist revolution had won a basic victory in the ownership of the means of production. In 1957, the rectification campaign "against the Rightist" had won a basic victory in the socialist revolution on the political and ideological fronts. Now, he had won a basic victory in the socialist revolution on the political and ideological fronts. In order to bring about a technological revolution, it was necessary to focus the Party's work on the question of technological revolution. This idea of shifting the focus of work was also the continuation of the correct strategic thought repeatedly emphasized before and after the First Session of the Eighth National Congress, which had changed from revolution to construction, but it could not be unified with the main contradictions identified at the Third Plenary Session of the Eighth Central Congress.

This serious self-contradictory situation demonstrated that the understanding of class struggle as the main contradiction at that time was preliminary and unstable. On the surface, it seemed that there were still many possibilities for development. But in fact, once such a major contradiction was established, it had a self-reinforcing function, especially when it was combined with a highly centralized planned economy and leadership system, because this combination itself could only greatly weaken socialist democracy, hardly tolerating different opinions, contention, and equal discussion of various opinions. The easiest way to suppress dissent at any time was to accuse the other party of being bourgeois or influenced by the bourgeoisie. The most obvious example was that at the Lushan Conference in 1959, Mao easily took the differences in the Party's internal economic construction as the reflection of class struggle within the Party, thus extending class struggle into the Party and launching a large-scale "anti-Rightist" struggle, which not only further developed economic mistakes, but also expanded class struggle. Greater mistakes would be further developed. If the main contradictions and tasks were still in a contradictory, unstable, dualistic state before, the contradictions would be rapidly reduced and the unstable dualistic state would gradually end after the Lushan Conference.

The rise of the trend of socialist reform in the 1950s and the emergence of ideological emancipation provided the Communist Party of China with a rare historical opportunity to depart from the Stalinist model and realize the "second combination" of Marxism with China's actual situation, but departure from the old model was not necessarily a smooth way to find a new correct model, and sometimes the subjective thinking of breaking free from the old model was actually merely breaking free from superficialities, but not touching the root. Clearly, there were some cognitive difficulties, but the most fundamental cause lay in the destruction of socialist democracy caused by the expansion of class struggle. Once this kind of democracy had been weakened, the localization of Marxism would lose its basis for survival. Because of the mistakes made in the main contradictions, the Party's exploration of the socialist path deviated from the correct direction, and the "second combination" of Marxism and China's actual situation also went astray.

II

The Great Leap Forward: An Extremist Catching-up Strategy

In addition to the main contradictions of socialism, the basic problems to be solved in exploring the path of building socialism in China included the scale, speed, and methods of socialist construction. From 1957 to the end of the Cultural Revolution, the Party made serious mistakes on both basic issues. After 1957, while making wrong judgments about class struggle in the socialist period, the Party committed serious errors in the construction of socialism in that it sought to rush the process.

1. Adventure and Counter-Adventure

Generally speaking, the newly independent nation-states after the Second World War could no longer follow the same path to industrialization as the old capitalist countries. They often adopted the strategy of catching up with and surpassing the old capitalist countries economically, striving to develop their own economy in a short period of time through a "rushed march" in economic construction. This was the development strategy generally adopted by socialist countries at that time. Under the current conditions, this development strategy had a certain rationality and inevitability. The strategy of catching up and surpassing formed by the Party after the founding of New China manifested not only the influence of the Soviet model, but also a profound understanding of China's national conditions and the severity of the international situation at that time. As Mao Zedong said, the current situation of "weak economic and cultural foundations" had "made us remain in a passive state, mentally bound, and we have not been liberated in this respect."[18] If the Party did not develop production as quickly as possible, it would be deprived of the "membership of this planet." This raised the strategy of catching up and surpassing to a political level that was vital to the life and death of Chinese socialism.

The proposal of the Great Leap Forward reflected the Party's efforts and attempts to combine Marxism with China's socialist construction, to shake off its dependence on the Soviet model, and to explore its own road to building socialism. As early as the middle and later stages of the First Five-Year Plan, in the process of agricultural cooperation, there was a tendency toward making a rash advance in economic construction. After the acceleration of socialist transformation in the first half of 1956, higher requirements and standards were put forward for the scale and speed of national economic construction. At the beginning of preparations for the Eighth National Congress, Mao put forward the central idea of the report of the Eighth National Congress, which was to oppose Rightist conservatism. He demanded that the Communist Party should be a "promotion association." Everyone should be a progress promoter instead of a retreat promoter. In early 1956, due to the accelerated development of all sectors of society, financial and material tensions were created. Leaders in charge of the economic work of the Central Committee and the State Council promptly discovered the tendency toward rash and aggressive progress and made efforts to correct it. Zhou Enlai, Chen Yun, Liu Shaoqi, and others proposed that while they opposed the right-leaning conservative thought of economic construction, they also opposed the tendency of being rash and aggressive. On June 20, 1956, in accordance with the spirit of the meeting of the Politburo, the *People's Daily* published an editorial entitled "To Oppose Conservatism and Impetuosity," which played an important role in mobilizing the entire Party, especially the leading cadres at all levels, to pay attention to correcting impetuous and aggressive tendencies in economic work. In this way, after several months of effort, the momentum of blind and bold progress in economic construction was initially curbed.

However, after the anti-Rightist movement, Mao more clearly expressed his dissatisfaction with "anti-rash progress." He believed that "anti-rash progress" not only frustrated the enthusiasm of the broad masses in building socialism, but also provided a pretext for Rightist attacks. The victory of the rectification campaign against the Rightists boosted the enthusiasm of the broad masses at an unprecedented scale, and so economic construction was expected to move faster. Mao's speech at the Third Plenary Session of the Eighth Central Committee changed the judgment of the First Session of the Eighth National Congress on the main contradictions in Chinese society, as well as the anti-conservative and anti-aggressive policy affirmed at that meeting. Those opposed to the "anti-rash progress" revived the rush for success in the Party.

2. The Rise of the Great Leap Forward Movement

During the rectification movement, some factories and the countryside witnessed rapid growth in production, which made it possible for many people to build at a much faster pace than dictated by the Five-Year Plan nationwide. This strengthened Mao's absolute understanding of the reaction of the superstructure and the role of class struggle, reinforcing his determination to fight against "rash advance." In late October 1957, the Third Plenary Session of the Eighth Central Committee announced the National Outline for Agricultural Development from 1956 to 1967 (Draft Amendment). On October 27, the *People's Daily* published an editorial entitled "Great Program for Building Socialist Rural Areas." The editorial called for "a great leap forward in all aspects of agriculture and rural work within twelve years in accordance with the necessity and possibility," thus putting forward the slogan of a "Great Leap Forward" in the newspapers of the central organs of the Communist Party. On November 13, the *People's Daily* also published an editorial entitled "Initiating All the People to Discuss the Forty Items and Setting Off a New Climax in Agricultural Production." The editorial criticized "some people for holding onto right-leaning conservatism and crawling as slowly as snails. They do not understand that after the agricultural co-operation, we have the conditions and need to make a great leap forward on the production front." According to the editorial, the achievements of 1956 fully reflected the correctness of this leap forward development. People who held to right-leaning conservative thought regarded the correct leap forward as a "bold advance." Influenced and stimulated by the Soviet Union's proposal to catch up with the United States in fifteen years at the Moscow Conference, as suggested in 1957, Mao proposed in November 1957 that China should catch up with Britain in steel production within fifteen years. The Central Committee accepted Mao's slogan of catching up with Britain and declared this the goal. The *People's Daily* published an editorial, requiring all regions and departments to criticize "right-leaning conservative" thinking and revise the original development plan in accordance with the requirements of the Outline of Agricultural Development and "catching up with Britain." Soon, new high targets were put forward from the central government to the local government, which set off a climax of agricultural production and opened the prelude of the Great Leap Forward movement.

The rise of this agricultural production climax further convinced Mao that carrying out political struggle to criticize right-leaning conservative thought and launching a large-scale mass movement could completely speed up economic construction. At a series of central meetings held in the first half of 1958, Mao more severely criticized the "anti-rash progress" and put forward a series of tasks, targets, slogans, and methods for launching the Great Leap Forward campaign. In fact, he denied that during the period from the recovery of the national economy to the First Five-Year Plan, the Party and the people accumulated in practice and up until the Eighth National Congress. In fact, the valuable successful experience summarized at the first meeting negated the experience and wisdom of the central leadership. After the anti-Rightist movement, the principle of collective leadership and the democratic centralism of the Party were destroyed. It was difficult for the Party to effectively prevent and correct major mistakes in decision-making caused by the mistakes of the Party's main leaders' personal understanding. These meetings made sufficient ideological and public opinion preparations for the launching of the Great Leap Forward movement.

In May 1958, the second meeting of the Eighth National Congress was held. On the initiative of Mao Zedong, the conference adopted the general line of "building socialism with full drive and striving for the upper reaches quickly and economically." The proposal of the general line of socialist construction reflected the desire of the broad masses to urgently change the backward situation of China's economy and culture, but ignored objective economic law, negated the comprehensive balance law of the national economy, exaggerated the reaction of subjective desire and human will, and made a blind pursuit of rushing the ruling party in its economic work. In the second half of 1956, the conference also strongly criticized the "anti-rash progress" work, calling on all departments in various regions to "take down the white flag and erect the red flag," further contributing to the wave of exaggeration and further expanding the Leftist thinking and eagerness for success. After the meeting, the Great Leap Forward campaign was launched at all levels throughout the country, quickly reaching its climax. At the same time, theorists, scientists and technicians, and sports and health professionals had also put forward their own "leap forward" plans and proposed many unrealistic goals for future generations. For example, many places proposed that everyone should be able to read, write, calculate, watch movies, sing, paint, dance, perform, and create. Writers and artists were required to make their own "leap forward" plan and release "creation satellites" under the requirements of "writing about the center," "singing about the center", and "painting the center."

The expanded meeting of the Politburo held in Beidaihe in August 1958 did not make any effort to correct the exaggerated and chaotic phenomena in real life, but supported them, thus pushing the Great Leap Forward movement to a climax. After the meeting, the Leftist deviation errors, marked by high targets, blind commands, exaggeration, and the "Communist style," spread throughout the country and greatly undermined social productive forces. After the Lushan Conference in 1959, under the call of the "anti-Rightists," the new Great Leap Forward climax and Communist-style errors again flooded in, directly leading to three years of serious struggle in the national economy.

On the surface, the Great Leap Forward had some similarities with the practice of the Soviet Union and other socialist countries in pursuing a catching-up strategy during the same period. But from the beginning of this movement, Mao regarded it as an attempt to break through the Soviet model and an innovation and development of the localization of Marxism in China. He believed that the construction of the Soviet Union did not fully mobilize the masses, give full play to the superiority of the socialist system, use communist ideology to educate and mobilize the masses, or engage in mass movements, so it was not widely accepted, which could not help but reduce the speed of the construction in the Soviet Union. However, because of the anti-Rightist struggle, China had won a victory over the bourgeoisie and its ideology, and the people's spiritual state had greatly improved, which created superior political and spiritual conditions for surpassing the Soviet model and promoting economic development at an accelerated rate. This relatively stereotyped understanding in 1957 and 1958 developed into "grasping revolution and promoting production" during the Cultural Revolution. The Soviet model really needed reform and breakthroughs, but because of the unfamiliarity with modern economic laws, the simple and empiricist duplication of the methods of mass movements in the war years, and the simple and dogmatic duplication of some ideas of classical communist writers, this strategy of catching-up and surpassing quickly went beyond reasonable boundaries and allowed subjectivity, empiricism, and voluntarism to expand rapidly, thus seriously undermining the development of productive forces in China.

The Great Leap Forward, an extreme catching-up strategy, was indeed different from the Soviet model and a breakthrough for this model. However, it did not conform to the basic principles of Marxism, but was instead totally divorced from China's actual situation. In fact, it distorted the correct direction of the localization of Marxism.

III

The People's Commune Movement Rushing into Transition

The people's commune movement accompanying the Great Leap Forward concerned construction speed and served as the Great Leap Forward for production relations, the forms of production and organization of daily life, and the transition from socialism to communism.

1. Origin of the People's Commune Movement

This sudden change in production relations was initially triggered by the movement of small cooperatives merging into large ones in high-level agricultural production cooperatives, which was originally a special demand under the circumstances of water conservancy construction and the large-scale construction of farmland. After socialist transformation and rectification of the "anti-Rightist" movement, the Central Committee believed that the socialist revolution on the economic, political, and ideological fronts had won great victories, which was bound to greatly inspire the enthusiasm and drive of the broad masses of the people in socialist construction and would inevitably push forward economic construction at a speed faster than that of the Soviet Union. In this context, from the winter of 1957 to the spring of 1958, there was a climax in farmland and water conservancy construction in rural areas. During this climax, many places began to expand beyond the existing scale of agricultural cooperatives, demanding mergers and attempting to settle the issues of unified planning and centralized labor, materials, and funds. During this period, the merger movement played a certain role in promoting the collective cooperation in some areas and strengthening the infrastructure of farmland and water conservancy. Mao attached great importance to this issue, once more raised the issue of running a community, and directed the drafting of documents on the issue. After his affirmation and advocacy, the merging work was carried out quickly. With the exaggeration and promotion of the atmosphere of the Great Leap Forward, the merger quickly developed into a mass movement eager to promote the transition of agricultural collective production organizations to so-called higher forms, regardless of the actual conditions. At that time, Mao and other central leaders believed that the larger the scale of agricultural cooperatives and the higher the degree of public ownership, the more productive they could be. The large cooperatives formed by the merging of smaller cooperatives were an effective form of organization for the Great Leap Forward in agricultural production.

At the beginning of the merger, the large-scale cooperatives were only a little larger than the original ones, and they were not quite the same as the later people's communes that served as both administrative and economic organizations. But after preparations for several meetings of the Central Committee in early 1958, Mao Zedong and Liu Shaoqi, the leaders of the Central Committee, began to deliberate on changing the rural grassroots organizational structure and conducting the integration of community and township. On different occasions, they talked about the idea of running "communes." In late April, while traveling to Guangdong by train, Liu talked with Zhou Enlai and Lu Dingyi about "trumpeting the news of communes, Utopia, and the transition to communism," as well as "fantasy socialism, nurseries, collectivization, collectivization of life, schools run by factories, factories run by schools, and half-work and half-study."[19] In late April, speaking with Liu Shaoqi and others about the organizational form of the future rural areas in China, Mao said that by then there would be many Communist communes in the Chinese countryside. Each commune would have its own agriculture and industry, universities, primary and secondary schools, hospitals, scientific research institutions, shops and service industries, transportation undertakings, nurseries, canteens, clubs, policemen, and so forth. Several rural communes would surround the city and become larger Communist communes. The conception of previous generations about "Utopia" would be fulfilled and surpassed. China's educational policy and other cultural and educational undertakings would also develop toward this goal.[20] Mao Zedong, Liu Shaoqi, and other leading comrades' ideas were disseminated through the speeches of some delegates during the Second Session of the Eighth National Congress of the Communist Party of China. In a few areas, organizations under the name of "commune" emerged in June. On June 30, Liu Shaoqi made it clear in a talk that "grassroots organizations in Communist society are now beginning to conduct experiments... I'm afraid we can't be confined to mere farming or industrial work as we are. Now we need to be engaged in industrial, agricultural, commercial, educational, and military work. Now agricultural cooperatives have started to run factories, businesses, banks, services, laundries, canteens, and schools. In the future, shooting drills will be conducted in factories, the countryside, and schools, thus integrating industrial, agricultural, commercial, educational, and military work... In my view, in thirty or forty years, we can build a Communist society."

In July, in the third and fourth issues of the *Red Flag*, Chen Boda published two articles, entitled "New Society, New People" and "Under Comrade Mao Zedong's Banner," which disclosed Mao's thoughts on running people's communes. He wrote, "Comrade Mao Zedong said that our direction should be to systematically form a large commune of industry (industry), agriculture (agriculture), commerce (exchange), learning (culture and education), and soldiers (militia, that is, the armed forces of the whole people), thus constituting the basic units of our society [...] Turning a cooperative into a grassroots organizational unit with both agricultural and industrial cooperation is actually a people's commune combining agriculture and industry." In August, Mao visited the countryside in Hebei, Henan, and Shandong Provinces, with the purpose of encouraging the merger and establishment of large cooperatives. He said several times, "I think farms are not as good as people's communes" and "people's communes are better."[21] Since then, he repeated this idea on many occasions and pointed out that the characteristics of the people's commune were first, that these communes were large, and that they were public communes. Their advantage was that they could combine industry, agriculture, commerce, education, and military work to facilitate management. After these ideas were published in the newspapers, the whole country was motivated by the news and promoted the establishment of people's communes nationwide.

Under these circumstances, the Beidaihe Conference, held from August 17-30, 1958, formally decided to establish people's communes in rural areas throughout the country and adopted the Resolution of the Central Committee of the Communist Party of China on the Establishment of People's Communes in Rural Areas (hereinafter referred to as the Resolution). The Resolution held that the merger and transformation of small-scale agricultural production cooperatives into large-scale people's communes with the integration of industry, agriculture, commerce, education, and military work, with its administrative and economic functions and a higher degree of collectivization, was the inevitable trend of the rapid development of rural production and the great improvement of farmers' awareness. "It is a basic principle that must be adopted to guide farmers to accelerate socialist construction and build socialism ahead of time and gradually move to communism."[22] In terms of ownership, although the Resolution pointed out that it was important not to rush to change from collective to public ownership, it emphasized that there were some elements of public ownership in the collective ownership of people's communes. This kind of ownership by all the people would continue to grow in future developments, the fastest being accomplished within three or four years and the slower in five or six years or more. It would gradually replace collective ownership. Such provisions were evidence of the rush into transition and the blowing of the "Communist wind" in the people's commune movement. The Resolution also endowed the people's commune with great strategic significance, believing that it would "be the best form of organization for building socialism and gradually transiting to communism, and it will develop into the grassroots units of the future communist society." It added, "We should actively use the form of the people's commune to explore a transition to communism in specific ways."[23] The people's commune movement and the resulting system reflected Mao's and the Party's understanding of socialism and the ardent pursuit of communist ideals at that time, as well as the Party's earnest intention of "Sinicizing" and "modernizing" Marxism. But history later proved that the people's commune movement was simply the product of the combination of the traditional socialist model and some historical Chinese traditions. Behind this "new thing" were merely old ideas and traditions.

2. Characteristics of the People's Commune Movement

After the Beidaihe Conference, the entire Chinese countryside rushed to launch the work and hurried to build people's communes "ardently and quickly," regardless of the actual conditions, starting a surge of large-scale people's commune movements, which completely went beyond Mao's requirements of first piloting and then realizing communalization in the spring of the following year. By the end of October, 26,000 people's communes had been established in most areas of China, and more than 99% of the total peasant households had joined the communes. At this point, in less than two months, people's communes were built up in rural areas throughout the country. At the same time, some provinces and municipalities carried out pilot campaigns of people's communes in cities.

The people's communes had a strong flavor of utopian socialism and military communism. One of the cores of this socialist view was equality. "Equal" socialism was embodied in the people's communes, that is, in the pursuit of the socialist purity of "large scale and great public ownership." Mao repeatedly emphasized that the characteristics of the people's communes are "large scale and great public ownership," with "large scale" referring to the expansiveness of the people's communes, and "great public ownership" pointing to the high degree of public ownership. People's communes were basically in the form of joining one village or several into one commune, or one county into one commune. The economic functions of the people's commune included almost all fields, such as industry, agriculture, forestry, animal husbandry, side-industries, fisheries, finance, education, health, military work, and so on. People's communes became the de facto grassroots organizations of state power. This five-in-one organizational form of integrating politics, society, industry, agriculture, commerce, learning, and military forces promoted a "militarized organization, combat action, and collectivized life" mode of labor organization and lifestyle, weakening the social division of labor and exchange, excluding material interests and the market economy, pursuing both the "big and complete" and the "small and complete," and remaining both self-contained and self-enclosed. What was more serious was that the people's communes were in a rush to make the transition to a single form of public ownership. Pushing all levels to assign all the means of production and private property of high-level communes to the communes themselves, without any compensation, relied heavily on orders from administrative powers at all levels. The reserved land, livestock, woodlands, some of the larger production tools, and even private houses and livestock reserved by members of the communes in the process of agricultural co-operation were regarded as remnants of private ownership, and all of them were transferred to the communes. At the same time, in order to vigorously eliminate the so-called "bourgeois legal power," the commune implemented the equalitarian supply system.

At a deeper level, the emergence of the people's communes aimed to simplify the understanding and application of some Marxist theories of socialism and to simply duplicate the successful experience of the war years to the results of economic construction in peacetime. It blurred the boundaries of collective ownership and ownership of all the people, socialism and communism, and the boundaries of different stages of socialist development, showing a distinct flavor of fantasy. The original intention of the people's commune movement was to use and surpass Marxism. In fact, it misinterpreted Marxism through its dogmatism and empiricism, and was a retrogression of the socialist outlook.

In order to develop social productive forces rapidly, the people's commune movement was launched by Mao and the Party too rashly, in the absence of experience in socialist construction and with insufficient understanding of the laws of economic development and the basic situation of China's economy. This was a major failure of the Party in the process of exploring the path of socialist construction, and also a setback of the localization of Marxism in the period of socialist construction. Like the Great Leap Forward, although the people's commune movement itself had a strong Chinese flavor, its ideas and methods were not only divorced from China's actual situation, but also from the inherent requirements of Marxist modernization. The fundamental reason lay, as Deng Xiaoping said in questions such as, "What is socialism? What is Marxism? Our understanding of this issue in the past was not entirely clear-headed."[24]

CHAPTER 7

Deepening the Understanding of Socialism in the Initial Rectification of the Left-leaning Errors

Reflection on the Nine-month Rectification of the Left-leaning Errors

1. Mao Zedong's Leadership in Correcting Left-leaning Errors

The serious consequences of the Great Leap Forward and the indiscriminate development of the people's commune movement were clearly presented in the autumn and winter of 1958. Mao Zedong was an active advocate and promoter of the Great Leap Forward and the people's commune movement, but also a leader of the Party Central Leading Group who made early detection of serious problems in the movements through investigation and research and took effective measures to correct them. From November 1958 to July the following year, under the chairmanship and promotion of Mao Zedong, the Central Committee successively convened the first Zhengzhou Conference (November, 1958), the Wuchang Conference and Sixth Plenary Session of the Eighth Central Committee (November and December, 1958), the second Zhengzhou Conference

(February and March, 1959), the Shanghai Conference and Seventh Plenary Session of the Eighth Central Committee (March and April, 1959), and the Lushan Preparatory Conference (July, 1959). These meetings objectively analyzed the situation, summed up the experience, and proceeded to correct the left-leaning mistakes that had been found. At these meetings, Mao took the lead in criticizing the aggressive mood, advocating a "compressed air," calling for cooling down, calming the minds of the participants in varying degrees, actively studying and taking measures to adjust some policy indicators, and initially curbing the chaos caused by the Great Leap Forward and the people's commune movement. From an objective point of view, the process of rectifying the left-leaning errors could not be a process of going back to the beginning and understanding afresh the actual situation in China, the socialist theory of classical Marxist writers, Stalinist theory and Marxist socialist theory as interpreted by the Soviet Union. These were all problems that had to be solved in the process of the localization of Marxism at that time. As a result, the process of correcting Leftism was also a process of advancing the localization of Marxism through the various detours that came with it.

At the end of 1958, Mao found that during the people's commune movement, many people had confused ideas that led them to announce prematurely the trend of public ownership, abolishing commerce and eliminating commodity production, which in turn caused serious consequences in the practical work. At the second Zhengzhou Conference, Mao admitted that since September 1958, "there has been a great adventurist mistake" and "the main error within the Party is still left-leaning." He said that he should take responsibility for his mistakes and said, "The central government may say nothing, but I can say it personally. As soon as I say it, I will have no burden." He hoped to persuade his feverish comrades to calm down. After several meetings involving deliberation and discussion, the Sixth Plenary Session of the Central Committee, held from the end of November to the beginning of December 1958, adopted the Resolution on Issues in the People's Commune (hereinafter referred to as the Resolution). While highly evaluating the people's communes, the Resolution pointed out that the boundaries between collective and public ownership should not be blurred, let alone socialism and communism. Further, the people's communes were still basically economic organizations under collective ownership, and agricultural production cooperatives were transformed into people's communes, rather than moving from collective ownership to public institutes. It was impossible to succeed if the Party sought to prematurely deny the principle of distribution according to work and replace it with distribution according to need before the conditions were ripe. An overly eager transition could only promote the tendency of petty bourgeoisie equalitarianism, but was not conducive to socialist construction. Many similar issues were raised during the session.

In response to the erroneous tendency toward attempting to prematurely abolish commodity production and exchange, the Resolution pointed out that in a specific period in the future, commodity production in the people's communes, as well as commodity exchange between the state and communes and between the communes themselves, must see great development. It was not capitalism to proceed on the basis of socialist public ownership. Rather, the continued development of commodity production and maintaining the principle of distribution based on work were two major principles for the development of the socialist economy which needed to be universally recognized by the Party.

2. Solving the Problems of Ownership and Distribution Within Communes

After rectifying the people's communes and initially curbing the momentum of rash transition to public ownership and communism, Mao proceeded with the problems of ownership and distribution within the communes and further corrected the "communist" trend to rectify the tendency of equalitarianism and over-centralization within the communes. At the second Zhengzhou Conference, he stressed that the main problem of the people's communes was that they progressed too far forward in improving production relations and in the ownership of the commune. Understanding the ownership of communes also required a process of development. As soon as the commune was established, it abolished the ownership of the production team and implemented the complete ownership of the commune, and the "equal distribution of income within the commune, transfer of team or individual property without charge, and banks' taking back loans to the rural areas," which caused great panic among the farmers. This was the root cause of the tension between the Party and the farmers at that time. He emphasized that the tendency of equalitarianism denied that the incomes of production teams and individuals should be different, that is, the socialist principle of distribution-based work and higher pay for more work. The tendency toward over-centralization denied the ownership of production teams. These two tendencies included the idea of negating the value rule and equivalent exchange. Equivalent exchange was an economic law that could not be violated in the socialist period. If it were violated, it would mean possessing the fruits of other people's labor gratuitously. The Party had not yet utilized the method of depriving the national bourgeoisie without compensation. How could it then take possession of the farmers' achievements without compensation? He emphasized that only by accounting could the Party implement the objective law of value, which was a great school of thought. Only by using it could the CPC lead tens of millions of cadres and tens of thousands of people to socialism. In his speech and criticism during the meeting, Mao further pointed out that this was "left-leaning adventurism" and that the Party's main front should be against Leftism. In just a few months, the precious work of acquiring such an understanding on several basic issues concerning socialist economic construction and upholding and developing Marxism was undertaken.

Mao's opinions were accepted by the Party's senior cadres. In the Draft Provisions on the Management System of People's Communes formulated by the Second Zhengzhou Conference and the Eighteen Issues Concerning People's Communes formulated by the Shanghai Conference, it was stipulated that production teams (in some places called production brigades, roughly equivalent to the scope of former high-level communes) were the basic accounting units of the people's communes. At present, the ownership of production teams was still the main basis of communes, which smaller production teams under the production teams (called production teams in some places, roughly equivalent to the original primary communes) should also have partial ownership and management authority as contracted production units. The old accounts of transferring property in the process of communalization, which was not calculated as originally stipulated, needed to be settled. Generally speaking, all the labor, capital, and personal belongings of the production teams and the members transferred by communes was to be cleaned up and returned as full or partial compensation. In May and June 1959, an urgent directive issued by the Central Committee stipulated that rural reserved land should be restored to allow members to raise livestock and poultry, and that members should be encouraged to make full use of scattered idle land beside houses and roadsides to grow crops and trees without those being taken as public grain or included in public ownership. The Central Committee also clearly pointed out that the small private ownership in such a large collective was necessary over a long period of time, and to allow such small private ownership was actually to protect the fruits of the members' work outside the collective working time, not to "develop capitalism."

In the previous nine months, in addition to a series of important adjustments in production relations, the Central Committee had downsized some of the high indicators that could not be reached at all during the 1958 climax of the Great Leap Forward, although these measures were far from settling the problem of high indicators and were often not effectively implemented in practice.

Admittedly, the nine-month rectification of Leftism was not carried out with the intent of completely abandoning it. Mao did not believe that the fundamental guiding ideology was wrong. In his view, the general line, the Great Leap Forward, and the people's commune were absolutely right. This is what he meant by saying "the line and the spirit remain the same." He proposed "to be low key" and "to compress the air," but also "to change the indicators" and "to solve the problem of working methods" so as to make a better leap forward, and so on. On the basis of such an understanding, it was not possible to correct Leftism without many limitations, and it was also difficult to avoid various obstacles and challenges.

In particular, it should be noted that this short period of history was an important link in the process of the localization of Marxism after the founding of New China. The positive and negative experiences and lessons provided a special perspective, which was of great significance for the Party in understanding the basic characteristics and laws of the localization of Marxism under socialist conditions.

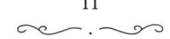

II

Investigation and Research into Rectifying the Ideological Line

1. Further Investigation and the Anti-Leftism Movement

The most important theoretical trait of Marxism was to respect the authority of practice and to stick to starting from reality and seeking truth from facts. Delving into the actual situation, investigating and researching, and correctly grasping the national conditions were the basic requirements for the integration of Marxism into China. In the course of rectifying the Leftism of the previous nine months, there was a prominent phenomenon throughout. That was, Mao and other central leaders eagerly investigated and studied deeply into the actual situation, and in fact began a new round of establishing a fresh understanding of the national conditions as a guide to correct the left-leaning errors.

If the Great Leap Forward and the people's commune movement were guided by separating themselves from the national conditions and accompanied by serious exaggeration, then the efforts to rectify Leftism were closely linked with in-depth investigation and research from the very beginning. Just as in the period of democratic revolution, Mao again advocated investigation and research in order to oppose dogmatism. From October 1958, in order to rectify Leftism, Mao once again delved into the actual situation and conducted investigation and research. In the previous nine months, Mao visited different places three times after mid-October 1958, including three trips to Henan and Hubei, two to Hebei alone, and one each to Shandong, Guangdong, Shanghai, Zhejiang, and Hunan, over a total of more than four months. In addition, he sent his staff to the grassroots level to conduct research, giving them specific, detailed guidance, in hopes that they could provide some real, reliable information about the grassroots situation. It was these in-depth investigations that gave him some real insights into the problems and their causes at the grassroots level.

On the eve of the first Zhengzhou Conference, Mao set out to inspect the situation from October 13-17. During those days, he talked to and held meetings with the secretaries of Tianjin, Hebei, Baoding Prefectural Committee, Tangxian, Zhengding, Xushui, and Anguo counties. From October 19-29, he sent four letters to Chen Boda and others, specifically arranging the contents and methods of their investigation and research in several communes in Henan Province, to "practice the methods and attitudes of investigating from the working people and to become skilled at investigation and asking questions," then to report to him. On October 26, he sent Wu Lengxi and Tian Jiaying to Xiuwu and Qiliying for investigation. On October 31, he traveled by special train past Baoding, Shijiazhuang, Handan, and Xinxiang to the south, where he talked with Party members in charge of local provincial, prefectural, municipal, and county committees and conducted investigations. After the Zhengzhou Conference, from November 11-20, he continued to conduct investigations and studies in Henan and Hebei, and he talked with cadres at all levels of provinces, prefectures, counties, and communes, as well as relevant leading comrades of the central government and cadres delegated by central organs, so as to understand all aspects of the situation. After the Sixth Plenary Session of the Eighth Central Committee in late November, he talked extensively with local comrades in charge on his way back to Hubei, Hunan, and Beijing, and continued to conduct in-depth practical investigations. From February 23-26, 1959, on the way to Zhengzhou to hold the second Zhengzhou Conference, he talked with responsible Party members in various prefectures and municipalities in Tianjin, Hebei, Shandong, and Henan. After extensive and in-depth investigation, he captured the actual situation in his theory. At the first Zhengzhou Conference, he proposed to distinguish between two kinds of public ownership and to stick to equivalent exchange. He criticized the tendency to cancel commodity production and rush ahead. At the Wuchang meeting, he said, "In our country, at present, some people are a little too enthusiastic. Besides, we are bragging too much now. I don't think it's practical. We need to sing a low-key song and cool down." He admitted that he had made a "rash" mistake, which was a real misfortune. He even said that in the past, people opposed his aggressiveness, but now he opposed others' aggressiveness. Following his opinions, the Resolution on Several Questions of the People's Commune, adopted by the Sixth Plenary Session of the Central Committee, proposed that the boundaries between collective and public ownership and between socialism and communism should be distinguished, emphasizing that "the continuing development of commodity production and the continuing maintenance of the principle of distribution based on work are two major principles for the development of the socialist economy."

At the beginning of 1959, Mao Zedong further calmed the situation. In January, he said in a conversation that "I need to observe" to see whether the general route was correct. In February, he said, "We are still at the infancy stage in economic construction [...] We should admit that, to work in the natural world on the planet earth, we just don't, or cannot, yet understand the strategy and tactics." At the second Zhengzhou Conference,' he pointed out that the "Communist wind" that had blown up after the establishment of the people's communes caused great panic among the farmers, which made the relationship between the Party and the farmers quite tense about some issues. The reason was that the Party did not discuss the law of value and went a little too far on the issue of the ownership of the commune. These analyses clarified some confused understandings and accurately grasped the crux of the people's commune system. According to his request, the meeting established the policy of rectifying and building the people's communes, forming the important summary of the Zhengzhou Conference. After the second Zhengzhou Conference, he made suggestions on several major policy issues, such as whether the basic accounting units should be placed in big or small groups, whether the old accounts should be counted, and whether the small groups should have partial ownership, so as to return the basic ownership of the commune to the scale of the former high-level or part of the primary communes.

From mid-October 1958 (less than five months before the launch of the Great Leap Forward) to early 1959, Mao worked virtually around the clock, with no time for proper meals or sleep as he rushed to make investigations and do research. On this basis, after two Zhengzhou Conferences, the Wuchang Conference, the Sixth Plenary Session of the Eighth Central Committee, the Shanghai Conference, and the Seventh Plenary Session of the Eighth Central Committee, the Party finally took a step to rectify Leftism and bring the Party's policy in line with the actual situation once again. This change was a result of Mao and the leading group of the Central Committee directly going deep into the actual situation, investigating and studying, listening to the voices of the masses, and deepening their understanding of the national conditions, which injected a strong impetus into the progress of the localization of Marxism during this period. This was similar to the adjustment in the early 1960s, which was led by a large-scale investigation and research conducted by the Party.

2. Prerequisites for Investigation and Research

In-depth investigation and research was the premise and foundation for rectifying Leftism. However, could it be said that when correcting the left-leaning problem, an investigation was carried out, and when making the left-leaning mistake, no investigation was made? No. In fact, in the course of launching the Great Leap Forward and the people's commune movement, Mao had also gone deep into factories and the countryside to familiarize himself with the on-the-ground situation. He repeatedly emphasized that central and provincial leading cadres should go outside the organs for several months a year and should work as ordinary laborers, "go the distance," and treat the masses with equality so as to understand the actual situation. However, this investigation did not guarantee Mao's understanding of the real situation. Instead, it led him to make the determination and draw conclusions such as catching up with Britain in "only two to three years" (June 22, 1958), "more food provided on a supply system at no charge" (August, 1958), steel production "doubling dramatically, without delay" (August, 1958), and so on. Apparently, advocating or conducting investigations did not guarantee an understanding of the national conditions or obtain the practical basis for the localization of Marxism in China. Without investigation, one had no right to speak. Only through investigation and research could one accurately grasp the national conditions. This worked in terms of general laws, principles, and methods. However, for a specific historical period and for an individual, the investigation and research may not guarantee the understanding of the national conditions. In addition to the limitations of subjective and objective conditions such as the stage of development, the degree of exposure to problems, and the amount of experience accumulated, there were other factors that led to such a "failure in investigation." For example, starting from a strong subjective desire and some dogmatic or empiricist formulas, the Party attached more importance to facts or opinions that conformed to its own views, hoping to investigate and verify its existing understanding. It could not accept the conclusions obtained by other people's surveys that were different from its own. In addition, there were some deep reasons that could not be avoided. For example, in the context of the expansion of the anti-Rightist movement and the escalation of criticism of Zhou Enlai and other "anti-rash advances," the expansion of class struggle seriously harmed democracy inside and outside the Party, and the "one dominating voice" within the Party began to take shape. Even the truth became a "scarce resource," and telling the truth required the Chairman of the Central Committee to ask how the quality of the survey would be guaranteed, and who would decide whether the survey results were correct. For example, the nine-month rectification of Leftism or the large-scale investigation and research conducted by the whole Party in 1961 were carried out on the premise that Mao had some understanding of left-leaning errors, and his attitude was relaxed. But what if his attitude had not been relaxed? These questions needed to be clearly thought through.

It can be said that because that the Party was in power, the important question was not whether to investigate and research, but whether to investigate and research scientifically and effectively and whether to put good intentions into practice. In order to truly realize these good intentions and grasp China's reality, it was important to investigate and study several important conditions.

III

Specific Marxist Principles as the Guideline for Practice

1. Reading and What to Read

In addition to investigation and research, another basic element of the localization of Marxism in China lay in upholding the stand, viewpoint, and method of Marxism. There was no doubt or controversy about this point in socialist countries or in proletarian political parties. But then another equally important question arose, which was what kind of Marxism China should adhere to, and how to ensure the correct understanding, grasp, and application of Marxism. In order to solve this problem, it was necessary to pay special attention to what was called Marxism, among other conditions, which must have the characteristics of modernity. This was the same as asking why the new democracy became a successful example of China's localization efforts, which included Mao grasping the characteristics of China from the perspective of "contemporary" Marxism. Without this, the task of "Sinicization" would not be carried out.

In the course of rectifying the left-leaning errors over the previous nine months, alongside a series of practical and effective investigations and studies, there was a prominent phenomenon. After the initial rectification of Leftism began at the end of 1958, Mao urgently asked at a series of important meetings that the leading cadres of the Party read books "in connection with the socialist economic revolution and construction of China" to "get a clear view to guide our great economic work." He believed that "during the Great Leap Forward and the people's commune period, reading such books was the most interesting" and "could clarify a lot of confused ideas."[2] At the beginning of the Lushan Conference in 1959, among the nineteen agenda items drawn up by Mao, the first was reading. On July 2, he said at the opening ceremony that, in view of the fact that the previous year, many leading comrades did not know much about the socialist economic problems and did not understand the laws of economic development, and that there was still a measure of transactionalism in their work, they should study hard armed "with last year's practice, and remember that it is better to read more."

One more thing worth noting was that Mao put special emphasis on the contents to be studied by leading cadres at all levels in the Party, which were the three important works, *Socialist Economic Problems of the Soviet Union*, *Communist Society in the Theories of Marx, Engles, Lenin, and Stalin* and *Socialist Political Economy of the Soviet Union* (textbook). This contrasted with his repeated emphasis on eliminating superstition, emancipating the mind, and overthrowing dogmatism in launching the Great Leap Forward, and his repeated recommendation of reading "The Theories of Marx, Engels, Lenin, and Stalin on Communist Society." The change in what to read directly reflected the change of guiding ideology from left-leaning to left-leaning rectification, reflecting what kind of Marxism was used to guide practice and what kind of attitude was applied to Marxism.

2. Implementing the General Line of the Transitional Period and Learning the History of the Soviet Communist Party (Bolshevik)

As mentioned in Chapter 3 of this volume, the Party put forward the general line for the transitional period in 1953, from the implementation of the New Democracy Outline for the Founding of the People's Republic to the socialist transformation and the construction of the First Five Year Plan with the Soviet model as its standard and objective. At the behest of the Central Committee, the Party initiated within its scope a surge in study of *The History of the Soviet Communist Party (Bolshevik)* (Chapter 9–10) and *Soviet Socialist Economic Issues*. The relevant chapters of the *Concise Course on the History of the Soviet Communist Party (Bolshevik)*, written in 1938, systematically discussed the history and experience of the Communist Party of the Soviet Union in leading the people to restore the national economy, industrialization, and agricultural collectivization, and emphasized the significance of giving priority to the development of heavy industry and realizing socialist industrialization. It was a classic summary of the system of the Stalinist model. In *Socialist Economic Problems of the Soviet Union*, published in 1952, Stalin systematically discussed some basic laws in socialist economic work based on the experience of socialist construction in the Soviet Union. Although these understandings were inevitably limited by the times, they were developed in comparison with the Soviet model in the 1930s and the relevant discussions in *History of the Soviet Communist Party (Bolshevik)*. They should be regarded as an important achievement in the process of the modernization of Marxism, which was highly praised by the Chinese Communists at that time. "Stalin left us works such as *Socialist Economic Problems of the Soviet Union* and his speech at the Nineteenth Congress of the Communist Party of the Soviet Union, which creatively enriched and developed Marxism-Leninism and gave us a brand new and extremely sharp theoretical weapon [...] We must also work harder to study Stalinist theory," so that "we can really become good students of Stalin."[3] In the initial stage of industrialization, the basic theory the CPC followed was Stalin's theory, which meant, in Mao's words, "the direction and the content remain unchanged."

After 1956, with the completion of the three major reforms, and especially after the Twentieth National Congress of the Soviet Communist Party and the subsequent events in Bosnia and Hungary, Mao and the Central Committee of the Communist Party of China clearly felt the drawbacks of the Soviet model and the need for its reform. They proposed that the Party should act in accordance with the actual situation and not be bound by the existing practices of the Soviet Union, so as to set the path of socialist construction with Chinese characteristics. When Mao wrote *On Ten Relations*, the idea of "learning lessons from the Soviet Union" was clearer. Mao stressed, "In the past, we took less detours due to their experience and lessons. Now, we should definitely take their experience as a warning." He noted, "What we want to learn is the universal truth, and learning must be combined with the actual situation in China. It is impossible to duplicate every sentence someone says, including Marx. Our theory centers on the combination of the universal truth of Marxism-Leninism and the concrete practice of the Chinese revolution."[4] He later said, "The first eight years have been duplicating foreign experience. But since 1956, when the ten major relations were put forward, we began to find our own route suitable for China."[5] However, finding the limitations of the Soviet model and opposing dogmatism in the Soviet experience only constituted the first step in exploring the right path. Whether the Party would find the right path for China depended on how the second step was made.

3. Launching the Great Leap Forward and Reading the Theories of Marx, Engels, Lenin, and Stalin on Communist Society

In the process of preparing and launching the Great Leap Forward, Mao repeatedly criticized right-leaning conservatism, stressed that superstition should be broken, and opposed dogmatism and blindness in studying the Soviet Union. The themes of his four speeches at the Second Session of the Eighth National Congress were to break down superstitions, emancipate the mind, and to dare to think, speak, and act. He believed that much of what the Party had done and practiced had surpassed Marx, so all superstitions had to be broken, "not fearing scholars, and not fearing Marx."[6] He believed that after the rectification campaign against the Rightist and the great victory on the political and ideological fronts, there would inevitably be a climax of economic construction. The Great Leap Forward and the people's commune movement were attempts to break through the Soviet model in terms of the speed of construction and the transitional period. In this context, the *Socialist Economic Problems of the Soviet Union* seemed to have been neglected for a time, because its main contents (such as commodities, the law of value, "planned, proportionate development," "technology deciding everything," and "cadres deciding everything") could not be done precisely according to the development of classical theory based on practice. The Great Leap Forward and the more extreme radicalization of the people's communes provided a theoretical basis.

With the encouragement of emancipating the mind and eliminating superstition, and the ever-rising situation of leaping forward and the surge of a rash transition, Lenin's new economic policy did not align with reality. To varying degrees, the Stalinist model, which had some defects, such as the Great Leap Forward and the people's communes movement and a "rash transition," was no longer mentioned. China seemed to suddenly find itself in some kind of "mode vacuum" or "theory vacuum." Against the background of the general simplification and idealization of socialism and communism in the socialist countries at that time, with the inspiration of the experience of the war years, the early descriptions of the future society by classical writers resonated with the leadership of the Party. In February and March 1958, Mao Zedong mentioned in a conversation that the integration of the township and community would be the foundation of communism, governing everything, including industry, agriculture, commerce, education, and military work.[7] In April 1958, when Liu Shaoqi and Zhou Enlai talked about the new rural grassroots organizational structure, they talked about communes, utopia, utopian socialism, and the transition to communism. They were asked to compile two books, *Utopian Socialism* and *The Theories of Marx, Engels, Lenin, and Stalin on Communist Society*. In June, *The Theories of Marx, Engels, Lenin, and Stalin on Communist Society* was compiled. The first sentence in the preface of this book stated, "In the situation of the Great Leap Forward of socialist construction in our country, which is the equivalent of twenty years in a single day, people cannot help but care about how our country will gradually transit from socialism to a communist society."[8] It went on, "The early descriptions of the communist society by some of the classical writers compiled in this book have become the theoretical basis and spiritual motivation for the eager transition, the first and second steps. For example, the first quotation listed in this book is Engels' speeches on communist society in his 1845 Speeches in Elberfeld. Two of them refer to the grassroots organizations of communist society called communes." Similar arguments seemed to have contributed greatly to Mao's final decision to call the newly merged community the people's commune. Another example was to copy Marx's exposition of "bourgeois legal power" to demonstrate the significance of implementing the supply system, narrowing down or even eliminating various differences, to copy the classical writers' assertion that "one day equals twenty years" in the revolutionary period as a basis for estimating the speed of productivity development in the socialist period, and to take many things that classical writers said as a basis for estimating the speed of productivity development in the socialist period. Primarily, it was a judgment carried out in the military, which served as the basis for the militarized management of the people's communes, and so on. In August, at the Beidaihe Conference, which launched the people's commune movement, Mao recommended the book to the General Assembly for publication and wide dissemination in order to provide a theoretical basis for the transition to communism.[9] He thought the book was inspiring, but it was quite inadequate. Many words were vague because they lacked experience at that time.[10] It seemed logical to call for the study of such a book when it was believed that "the realization of communism in our country is no longer something in the distant future."[11]

In an atmosphere of opposition to dogmatism and eagerness for transition, the Party directly applied some of the early expositions of classical writers, without considering the great differences and changes in times and national conditions. In fact, it used the dogmatism of classical writers to replace dogmatism of the *History of the Soviet Communist Party (Bolshevik)* and Stalin's *Socialist Economic Problems of the Soviet Union*. Some more traditional conclusions served as the basis for transcending and replacing the outdated Soviet model, thus seeking a theoretical basis for extreme practices such as the Great Leap Forward. From the perspective of the history of Marxist development, the process of launching the Great Leap Forward and the people's commune movement was to take dogmatism as the intermediary and replace the process of modernization with traditionalization.

4. Two Books Focused on Learning in the Nine-month Rectification of Leftism

After the left-leaning rectification began in November 1958, Mao's attention to the content for study changed significantly from the previous few months' call for reading books on communism. During the preparation and convening of the first Zhengzhou Conference, what he carefully discussed and repeatedly called on the whole Party to study earnestly was Stalin's *Socialist Economic Problems of the Soviet Union*. "To study the nature of communes and exchange, the transition from socialism to communism and from collective to public ownership, we can refer to Stalin's *Socialist Economic Issues of the Soviet Union*." He added "Now we must look at it differently than when it was published. At the time of its publication, none of us thought of these questions."[12]

On November 9, in order to clarify the ideological confusion in the Great Leap Forward, in his famous "Suggestions on Reading," Mao asked the members of the Party committees at the central, provincial, municipal, autonomous region, prefectural, and county levels to carefully read Stalin's two books, *Socialist Economic Issues of the Soviet Union* and *Marxist Theory of Communist Society*, reading each three times. In the future, they were to continue to read *The Textbook on Soviet Political Economy*. "We should read these two books in connection with China's socialist economic revolution and construction so that we can get a clear view to guide our great economic work. Now many people have numerous confused ideas, and reading these two books will help to clarify them [...] In the period of the Great Leap Forward and the people's commune movement, reading such books is the most interesting."[13]

On November 9-10, when explaining the first, second, and third chapters[14] of the book to the Party members attending the first Zhengzhou Conference, Mao said, "We were not interested when we read them earlier on, but now things are different. There are many noteworthy things in these three chapters."[15] He also said, "The book should be read from beginning to end. It should be read chapter by chapter, then discussed."[16] He focused on Chapter 2 and the "commodity economy" and "the attempts to copy Stalin and continue to persuade some comrades."[17] In response to the words and deeds related to abolishing commodities and the rush for transition prevalent during the Great Leap Forward movement, he repeatedly quoted and developed Stalin's expositions on commodities, emphasizing that "socialist commodity production and exchange have a positive role to play."[18] He pointed out that "commodity production should not be confused with capitalism. Why are we afraid of commodity production?"[19] He repeatedly criticized the tendency to blur the boundaries between collective and public ownership. On November 13, he also suggested discussing the first, second, and third chapters of Stalin's "Opinion on the Soviet Union's Economic Issues" in order to "make mental preparations for the Wuhan Conference (expanded meeting of the Politburo)."[20] At the Sixth Plenary Session of the Party Central Committee, he called for "the study of economic theory in the light of reality for our cause," adding that, "at present, study of this issue is of great theoretical and practical significance."[21]

This period of intense and in-depth reading had an important impact on Mao Zedong. During the first Zhengzhou Conference, he revised the two important documents, "Forty Articles of Socialist Construction Outline Over Fifteen Years (1958-1972)" and "Resolutions of the Zhengzhou Conference on Several Issues Related to the People's Communes." He discussed what socialism was, what socialism had built, and the two ownership relations in socialism. This understanding basically reflected the thinking of *Socialist Economic Problems of the Soviet Union*.[22] In response to the trend of contempt toward planning and balance in the Great Leap Forward, Mao called Stalin's "law of planned development of the national economy" an "objective law" in his reading commentaries and asked, "Have we studied, mastered, and learned to apply this objective law skillfully? Have our plans reflected this objective law?"[23]

Unlike the classical writers' exposition of communism, *Soviet Socialist Economic Issues* was written on the basis of a certain practice of socialist construction and made some important developments in the traditional viewpoints of the

1930s. Although it still belonged to the traditional socialist model in general, its discourse on the socialist economy had gone far beyond the general description of the future society by the classical writers. Just as copying some of the expositions in *The Theories of Marx, Engels, Lenin, and Stalin on Communist Society* became a theoretical weapon for a more rapid transition, Stalin's book became an important theoretical weapon for Mao Zedong to correct left-leaning mistakes and unify the Party's ideology, that is, "to use Stalin, a dead man, to repress living ones."[24] The change in the focus of reading reflected in a sense the trend of returning from extreme behaviors such as the Great Leap Forward to the traditional Stalinist model, and also the desire to replace the mere duplication of classical Marxism with a relatively contemporary Marxism.

In the first half of 1959, with the deepening of the left-leaning rectification, on the basis of studying Stalin's works, Mao Zedong shifted the focus of his study to the third edition of the *Textbook on the Soviet Union's Political Economy* (Volume 2). Earlier, on November 20, 1958, Mao Zedong proposed that the "Important Revision and Supplement of the Third Edition of the *Textbook on the Soviet Union's Political Economy*," compiled by the Ministry of Philosophy and Social Sciences of the Chinese Academy of Sciences and published in the internal journal of the Ministry of Publicity, be printed and distributed to attendees of the Wuchang Conference.[25] The next day, he put forward that "we should read textbooks on the political economy" and "we should look at the socialist part first."[26] In June 1959, he ordered that textbooks be published in large print and distributed to leading comrades at the central and provincial levels. On July 2, he convened a meeting of some central leaders and directors of various cooperative districts and said that in view of the fact that many leading comrades did not know much about socialist economic issues or understand the law of economic development, and that there was still much mere practicality in their work, they should study hard. "Members of the central, provincial, municipal, and prefectural committees, including county Party secretaries, should read the *Textbook on the Soviet Union's Political Economy* (third edition)."[27] On July 3, Mao Zedong put as the first item in the list of the "Lushan Conference issues to discuss" reading by "senior cadres of the second volume of the *Textbook on the Political Economy* (third edition)." He noted, "Everyone, from the Central Committee to the Secretary of the County Committee, should read it."[28] On August 15, Mao also suggested that the central leading comrades read *The Soviet Union's Philosophical Dictionary* (third edition)[29] and the third edition of the *Textbook on the Political Economy*. Mao hoped that cadres at all levels of the Party would, in connection with the practice of the Great Leap Forward, study the economic theory of the Soviet Union's socialism in the mid-1950s and earnestly sum up their experience in correcting the left-leaning mistakes. Although the Lushan Conference reversed from rectifying Leftism to opposing the right, from the winter of 1959 to the beginning of 1960, Liu Shaoqi, Mao Zedong, Zhou Enlai, and other central leaders formed reading groups, carefully scouring the second volume of *Textbook on the Political Economy* (third edition) and holding several important discussions on what they read.

The third edition of *The Textbook on the Political Economy*, published in October 1958, was still generally in the Stalinist mode, but it also reflected to a certain extent the results of the initial reform of the Soviet Union after Stalin's death, and it deepened the understanding of what socialism was. Compared with the first edition of *The Textbook on the Political Economy* compiled by following Stalin's *Socialist Economic Problems of the Soviet Union*, it had been revised more, and the most amended and supplemented part was the socialist mode of production. It contained new expressions of the basic laws of the socialist economy, the law of planned and proportionate development of the national economy, the law of commodity production and value, and material encouragement. For example, in the discussion on the necessity of commodity production under socialist conditions, the third edition highlighted that the exchange of products between different owners must take the form of buying and selling commodities. Given the previous view that the means of production circulated within the state ownership system were not commodities, the third edition held that although such circulation did not change owners, it was still a commodity. As for the law of value under socialist conditions, the first and second editions mainly discussed the restriction and the third edition mainly discussed the utilization. When talking about economic accounting, the third edition emphasized its significance to collective farms, which had not been previously highlighted, and the principles of "material rewards" and "distribution based on work." The third edition was more important, and it was obviously different from the first two. For example, unlike the first and second editions, the third edition emphasized the role of the law of value and material interests under socialist conditions. These new viewpoints reflected the deepening of the understanding of socialist issues and should be considered an effort and achievement of the modernization of Marxism. In fact, after Stalin's death, the Party had gradually faced two Soviet models. One was the model of the Soviet Union that ended in 1953, and for which *The History of the Communist Party of the Soviet Union (Bolshevik)*, and especially the *Socialist Economic Issues of the Soviet Union*, could serve as a representative. The other was the model of the Soviet Union that had been constantly revised and reformed since then, and for which the first edition of the textbook could serve as a representative.

5. Talk on Mao Zedong and Liu Shaoqi's Reading of *The Soviet Textbook on the Political Economy*

Mao Zedong's talk on reading textbooks involved economic, philosophical, political, historical, international, and other issues. Based on his own experience and knowledge, he understood and elucidated some viewpoints in the textbooks, especially after misjudging Peng Dehuai at the Lushan Conference. Mao accepted some of the ideas in the textbook, strengthened some, and negated some. In these, there was not only a new understanding of the law of socialist construction, but also an adherence to or even development of the traditional Stalinist model. Some of his remarks broke through the traditional model. For example, in his understanding of the historical stage of socialism, Mao believed that socialism could and would be divided into stages. In particular, he put forward the viewpoint of "underdeveloped socialism" and "relatively developed socialism," which was a new and important methodology for the theory of socialist stages at that time, which developed the Party's understanding of the long-term nature of socialism. In order to achieve the goal of socialist modernization in China, he put forward that "building socialism originally required industrial, agricultural, scientific, and cultural modernization, but now it is necessary to add national defense modernization" and stressed that China must establish an independent and complete industrial system. In response to the rashness to transition to communism at that time, he stressed that it was an arduous task to complete socialist construction in China, and that the Party "should not build socialism too early." He proposed that under the condition of giving priority to the development of heavy industry, several measures should be taken simultaneously. Mao pointed out that those who advocated the abolition of commodities and the elimination of commodity production did not distinguish the essential differences between socialist commodity production and capitalist commodity production, nor did they understand the importance of utilizing commodity production under the socialist system. He also believed that the means of production could be commodities. He agreed with Stalin that commodity production was linked to certain economic conditions. He emphasized that workers should directly manage the country and achieve equality between workers and managers and between cadres and the masses. He also agreed with the main points in the book about the law of socialist economy, the speed of industrialization, the commodity economy, and so on.

On the other hand, some of the conversations reflected that he had not yet stepped out of the craze caused by the Great Leap Forward. For example, he still insisted on a high appraisal of the Great Leap Forward and the people's commune movement as the best form of the transition to communism. He also affirmed that the private concept of contracting production to households was the resistance of a part of the wealthy middle peasants to the people's communization, and he expressed dissatisfaction with the change of the Great Leap Forward to the Great Development in the third edition of textbooks, and hoped to find the basis for the Great Leap Forward and the people's commune movement from textbooks. He appreciated the idea that "poverty is the driving force," thinking that it was not good to be rich, and he agreed with the textbooks that socialism was not an independent and fixed social and economic form, but was a transition to communism. He talked more about the necessity of transition. In fact, like other socialist countries at that time, he did not realize the long-term nature of the socialist stage. In terms of the motive force of socialist development, on several occasions, he criticized textbooks for failing to recognize that social contradictions were the motive force of socialist development, while he appreciated the statement that the main economic contradiction in the transitional period mentioned in various textbooks was that seen between socialism and capitalism. He highly valued the previous supply system and criticized textbooks for overemphasizing material interests, and he criticized textbooks for exaggerating the role of the law of value and believed that the law of value could not be taken as the main basis for planning work, because "the Great Leap Forward was not carried out according to the requirements of the law of value."[30] He embraced numerous ideas of this sort. In fact, such comments fell behind the standard of *Socialist Economic Problems of the Soviet Union*. Some of the ideas reflected that his evaluation of the textbooks was lower than his view of this volume. Between the two, he tended to stick to the traditional Stalinist model and criticize the new viewpoints of the textbooks.

This was more evident in his systematic reading after the Lushan Conference. He believed that the textbook "has serious shortcomings and principled errors," such as "deleting some of Stalin's good points and adding the negative ideas of the Twentieth Congress, which is a great step backwards." He added that "it can be considered a book of Marxism with serious errors."[31] In particular, the criticism of material rewards throughout the conversation reflected Mao's attitude toward the reform of socialist countries at that time. "In this book, some basic ideas are wrong. The book does not emphasize political leadership, the mass line, or two-pronged progress, but puts emphasis on personal material interests and promotes material incentives." These ideas, which were often expressed in budding form when reading the textbooks, developed further in the 1960s, when class struggle expanded and the debate against revisionism started, and developed into a complete theoretical form in the "theoretical instructions" of 1975.

Liu Shaoqi also made some important comments in his speech on reading textbooks. Many of them shared Mao's views, but there were many important and unique views as well. For example, in terms of the motive of socialist development, his view remained somewhat in line with the correct conclusion of the Eighth Congress resolutions. He believed that the contradiction between socialism and capitalism was still fierce, but would gradually decrease in the future. He noted, "The contradiction between production and demand (including production and life) promotes social development."[32] On the issue of the dictatorship of the proletariat, he believed that from the perspective of the trend of the development of state functions, the role of dictatorship in China was becoming smaller, "and the function of organizing and educating the masses will still exist in ten thousand years."[33] On the issue of ownership, he proposed that attention should be paid to solving the contradictions within the ownership system, saying, "Under the socialist public ownership, there is huge space for development, and constantly adjusting the internal relations can help productivity develop better." On the issue of distribution based on work, he believed that "material stimulation is still necessary, but we cannot rely on it alone," and so on.[34]

From imitating the Soviet model in 1953 to breaking through the model in 1956, then to the return to the classics in the Great Leap Forward, and later to rereading *The Soviet Socialist Economic Issues* when correcting left-leaning errors and returning to the Stalinist model, and finally to the choices and judgments made when reading the third edition of the textbook, the specific point of view of reading reflected, to some extent, that in a short period of time, Mao and other central leaders had experienced the choice of three modes (classical mode, Stalinist mode, and the Soviet mode with some traits of reform, although the latter two modes were not very different), and the process of identifying, breaking through, and returning to the Stalinist mode. In spite of the complicated forms, given the relationship with the traditional model, the CPC only touched the branches and leaves, but the trunk was not or could not be touched. As Mao said, "The principles are the same as those of the Soviet Union, but the methods are different."[35] Between the two Soviet models, the CPC preferred the former Stalinist model, while between traditional Marxism and the Marxism in the process of modernization, it seemed to prefer the former. On the surface, practices such as the Great Leap Forward were a breakthrough in the Soviet model, seemingly more radical, but in fact also more retrogressive than the original model, especially in relation to the reforms that had already begun.

Whether launching the Great Leap Forward and nine-month rectification of the left-leaning errors, the call and action of studying Marxism ran through all these projects. But practice proved that it was not enough to call on or study Marxism in general, and that it was difficult to avoid dogmatism, pragmatism, and formalism. What was more important was what kind of attitude one should take towards Marxism, how to advance the modernization of Marxism with the times, and how to combine contemporary Marxism with China's actual situation so as to realize the integration of Marxism into China under the new historical conditions.

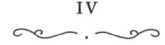

IV

Democratization and the Localization of Marxism in China

1. Interruption of Democratization and the Reversal of Anti-Leftism

In mid- and late July 1959, the work of rectifying the left-leaning tendency, which was improving, came to an abrupt end in the latter half of the Lushan Conference. The subsequent anti-Rightist movement not only brought about serious political and economic consequences, but also hindered the process of the localization of Marxism, which had just begun to improve in the nine-month rectification of the left-leaning tendency. This reversal attracted researchers' attention for a long period because it happened at a time when they had some understanding of the Great Leap Forward, the mistakes of the people's commune movement, the deepening of their understanding of the situation, and the progress of their understanding of the modernization of Marxism. As far as the entire Party was concerned, their understanding had developed and problems had been noticed. However, things moved constantly backwards as new situations occurred, which happened several times in the 1950s and 1960s.

For example, when summing up the lessons of the Great Leap Forward in the early 1960s, Mao had already felt quite profoundly that the lack of democracy inside and outside the Party was an important factor that could not be avoided. So at the beginning of his speech at the Seven Thousand People's Congress, he said, "The central point is to talk about a problem of democratic centralism," emphasizing that "we should have a full democratic life both inside and outside the Party."[36] But this strong desire had not changed the deterioration of democratic life inside and outside the Party since that time. In another instance, in May 1963, Mao added a note concerning "where the correct thought of man comes from" in the guiding principle document, The First Ten Articles, emphasizing that the correct thought of man can only come from social practice. Even so, this did not prevent the Four Clearance Movement from repeatedly miscalculating the class struggle. As a final example, in the Cultural Revolution, Mao repeatedly called on the Party and the entire country to study the works of Marxism and Leninism, but the basic principles of Marxism were distorted to an unprecedented degree during that decade. Although there were some historical limitations and accidental factors, the most fundamental reason lay in the lack of democracy inside and outside the Party and the drawbacks of the national political system. Here, another basic element of the localization of Marxism – the institutional factor – was introduced. Moreover, the Lushan Conference proved that under socialist conditions, institutional factors seemed to play a more important role than the previous two factors.

Just as the first historic leap in the localization of Marxism in the period of democratic revolution was built on the premise of weakening or even eliminating the Comintern's highly centralized "blind command" of China and achieving a certain "democratic right" of independent thinking,[37] under the socialist conditions, the localization of Marxism was bound to be broad and extensive. Extensive democracy inside and outside the Party, linked with ideological emancipation and theoretical innovation, would inevitably rely more directly on China's democratization process. For the innovation and development of Marxism, democracy was as indispensable as water and air. Moreover, such democracy must be an internal democracy in a system based on relatively developed productivity and a market economy, not just a democracy in style.

The Great Leap Forward, the people's commune movement, and the reversal of the Lushan Conference were the first results of the destruction of the Party's collective leadership principle and democratic centralism, and the frustration of China's democratization process. Once democracy became a scarce thing, it was not only impossible to talk about the second leap, but also became even more valuable to tell the truth. In the course of correcting the left-leaning movement of the previous nine months, Mao was more aware of the problems among cadres who did not dare truthfully reflect on the situation to their superiors or put forward different opinions. In early April 1959, at the Eighth Plenary Session of the Seventh Central Committee, he called on leaders to learn from Hai Rui to tell the truth. He even said that CPC members were nowhere near as brave as Hai Rui.[38] In the same month, he wrote "Intra-Party Communications" directly to cadres at all levels from the provincial level down to the production teams, emphasizing the issue of telling the truth, saying, "Honest people, those who dare to tell the truth, in the final analysis, are beneficial to the people's industry and do not suffer losses themselves," and pointed out that "it should be said that there are many falsehoods pressed down from above."[39] After that, Liu Shaoqi and other leading comrades of the Central Committee also focused on this issue in summing up their experience, saying, "In recent years, democratic centralism has been greatly weakened in the life of our Party and our country, and in some places it has been practically destroyed."[40] And, "speaking according to the intention of the leaders and providing information based on what the leaders prefer – this situation is probably quite common and has become a popular style in many places."[41] Further, they noted that "life inside the Party has been abnormal in recent years. It's a very dangerous trend for people to 'tell the partial but not the whole truth.'"[42] The Five Tendencies,[43] which had become more intense and could not be cured for some time, were only the external manifestations of a systemic disease strengthened by the anti-Rightists and anti-Rightist expansion.

2. Drawbacks of the Traditional System Hinder the Localization of Marxism

It was generally believed that the traditional Stalinist model had several basic characteristics. The first was a highly centralized power structure and decision-making system of one party in power. Second, there was no distinction between Party and government, and no distinction between government and enterprise. Third, there was direct operation and management of enterprises by the party and the state through state power and administrative orders, regulating economic operations and allocating social resources. The fourth was the single public ownership structure and directive planned economy system that basically excluded any market mechanism. Finally, it involved a huge, omnipotent, top-down hierarchical authorized leadership system, and a leading official ideology and strict Party organization with strong mobilization ability and with Marxism as the core. In the early stage of socialism, this mobilization system, which emphasized unity, obedience, consistency, solidarity, and political and spiritual mobilization, had strong social mobilization functions and resource allocation abilities. It had effectively promoted economic recovery and productivity development and accomplished the mission of the early stage of industrialization, although at considerable cost.

This classical socialist system caused its own unique problems, which was even more obvious in the case of lagging reform. The blind pursuit of the degree of public ownership of the means of production made the unclear entity of property rights more prominent. In fact, it often made officials at all levels become an entity of property rights at different levels, and the vagueness of the source of power caused the people's rights not to be respected. The system structure gave government agents at all levels obvious advantages over other social groups in the decision-making process, making the leadership at the core of the system supreme in the decision-making system, which inevitably led to the formation of various forms of "one domineering voice." While creating material wealth, the planned economy was constantly reproducing the authority of the superior to the subordinate and the latter's obedience to the former. The hierarchical appointment system made officials at all levels pay more attention to their responsibility to their superiors and their preferences and intentions, so that the former would collect and process information according to their superiors' intentions and preferences, which became a stubborn disease. The highly centralized system greatly limited the Party's ability to reflect the situation from bottom up and its supervision, reducing the masses' enthusiasm for participation and making it better at rapid decision-making and effective implementation, though still lacking a timely and effective self-regulation ability and error-correcting mechanism. The scope of planning often went beyond the economic field to extensively permeate the political, ideological, and even private space, which made it difficult for a society that had been lacking vitality due to the weakening of the commodity economy to follow and gain the motivation to "activate." Moreover, the centralization and hierarchy inherent in the traditional system not only easily resonated with the hierarchy in some pre-capitalist societies and derived personal worship, but was also further strengthened under the conditions of the threat of war, economic difficulties, and the expansion of class struggle.

In brief, while this highly centralized and unified system demonstrated its huge institutional advantages and performance, there were institutional weaknesses, such as a low degree of democratization, inadequate participation of the masses, and a lack of vitality in society, which weakened the drive and ability in theoretical innovation. Just as it was impossible to imagine a decentralized political system and a pluralistic ideological system under a highly centralized planned economy, it was impossible to imagine that such a system could provide ample space for academic contention, independent thinking, equal discussion, and open thinking. Further, just as it was difficult to cultivate the modern concept of equality in the hierarchical obedience system, this system could not get rid of the chronic illness of adjudicating academic disputes by administrative power and judging the truth by status, thus making theoretical innovation the patent and privilege of leaders, and making "leader-orientation" the intrinsic compulsory requirement of the system and dampening people's enthusiasm for theoretical thinking. In the traditional system, under the condition of weakening economic leverage and shrinking the commodity economy and of economic development while reform lagged behind, if the Party made a wrong judgment in relation to the class struggle in the socialist period, the subjectivity and compulsion of the system would be more prominent. Further, the compulsory political and administrative means of the economy would be strengthened, and the role of ideology would expand and its uniqueness, absoluteness, and mandatory features would be more obvious. Such institutional defects seriously hampered the development of Marxism and weakened the motive of theoretical innovation. They were far from meeting the necessary conditions for the localization and nationalization of Marxism. This was the deeper reason that dogmatism prevailed in all socialist countries after the war, and that stereotypes, empty words, and formalism overflowed. It was also the deeper reason that the modernization and nationalization of Marxism were so difficult, and why the second leap of the localization of Marxism was not realized between 1949 and 1978.

This system defect was not man-made, but a common problem with regularity in the socialist construction of backward countries. It could only be explained by the backward productivity and social development level once power had been seized, the radical political revolutionary tradition, the severe international situation during the Cold War, and the catch-up strategy of backward countries in the early stage of industrialization. It could not be abstractly criticized without considering historical conditions, let alone resorting to the criticism of pan-moralism. The history of modernization in the world showed that, unlike developed countries, non-economic factors such as politics and ideology had to be prioritized over economic factors as the initiating factors of modernization in backward countries. The country's political system and ideology played a leading role in the early stage of development. The country solved various problems in the early stage of industrialization through different degrees of political and economic concentration. This choice of political-economic system was determined by the conditions of the times and the domestic environment. Generally speaking, any country that experienced a long-term revolution or war and had a vast territory would have a higher demand for the centralization of political power. The more backward the country before the revolution, the more powerful political authority and domination would need to be in the process of industrialization, and the strategy of catching up at a faster rate and the priority of heavy industry would be pursued.[44]

After the fierce political revolution, China, being a backward eastern power, relied on the socialist system, took the highly centralized power as a mighty lever to promote social and economic transformation and development, and accelerated its social transformation and development through the planned economy rather than the market economy. Facing a severe international situation, China encountered a serious challenge. The choice of the above-mentioned system had its historical inevitability and rationality, and it was a historical progress to start the rapid march of modernization in the Cold War environment. Here, there was not only the following of traditional socialist theory and ideology, but also the very realistic economic considerations of non-ideology. It was like the post-war era when "even western market economies realize that a strong government is needed to restore their economies. Even countries that have always advocated liberalism tend to adopt economic policies that were previously labelled as 'socialism' and planned by the state." Even some active supporters of economic liberalism became enthusiastic supporters of the planned economy, although they were still enemies of socialism.[45] China's subsequent failures were not mainly due to the choice of this model in the early days of the founding of New China, nor to the failure to put forward the task of reform in a timely manner, but to the deviation of direction when the Party was eager for reform and, under the influence of various complex factors, to regard a more rigid model than Stalin's as the development and improvement of contemporary Marxism.

The centralized planning system adapted to the needs of the development of productive forces at that time, but it could not provide a mature democracy rooted in the full development of the commodity economy and the relative development of the market economy in a short time. The restrictions imposed by this institutional feature on emancipating the mind, theoretical innovation, and the localization of Marxism in China were not compensated for by the general call for the development of a democratic style of work. Moreover, just as the economic development of backward countries could not be achieved overnight, the transition from a traditional system to a modern democratic system was not achievable in the short term. In this way, the Party faced a dilemma. The localization of Marxism had to rely on the development of socialist democratization to a certain extent, but this democratization was faltering due to the defects of the system and the expansion of class struggle. As an example, the previous nine months of left-leaning rectification ended at the Lushan Conference. This contradiction not only explained to a considerable extent the reason the second leap in the localization of Marxism was not completed between 1949 and 1978, but also pointed out that the realization of the "second leap" could only depend on the reform of China and the development of democracy inside and outside the Party.

From the first Zhengzhou Conference to the early Lushan Conference in 1959, after nearly nine months of intensive efforts, the serious consequences of the Great Leap Forward were initially curbed and the situation began to change for the better. During this period, the leading comrades of the Central Committee went deep into practice, investigated and studied some works of Marxism, and put forward some correct theoretical views and policy ideas, which had important long-term significance. But at that time, Mao and the majority of the Party still lacked a clear understanding of the seriousness of the errors, and the left-leaning errors were far from being completely corrected. It was this background that provided the potential for major repetition in the later stage of the Lushan Conference.

The previous nine months of rectification of Leftist error and its repetition revealed several regularity problems in the process of the localization of Marxism. First was the lag of the modernization of Marxism and the reform of the system, which greatly restricted the efforts to rectify the left-leaning tendency and the process of the localization of Marxism, which was the basic reason for the stage of "extension and preparation" in the process of localization from 1949 to 1978. Secondly, this lag was more a limitation of the times. And finally, under socialist conditions, the development of the localization of Marxism could not be separated from the promotion of socialist democratization and the reform of the political system.

CHAPTER 8

Two Trends of Development in Adjustment

In *Seventy Years of the Communist Party of China*, edited by Hu Sheng, there is a classic summary of the ten-year exploration from 1956 to 1966, which states that "during the ten-year exploration, the Party's guiding ideology had two trends of development. One was the correct or relatively correct trend, or the correct and relatively correct theoretical viewpoints, principles, and policies formed by the Party in the process of exploring China's own road to building socialism, and some correct and relatively correct practical experience that had been accumulated. This mainly referred to the positive results achieved in the exploration of more than one year before and after the First Session of the Eighth National Congress in 1956, the eight- or nine-month exploration before the Lushan Conference in 1959, and the exploration of the five-year readjustment after the winter of 1960. The other was the wrong trend, or the wrong theoretical viewpoints, policy ideas, and practical experience formed by the Party in the process of exploring China's own path to building socialism." It goes on, "At the same time, it is worth noting that during the ten-year exploration, the correct development trend and the wrong development trend were not entirely separated. Many times, they were interpenetrating and interacting with each other. They coexisted not only in the process of the common exploration of the entire Party, but also in the process of the cognitive development of the individual person. Sometimes this trend prevailed in the Party, while sometimes that trend prevailed, or different tendencies coexisted in different fields at the same time."[1]

From the point of view of basic content and process, although there were some differences in the three stages from September 1956 to early July 1959, from November 1958 to early July 1959, and from the end of 1960 to 1966, in terms of the degree and length of the process, the intrinsic basic elements and development trend were basically the same. In these three periods, when the correct and relatively correct development tendencies dominated, the six-year adjustment from the end of 1960 to 1966 had the most severe context, the longest period, and the greatest achievements (mainly in the economic aspect), but it ended with the outbreak of the Cultural Revolution, which also ended the two previous rectifications of Leftism. To some degree had in the context of not touching the provisions of the main contradictions of socialism, the political system, and the leadership system, the end of rectifying Leftism could only be so. The experience of rectifying Leftism and its outcome profoundly revealed some phenomena in the regularity of the development of socialism in China and revealed some changes in the process of the localization of Marxism.

I

Intra-Party Investigation and Research into Rectifying the Line of Thought

1. Re-initializing the Rectification of Leftism in the Face of Serious Difficulties

The reversal from rectifying Leftism to opposing Rightism in the latter part of the Lushan Conference undermined the process of rectifying Leftism that had just begun. The large-scale anti-Rightist struggle that was launched nationwide after the conference not only brought serious political consequences, but also interrupted economically the positive process of rectifying Leftism. Heeding the call of the anti-Rightist movement, the new Great Leap Forward surge was again set off, and the Five Surges again overflowed. Some errors that had been corrected since the first Zhengzhou Conference grew more serious. In addition, the Great Leap Forward destroyed productivity and caused serious difficulties in the national economy.

By the second half of 1960, the deteriorating situation had reached a point where the whole national economy could not be sustained without adjustment. In November 1960, the Central Committee issued the Emergency Directive Letter on Current Policy Issues of Rural People's Communes (referred to as the Emergency Directive Letter). The core of the Emergency Directive Letter was to ask the whole Party to do its utmost to correct such mistakes as the communist style. In fact, it was to restart the process of rectifying the Leftism that had been interrupted by the anti-Rightist struggle after the Lushan Conference, and it had become the starting point of reversing the serious situation in rural areas. In January 1961, at the Ninth Plenary Session of the Eighth Central Committee of the Communist Party of China, the policy of "readjustment, consolidation, enrichment, and improvement" was adopted for the national economy after 1961. These two events marked an important change in the Party's guiding principles at this historical stage. Serious difficulties and losses deepened people's misunderstanding of the Great Leap Forward and the people's commune movement. They had realized that the breakthrough of the Soviet model, the application and development of Marxism, and the localization of Marxism, as they had existed in 1958, actually deviated from the correct direction. In the late 1950s, Tian Jiaying, Mao Zedong's secretary, said in a scholarly discussion that "if we could start socialism from scratch, I would do it in another way."[2] At that time, there were probably a number of people who shared his view.

In the process of adjusting policies and overcoming difficulties, the Party renewed its efforts to rectify Leftism from the first Zhengzhou Conference to the early Lushan Conference, and it continued its efforts before and after the First Session of the Eighth National Congress in order to further explore China's own path to building socialism. Whether or not it was recognized at that time, this process was also one of recognizing afresh "what socialism is" in practice and exploring the correct path of the localization of Marxism in China.

On June 18, 1960, Mao Zedong summarized the experience and lessons of revolution and construction since the founding of New China in a famous article entitled "Ten-Year Summary." In it, some opinions were correct because they had gained new insights and leaps after taking a detour, while others were still continuing the views of Great Leap Forward and the people's commune movement. "The first eight years have been copying foreign experience," the article said, "but since 1956, when the Ten Relations were put forward, we began to find our own route more suited to China." He admitted, "I have made many mistakes myself, and some were committed by others… It seems impossible not to make mistakes… Our Party's general line is correct and its actual work has basically been done well. Some of the mistakes were likely unavoidable. Where is the so-called saint who makes no mistakes and achieves truth all at once? Truth is not accomplished all at once, but gradually. We are epistemologists of dialectical materialism, not of metaphysics. Freedom is the transformation of the necessary knowledge and the world. The leap from the realm of necessity to that of freedom is gradually completed through a long process of understanding. For our socialist revolution and construction, we have had ten years of experience and learned a great deal, but we are still quite blind about the revolution and construction in the socialist period, with a great unknown realm. We don't know it yet. We should investigate and study it in the second decade, and discover its inherent laws so as to use them to serve the socialist revolution and construction."[3] Mao's article focused more on summing up experience from an epistemological perspective. It was the forerunner of correcting the direction of the ideological line and exerted a great influence within the Party. It had prepared the ideological basis for deeply summing up experience, comprehensively adjusting and correcting the direction of the localization of Marxism. However, it was only preliminary to sum up experience in this way. As mentioned above, to correct the mistakes such as the Great Leap Forward really required several equally important factors, such as intra-Party democracy. At that time, the progress in this regard was not obvious.

2. Surge of Investigation and Research in the Party

At the beginning of the adjustment, Mao made strict demands in some important directives and instructions that Party committees at all levels must make up their minds to completely correct the Five Surges with the focus on the "communist surge" that would occur within a few months. In a comment drafted for the Central Committee, he admitted that "I have made mistakes and must correct them,"[4] so as to lead the majority of cadres to realize that "now is the time to make up their minds to correct mistakes."[5] He believed that the errors in recent years were directly caused by subjectivism and one-sidedness in ideological methods, so he repeatedly stressed the need to restore the fine tradition of seeking truth from facts and investigation and research. He said that the Party was realistic and traditional, that is, it combined the universal truth of Marxism-Leninism with the actual situation in China. But after the founding of the People's Republic of China, especially in recent years, the Party had not been very sure about the actual situation. He called on the entire Party to vigorously develop the style of investigation and research, proceeding from the actual situation and demanding that 1961 be a year of seeking truth from facts and of investigation and research. After this, the Central Committee issued a letter to the Central Bureau and provincial, municipal, and district Party committees concerning serious investigation, along with an article entitled "On Investigation" (later changed to "Opposing Doctrines" when disseminated publicly), written by Mao Zedong in 1930, which had been lost years earlier and only recently rediscovered, requiring the leading organs at and above the county level to study it in-depth, connecting it to practical concerns. The letter demanded, "Everything proceeds from reality. Without investigation, we have no right to speak, which must serve as the primary criterion for the thinking and action of all Party cadres… When conducting an investigation, we should not be afraid of substantial and dissenting opinions, nor of overturning them by actual tests the judgments and decisions already made." It further raised the question of rectifying the ideological line for the leading cadres of the whole Party. Emphasis was placed on practice such as the criterion for testing truth, rather than on judgments made in the past, which opened the way for correction based on practice and testing past wrong decisions.

After the Ninth Plenary Session of the Eighth Central Committee of the Communist Party of China in 1961, Mao directly organized and directed three investigative groups to investigate rural areas in Zhejiang, Hunan, and Guangdong Provinces. Liu Shaoqi, Zhou Enlai, Zhu De, and Deng Xiaoping also went to Hunan, Hebei, Sichuan, and Beijing to conduct in-depth investigation and research at the grassroots level. Liu Shaoqi sincerely apologized to the members during the investigation in Ningxiang County and Changsha County in Hunan Province, saying that the Central Committee had done something wrong and was sorry for it, and that to correct the mistake, the Party needed to know the real situation, and it hoped all present could help him and provide him with accurate information. After a preliminary investigation, he had a clearer idea that "the canteen was reluctantly built, and extremely unpopular. On this issue, we have made mistakes and worked for three years without understanding it. Such a canteen should have been long gone."[6] After in-depth investigation and research, Liu felt that the main reason for the difficulties in the local rural areas was not natural disasters, but the mistakes in the Party's work, as the local farmers said, "the disasters were 30% natural and 70% man-made." A commune member said directly to Zhou Enlai during his investigation in Hebei, "Life during these two years has been getting worse and worse… If it goes on like this for another two years, even you will not have any food." After the investigation, Zhou raised several main problems in his telephone report to Mao, including that the overwhelming majority and even all members of the commune wished to "go home to cook," members disapproved of the supply system, members of the masses urgently needed to restore the method of assessing work marks based on labor in senior communes, and so on. Less than a year before, the problems of canteen, supply system, and ownership of communes were still regarded as socialist camps and needed to be upheld. This was highly affirmed by Mao and regarded as the focus of the struggle between socialism and capitalism. In the Party's in-depth investigation, these seemingly unshakable things had been denied.

Following Mao's instructions, the entire Party developed a trend of investigation and research. The heads of the central bureaus and Party committees of provinces, municipalities and autonomous regions, central and state organs and provincial, municipal, and district Party and government departments had also gone on to conduct key investigations in counties, societies, and teams. The in-depth investigation gradually unified the Party's understanding on such issues as canteens, the supply system, family sidelines, and reserved land, which directly promoted the adjustment of rural policies and other fronts.

One of the basic preconditions for the localization of Marxism in China was to truly understand the national conditions based on facts. An important reason for the Great Leap Forward and other movements was the superficiality and confusion of this understanding. At the beginning of the readjustment, Mao and the Party Central Committee began with the emphasis on investigation and research, thus restoring to a certain extent the ideological line of seeking truth from facts and laying the ideological foundation for the overall readjustment, correcting the direction of the localization of Marxism to a certain extent. From the basic level, this process was consistent with the process of rectifying Leftism which began in 1956, and was ramped up in November 1958.

II

Intra-Party Adjustment Toward a Deeper Understanding of Socialism

1. Adjustment of Rural Policies

With the deepening of investigation and research and the initial rectification of the ideological line, the adjustment of the rural policy was also deepened.

In a large-scale investigation and study, leaders at all levels from the central to the local governments found that although specific measures had been formulated to implement the Emergency Directive Letter on Current Policy Issues of the Rural People's Communes, there were still some places where the work was done in a perfunctory way, and the Emergency Directive Letter itself did not completely resolve the major issues of equalitarianism between the production teams of a production brigade of the people's communes and between the members of the production team. In order to systematically resolve various serious problems of rural people's communes, including these two forms of equalitarianism, Mao Zedong presided over the formulation of Rural People's Commune Work Regulations (Draft) in Guangzhou in March 1961 (referred to as the Sixty Articles of Agriculture), sending them to all rural Party branches and commune members for amendments. After repeated discussions and pilot projects by the cadres and the masses, several major revisions were made to the Sixty Articles of Agriculture. In the pilot amendment draft issued that June, the partial supply system and public canteens generally opposed by farmers were abolished, a decision greatly welcomed by farmers. These two items, which were called the "new things" of communism in 1958, caused great damage to rural productivity. When canceling or proposing to cancel public canteens in 1958 and the second half of 1959, they were regarded as a major part of "right-leaning opportunism." Up to the end of 1960, the Emergency Instruction Letter and the preliminary draft of the Sixty Articles of Agriculture in March 1961, the two things were still considered something that "must be done well" and "must be adhered to." In September, on the basis of the opinions of several provinces, Mao proposed that the basic accounting units of the people's communes should be decentralized to production teams of the same size as the primary communes. In his letter to the Central Committee, he said that the serious egalitarianism in agriculture had not yet been completely resolved, leaving the lingering issue of the right to production being confined to the small group, while the right to distribution was in the hands of the large group. This serious contradiction still restricted the enthusiasm of the masses for production. "On this issue, we have spent six years in confusion (since the founding of the Senior Society in 1956) and should wake up in the seventh year."[7] According to Mao's view, the final revised Sixty Articles of Agriculture stipulated that the three-level collective ownership of rural people's communes based on production teams was the fundamental system implemented over a long period of time.

The Sixty Articles of Agriculture was an important document for the Party to adjust the country's rural production relations and promote the recovery and development of agricultural production. On the premise of maintaining the general framework of the people's communes, this regulation corrected some outstanding errors in rural practical work after the communization and resolved the most pressing problem of the masses' opinions at that time. Although it failed to completely resolve some fundamental problems of the people's commune, it played an important role in mobilizing farmers' enthusiasm, and in restoring and developing agricultural production. For quite some time afterwards, even amid periods of turmoil like the Cultural Revolution, it played an active role in curbing the revival of the Communist Surge. From the Emergency Directive Letter to the revised Sixty Articles of Agriculture, the Party's major adjustment of the people's commune system was not only the continuation of the first Zhengzhou Conference in 1958, but also traced back to the efforts made to adjust the internal relations of the cooperatives after the climax of the agricultural cooperative movement. In a sense, it was also a sort of return to the primary society that was quickly replaced by the senior society, and a denial of the sharp upgrade of rural production relations in the mid and late 1950s. This "retrogression" reflected some advances in the understanding of socialism and brought it closer to the reality of China.

During this period, in accordance with the same spirit, the Party Central Committee had also begun to solve the problems of the handicraft industry and commercial policy in urban and rural areas. In June 1961, the Thirty-Five Articles of Handicrafts issued by the Central Committee clearly pointed out that "in the handicraft industry of the entire socialist stage, collective ownership is the main issue. Individual ownership is the necessary supplement and assistant to the socialist economy, and public ownership can only be part of it. Too early a transition to ownership by all the people is not conducive to production. At the same time, the Forty Articles of Commerce affirmed that at this stage, besides state-owned commerce, supply, and marketing cooperative commerce, there is also rural market trade, which is a necessary supplement to the first two channels. The formulation and implementation of these policies put an end to the mistakes made since the Great Leap Forward in abolishing the rural market trade and peddlers and in transforming collective handicraft and commerce into ownership by all the people."

2. Industrial Adjustment

The first step in industrial adjustment was to slow down the speed and lower the target. However, it was not easy to achieve this in a short period of time under the background of the high index and high speed that had expanded to the extreme since 1958. Although the eight-character policy of adjusting the national economy was put forward in September 1960, it was not until the second half of 1961 that it began to gradually come into effect. At the Central Working Conference in September 1961, Zhou Enlai stressed that the targeted indicators should be resolutely lowered so as to leave room for rectification that year.

Deng Xiaoping pointed out that the general policy of adjustment aimed to protect agriculture, light industry, and national defense, so the battle line should be shortened accordingly. In the Directive of the Central Committee of the Communist Party of China on Current Industrial Issues adopted at the meeting, it was pointed out that the Party had lost a whole year and could hesitate no longer. It was important to make a decisive choice at the right moment. The Party needed to slow down and lower the targeted indicators of industrial production and capital construction to a level that was reliable and had room for improvement. In the next three years, when implementing the eight-character policy, it was important to focus on readjustment. A failure to make this determination and continue to adhere to those unrealistic targets, remaining stubbornly unwilling to go up or down, would result in industry and even the whole national economy falling into a more passive, serious situation. After the meeting, with the approval of the Central Committee, the State Planning Commission made a major adjustment to the 1961 plan. The decline of production indicators was the result of denying the fanaticism of the Great Leap Forward and deepening the Party's understanding of the national conditions. That is to say, in the adjustment of correcting the Leftist deviation, the localization of Marxism in China had taken an important step in the right direction.

Another aspect of industrial restructuring was to rectify the production order that was disrupted by the Great Leap Forward. The movement was a bold attempt to break through the Soviet model, but because of the restrictions of backward productivity and the misunderstanding of "emancipating the mind," "breaking superstition," and "mass movements," these attempts often turned into scorn for large production by small production and the exclusion of production order by blind revolutionary enthusiasm, resulting in repercussions in the management of modern industry and many problems for enterprises, including confusion in management, a slack responsibility and economic accounting system, damage to equipment, prevailing equalitarianism in the distribution system, lower product quality and labor productivity, and so on. During the period of readjustment, Deng Xiaoping emphasized on many occasions the need to rectify industrial enterprises and deal with the chaos. In the process of formulating Sixty Articles of Agriculture, Mao put forward the opinion that "cities should also have dozens of articles." Accordingly, under the chairmanship of Deng Xiaoping, Li Fuchun and Bo Yibo were responsible for dispatching eleven working groups to many industrial and mining enterprises for investigation. On the basis of extensive investigation and study, after discussion and modification, the draft Regulations on the Work of State-Owned Industrial Enterprises (abbreviated as Seventy Articles of Industry) was formed. After discussion and adoption at the Lushan Central Working Conference, it was issued by the Central Committee for trial implementation in September 1961.

The Seventy Articles of Industry systematically summarized the experience and lessons of industrial management since the founding of New China, especially since the Great Leap Forward. It also put forward some guiding principles for the management of state-owned enterprises in China and made many specific provisions. The regulations stipulated that the state would implement the Five Determinations[8] for enterprises and the enterprises implement Five Guarantees[9] for the state. The regulations also specified in detail the factory director's responsibility system under the leadership of the Party Committee, the staff congress system, and the operation and responsibilities of the unified production administrative command system headed by the factory director. The Regulations required the establishment of strict responsibility systems at all levels, in all aspects, and in all links, the implementation of comprehensive economic accounting, and the pursuit of economic results. The Regulations emphasized strengthening the management of state-owned enterprises in accordance with the strict directive planning system. It not only restored the rules and regulations of industrial enterprises and normal production order that were negated and disturbed by the Great Leap Forward, but also established some systems which were not established before the Great Leap Forward, so that the management of industrial enterprises in China had, in the process of adjustment, taken a step toward standardization and sound development. The Seventy Articles of Industry were supported by cadres and workers as soon as it was issued. As a result of the implementation of this regulation, a series of necessary rules and regulations for state-owned enterprises had been restored and established, which played a positive role in the adjustment, consolidation, enrichment, and improvement of industry.

3. Adjustment in the Field of the Superstructure

The anti-Rightist movement and the serious Leftist mistakes in the Great Leap Forward and the people's commune movement involved the economic foundation, superstructure, and ideology. As a remedy for these errors, the adjustment in the early 1960s would inevitably cover all these areas. As the readjustment in the economic sphere gradually deepened, the readjustment in the fields of politics, ideology, science, education, culture, united front, religion, ethnic, and other concerns had also been carried out.

In 1957, the anti-Rightist movement caused serious harm to intellectuals in the fields of the superstructure and ideology. Later, the Great Leap Forward and anti-Rightist movements in the fields of science, education, literature, and art proved to be prone to exaggeration and blind command. The continuous political movements had a great impact on the work of science, education, literature, and art. Normal working order was disrupted, and the enthusiasm of intellectuals was seriously frustrated. This, in turn, had a serious negative impact on economic work.

In the early 1960s, the adjustment in the fields of science, education, and culture began with the formulation of regulations on science, education, literature, and art. After the winter of 1960, under the chairmanship of Nie Rongzhen, after repeated investigations and a long period of listening to the opinions of the scientific community, the National Science and Technology Commission put forward in 1961 Fourteen Opinions on the Current Work of Natural Science Research Institutions (Draft) (referred to as Fourteen Articles of Science). In July, it was discussed and approved by the Politburo and issued for trial implementation. In the field of education, after 1961, the Party Group of the Ministry of Education held a special symposium to invite leaders and professors of several universities to offer their opinions. Under the chairmanship of Deng Xiaoping, the Party Group of the Ministry of Education and the Central Propaganda Department drafted the Provisional Regulations on the Work of Institutions of Higher Education Directly under the Ministry of Education (Draft) (hereinafter referred to as Sixty Articles of Higher Education). In September, the draft was discussed and adopted by the Lushan Central Working Conference and released for trial implementation. While drafting Sixty Articles of Higher Education, the Ministry of Education began to draft regulations on primary and secondary education according to the instructions of the Party Central Committee. Later, the Temporary Regulations on Full-time Secondary Schools (hereinafter referred to as Fifty Articles of Secondary Education) and the Temporary Regulations on Full-time Primary Schools (hereinafter referred to as Forty Articles of Primary Education) were drawn up and approved by the Party Central Committee for trial implementation in March 1963. Under Zhou Enlai's supervision, the Party Group of the Ministry of Propaganda and Culture and the Party Group of the National Federation of Literature and Arts drafted the Opinions on Current Literature and Art Work (Draft) (hereinafter referred to as Ten Articles of Literature and Art) in the first half of 1961 on the basis of a large number of investigations and studies. Later, according to local opinions, it was changed into the Eight Articles of Literature and Art and approved by the Party Central Committee for nationwide implementation in April 1962.

These regulations on science, education, literature, and art summarized the experience and lessons of the People's Republic of China since its founding, especially since the Great Leap Forward. They not only affirmed achievements, but also pointed out the shortcomings and mistakes in the past three years of work. They further put forward a series of policies to adjust relations, stabilize the working order, mobilize the enthusiasm of intellectuals, and provide specific provisions. A central issue in these regulations was to adjust the relationship between the Party and intellectuals. Since the Great Leap Forward, many intellectuals had been excessively and erroneously criticized by means of pulling out the "white flag," criticizing the "white professional" path, and breaking the "bourgeois academic authority." Some Party members and cadres in cultural and educational units even believed that since most of the intellectuals were the bourgeoisie, they were appropriate revolutionary targets in the period of socialist revolution. After the anti-Rightist struggle in 1959, this Leftist tendency expanded further. It was in response to this situation that these regulations particularly emphasized the need to treat knowledge and intellectuals correctly in order to adjust the relationship between the Party and intellectuals. In its comments, the Central Committee pointed out that it was very important to do a good job in the work of intellectuals. In recent years, many comrades had developed one-sided views on the issue of knowledge and intellectuals, and taking overly simple, direct means to address the issue, which deserved serious attention if the direction was to be corrected. In academic work, it was important to stick to the policy of a hundred flowers blooming and a hundred schools of thought contending, rather than posting labels, imposing restrictions, or poking holes, in order to fully mobilize the enthusiasm of the intellectuals so that they could do their work safely and responsibly. All departments and units in which intellectuals worked should clean up the criticisms made on the intellectuals after the struggle against the Rightists. Those proper criticisms could continue, but for those wrongfully accused, it was important to distinguish facts from stories and right from wrong, to correct the wrong, and to remove wrong labels in order to relieve the ideological knots, promote democracy, and strengthen unity.

Another important notion contained in these regulations was the implementation of the policy of "letting a hundred flowers bloom and a hundred schools of thought contend" in scientific and literary work, which was closely related to the adjustment of the relationship between the Party and intellectuals. These regulations put forward that on academic issues of the natural sciences, various schools and academic opinions must be encouraged to explore, debate, and compete freely. In philosophy and social sciences, it was necessary to critically inherit historical and cultural heritage and absorb all the valuable things. Among the masses and in

Marxist circles, it was important to allow different opinions to be freely discussed when addressing various academic issues. In literary and artistic creation, writers and artists had full freedom to choose and deal with subjects, advocate diversity of styles, and develop different artistic schools. In literary and artistic criticism, they had the freedom to discuss and criticize different opinions on literary and artistic works and literary and artistic theories, as well as freedom to reserve opinions and criticize them. These regulations also elaborated and stipulated a series of specific policies for implementing the "two hundreds" policy, emphasizing that political struggle should not be used, let alone a struggle against the enemy, to deal with different views within the people on academic and artistic issues.

In view of the chaotic phenomena of excessive productive labor and social activities in the departments of science, education, literature, and art after the Great Leap Forward and the exaggerated and blind conduct in the work of the Party, as well as the widespread problems, such as the overwhelming interference of the Party committees in the work and administration or managers and business personnel not daring to work boldly, some regulations clearly stipulated that the fundamental task of scientific research institutions was to produce results and talent, and to serve socialism. Further, the stability of scientific research work had to be guaranteed, and scientific researchers needed to spend at least 40% of their time in professional work. Schools were to be teaching-oriented and students learning-oriented. Literature and art could not be understood too broadly for political service, nor could they be understood too narrowly. Only the revolutionary enthusiasm of the people should be encouraged and their ideological awareness raised. They should be given proper artistic enjoyment and healthy entertainment. All works that met any of the above requirements were in the service of the people and socialism. The main tasks of Party committees in scientific research institutions, institutions of higher learning, and departments of literature and art were consistent. It was important to implement the Party's principles and policies thoroughly and prevent everything from being superseded and arbitrary.

The formulation and implementation of these regulations exerted a positive influence on intellectuals both inside and outside the Party. It eased the tension between the Party and intellectuals, restored the working order, and played an important role in gradually forming a set of principles, policies, and specific systems for the scientific, educational, and cultural undertakings of socialism in China. Although the problem of the expansion of the anti-Rightist struggle had not yet been resolved, most intellectuals were in a relatively content mood at that time, and the conditions for devoting themselves to professional work were generally available.

III

The 7,000 People's Congress and Subsequent Adjustments

1. Reflections on the 7,000 People's Congress

After more than a year of adjustment, the serious economic difficulties caused by the Great Leap Forward saw some relief, production order was restored, and various relations were initially adjusted, but the overall situation was still quite grim. Faced with this situation, there were various doubts and divergences in the ideological understanding inside and outside the Party. In order to further sum up the experience and lessons learned after 1958, unify and enhance the understanding of the whole Party, strengthen unity, and mobilize the whole Party to implement the adjustment policy more resolutely and strive to overcome serious difficulties, the Central Committee convened an expanded Central Working Conference in Beijing from January 11 to February 7, 1962, historically known as the 7,000 People's Congress.

In his written report at the meeting, Liu Shaoqi focused on the main shortcomings and mistakes in his work, analyzing their causes. On the one hand, he pointed out that the reasons for the mistakes were the lack of experience in construction work, while on the other, the lack of modesty and prudence of many leading comrades in the Party, which violated the Party's tradition of seeking truth from facts and the mass line, weakened the principle of democratic centralism and prevented the Party from discovering and correcting the mistakes as quickly as possible. In his speech at the General Assembly, he made some important comments on some of the most questionable issues within the Party, including the need to admit that it was facing considerable economic difficulties at present. Regarding its achievements and mistakes, in the past, it often compared shortcomings and mistakes to the relationship between one finger and nine fingers. He noted that this could no longer be so widespread, extending across the country. He noted it was more like the relationship between three fingers and seven fingers, and some regional mistakes could be seven fingers. As for the causes of economic difficulties, on the one hand, they were due to natural disasters, while on the other, to a large extent, they were the result of errors in work. In some places, they were "30% because of natural disasters, and 70% because of man-made disasters." With regards to the "three red flags," the Party would not cancel those yet, but would continue to maintain them. Some problems were not yet clear, but in five or ten years, the Party would sum up its experience, and then it could draw further conclusions. At that time, it was difficult to criticize the "three red flags" positively or discuss them in formal circumstances. Liu's reservations were heartily supported by many people because he reflected the views of many people at that time. His written report and speech were warmly welcomed by everyone.

In his long speech on January 30, Mao focused on democratic centralism. He stressed that both inside and outside the Party there should be full democratic centralism and the masses should be allowed to speak. Democratic centralism was embodied in the Party Constitution and the Constitution. It was impossible to overcome the difficulties the Party faced without democratic centralism. If there were mistakes, it was important to engage in self-criticism and let the people offer criticism. He offered a self-criticism, saying, "I am directly responsible for all the mistakes made by the Central Committee, and indirectly I am also responsible for them, because I am the Chairman of the Central Committee." He also stressed that the Party still had a great deal of blindness in its socialist construction. There were still many unknowns in the socialist economy. In the future, it was necessary to work hard to investigate, study, and gradually deepen the Party's understanding in practice. He pointed out that China's large population, weak foundation, and backward economy made it impossible to develop its productive forces to catch up with and surpass the most advanced capitalist countries in the world in less than a hundred years. For this reason, it was important to combine the universal truth of Marxism-Leninism with the concrete reality of China's socialist construction and the concrete situation in the future world revolution as well as try to better systematically understand the objective law of struggle through practice. From this point of view, there were many advantages to assuming a longer period, but it was harmful to imagine a shorter one. In connection with the three-year Great Leap Forward, he acknowledged that there was still a great deal of blindness in socialist construction, which indicated that he had made new progress in his understanding. This played an important role in further summarizing the construction practice in recent years and correcting the mistakes in the Party's work.

If Mao's emphasis on seeking truth from facts and investigation and study at the beginning of 1961 was to highlight a basic element in the localization of Marxism in China, then nearly a year later, after some progress had been made in the adjustment, Mao corrected the Leftist mistake and realized democracy, another basic element of the localization of Marxism in China. The anti-Rightist movement seriously damaged democracy inside and outside the Party, which was an important reason for the serious mistakes made in economic construction. If these errors were ignored, there would be no other adjustment. This conformed to the law of knowledge and also met the need for further adjustment. However, the limitations of this kind of democracy mentioned by Mao at the meeting were also obvious. First, there could be no real socialist democracy without a correct understanding of the main contradictions in a socialist society. Second, it was obviously not enough to interpret democracy only as "letting the masses speak" and "letting people criticize." This was still a kind of "top-down" and "giving" democracy. Although it was better than not letting people speak, it could be "revoked" under various names at any time because of the change of leaders' understanding and attitude. Such democracy was still far from a real socialist democracy. True socialist democracy was not given by anyone, but was endogenous to its level of productivity, economic base, and superstructure, and it was the inalienable power of every Party member and the masses. This kind of democracy with authority limitations played a role in the initial stage of adjustment, but it could not guarantee the need for further adjustment, because the deeper the adjustment was, the more obvious the divergence on the question of the nature of socialism. Once class struggle had been determined to be the main contradiction, it was more likely to raise this divergence to the "height" of class struggle, thus "exceeding" the limits of democratic application and ending some adjustments. The democracy needed for the localization of Marxism in China could not be this sort of democracy with great limitations.

Deng Xiaoping and Zhou Enlai addressed the General Assembly and offered self-criticism on behalf of the Secretariat of the Central Committee and the State Council respectively. Deng Xiaoping pointed out in his speech that the Party's leadership and work had serious shortcomings. As far as the whole Party was concerned, the Party's fine traditions had been weakened to a considerable extent, especially the neglect and damage to the traditions of seeking truth from facts, the mass line, and democratic centralism, which brought great harm to the work. Zhou pointed out in his speech that in recent years, the Party's work tended to focus only on subjective needs, regardless of objective possibilities. It rested only on current requirements, without long-term plans, but it delayed results. He emphasized telling the truth, making real effort, doing actual work, and reaping substantial results. In their speeches, Zhu De and Chen Yun also focused on correcting the Leftist mistakes and the problems of democratic life within the Party.

The 7,000 People's Congress brought important achievements to the historical conditions at that time. To some extent, the conference promoted intra-Party democracy, which was essentially an adjustment in intra-Party relations. On this basis, the conference adopted a more realistic attitude toward shortcomings and mistakes and summarized its experience and lessons objectively and thoroughly. The spirit of democracy and self-criticism at the conference encouraged the whole Party, made the majority of Party members feel more comfortable, and played a positive role in mobilizing the entire Party to work together to overcome difficulties. Due to the limitations of historical conditions, the meeting still affirmed the "three red flags" in principle. For the anti-Rightist struggle, only the cases of the subordinate Party members who were wrongly criticized were screened and redressed, while Peng Dehuai's was still not redressed. For the assessment of the situation and the analysis of the reasons for the difficulties, there were divergent views within the party. All these indicated that under the current conditions, there were considerable limitations to the rectification of the mistakes of the Great Leap Forward and the anti-Rightist movement, in line with the guiding ideology.

The posture, depth, and achievements of the anti-Leftist movement of the 7,000 People's Congress were in sharp contrast to the criticism of the anti-rash, the Great Leap Forward, and the people's commune movement in the first half of 1958 and the anti-Rightist movement after August 1959. These achievements were due to the fact that the whole Party had earnestly learned lessons from its failures, abandoned some wrong socialist concepts, and added some socialist concepts suitable for China's national conditions, while also benefiting from the relatively active democracy within the Party in times of severe difficulty. After the

7,000 People's Congress, the entire Party still faced two basic choices. One was to continue the efforts to rectify Leftism that had begun in late 1960, and to continue the healthy development momentum. The other was to discount or even abandon the adjustment because it could not touch some more fundamental traditional concepts. The reason for this was not only the limitations of the times, but also the more direct role of the system. This had been evident in the interruption of the "counter-rash advance" and the interruption of nine months of correction of Leftism.

2. Further Readjustment after the 7,000 People's Congress

For some time after the 7,000 People's Congress, economic and political adjustments were further developed and further achievements were made in some areas.

Shortly after the 7,000 People's Congress, the Central Committee found that its estimate of the difficulty of the economic situation was still inadequate. According to the new analysis provided by the financial department, Liu Shaoqi pointed out at the Expanded Meeting of the Standing Committee of the Politburo in late February 1962 that the national economy would deteriorate further if decisive measures were not taken. Chen Yun spoke systematically at the meeting and was warmly endorsed. According to these guiding principles, at the Expanded Meeting of the Standing Committee held in May, the Party discussed and adopted a plan for further drastic adjustment of the national economy. This included vigorously streamlining staff and workers, further reducing the scale of capital construction, shortening the industrial front, further strengthening agriculture in all aspects, strengthening leadership at the grassroots level in rural areas, and so on. With these decisive measures and the arduous struggle of the whole nation, the readjustment work achieved rapid results. At the end of 1962, the national economic situation began to improve. Agricultural production began to pick up, the proportion of agriculture, light industry, and heavy industry improved, state revenue and expenditure were more balanced, the supply and demand of market commodities eased, and the people's lives in urban and rural areas began to improve.

With the deepening of readjustment work, people's minds were liberated, and some previously suppressed views and practices were revived. In addition, the difficult economic situation also prompted people to find many ways to tide themselves over during the difficulties. It was against this background that various forms of agricultural production responsibility systems emerged again, expanding rapidly. After the basic accounting units of rural people's communes were decentralized to production teams of the same size as the original primary communes, farmers' enthusiasm was greatly improved. But they were not satisfied with this "retrogression," hoping instead to combine their own earnings and labor more closely through a more effective form of accountability. In this way, various forms of "contracted production to households" were spontaneously carried out in many places. With this co-operation, whenever the Party proposed to adjust production relations within the agricultural collective economic organizations, the situation in which farmers spontaneously engaged in "contracted production to households" emerged. Despite repeated checks, it managed to return. This eloquently proved that, as a level of the collective economy, family management was suitable in many ways for the situation of productivity in rural China, which was dominated by manual labor, and for the needs of most farmers in China. As for the implementation of "contracting production to households," there were actually different views within the Party from the very beginning. In November 1961, the Central Committee decided in an instruction that the practice of "contracting production to households" and some disguised and single-handed practices were "inconsistent with the principles of socialist collective economy" and called for "change."[10] By the first half of 1962, however, not only had the contracted production to households not really been stopped, but it showed more vitality. In July of that year, more than 20% of the countryside in China had implemented various forms of "contracted production to households" with positive results, which was welcomed by farmers and many grassroots cadres.

Liu Shaoqi, Chen Yun, Deng Xiaoping, Deng Zihui, and other leading members of the Party Central Committee and relevant departments of the Central Committee also expressed positive support for it in the investigation and study. Liu said that the implementation of the responsibility system, one piece per household package, or one piece per group package, was entirely possible, making "contract production to households" legal.[11] After the investigation, Deng Zihui put forward in his written opinion to the Central Committee in May 1962 that members should be allowed to operate some "minor freedom and with minor private ownership" within a certain range, which was the most effective way to mobilize the enthusiasm and responsibility of farmers in the current stage of agricultural productivity development. He pointed out that the establishment of the responsibility system for production "is the fundamental link to doing well in collective production and consolidating collective ownership in the future."[12] After investigation, Chen Yun believed that contracting production to households was "an extraordinary method in a very specific period of time."[13] He even put forward that "it is not thorough to contract production to households, so it is better to distribute farmland to households than to contract production to households."[14] When Deng Xiaoping listened to the report of the Rural Office of East China Bureau in late June of that year, he said that in areas where farmers' lives were difficult, various measures could be taken. "Responsibility farmland" was a new thing, and it could be tried. In July, he quoted the famous Sichuan folk proverb often spoken by Liu Bocheng in a speech, saying, "No matter whether it is a yellow or black cat, if it catches mice, it is a good cat." He said, "I am afraid we need to adopt an attitude in terms of the form of production relations that takes the form that can most likely and most quickly restore and develop agricultural production in any place, and the form that the masses are willing to take, legalizing it if it's not yet legal." The viewpoints and methods embodied in this easy-to-understand language were the theoretical cornerstone of the Reform and Opening Up, namely, the productivity standard.

In terms of adjusting political relations, on behalf of the Central Committee, Liu communicated the spirit of the 7,000 People's Congress to non-party democrats at the Supreme State Conference, the Third Session of the Second National People's Congress and the Third Session of the CPPCC held in March and April 1962, explaining the shortcomings and errors of the domestic work in recent years. He noted that the main responsibility lay with the Central Party Committee. Zhou Enlai offered sincere self-criticism on behalf of the State Council on issues in government work. The democratic parties present at the meeting were inspired by the solemn attitude of the CPC in its efforts to be frank, daring to admit mistakes, and seriously correcting them. They expressed their willingness to work with the CPC and to be united to overcome difficulties.

In order to further strengthen and improve the work of the united front, the United Front Ministry of the Central Committee of the Communist Party of China, the National Committee for Nationalities of the National People's

Congress, and the National Commission for Ethnic Affairs convened the National United Front Work Conference in April 1962 and the National Ethnic Work Conference the following month. The two meetings focused on examining some serious Leftist errors in the implementation of the united front and ethnic and religious policies enacted since the Great Leap Forward. They studied the principles, policies, and specific measures for solving these problems. The meeting pointed out that the Party must actively adjust its relations with intellectuals, business and industry, democratic parties, democrats, religious circles, ethnic minorities, returned overseas Chinese and other patriots, and promote democracy, strengthen solidarity, fully mobilize all positive factors, work together to overcome current difficulties, and complete the task of adjusting the national economy. The National United Front Conference also proposed that the Party should do a thorough job of screening and eliminating non-Party people who had been injured in the political movement, the placement of those who have taken off their Rightist hats and those who still wore them, and not discriminate against the families and children of those who have been classified as Rightists in schools, employment, or other areas of life. At the same time, the Central Committee made corresponding adjustments to the policy on overseas Chinese affairs. The National Symposium on Ethnic Work put forward that adjusting ethnic and other relations in accordance with the central policy was the top priority in ethnic minority areas during the period of adjustment, and other undertakings were to be subject to this general purpose. Through adjusting national relations and strengthening national unity, the unity with all patriotic nationalists, and the alliance of workers and peasants, it was important to mobilize the enthusiasm of the people of all ethnic groups and concentrate on the recovery and development of production. In 1961, the Central Committee for Ethnic Affairs had drafted the Provisions on Policies Concerning Ethnic Minority Pastoral Work and Pastoral People's Communes (Draft) (hereinafter referred to as Forty Articles of Pastoral Work), which made a number of adjustments to the policies of ethnic minority areas and strengthened support to these areas.

After the 7,000 People's Congress, with the overall adjustment of the national economy, the adjustment of the Party's policy towards intellectuals was further deepened. The regulations on science, education, literature, and art formulated and implemented in 1961 gradually rectified the direction of the work of intellectuals and initially mobilized the enthusiasm of the majority of intellectuals. The deepening of this adjustment inevitably involved a new scientific judgment on the class attributes of the intellectuals. After the anti-Rightist struggle in 1957, the judgment of the class attributes of intellectuals changed and they were all "bourgeois intellectuals." This "hat" made it difficult to arouse the enthusiasm of intellectuals. In February and March 1962, Zhou Enlai resolutely restored, in essence, the Party's basic estimate of the status of China's intellectuals at the 1956 Intellectuals Conference at the Scientific and Technological Work Conference and the Literary and Art Work Conference held in Guangzhou, affirming that the overwhelming majority of intellectuals were already intellectuals belonging to the working people, not the bourgeoisie. In his speech at the meeting, Chen Yi emphasized that after twelve years of testing, especially through the severe difficulties in recent years, the majority of intellectuals in China had proven to be patriotic, believing in the Communist Party and sharing the joys and sorrows of the Party and the people. If a person could not be identified in eight, ten, or twelve years, then the Communist Party was blind. He declared that he would "take off the hat" (i.e., the hat of "bourgeois" intellectuals) and "crown" them (i.e., the crown of "working class" intellectuals). Zhou reiterated this scientific conclusion in his report on the work of the government at the subsequent Third Session of the Second National People's Congress. Further readjustment of intellectuals' policies greatly aroused their enthusiasm and made the spring of 1962 an unforgettable time for them.

While adjusting the political relations outside the Party, the Central Committee took important steps to adjust the political relations within the Party as well. In June 1961, the Central Committee issued an instruction on the screening of Party members and cadres who had been criticized and punished in the anti-Rightist movement over several years. After the 7,000 People's Congress, the Central Committee accelerated the progress of this work. In view of this unbalanced progress, in April 1962, under the chairmanship of Deng Xiaoping, the Central Secretariat formulated and issued the Notice on Accelerating the Screening of Party Members and Cadres, then, based on the experience of the army, proposed a package solution for cadres below the county level throughout the country, that is, cadres who had made mistakes in the past or had made fundamental mistakes. In order to rectify the situation, it was important not to "leave a tail," but to resolve it all at once, except for in a few of the more serious cases. In this way, the screening of counter-revolutionaries within and outside the Party was carried out rapidly and comprehensively. By August 1962, the cases of more than 6 million cadres, Party members, and the masses had been redressed throughout the country.

In addition, in the field of foreign affairs, there were also requirements for correcting Leftism. In the spring of 1962, in view of the Leftist tendency gradually developing in foreign affairs, Wang Jiaxiang, Minister of the Central Committee of the Commonwealth of China, suggested to the Central Committee that it was necessary to strive for a relative easing of foreign relations in order to gain time to sustain the country through it difficulties and speed up construction. He noted that strategies should be given attention in the struggle with the United States and the Soviet Union, and that foreign aid should be realistic and measured. It was important also to emphasize the peace movement, not just the national liberation movement. These opinions advocated the policy of easing foreign policy, which was a revision of the tendency of expanding the scope of attack and increasing the harsh tone of voice in the international struggle that had emerged at that time.

In short, during the six month period after the 7,000 People's Congress, the readjustment work showed a stronger momentum of development. This was not only reflected in its wide range of coverage, but also in the depth achieved in practice and theory. It was in the process of deepening the adjustment that some substantial progress was made in the localization of Marxism in China.

If this healthy momentum had been developed smoothly, the subsequent Cultural Revolution would not have been possible. Perhaps China's reform would have started relatively early and gone more smoothly. The question remained whether the conditions of understanding and the system at that time could provide the atmosphere needed for the sustained development of this momentum.

IV

Conflicting Patterns Resulting from Divergent Directions of Economic and Political Development

1. The Adjustment to Correct Leftism

The adjustment in the early 1960s began from addressing the imminent economic difficulties at that time, but it inevitably embarked on a road different from the "three red flags" in 1958, which in fact formed another climax in the localization of Marxism after the founding of New China. After the Emergency Directive Letter was issued at the end of 1960 and a large-scale investigation, exploration, and promotion was conducted by the Party in 1961, the readjustment was carried out in an all-round way from the end of 1961 to the 7,000 People's Congress. After the Congress, both in breadth and depth, the readjustment showed a trend of rapid development. The adjustment of continuous in-depth development not only achieved remarkable economic results very quickly, but also corrected some major errors in the fields of production relations, superstructure, and ideology that had existed since 1958 to varying degrees. It gradually displayed features different from the Great Leap Forward and the people's commune model. A road that combined Marxism with China's actual situation had gradually corrected the direction of the localization of Marxism in China.

The revision of the main contradictions in socialist society after the anti-Rightist movement in 1957, and the "three red flags" in 1958 were considered to be transcendence of the Soviet model, an important development of Marxism, and a new achievement in the localization of Marxism. However, in terms of the speed of its construction, its pursuit of "large scale projects and publicizing property" in the form of ownership, its establishment of the main contradictions of socialism as class contradictions, its short estimation of the historical stage of socialism, and its more eager transition to communism were essentially a more extreme and rigid socialist model than the traditional one seen in the Soviet Union. While it did have distinct Chinese characteristics, it was not only divorced from China's actual situation, but also ignored the inevitable trend of the modernization of Marxism, so that the correct development trend of Marxism in the contemporary era was regarded as revisionism, which inevitably deviated from the correct direction for the localization of Marxism in China. In fact, on the basis of its divorce from the actual situation in China, it dogmatized some conclusions of classical Marxist writers about socialism and communism that had been developed nearly a hundred years earlier and copied some concrete experiences of the revolutionary war era, supplemented by the ideals and practices of a society of great unity in traditional Chinese culture.

The essence of the adjustment in the early 1960s was to a large extent the correction of the Leftist deviation in the fields of economy and politics after the Great Leap Forward in 1958, and the negation and correction of a wrong socialist outlook to a certain extent. The new understanding, new generalization, and economic restructuring of the socialist development stage by the central leaders such as Mao Zedong and Liu Shaoqi was a negation of the "rush" and eagerness to achieve success. The Sixty Articles of Agriculture was a negation of "large scale projects and publicizing property," "supply system," and public canteens. The Seventy Articles of Industry was a negation of the destruction of the production order, the practice of bringing everything under Party organizations, the lack of division between enterprises and governments, disregard for the economic law, and the economic effects and material interests since "the Great Leap Forward." The Fourteen Articles of Science was a negation of the neglect of the laws of scientific research and the disrespect for scientific and technological personnel. The Eight Articles of Literature and Art was a negation of disrespecting the laws of art and artists, and the Sixty Articles of Higher Education was a negation of disregarding the laws of teaching and disrespecting intellectuals.

With the deepening of the adjustment, this type of negation and amendment was not only more in-depth in content, but also followed the trend of accelerating development. The more realistic estimation of the severe economic situation after the 7,000 People's Congress was the basis for further adjustment and objectively reflected the absurdity of the Great Leap Forward. Zhou Enlai and Chen Yi's speeches on the class attributes of intellectuals at the Guangzhou Conference negated the mischaracterization of intellectuals after 1957, and in the first half of 1962, under the chairmanship of Deng Xiaoping, the work of speeding up the screening of Party members and cadres was to a great extent a negation of the Anti-Rightist struggle in 1959, which began to touch upon the expansion of the anti-Rightist struggle in 1957. Wang Jiaxiang's proposal to the Central Committee on foreign relations in the spring of 1962 was a correction of the Leftist deviation in foreign affairs at that time. The rapid development of "household-based production" in many rural areas broke through the bottom line of "three-level team-based" ownership, in Sixty Articles of Agriculture. In fact, it also implied a revision of the rash and radical socialist transformation of agriculture in 1956. Deng Xiaoping's "cat theory" of supporting "household-based production" actually included replacing the 1958 standards of production relations and ideology with productivity standards. Compared with the two Leftist rectifications, in the first half of 1956 and from the second half of 1958 to the first half of 1959, various specific adjustment measures and understandings of the previous five years showed that the adjustment was no longer limited to the correction of the 1958 extreme socialist model and the restoration of the traditional model, and also indicated the transcendence and the overcoming of the Soviet model. Some reforms occupied a place in the tide of socialist reform at that time.

But the limitations of the adjustment were also obvious. This was mainly manifested in, first, the fact that the important progress of adjustment was mostly reflected in the economic aspect, while the progress in the political aspect and the political system was often very limited, and the development between the two was not synchronous and balanced. Further, some deep-seated basic problems concerning what socialism was were not yet broken through, and before these problems were solved, other adjustment results were not solid. It was the asynchronization of political and economic development that provided the conditions for the development of erroneous or comparatively erroneous trends to develop again.

But under the conditions at that time, whether in China or in the Soviet Union and other socialist countries, the conditions for comprehensive reform were far from mature. While the traditional model was touched by some factors, some basic aspects of it were still regarded as sacred and undeniable, and this was still the consensus of the entire Party, as was typical in socialist countries at that time. Against this background, deep adjustment could not fundamentally correct the Leftist deviation in the Party's guiding ideology. In fact, there were still many divergent views on the situation and policy within the Party, especially in the Party's leadership. On the premise that the criticism and accusation of the "anti-rash advance" in 1956, the anti-Rightist struggle in 1957, the "three red flags" in 1958, and the Lushan Conference in 1959 could not be touched at all, and the deepening of adjustment and the development of understanding could not help but widen the differences. In the face of serious difficulties, when adjustment had not yet touched upon some more fundamental problems, these contradictions and differences had either not been fully demonstrated or were temporarily latent. After the situation gradually improved, with the further deepening of the domestic policy adjustment, the further intensification of the Sino-Soviet debate at that time, and the intensification of tensions with some neighboring countries and regions, the differences in the assessment of the situation and work guidance within the Party steadily developed. What was more serious was that, in the view of the traditional socialist model and even more extreme model, this divergence was regarded as a class struggle. As a result, a new round of class struggle was expanded by further adjustment.

2. The Tenth Plenary Session of the Eighth Central Committee

In August 1962, the Central Committee held a working conference in Beidaihe at an important moment when the Central Committee led the people of the whole country to overcome serious difficulties and adjust constantly in all aspects. The original topic of the meeting was to discuss agriculture, finance, and trade, and it included the issue of contracting production to households. At the beginning of the meeting, Mao raised the issues of class, situation, and contradiction and asked everyone to discuss them. In this way, the focus of the Beidaihe Working Conference shifted to the discussion of class struggle. From that time, this topic became the theme of the preparatory meeting for the Tenth Plenary Session of the Eighth Central Committee. At the Beidaihe Working Conference and the Tenth Plenary Session of the Eighth Central Committee, Mao repeatedly raised the issue of class and class struggle in China in connection with his criticism of the views of Khrushchev and the measures taken to adjust the domestic situation, especially after the 7,000 People's Congress. He regarded some differences of understanding in the Party as a reflection of class struggle, some opinions which he disagreed with but which actually conformed to the objective situation, as manifestations of right opportunism, namely revisionism, and called them a "dark wave," "single-handed work," and a "redressing wave."

From the end of 1961 to the 7,000 People's Congress, the central leaders, including Mao Zedong, recognized the serious economic difficulties. However, there were still different opinions on the severity of the difficulties and whether they had come out of the most serious difficulties. For example, according to estimates made before and at the 7,000 People's Congress, by 1962, the national economy had come out of its most difficult "trough" and begun to recover. After the 7,000 People's Congress, at the Expanded Meeting of the Standing Committee of the Politburo (i.e., the West Building Meeting) held by Liu Shaoqi in February 1962, according to the analysis of the financial department, Liu pointed out, "The Central Working Conference (i.e., the 7,000 People's Congress) is not thorough enough to understand the difficult situation and is unwilling to expose any problems, for fear of darkness. What are we afraid of? We are merely getting to the bare truth. It may make people pessimistic but that can stimulate people's courage to struggle against difficulties."[15] This realistic estimate turned out to be the basis for the Central Committee to make further adjustments, but it caused Mao great discontent. At the Beidaihe Work Conference, Mao said that some people now viewed the situation as a dark one. They were confused, lacking confidence, and failing to see the light. Therefore, they thought that socialism did not work, and they had to work on their own. The wind blew higher and higher. He criticized some leaders of the Central Committee for supporting the idea of contracting production to households, representing wealthy middle peasants and demanding independence, and even opposing socialism from the standpoint of landlords, rich peasants, and the bourgeoisie. He also expressed his dissatisfaction with the screening of the anti-Rightist movement at that time, saying that the recent redress was wrong and that the anti-Rightist movement in 1959 could not be done alone. In short, several important aspects of further readjustment after the 7,000 People's Congress were almost regarded as important manifestations of class struggle.

In revising the communiqué of the Tenth Plenary Session of the Eighth Central Committee, Mao added a paragraph emphasizing the existence of class struggle between the proletariat and the bourgeoisie and the struggle between socialism and capitalism in the "whole historical period of the transition from capitalism to communism." In this historical period, "the overthrown reactionary ruling class is not willing to perish. They always try to restore their power. At the same time, there are still bourgeois influences and customary forces in the old society, and there are spontaneous capitalist tendencies of some small producers […] Under these circumstances, class struggle is inevitable. This is a historical law that Marxist-Leninist doctrine has elucidated for a long time, and we must not forget it." Mao Zedong also said that from then on, it was crucial to talk about the danger of class struggle and the restoration of capitalism year after year and month after month, so that the Party could have a clear understanding of this problem and have a Marxist-Leninist line. In this way, determining how to recognize and deal with the important and complex problem of class struggle in a socialist society was once again raised throughout the Party in a serious and extremely simple way. In a socialist society, class struggle would exist in a certain range for a long period and it may intensify under certain conditions, but it was not the main contradiction of socialism. In 1957, the main contradiction in a socialist society was defined as class contradiction because of the expansion of the anti-Rightist struggle. This misconception continued to develop until the Tenth Plenary Session of the Eighth Central Committee further asserted that the main contradiction existed before the arrival of the high stage of socialism. This symbolized the further systematization of the viewpoint of the enlargement of class struggle and made theoretical preparations for the re-development of the Party's Leftist errors on this issue. Like the "three red flags" of 1958, the idea that "class struggle is the core" was different from the Soviet model, but it also went against the correct direction of the localization of Marxism. What was more serious was that the establishment of this "outline" further weakened the Party's ability to correct errors and greatly increased the difficulty of returning to the correct direction of the localization of Marxism.

After the Tenth Plenary Session of the Eighth Central Committee, the work of the whole Party and the whole country entered a complex situation. On the one hand, the Leftist error of expanding political class struggle further developed, while on the other, the task of economic adjustment and recovery could basically continue to be carried out according to the original plan. The two were contradictory, but the contradiction was temporarily controlled within a certain range. It could be imagined that in such a contradictory pattern, the more thorough the economic adjustment and the greater the results, the more likely political Leftist thought would develop, ending this contradictory pattern with a movement similar to the "anti-aggressive" and "anti-Rightist" movements of the 1950s.

According to the analysis of the class struggle situation at that time and the theory of the expanding class struggle, the Central Committee decided to launch a general socialist education movement in urban and rural areas. In the first half of 1963, Mao summed up and put forward the idea that "class struggle should be carried out as soon as possible." He decided to carry out the socialist education campaign with the Four Clean-ups[16] as its main content in the countryside and the Five Oppositions[17] campaign in the cities. By the spring of 1964, a large number of rural social teams had carried out the Four Clean-ups and a few cities had carried out the Five Oppositions pilot projects.

These "major strategic measures" under the guidance of the Leftist inclination in turn developed the Leftist inclination theory. During the campaign in the second half of 1963, the policy of "taking class struggle as the main line" was clearly put forward. In the first half of 1964, a serious estimate was made that about one third of the leadership of grassroots units in the country was not in the Party's hands but in the hands of the enemy and its allies. By the second half of 1964, tasks such as "seizing power" were put forward, and the main danger at present was that right-leaning and left-leaning errors would be further developed. At the Central Working Conference held from the end of 1964 to the beginning of 1965, although some of the Leftist practices in the local movements were partially corrected, it emphasized that the nature of the movement was to solve the contradiction between socialism and capitalism, and that the focus of the movement was "to consolidate the Party's authoritarians who took the road of capitalism." This would focus the spearhead of the struggle on the leaders at all levels of the Party, so as to develop the Leftist ideology of the expansion of class struggle to a new stage, that is, to artificially and systematically create the so-called "class struggle" stage.

At the same time, in the field of ideology, excessive and wrong criticism and struggle had been carried out. In December 1963 and June 1964, Mao Zedong stated in his criticism in two directives concerning literary and artistic circles that "many Communists are keen to advocate feudal and capitalist art, but not socialist art." In recent years, they had fallen to the edge of revisionism. He said that if the Party did not reform this seriously, it would become a group like the Petöfi Club in Hungary. Prompted by these two instructions, criticism in the field of literature and art escalated after 1964, rapidly expanding to academia and education. With the development of overheated criticism in these fields, the "two hundreds" principle was seriously undermined, and the majority of intellectuals were all soldiers and self-endangered. Most of the intellectuals were once again called "bourgeois intellectuals." Many adjustments in the fields of culture were interrupted in the early 1960s.

After the Tenth Plenary Session of the Eighth Central Committee, although the Leftist errors in politics, ideology, and culture developed again, they did not become the errors that dominated the overall situation until the launch of the Cultural Revolution. The main focus of the Party and the people throughout the country was still on adjusting the national economy and restoring and developing production. After 1963, the national economic situation began to improve overall. By 1965, after five years of readjustment, industrial and agricultural production had been restored and developed, market supply had been improved, price stability and market prosperity had been maintained throughout the country, and the task of readjustment had been successfully completed. At the Third National People's Congress held from the end of 1964 to the beginning of 1965, on behalf of the Central Committee, Zhou Enlai declared that China's national economy was about to enter a new period of development. In 1966, the Third Five Year Plan would be implemented. All the people of the country should strive to gradually build China into a strong socialist nation with modern agriculture, industry, national defense, and technology.

From the completion of the three major reforms to 1966, there were two trends in the development of the Party's guiding ideology. One development trend was correct and relatively correct, and the other was wrong. All the correct development trends were able to correctly grasp China's national conditions, promote its modernization in the process of the localization of Marxism, and adapt it to the international environment that had undergone great changes and the needs of contemporary socialist development. Any violation of these two articles would inevitably lead to a wrong trend of development. However, whether the trend be correct or wrong, it was the product of the process of exploring the localization of Marxism, and it also provided the conditions for the ultimate realization of localization.

The accumulation and development of Leftist errors in the previous ten years finally temporarily overwhelmed the correct trend of development and led to the launching of the Cultural Revolution.

Chapter 9

The Destiny of the Localization of Marxism in China During the Cultural Revolution

With the completion of the task of national economic adjustment in 1966, China launched the implementation of its Third Five Year Plan, ushering the country into a new period of economic development. To overcome the serious national economic difficulties and encourage confidence among the cadres and the masses, great effort was put into production, with a strong hope that the economy would improve rapidly. Unfortunately, it was at this time that the Cultural Revolution broke out.

The Cultural Revolution was part of the CPC's process of exploring ways for China to forge its own path toward socialism. Under the banner of defending and developing Marxism, a serious Leftist error emerged. It was the strong desire for Chinese Marxism that led the pursuit astray.

The Cultural Revolution was a negation of the policies and theories enacted since the founding of New China, particularly in the 1960s. It was a mistake in the CPC's movement toward socialism, in which Marxist theory was adapted to the real situation in China in inappropriate ways. It was also a misguided response to the contemporary socialist revolution and the global trend of modernism. This misguided response reflected a thought and practice that were typical in a world going through the process of modernization.

In declaring the "fully victorious" Cultural Revolution, the Political Reports of the CPC's Ninth National Congress emphasized that Mao Zedong Thought embraced "the complete collapse of imperialism and an age of the global victory of Marxist-Leninist Thought" and "combined the universal truth of Marxist-Leninist ideology with revolutionary practice, inheriting, defending, and developing Marxist-Leninist Thought in political, military, economic, cultural, philosophical, and other aspects, to elevate it to a new stage." The Reports also argued for the theory of "continuing revolution under the dictatorship of the proletariat," which was "the theoretical foundation of the Great Proletarian Cultural Revolution." In fact, Mao Zedong launched the Cultural Revolution based on this theory, seriously distorting the scientific implications of Mao Zedong Thought and departing from basic Marxist principles. It was also a serious departure from the task of integrating Marxism into the realities of the Chinese situation.

I

The Concept of Socialism at the Beginning of the Cultural Revolution

The Cultural Revolution was launched and led by Mao Zedong. He hoped it would allow China to choose a different path to social development, something other than the traditional Soviet model. At the same time, it was a response to the drawbacks of contemporary capitalist modernization. It was his answer to the burning questions of the 1960s, of what socialism was and how a socialist society should be built. It was also his great effort to further localize Marxism in the face of current conditions. The Cultural Revolution was a deviation from contemporaneous global trends toward modernization, and it brought disastrous results to the Party and to national development, going astray from the overarching aim of integrating Marxism into the realities of the Chinese situation.

1. China and the Radical World

The Cultural Revolution was the product of a socialist concept that was closely related with the Leftism and radicalism rampant in the decade of the 1950s and

1960s. At the time, China's development was typical of the classic notion of generalized changes around the world: there was great turbulence, great division, and massive reorganization. Looking back now, forty years later, this assessment seems even more accurate. At that time, in many different regions and countries, a great variety of groups or factions each went in more radical or more conservative directions, but on the whole, the leading trend was a move toward radicalization.

Since the 1950s, Third World nations had opposed imperialism and both old and new forms of colonialism. In many places, people took up arms in national independence and liberation movements. Good news spread in wave after wave. The international order of old colonialism collapsed and numerous conflicts emerged in the capitalist system. To Third World nations, the 1960s was a period of anti-imperialism, the age of revolution against old and new forms of colonialism, and a movement against hegemony. Armed uprisings, guerrilla warfare, military coups, foreign interventions, bloody killings, and political turmoil were all clear signs of that decade. The liberation movements in Third World countries reached a climax in the 1960s, basically completing the mission of national liberation and independence.

After the Second World War, developed capitalist countries were going through their own adjustments, to varying degrees adapting to the demands of development in the new technological revolution, easing or delaying economic crisis, and accelerating productivity. For some major capitalist countries, this period was a "golden age." The vast majority of workers, farmers, and intellectuals became the beneficiaries of this prosperity, easing the class tensions in the Western world. But amid the process of capitalist modernization, there were several drawbacks, resulting in the rise of left-wing groups, students' movements, movements protesting racial discrimination, and other such activities. This was especially true in the 1960s after the escalation of the Vietnam War, which set off an anti-war movement that was unprecedented in Western developed countries, dealing a heavy blow to the American and other governments. In 1968, student groups around the world stirred up trouble, leading to students' movements, from Western countries such as the US, France, Britain, and Germany, to Japan and across socialist countries such as Poland, Czechoslovakia, and Yugoslavia. Young people were not content to become materially wealthy under a capitalist system of modernization. Their dissatisfaction with, anger at, and rebellion against the expanding material desire, the spiritual degradation, the prevailing instrumental rationality, and the repression of the individual all merged into a surging tide. Maoist thought gained great prestige among Western left-wing intellectuals. In April 1969, the *Political Reports of the Ninth CPC National Congress* pointed out that in the heart of capitalist territory in Japan, Western Europe, and North America, there had been an outbreak of unprecedented revolutionary activity and that more and more people were undergoing an awakening.

Compared to the evolution of Leftist radicalism in Third World countries and in developed capitalist nations at the time, reform in socialist countries was lagging behind, revealing a hidden tendency toward conservatism. After the Second World War, a strong socialist camp emerged. As socialist countries made great strides in eradicating exploitation, developing the economy, promoting equality, and safeguarding peace, progressive movements around the world were encouraged to stand against imperialism and all forms of reactionary forces. Since the mid 1950s, the international communist movement had started reflecting on the Stalinist model, and most socialist countries began their reforms based on the Soviet model. The reforms had brought great vitality to the politics and economy of those socialist societies, but it was inevitable that their historic traditions, geopolitics, national conditions, divergent understandings of Marxism, rigid political systems, and other factors would lead to divergence in their understanding and practice in their reforms, leading to divergence or even outright division in the socialist camp. It should be noted that such debates, disagreements, and divergence in the development of contemporary socialism were inevitable. While this brought great losses to the international communist movement, it also drove the development of socialist theory and practice. In this process, whatever achievements or setbacks the socialist countries, workers' parties, or the Communist Party around the world underwent, they were reflections of socialism moving along the inevitable historical path from classic to modern and further to a contemporary form.

In the absence of precedence for reform, Soviet leaders such as Khrushchev and Brezhnev sought to make a few attempts and achieved certain results, but because of the limitations they faced, they met with numerous obstacles and much opposition. Most noteworthy is that though the revolutions were still in the preliminary stages, there was a certain degree of negation to the original models and traditional ideas. In the eyes of those socialist countries where the economy was already more developed, where material conditions were more mature, and where there was already a high degree of socialization, this was a natural historical process. But among those countries where productivity was still relatively backward and where the top priority was to develop the economy quickly under a new system, and in countries that had just ended massive revolutionary wars where vigorous class struggle movements retained a great deal of inertia, it was difficult to understand or accept anything different from classical theory, and even more difficult to absorb practices different from the traditional practice of reform through war.

After the death of Stalin, the great power and chauvinism retreated for a while in the Soviet Union, but before long, it bounced back and intensified, causing dissatisfaction and opposition from socialist parties in various countries. Partly because of differences over the issue of reform, but also because of chauvinism and hegemonism on the part of the Soviet powers, Sino-Soviet relations continued to deteriorate to the point that a major debate impacted the world in the 1960s. Mao Zedong believed the Soviets had already become a revisionist party through "peaceful evolution," betraying the cause of communism. Parties in Europe, Asia, and South America were likewise evolved or in the process of evolution. The changes in the Soviet and other parties were not accidental, but were the result of interference on the part of the new domestic bourgeoisie or foreign imperialist forces. If China did not take urgent action to block it, struggling against imperialist "peaceful evolution" and modern revisionism, the tragedy that had occurred in the Soviet Union would be repeated in China. In the first half of 1966, Mao Zedong said several times that the majority of the parties in the world stood on the side of revisionism. In July of that year, with a heavy heart and with great concern, he wrote a letter in which he said that of the more than one hundred Communist Parties in the world, most no longer believed in Marxism and Leninism, and that Marxist-Leninist Thought had been shattered. This reflected his view that the socialist ideas and movement were then undergoing significant and profound changes all over the world at that time.

After the 1960s, China found that there had been a major change in its environment. Two superpowers, the US and the Soviet Union, exerted pressure on China, one from the north and one from the south, even threatening naked aggression. This situation gave Mao Zedong a sense of impending crisis. He often mentioned to the whole Party that imperialism would encroach on China, but

China had no way to fight off subjugation. His concerns were not without reason, but as he considered this issue, he failed to pay sufficient attention to the major economic and political changes in the post-war capitalist nations, the new features in the global economy, and the new trends and traits in the global environment ushered in by the rise in the technological revolution. He drew several conclusions about war and revolution from Marx and Lenin, particularly the belief that war and revolution should continue to be the main features of the current era. The general pattern around the world was that either revolution put an end to war, or war brought about revolution. He encouraged the whole Party not to fear war, but to be prepared to fight. They should make all preparation, be prepared even to fight the US, and be especially prepared to fight revisionism. He overestimated the urgency to prepare for the outbreak of war and overestimated the possibility of revolution being triggered by such wars around the world. On the one hand, these overestimations gave him confidence and optimism about the future of revolution around the world. On the other hand, with two superpowers pressing down on him on either side, he worried about national security.

With the movements opposing imperialism and colonialism around the world and the upsurge in Leftist movements and ideology in the 1960s, revolution in socialist countries had met with many obstacles, or even come to a standstill in some instances. The sense of urgency surrounding the possible imminent outbreak of war had a profound impact on heads of state and of the Communist Party of China in their views of the global situation and the continued progress of socialism and the contemporary development trends in Marxist thought, which in turn profoundly impacted their views on the domestic situation and influenced the future direction taken by policy-makers.

2. What is Socialism?

By 1956, the Three Great Transformations had just been completed, and Mao Zedong had put forward the task of reform according to the Soviet model. He told the Party that Chinese socialism must proceed from China's own national conditions and with liberated thought based on the Soviet experience, relying on Marxism for development and progress. This understanding reflected the common aspirations of some socialist nations at the time concerning the proper direction socialist countries should then pursue in their reform. But once this issue had been settled, another more complicated and arduous task lay ahead of them, the question of how thought should be liberated and how the Soviet model could be surpassed. What, in fact, should the socialism they were pursuing ultimately look like? What was the path to Chinese Marxism? How could the tenets of the original Marxist doctrine be applied to the Chinese situation? It was not so simple a thing as just denying the Soviet model and moving smoothly along the path to reform. Socialist countries met with many obstacles in the process of reforming the Soviet model, putting in a great deal of effort, and many had to pay a very heavy price. In their own explorations, Mao and the CPC expended great effort and endured a torturous path to development. The Great Leap Forward, for instance, was a failure, but it showed the Party's ardent desire to transcend the Soviet model. The people's commune movement had a strong Chinese flavor to it, but it was not Marxist. The Cultural Revolution was a complete mistake, but it was also a huge step away from the Soviet model.

The successful reform of the Soviet model required not only in-depth observation of the practical experience of Soviet socialism, but also a deep understanding of one's own national conditions, while also gleaning wisdom from decades of rich practices of the international communist movement and the changing themes of the times to liberate thought and promote the development and modernization of Marxism. At the same time, it was important to also have a profound grasp of capitalism and a deep, comprehensive understanding of the time and its contemporary trends. Most importantly, smooth reform required a certain level of development of socialized mass production and a commodity economy — that is, the development of productivity — as the material basis. If just one small agrarian economy accounted for the majority of the nation, an understanding of things such as the law of value, modern management, and use of modern credit systems would be lacking. This lack of attention and use of these things would result in such countries lagging far behind developed industrial nations. Likewise, observation and understanding of the drawbacks of the Soviet model showed that an obvious discrepancy often existed between the conclusions drawn by developed and undeveloped nations.

Mao Zedong used various resources for the reform of the Soviet model. Besides his observations and contemplations on the Soviet revolution and construction model, he relied on his particular understanding of the basic tenets of Marxism formed in the long-term revolutionary struggle. His reform was also based on his understanding of Chinese history and its relation to the world at large, the impact of the "New Village" activities in his revolutionary career, and the influence of the wealth and power of militant communism and its influence during the period of the Chinese revolutionary war. It was the interaction of these material and ideological conditions that determined many of the characteristics of China's reform at that time. Though the Great Leap Forward came with a strong desire to transcend the Soviet model, many of its underlying tenets are not aligned with the direction contemporary socialism had taken, such as its neglect of the role of economic laws in socialist construction, its neglect of and unfamiliarity with modern management systems and the legal system, its concern over the potential of "bourgeois law" as a result of a commodity economy and distribution of income based on one's performance under socialist conditions, its advocacy of the use of mass movements and militant communism for economic construction, its deep concern over the emergence of "bourgeois thinking" and "revisionism" that material benefits might produce, and a belief that a life of simplicity and poverty would engender and sustain a sufficient revolutionary spirit, which could in turn provide a strong impetus for socialist development.

From the adjustments of the early 1960s, the traditional model was both restored and reformed. The more realistic adjustments and deeper explorations yielded a number of quick preliminary results. More importantly, in many different ways, these efforts reflected new understandings of socialism. But under the conditions at that time, the modernization of Marxism did not make significant progress. Reform in socialist countries was still faltering, and there were no substantial breakthroughs behind the scenes. With China's underdeveloped economy, the basic issue of the people's understanding of the nature of socialism was restricted to varying degrees. In an environment in which political adjustments and adjustments to the political system lagged behind economic adjustments, coupled with the international situation at that time, conditions were not yet ripe for China's socialist reform. As a result, the new understandings of socialism and correspondingly new measures produced in the adjustment period deepened and intensified their contradictions with traditional concepts of socialism. From 1964 onward, Mao's criticism of revisionism in his conversations with the Party became increasingly sharp. At a deeper level, these sort of concerns reflected the contradictions between Mao's ideal form of socialism and the realities of China's internal situation at that time. At the same time, they also reflect the contradictions between the reforms socialism was undergoing in the rest of the world and the ideal form of socialism according to Mao.

On May 7, 1966, the eve of the launch of the Cultural Revolution, Mao Zedong gave Lin Biao a set of instructions, called the May 7 Instructions, in which he once again systematically laid out some basic views on socialism. He said that the army should be a big school that could do all sorts of work beyond the waging of wars. During the eight years of the Second World War, China had used its anti-Japan base in just this way. In this school, one could study politics, military tactics, or literature, engage in agricultural and sideline production, and work in small or medium sized factories. They would produce enough for their own needs, and the surplus would be exchanged for other products with other parts of the country. It would engage in mass production and participate in the Four Clean-ups Movement (i.e., Socialist Education Movement) in factories and rural areas. When the Four Clean-ups Movement was complete, there would be other work for the masses to engage in, creating lasting unity within the military. Even more, the military might take part at any time in the struggle for cultural revolution through criticism of the bourgeoisie. In this way, military studies, military industry, and military and civilian activities could be integrated. But in order for these to be deployed appropriately, any particular army could incorporate only one, or at most two, of agriculture, industry, and other civilian activities, but not all three at once. In this way, the might of millions of troops might be well utilized.

He believed the workers were the same, that while they would take production as first priority, they would also be trained in military affairs, politics, and culture, while participating in the Four Clean-ups Movement and the criticism of the bourgeoisie. When possible, they should also be engaged in agricultural and sideline industry production, as the case in the Daqing Oilfield. Farmers would take agricultural work (including forestry, animal husbandry, sideline, and fishing) as their primary responsibility, while also studying military affairs, politics, culture, and when possible, engage in light industry and criticizing the bourgeoisie. Students would do the same, taking studies as their primary responsibility while learning other skills. They would not only study, but also learn industry, agriculture, and military affairs, while also criticizing the bourgeoisie. The school years were to be shortened. Education was to be revolutionized, and the rule of schools by bourgeois intellectuals would not be allowed to continue. Commerce, the service industry, and the Party and government organizations would follow a similar practice whenever conditions allowed.

Finally, Mao pointed out that these ideas were not new suggestions or innovations. They had, in fact, been implemented for many years, but were not yet popular. The military had already been functioning in this way for decades, but now it was necessary to develop it even further.

These suggestions of Mao's reflected some of his basic assumptions about socialism at that time. These ideals had been played out in a certain degree in the Great Leap Forward and the people's commune movement. During the period of adjustment that followed, according to his own experience and reflections in 1958, Mao further explored the issue of what socialism really was. Abandoning some of the impractical ideas behind the Great Leap Forward, he developed an understanding of the long-term construction and development of socialist revolution. With the deepening differences in views in the Party on socialist construction and the expansion of class struggle, Mao's concept of socialist construction increasingly emphasized class struggle. These new developments are more fully attested to in several documents issued just before the outbreak of the Cultural Revolution, including the May 16 Notice and the May 7 Instructions.

In some important respects, the May 7 Instructions, the Great Leap Forward, and the people's commune movement were quite similar, reflecting Mao's unremitting desire for certain important features of socialism. This sort of socialism "took class struggle as the key link," relying on class struggle for the power and security of economic construction and social development. For individuals involved in production, then, class consciousness and the revolutionary spirit were the overriding source of inspiration for anything. In such a society, every member of the community, as a worker or a farmer who was physically and mentally competent, would be economically self-sufficient, or at least partially so. As for the production of goods, though it could not be neglected as a means of developing the economy, it belonged to the bourgeoisie, so must be limited. Although social division of labor was a must for the future, it would lead to inequality among the people in the production process, so it too must be limited, with conditions gradually being created to narrow it. In the field of distribution, differences should also be narrowed, or even implemented on a system of supply on a largely equal basis. The fact that human desires were always led by their material interests presents a direct threat to pure, noble virtues, and even led to a downfall of the spirit, so it was revolutionary ideals and class consciousness that could lead to the greatest, most lasting power, making workers happy and willing to endure the trials of hard labor and taxing mental work. Such a society may not be wealthy, but would be a superior system, because those in affluent societies tended to pay the spiritual price, suffering depression as socialist values deteriorated.

Mao Zedong's understanding of socialism included century-old Marxist notions about the future direction of society, as well as his sense of overcoming the drawbacks associated with Soviet models. It likewise bore the deep imprint of China's experience of base construction and militant communism during the period of revolutionary war, layered on top of a long history of Chinese traditions and culture. While containing some bold ideas and imaginative thoughts and reflecting some sharp criticisms of contemporary capitalist modernization in an embodiment of an idealist pursuit, the May 7 Instructions presented a socialist model that, overall, was not very realistic. It ignored the decisive role of the level of development in production to the form of a society, detached from developing productivity as the core of socialism, ignoring the significance of a commodity economy to the development of socialism. Further, it took the remnants of class struggle as the main spearhead for ongoing socialist struggle, hoping to achieve victory over the bourgeoisie through uninterrupted class struggle, limiting the division of labor, limiting differences, limiting material interests, and other similar means. All of this held a flavor of empiricism and utopianism. Mao put forward these ideas because, as he himself said, since they were proven methods from the War of Resistance Against Japanese Aggression, the army had "already been doing this for decades." But he did not seem to notice that what was an appropriate approach during a revolutionary war would not be able to unconditionally promote what was needed for society at large, particularly not for a comprehensive construction of socialism. Socialism required development and reform, but these things had to start from the point of present circumstances and the current level of development of production forces. Socialist construction required revolutionary tradition and heroism during the war, but these things could not simply be forced directly into a society. The basic principles of Marxism could not be violated, but they must follow the development of the times, and the correctness of these developments could only be tested by practice and experience.

On May 15, the Central Committee forwarded this missive to the entire Party. The forwarding of the May 7 Instructions showed that a "new period of the development of Marxist-Leninist Thought has dawned." On August 1, Mao Zedong published an article in the *People's Daily* celebrating the 39th anniversary of the army, entitled "The Entire Nation Should Become a School for Mao Zedong Thought: Commemorating the 39th Anniversary of the Chinese People's Liberation Army." An excerpt of the May 7 Instructions was published with it, along with a very favorable review, which read, "We heartily commend as our guideline Comrade Mao Zedong's proposal that people from all walks of life who are physically and mentally competent engage in agricultural and industrial work, as at a school for revolutionary thought. If we carry out all that Comrade Mao has said, it will greatly raise the consciousness of the proletariat, revolutionizing the people's thought… In this way, the gap between workers and peasants, rural and urban peoples, and blue collar and white collar workers could be reduced… and a fully militarized population be achieved… China's 700 million people can all be made critics of the old world order, and builders and defenders of the new world. They would each pick up a hammer to build, a hoe to till, a gun to defend, and a pen to write. In this way, the entire nation will be schooled in Mao Zedong Thought, which is to be schooled in communist thought."

The basic ideas and specific requirements laid out in the May 7 Instructions were implemented in 1969 in the Struggle, Criticism, and Reform Campaign. It entered deeply into the realm of nearly every department and every field, involving countless experiments, case studies, and a dazzling array of activities. This understanding of socialism and the consequent disputes it provoked within the Party turned out to be the key contributing factors of the Cultural Revolution. It was the pursuit of this model of socialism that became the core element of the Cultural Revolution. With this sort of standard of socialism it was inevitable that an increasing number of class enemies would be identified, the danger of restoring capitalism would be greater, and class struggle would be escalated.

3. Lagging Marxist Modernization and Erroneous Judgment

With the revolutionary economic, political, and other changes happening in the international arena, Marxism itself faced the urgent task of making itself more contemporary – that is, of adapting to the current, developing conditions in various countries around the world, and finding a way to advance with the times. This required not only adherence to the basic principles of Marxism, but also the sublation of some conclusions about Marxism that had proven outdated and the introduction of new developments within Marxist thought. Without this sort of effort toward making Marxism more contemporary – or to put it more precisely, without *proper* effort toward making Marxism more contemporary – Marxism would become outdated, and the hope of integrating Marxism into China would come to naught.

During the democratic revolution, Mao had resolutely opposed dogmatism. He opposed the process of dogmatizing Marxist thought, and proposed that Marxism be integrated into China scientifically, founding Mao Zedong Thought, and thereby achieving the first great leap in localizing Marxism. Once comprehensive socialist construction was underway, despite the strong development of Marxism and the hope of promoting Chinese Marxism, for reasons beyond China's control – including the lag in innovations in Marxist ideas around the world and the limitations of China's current situation – some dogmatism or misunderstandings of the original tenets of Marxism's guiding principles began to creep into China's socialist construction, without proper attention to its specific situation. For instance, because of the vision for the future found in the works of many classical Marxist writers, the long-term nature of socialist revolution was greatly underestimated, and the fundamental importance of developing productivity to China's revolution and construction was overlooked. During the Great Leap Forward and the people's commune movement, the attitude toward "communes," "bourgeois rule," and other issues contributed directly to the use of classical writers' descriptions as a basis for a future society. During the period of adjustment of the national economy, some of the assertions made by classic writers were misinterpreted, taking some appropriate adjustment measures as signs of revisionism or capitalism and hence affecting the Party's judgments of the national situation and that within the Party, so that class struggle could progress step by step. In the debates over the development within the International Communist Party in the 1960s, this sort of tendency went even further. For instance, in June 1963, in *On the General Line of the International Communist Movement*, it was said, "Prior to the stage of a communist society is the transitional period of transition from capitalism to communism, i.e., the period of the rule of the proletariat." This statement caused some confusion in the recognition of two different transitions in the stages of social development, that is, from the new democracy to socialism, and from capitalism to socialism.

Another example of a departure from Marxism occurred in the use of excerpts from classical Marxist writers' works from more than a hundred years earlier. Ignoring the realities and great changes of the postwar world, Marxist thinkers lagged behind in their understanding of capitalism and socialism, the transition from capitalism to socialism, the characteristics of the times, how to deal with war and peace, and a series of other major issues. As a result, when Soviet and other leaders proposed ideas such as "peaceful coexistence, peaceful competition, and peaceful transition" after World War II, these were harshly criticized by China. The CPC believed that the world was still in the ongoing imperialist and proletarian revolution era that Lenin had pointed to, and that "global capitalism and imperialism must be destroyed, and socialism and communism brought to victory."[1] Further, "the general trend of the world today" could be summed up in Mao's words, "the enemy rots as we get better day by day."[2] Such a judgment of the times and understanding of the situation around the world were continually reinforced during the Cultural Revolution. In fact, they were recorded in the preface to the reprint of *Quotations of Chairman Mao* and circulated widely, and were adopted and added to the constitution of the Party at the Ninth National Congress of the CPC. With such major divisions on the nature of the times, other conflicts were bound to develop.

In the context of Marxism's lagging behind in its efforts to become more contemporary, not only did varying degrees and forms of dogmatism develop with the international communist movement, but conflicts also emerged internally, affecting domestic policy. These developments, heightened by misreadings of the international situation, were important factors behind the launching of the Cultural Revolution.

4. Development of Errors in the Theory and Practice of the Expansion of Class Struggle

After a long revolutionary war, the Communist Party of China finally entered a socialist society. With the influence of this practice, experience, and habit of intense class struggle, after the anti-Rightist struggle in 1957, Mao Zedong changed the Party's conclusions at the Eighth National Congress of the CPC on the major conflicts in a socialist society. This was the starting point and theoretical root for the errors that occurred in the development and expansion of class struggle. During the Lushan Meeting in 1959, Mao not only wrongly launched a criticism of Peng Dehuai, but also called this conflict "a class struggle" and "a continuation of the life-and-death struggle between the bourgeoisie and the proletariat," bringing class struggle into the Party. This was a serious escalation of class struggle. By the time of the Tenth Plenary Session of the Eighth National Congress of the CPC in 1962, Mao had developed an understanding of the differences within the Party as reflections of class struggle and sought to expand and bring to an extreme the class struggle that was bound to exist to some degree in any socialist society. He further asserted that a period of class struggle as the main conflict should be extended until the advanced stages of communism had been ushered in. Later, this assertion was called the "basic theory" of the Party, and during the Cultural Revolution, it was called "the basic line of the Party throughout the history of its move toward socialism."[3] This indicated that the idea of the expansion of class struggle had been further systemized. Between 1963 and 1965, the socialist education movement put forward a policy of "class struggle as the key link." In January 1965, the "Twenty-Three Propositions" drawn up under Mao's leadership stressed that the essence of this campaign was to solve the contradictions between the doctrines of socialism and capitalism. The target of the movement was to "take on those within the Party who followed the capitalist path." This put the focus of the struggle squarely on Party leaders at all levels, which resulted in Leftist thought developing to a stage where "class struggle" was systematically created in an artificial and arbitrary way, which became the main basis for the Cultural Revolution and for the theory of "continuing revolution under the dictatorship of the proletarian."

From this theory, Mao continued to make further errors in his judgments of domestic and the Party's political situations and major tasks. On the eve of the Cultural Revolution in 1966, he gradually formed a more cohesive, systematic view, from which the Cultural Revolution was launched. He believed that a large number of representatives of the bourgeoisie and reactionary revisionists were intermingled with the Party, government, military, and cultural fields, and that the leadership in a majority of sectors was no longer in the hands of the Marxists and the people. In addition, a faction within the Party was taking the capitalist road, forming a bourgeois leadership within the Central Government that was taking a revisionist political and organizational line, with representatives in the provinces, municipalities, autonomous regions, and the central government. He further believed that in the past, all manner of struggle had not been able to settle the issues and that only the implementation of a great cultural revolution that was open and comprehensive, working from the bottom-up to mobilize the masses to expose the darkness would be able to recapture power from the capitalists. Finally, this was essentially a class struggle to achieve another stage in the great political revolution, and it would ultimately have to be repeated numerous times. In this way, Mao launched a comprehensive, systematic theory of the Great Proletarian Cultural Revolution. This more typical theory of "continuing revolution" formed the theoretical foundation for the Cultural Revolution.

In the mid 1960s, in the process of correcting the Leftist error of the Great Leap Forward and adjusting the national economy, on the one hand, China continued in accordance with the original plan for the task of economic adjustments and recovery. On the other, the Leftist error continued on the political front, mainly symbolized by the expansion of class struggle, but right up until the launch of the Cultural Revolution, it had not yet reached a position of dominance. Within the Party, since the eighth National Congress of the CPC, the two trends had continued to cross and intertwine in the process of exploring China's own forging of a socialist path, and conflicts had developed.

In the end, because of the influence of the dogmatic understanding of Marxism at that time and the arbitrariness of some individuals, among other factors, Leftist error tended to temporarily overwhelm proper development trends, which eventually led to the launch of the Cultural Revolution.

With a guiding idea of "class struggle as the key link," the Party leadership – both Mao himself and other leaders – launched a decade-long initiative, lasting from 1966 through 1976, that aimed to "topple the capitalist faction within the Party." The "world of chaos" the Cultural Revolution brought to the Party, the state, and the people had disastrous results.

II

The Theory and Practice of Continuing the Revolution Under the Dictatorship of the Proletariat

1. The Formation and Content of the Theory of Continuing Revolution

The theory of "continuing the revolution under the dictatorship of the proletariat (referred to as the Theory of Continuing Revolution was the guiding ideology and basic theory undergirding the Cultural Revolution, written into the Party's political reports and Party Articles approved at the Ninth and the Tenth National Congresses of the CPC and incorporated into the Constitution, and passed at the Fourth National People's Congress. It was understood to be the "third great milestone"[4] in the development history of Marxism. At that time, in the general understanding of the main aspects of the development of Marxism, it was referred to as "the consolidation of the theory and practice of the dictatorship of the proletariat, with prevention of the return of capitalism as a key topic."[5] History had already proved that the Theory of Continuing Revolution was not a development of Marxism, but a dual departure from Marxism and the basic conditions in China. The integration of Marxism into China had suffered major setbacks, resulting in serious consequences to the Party, the state, and all the people in the country.

The Theory of Continuing Revolution was the embodiment of the whole body of Leftist errors in socialist class struggle, which had been continually developed since the struggle against the right in 1957. Before the Cultural Revolution, the theory was still in its burgeoning, fermenting, and early development stages. In looking at the whole body of Mao's thinking and activities, this problem forms only one small part of his errors. After the full launch of the Cultural Revolution, the basic premises of this theory took shape, and it occupied a dominant position in his thought and activities of this time. At the Eleventh Plenary Session of the Eighth National Congress of the CPC, the Central Committee put forward a series of instructions by Mao Zedong regarding the Cultural Revolution, in which it was called "a great development in Marxist-Leninist thought" and a product of "Comrade Mao's inheritance, defense, and development of Marxist-Leninist thought in a genius, creative, and comprehensive way to usher it into a new stage." On May 18, 1967, *Red Flag* and the *People's Daily* ran a series of articles as "Great Historical Documents," which first proposed the concept of "revolution under the dictatorship of the proletariat," calling it the "third great milestone" in the development of Marxism. In 1967, the ninth issue of *Red Flag* ran an article entitled "Two Fundamentally Opposed Documents," which evaluated this theory and "the brilliant idea of revolution under the dictatorship of the proletariat." On October 1, 1967, the *People's Daily*, *Red Flag*, and the *Liberation Army Daily* ran the editorial article "Long Live the Cultural Revolution Under the Dictatorship of the Proletariat," in which the development was called "the glorious theory of continuing revolution under the dictatorship of the proletariat." This continued until June 1, 1976, when an article appeared in the *People's Daily*, *Red Flag*, and the *Liberation Army Daily*, entitled "The October Socialist Revolution Opens the Way Forward: Commemorating the 50th Anniversary of the October Revolution," which formally laid out the theory of continuing revolution under the dictatorship of the proletariat, summing up its theory and main content in six points, offering a detailed, "authoritative" explanation. Chen Boda and Yao Wenyuan oversaw the draft of this article, and it was personally approved by Chairman Mao, who gave the article a very positive evaluation. "Comrade Mao has completely inherited, defended, and developed Marxist-Leninist Thought, creatively putting forward the great theory of continuing revolution under the dictatorship of the proletariat, and personally launching and leading the first Great Proletarian Cultural Revolution in human history. This is a new stage in the development of Marxism, and a very important expression of Mao Zedong Thought." The theory of continuing revolution "ingenuously and creatively developed the concept of class struggle and the dictatorship of the proletariat in Marxist-Leninist Thought, the significance of which has shaped a generation, and has cultivated the third great milestone in the history of Marxism."[6] It went on to say, "The great October Socialist Revolution opened the way for the proletariat to seize power," and "China's Great Proletarian Cultural Revolution has opened the way for the consolidation of the dictatorship of the proletariat, prevented the return of capitalism, and opened the way to communism. Its basic experience reflects the struggle after the establishment of the dictatorship of the proletariat during a particular historical stage in the transition to communism." This article held that the center of the worldwide revolution had gradually moved to China, "producing Mao Zedong Thought."

The Party's Political Reports of the Ninth National Congress of the CPC further called the theory "a major new contribution to the theory and practice of Marxist-Leninist Thought," and said that according to this theory, the launching of the Cultural Revolution was "absolutely necessary, and very timely."⁷ Kang Sheng likewise publicized his opinion. He said that Mao had developed the Marxist theory of continuing revolution not only by advocating the theory of continuing revolution under the dictatorship of the proletariat, but also through his creation of a particular form of continuing revolution, the Great Proletarian Cultural Revolution.

On March 8, 1971, to commemorate the 100th anniversary of the Paris Commune, the *People's Daily*, *Red Flag*, and the *Liberation Army Daily* jointly issued an editorial entitled "Long Live the Victorious Dictatorship of the Proletariat," the main content of which was a discussion of the significance of the theory of continuing revolution. The editorial pointed out that the focus of Marxist continuous struggle against revisionism, the bourgeoisie, and the petty bourgeoisie was to determine whether to insistently use revolutionary violence to destroy the bourgeois state machine and to establish the proletariat, or to maintain the bourgeois state machine and oppose to the proletariat. The proletariat taking power was not the end, but merely the beginning of socialist revolution. In order to consolidate the dictatorship of the proletariat and avoid the return of capitalism, the proletariat must not only carry out socialist revolution on the economic front, but also on the political and ideological fronts, transforming the overall structure of society and implementing the dictatorship of the proletariat in every aspect of the culture, seeing socialist revolution through to the end. The article gave a positive review to the theory of continuing revolution, saying that "Chairman Mao has completely summed up the historical experience of the dictatorship of the proletariat, both its positive and negative aspects. He has inherited, defended, and developed the theories of the revolution and the dictatorship of the proletariat in Marxist-Leninist Thought, putting forward the idea of continuing revolution under the dictatorship of the proletariat and, in both theory and practice, working to consolidate the dictatorship of the proletariat and prevent the restoration of capitalism. This is the most significant new contribution to Marxist-Leninist Thought, allowing us to gain the victory by completing the establishment of the dictatorship of the proletariat."

In the later days of the Cultural Revolution, Mao brought a new development to this theory, proposing several theoretical issues in socialism and the dictatorship of the proletariat. On October 20, 1974, when meeting with the Prime Minister of Denmark, Paul Hartling, Mao Zedong said, "Overall, China is a socialist state. Before Liberation, we were basically like a capitalist state. Now in the areas of implementation of the eight-grade wages system, income distribution based on performance, and currency exchange, we are not much different from before. What is different is that ownership has changed."[8] In February 1975, the *People's Daily* published the editorial, "Learn the Theory of the Dictatorship of the Proletariat," which contained a transcript of a discussion with Mao. In it, he stated, "It is important to understand why Lenin said what he did about the dictatorship of the bourgeoisie. If one is not clear on this issue, it will result in revisionism... Now, China has already implemented a commodity system to a degree, the wage system is not equal, and we have the eight-grade wages system, and other such things. These can only be limited under the dictatorship of the proletariat. So if Lin Biao and others like him come to power, it is easy to fall into capitalism."[9]

Mao recognized that the distribution of income based on performance, the exchange of goods, and other such forms of equality were in fact systems of inequality, and were therefore the breeding ground for revisionism and capitalism. This was the main reason for the Cultural Revolution, and was the theoretical basis for his Leftist leaning economic policy. In fact, this sort of thinking was based on a misunderstanding of the works of Marx, Engels, and Lenin, and also contained a good deal of dogmatic interpretation, resulting in one-sidedness. Not long after Mao's instructions on theoretical issues were published, the *People's Daily* published works selected by Zhang Chunqiao and Yao Wenyuan for *A Compendium of Marx, Engels, and Lenin*, setting off a nationwide study of the theory of the dictatorship of the proletariat. Yao and Zhang also separately wrote articles entitled "The Social Basis for Lin Biao and the Anti-Party Faction" and "The Overall Dictatorship of the Bourgeoisie." The central message of the two articles was the discussion of the "overall dictatorship," and how socialism could be consolidated "with the overall dictatorship of the bourgeoisie in every area and at all stages of revolutionary development."[10] This completely obliterated the richness of the Marxist theory of the dictatorship of the proletariat, thus distorting the essence and the work of socialism.

2. Main Points and Core of the Theory of Continuing Revolution Under the Dictatorship of the Proletariat

According to the article "The Road Ahead for the October Socialist Revolution," the main points of the Theory of Continuing Revolution were:

1) Socialism must be viewed through the lens of the Law of the Unity of Opposites, as found in Marxist-Leninist Thought.
2) Socialist societies have long historical stages. In the historical stages of socialism, there are still classes, class conflicts, and class struggle. There will be a struggle between capitalism and socialism, and there will be a danger of falling back into capitalism. When the socialist revolution is basically completed in the ownership of the means of production, class struggle will not end. There will be class struggle between the proletariat and the bourgeoisie, and political struggle between various factions, and the ideological struggle between the proletariat and the bourgeoisie is long, circuitous, and even torturous. In order to prevent the reversion to capitalism, and to prevent "peaceful evolution," the socialist revolution must be seen through to the end on the political and ideological fronts.
3) Class struggle under the dictatorship of the proletariat is essentially a question of power. That is, the bourgeoisie will overthrow the dictatorship of the proletariat if the latter is not properly consolidated. The proletariat must have a full dictatorship over the bourgeoisie in the superstructure, including all the various cultural fields.
4) The struggle between the two classes and two paths in society are bound to be reflected in the Party. A handful of those in power within the Party who follow the capitalist path are representatives of the bourgeoisie. They are a counterrevolutionary revisionist group. When the time is ripe, they will seize power, moving from the dictatorship of the proletariat to that of the bourgeoisie. When we attempt to consolidate the dictatorship of the proletariat, we must continue to fully observe and take note of them, expose them, criticize them, and topple them, so that they cannot turn the tide and recapture power for those who have been usurped by the proletariat.

5) In continuing revolution under the dictatorship of the proletariat, the most important thing is to launch the Great Proletarian Cultural Revolution.
6) On the ideological front, the fundamental program of the Great Proletarian Cultural Revolution is to "repudiate egoism and revisionism." On the political, ideological, and theoretical fronts, revisionism must be criticized. Proletarian thinking must be employed to fight bourgeoisie egoism and all anti-proletarian thought, reforming education, the arts, and all in the superstructure that is not compatible with a socialist economic base, in order to uproot revisionism.

Looking at these six items, we can see that central to the theory of continuing revolution was the notion that in the context of the proletariat having obtained power and established a socialist system, it was necessary to undergo a revolution for class overthrow. The Cultural Revolution was the most significant form of "continuing revolution."

From the basic content of the Theory of Continuing Revolution, it can be seen that the main development of Marxism it proclaimed was essentially a serious departure that was based on a dogmatic understanding of Marxism. At that time, this theory was regarded as the most significant achievement in Mao Zedong Thought, and was seen as a development that would usher in a new stage of Marxism, the stage that came after Leninism and was called "the third milestone" in Marxism. It absolutized the theory of continuing revolution, betraying a normative intention to formulate a set of standards and stipulations for those across the world who would be willing to accept Marxism. As a result, the methods it employed were wrong.

III

The Theory of Continuing Revolution in Practice

1. The "Ideological Program" of the Theory of Continuing Revolution: Fighting Egoism and Repudiating Revisionism

The Cultural Revolution was promoted as "a touch of the people's revolutionary spirit." It took "Fighting Egoism and Repudiating Revisionism" as the ideological platform of the revolution. According to the understanding at the time, "fighting egoism" was an application of Marxism-Leninism and Mao Zedong Thought in which the word "egoism" was to be completely removed from the mind. The term "repudiating revisionism" was the application of Marxism-Leninism and Mao Zedong Thought to oppose revisionism and fight against the handful of leaders in the Party who followed the capitalist path. This sort of criticism was based on the idea that "the unbreakable truth of revolution is destruction for construction. If we do not use Mao Zedong Thought to criticize all sorts of anti-Maoist, revisionist, and reactionary thought, and if we do not criticize the bourgeois worldview in the political, economic, and cultural spheres, then the proletariat cannot really occupy the various positions in the ideological and cultural fields. Those positions are already occupied, but if we do not continue to carry out the revolution, there is a danger of them being recaptured by the bourgeoisie." So it was necessary to go through a mass, lasting overhaul of so-called revisionism and the bourgeoisie in the superstructure and ideological field, with the goal of preventing revisionism, overthrowing capitalism, transforming the worldview, and developing productive forces.

According to the Marxist point of view, transformation of the subjective worldview was not just about transforming ideology, but also included a transformation and development of the people's ability to understand. In order to address ideological and cultural issues, the people's worldview must first be addressed. The problem could not be solved through a coercive approach, but only through Marxist education and the development of scientific and cultural education, and its solution had to be done through the people's practice, in the form of criticism and self-criticism. Mao himself said, "If we take a brutal or repressive approach to the issue of ideology, it can only be harmful, with no benefit." But in the long period of time since the establishment of New China, any mention of the transformation of a worldview – the subjective worldview – was equated with the transformation from bourgeois or non-proletarian thought, while completely ignoring the transformation of the ability to understand or the question of how one thought. As a result, each transformation led even further away from Marxism. This was especially true during the Cultural Revolution. Practices like "fighting egoism and repudiating revisionism" resulted in either lip service, blurring the line between enemies and friends or between right and wrong, or chaotic struggles, which had nothing at all to do with Marxist thought and approaches. Through the decade of turmoil, not only were the old rules broken and new rules set, but the Party and the revolutionary tradition suffered great harm, with political consciousness and moral standards declining greatly, and anarchy and extreme individualism becoming widespread.

During the Cultural Revolution, "fighting" and "repudiating" campaigns of this kind reached almost every aspect of society, both ancient and modern. It directly destroyed a variety of production activities, confusing the people's thinking. It also displayed an extremely utopian, backward view of socialism, an inevitable result of an empiricist, dogmatic approach towards Marxism, and an ignorant and alienated view of the trend of modernization throughout the world. For instance, the Sixty Articles on the Rural People's Commune allowed the commune members to, in small portions, cultivate private plots of land, operate sideline family businesses, and sell produce and sideline products from family farms. But the "fighting" and "repudiating" campaigns denounced such activities as "capitalist tendencies," criticizing the sale of the remaining agricultural or sideline products at the market after the state rationalized tasks had been completed as "capitalist" or "speculative." The work scores system within the people's communes was criticized as "dominance of work scores." If factories, mines, and enterprises operating at high altitudes and temperatures offered workers sent into the mine shafts labor insurance, it was called a "material stimulus," and overtime wages, allowances for night work, and other reasonable subsidies were all canceled. Rules and regulations in factories and enterprises were called "revisionist control, supervision, and suppression" in criticism. Enterprises that pursued a reasonable profit were criticized as "profiteers." In schools, the slogan was, "We should further revolutionary criticism of the liberal arts, criticizing the counter-revolutionary bourgeois ideology within philosophy, history, literature, political economics, journalism, and other fields of education," claiming that the "old liberal arts colleges" would only be renewed through criticism.

Because of the ignorant, nihilistic view that ignored all the outstanding civic and cultural achievements of ancient and modern culture, frenetic criticism was even turned on the natural sciences. Such criticism happened all too frequently after the establishment of New China, reaching its peak in the Cultural Revolution. For instance, it was believed that, on the scientific front, an "outright counter-revolutionary revisionist line in the field of scientific research" had been followed for seventeen years since the founding of New China. Such a line undermined the Party's leadership, obliterated class struggle, downplayed the importance of the political mind, advocated the primacy of professional expertise, and promoted professional competence without a socialist mind, while establishing a series of "black" programs, documents, and various regulations, attempting to set China's science and technology sector on the wrong path. The Fourteen Articles for Scientific Research set in 1961 were viewed as representative of this "counter-revolutionary revisionist line in scientific research," criticized for stating that "we should not label separate schools or propositions in the natural sciences and technology as 'bourgeoisie,' 'proletarian,' 'capitalist,' or 'socialist,'" because the inevitable conflict between the two world views would be reflected in science and technology, unchanging with the human will, and to defile the serious struggle as "class labeling" was an attempt to reconcile this sort of struggle, or to whitewash it, which was absolutely not allowed. The Fourteen Articles for Scientific Research were also criticized for stating that "the debate over the academic issues in the natural sciences, even when concerning materialism and idealism, or dialectics and metaphysics, are academic in nature, and such conflicts are merely academic problems," because in "repudiating" campaigns, those debates in science and technology were seen as class struggles in ideology and to view the struggles as "academic problems" was to obliterate the struggle between the two classes.

Such criticism of the natural sciences was ridiculous. For instance, the Theory of Relativity was seen as "a typical example of natural science theory embedded with the bourgeois consciousness, which intervenes in the real class struggle." Einstein was "the greatest bourgeois academic authority," a "defender of the capitalist system," a "priest of imperialism," and "an enemy to socialism." In a criticism of the Big Bang Theory of Cosmology, it was said that "such a theory can only adapt to religious necessity, and to the needs of reactionary forces to paralyze the people in spirit." In an article entitled "Conflict and Opposition is the Impetus for the Development of Chemical Science," it was argued that chemistry was full of the struggle between dialectics and metaphysics, and that such a philosophical struggle was the result of class struggle. In an article about environmental pollution and energy, it was stated that the source of environmental pollution "did not depend on industrial production itself, but on the social system, on the nature of the production." Further, environmental pollution was "the congenital abscess brought by the fetus of capitalism" and "there are always two possible roads in dealing with environmental pollution, and these two roads represent two world views which will always be engaged in struggle." It also stated that the energy crisis reflected the "depletion" of the capitalist system, and was an incurable disease of capitalist society" and the "energy crisis… was essentially a crisis of the capitalist system, the twilight hours of capitalism, a precarious situation that could lead to real problems." In criticism of the Copenhagen School of Quantum Mechanics, it was said that the debate over quantum mechanics of the past half century had been a matter of materialism and idealism, a conflict between the dialectical and metaphysical philosophies and their understanding of physics. The Copenhagen School represented a reactionary, conservative trend, whose political motive was to vigorously "combine two in one," a doctrine of moderation, engaging in class reconciliations in an attempt to save the dying capitalist system. "It was a rotten product of the decadent, declining, dying imperialist system, serving reactionary politics." Therefore, it was certainly necessary to occupy this position with Marxism-Leninism and Mao Zedong Thought, holding onto the dictatorship of the bourgeoisie in the field of the natural sciences.

The fields of the humanities were likewise filled with such absurd criticism. In *A History of Western Music*, a book compiled at that time with "class and path struggles as guidelines," it was stated that "every achievement in Greek culture was made through class struggle among the masses." The book said that Schubert's music, viewed objectively, "often played a negative role that favored the restoration of feudalism," and that Bizet's works faithfully served the reactionary political faction in the Second Empire, representative of the interests of the bourgeoisie and the landlord class. It went on to say that Verdi's works employed bourgeoisie humanism, humanist theory, and theories of destiny to cover up and reconcile class conflict, using these as tools to sway public opinion. It further said that

Shostakovich had once again launched bourgeois forces to sway public opinion to restore capitalism and implement revisionism.

Throughout the Cultural Revolution, there was some criticism of the domestic policies of some socialist countries, in which some of the negative characteristics of the Cultural Revolution's pursuit of "socialism" can be seen. For example, in *The October Socialist Revolution Opened Up the Way Forward*, it was said that the Soviet Union "dressed itself in a coat of communist construction, replacing the socialist planned economy and distribution of income based on performance with capitalist rules of profits and free competition, turning entire ownership of enterprises and collective farmlands into capitalist enterprises and a "rich peasant" economy (i.e., a capitalist economy in rural areas)."

A paper entitled "Soviet Revisionism and the Hard Evidence of a Comprehensive Restoration of Capitalism in Rural Areas" argued three points in connection with the Soviet authorities. 1) It had implemented a "new system" with profits at its center, i.e., a "comprehensive economic accounting system" with profits as its core concern, placing profits above all else. In farms and farming villages, it promoted the division of farmland to separate groups and a system of production incentive packages, promoting "internal economic accounting" in "collective farming," stating to the accounting units that all products, including both agricultural and sideline products, were still goods and the relationship between production teams and livestock farms was based entirely on the commodity relations of capitalism. This series of measures restoring capitalism completely disintegrated the original production relations of the Soviet socialist agriculture, turning farms and farming villages completely into capitalist agricultural enterprises. 2) The Soviet authorities had supported privatization of the economy and encouraged people to engage in sideline enterprises. After they came into power, Brezhnev and Kosygin strengthened their support of the private economy, and the first step taken toward privatizing the agricultural economy was to relax restrictions on private plots and livestock to publicize the "extreme importance" of promoting and developing a private economy. With the Soviet Revisionist Group's encouragement, the area of privately owned land expanded rapidly and private livestock industry boomed. 3) The Soviet authorities had encouraged the free sale of agricultural products and allowed the free market to overflow, so that the current Soviet Union's urban residents had to increasingly rely on free market supplies for all non-staple food supplies.

In a paper entitled "See What Leninism has Turned Into Under Soviet Revisionism," it was argued that the group had long tried to carry out an "elite route" to promote a large number of bourgeois intellectuals to gain control of the Party leadership at all levels, so that the Party had gone from being representatives of the proletariat to becoming tools of the privileged bourgeois class. The Soviet Revisionist group placed "the economy above politics" and "made economic and production issues the Party's central activity, supplanting the primacy of Party organization," wantonly promoting and relying on "the national economic experts" at the expense of the majority of workers and peasant cadres who were excluded and replaced. In *The Communists*, the Soviet Revisionists publicly declared the Party's leaders must be "experts." In the development of new Party members, there was an increasing share of capitalist intellectuals. In 1966, of the members absorbed into the Soviet Communist Party, 40.6% were office staff, of whom three quarters were engineering or technical personnel and experts in various sectors of the national economy.

In an article entitled "The Fruit of the Soviet Revisionist Group's 'New Economic Policy,'" it was argued that the center of the Soviet Revisionists so-called "new policy" was to encourage enterprises to pursue profits through various measures and to promote production through material stimulation. It expanded the autonomy of business operations, vigorously promoted market regulation through market production systems, and increased the power of heads of enterprises responsible for the recruitment, discharge, punishments, and rewards of workers. This series of measures turned the state-owned socialist enterprises into capitalist enterprises, replacing the socialist planned economy with capitalist free competition.

In the paper "The Renegade Soviet Revisionist Group Opens the Door Wide for Western 'Tourists' through 'International Business Travel' to Launch Restoration of Capitalism," it was argued that the renegade Soviet revisionist group was making increasingly explicit efforts to restore capitalism, using "international business travel" to attract all types of "tourists" in the Western world and that such people would spread the shameless Western way of life throughout the Soviet Union, poisoning the Soviet people. There were signs that the Soviet revisionist group attempted to surrender to imperialism internationally and restore capitalism domestically, making use of "international business travel" under the banners of "peaceful coexistence" and "cultural exchanges." Because of Khrushchev's active revisionism, the "tourists" of Western capitalist countries were welcomed to "travel" into the Soviet Union. Since the new Soviet revisionist leadership had assumed power, not only had they inherited Khrushchev's mantle in this regard, but they even took it a step further. Over the past several years, the number of "tourists" to the Soviet Union had multiplied. In order to attract these "tourists," the Soviet revisionist leadership group had let them spread the Western capitalist way of life, and had disseminated large amounts of promotional and advertising material abroad, holding press conferences overseas, attending international fairs, and displaying all sorts of hype on film. At the same time, the Soviet revisionist clique simplified immigration procedures and entered into contractual agreements with hundreds of travel agencies, opening the door to Western "tourists."

In an article entitled "The Soviet Revisionists' Implementation of the 'Five-Day Work Week' is a New Scam to Step Up the Exploitation of the Workers," it was said that the Soviet revisionist renegade clique had been, over a period of more than a year, implementing the so-called "five day work week," a ploy to distract from the complete dissatisfaction the people felt with them, and that it was, in fact, a conspiracy for allowing the elite class of the Soviet bourgeoisie to exploit workers. The Soviet revisionist leadership group widely touted this "five day work week," proposing it at the 23rd National Congress of the Soviet Communist Party in 1966. Over two years, Brezhnev, Khrushchev, Kosygin, and others had employed their propaganda machine, often personally trumpeting and touting with all their might this "black" program. They put forward the "five day work week" with a good deal of hype, saying it was to "improve the material welfare of the Soviet Union" and was "meant to create a better environment for workers and allow them time to rest." They even put forward the nonsensical idea that it would be "one of the major achievements in all of Soviet Union's fifty year history." Actually the so-called "five day work week" was meant for workers to complete six days' worth of work in five to serve the Soviet revisionist privileged group. So the "five day work week" was in no way "meant to create a better environment for workers and allow them time to rest." On the contrary, it was a step toward greater exploitation of them.

In an article entitled "The Soviet Revisionist Clique is Implementing All Sorts of Revisionism in Education," it was said that, in order to consolidate its reactionary rule, the Soviet revisionist group had formed a renegade clique to cultivate revisionism in education and vigorously promote bourgeois products and implement a revisionist line. The group was implementing a bourgeois "expert-run schools" policy, so that the school had become a mechanism for reestablishing bourgeois values. The group's bourgeois worldview was in line with the Soviet Union's policy of restoring capitalism, and they were a faithful tool for the line of revisionism in education. In school, the bourgeois "experts" were autocratic and arbitrary, as they had a monopoly on all these assets. According to the *Soviet Revisionist* newsletter, "of the thirty-nine members of the Party committee at Moscow University, thirty are professors and associate professors. The situation is the same in the Party groups of separate departments." Further, positions such as president or provost of the college had to be taken by professors and associate professors. In order to nurture revisionist successors, the Soviet revisionist clique vigorously promoted a reactionary political service approach of "intellectual education first" in the schools. The head of the Soviet revisionist group, Maslov, in a meeting with all the schools, advocated the notion that the student's task was to "familiarize businesses." The education minister in upper and middle secondary education, Gennadiy Yagodin, even said, "The basic requirement of the young people in the university is to gain deeper, more solid knowledge." That is to say, the only criterion for admission was one's scores. In order to restore what was necessary for capitalism, the Soviet revisionist group introduced many toxic revisionist materials into the school curriculum. They compiled the *History of the Soviet Communist Party*, *The Origins of Marxism*, *Marxist Philosophy*, and other textbooks, along with newly published course materials, such as *Sociology* and *The Principles of Communism*, all of which were anti-Marxist-Leninist and anti-Maoist revisionist thought, and therefore "black" goods. These textbooks advocated a communism that was "humane," and were greatly opposed to Stalin and the dictatorship of the proletariat. They trafficked theories such as "the People's Party" and "the people's nation-state" for the purpose of restoring capitalism. The Soviet revisionist group set some "professional" courses in the schools, in the service of restoring capitalism. For instance, in 1965, after the Central Committee of the Communist Party of the Soviet Union made a strong push toward the restoration of a capitalist "new management system" at the Plenary Session in September, the Soviet revisionist group immediately decided to set up dozens of new economic departments in institutions of higher learning in the Soviet Union, to establish higher economics schools in several large cities, and to train a large number of "economists" to implement this restoration of capitalism. Reactionary bourgeois "authorities" had also responded to the preparation of the new economics textbooks and reference books that advocated the restoration of capitalism. The Soviet revisionist group took numerous measures and offered vigorous "material stimulation" to encourage students to pursue fame and fortune. They used the bourgeois "title" system to "stimulate" personnel in scientific research. If one wrote an "academic paper" that was appreciated by the group, it was possible to gain one title or another. When one gained a title, his wages would be greatly increased, as would his fame. In order to nurture revisionist successors, so-called "experimental secondary schools" were opened for "geniuses." In Siberia, the "Siberian Olympics" were held, which consisted of three rounds of examinations, selecting the so-called "genius" students. There were many other similar initiatives.

Such criticism is obviously absurd and ridiculous, which is not surprising, since it came out of a distorted understanding and pursuit of socialism. It was only within such a view of socialism that the Cultural Revolution was possible.

In fact, criticism of notions such as "old thought," "revisionism," and "capitalism" during the Cultural Revolution rarely conformed to the actual situation, because the methods employed were so completely antithetical to the principle teachings of Marxism. In a society that holds a negative view of, or even contempt for, material interests, a commodity economy will be viewed as a restoration of capitalism, a market economy viewed as the scourge of the community, knowledge and intellectuals held in contempt, democracy seen as a tool of pragmatism, knowledge of the law and legal system reduced below the level of agricultural societies, and the chanting of slogans such as "if you want socialist grass, you can't plant capitalist seedlings" or "knowledge breeds reactionaries" will abound. In such a society, it can be imagined what kind of answers it will offer to the questions related to the nature of revisionism, capitalism, or socialism, as well as "the big break" and "the big innovation" on this basis.

2. Opposing Revisionism Under the Theory of Continuing Revolution: The Cultural Revolution

With the deteriorating international situation in the early 1960s, the conflicting judgments and understandings within the CPC concerning domestic socialist construction prompted Mao Zedong to put forward the issue of revisionism and to carry out a socialist education movement on that basis, intending to "catch the spirit of class struggle." On the eve of the Cultural Revolution, he brought forward the concept of "leaders following the capitalist path," saying that those who did so had formed a "capitalist headquarter" within the central government, and that there was a revisionist political and organizational line that had agents in all the central and local departments. Further, the rural "Four Clean-ups," the urban "Five Oppositions" and criticisms in the ideological field were not sufficient to solve the problem. Instead, only when the masses were mobilized from the bottom up, fully and openly, could the power that had been usurped be recaptured. The best form of revolution was a Great Cultural Revolution. The distinctive features of this Cultural Revolution would be that it would go through "a world of chaos" to reach "a world of rule and order."

Prior to this, Mao had always adopted a philosophy of "if you don't destroy, you can't build." In the 1960s, because of serious miscalculations concerning "revisionism" and the "restoration of capitalism," he put his philosophy into direct action. He did not take into account that the Communist Party of China had come to power, turning from leading armed struggle and class struggle to leading socialist construction, and that China had become a socialist country led by the Communist Party. He did not believe a socialist country could progress peacefully or simply improve and develop on its own through reform or remedy, and so still held on to ideas and experience gained during the revolutionary war. In order to oppose "revisionism" and "capitalists," he waged a devastating battle for state power. In his letter to Jiang Qing of July 8, 1966, he pointed out, "The world of chaos is the way to the world of order. It will happen again every seven or eight years." In the Party's Report on Revising the Party Charter at the Tenth National Congress of the CPC, this "objective law" was reaffirmed. During the unrest, the Party organization suffered a shock at every level, leaving it in a state of paralysis or semi-paralysis. The Party's members were generally criticized, and Party activities basically came to a halt. Mao mistakenly saw this "chaos" as "chaos of the enemy and an exercise of the masses," and took it as a sign of the masses being fully mobilized. Later, he hoped to reach "order" through "chaos," to stabilize the situation by taking various measures such as establishing the revolutionary committee at every level as the authoritative body and restoring the Party's organizational life. In fact, in a people's democratic state, the power was to rest with the people, and unrest could only undermine the people's governance of the state, causing damage and loss of work in every respect. The reason for this, aside from the errors in the guiding ideology of the "world of chaos," was that the concept or definition of "revisionism" was blurred and wrong. What was "revisionism"? What was the real standard for "revisionism"? Was there even such a thing? Where was the line between "revision" and "reform"? These important theoretical questions remained unclear at the time. The tragedy of attempting to reach "order" through "chaos" in a "cultural revolution" lay in this failing.

3. The Theory of Continuing Revolution as a Guiding Principle and Model for Economic Development: "Grasping Revolution and Promoting Production"

After 1957, the idea continued to develop that revolutions in ideology and superstructure would bring about economic development. The Great Leap Forward in 1958 confirmed that a victory over the bourgeoisie had been gained in the field of ideology, and that the inevitable emergence of the building of production was at its climax. In 1963, this led to the development of "grasping the spirit of class struggle." During the Cultural Revolution, after extreme "revolutionary" measures had been employed to topple the "bourgeois command," it was believed that construction of the superstructure would lead to a decisive victory, eliminating "revisionism," "capitalist thought," and various rules and regulations of "controlling, supervising, and suppressing" workers and farmers to achieve the goal of revolutionizing the people's thought and inevitably allowing more work to be done faster and more efficiently through the development of production. In fact, this policy reversed the relationship between revolution and production, and turned the relationship between superstructure and the economy upside down. It made absolutes of the experience of wartime, exaggerating the role of production and inverting the priorities of production and ideology, which went contrary to the decisive Marxist principle of productivity. According to Lenin's view, the passing of state power from one class's hands to another was the basic, most important sign of revolution. However, the nature of "revolution" captured in the Cultural Revolution involved a special sort of struggle against "revisionism" and "bourgeois" politics, aiming to correct a number of measures and policies that had been implemented since the establishment of New China. This would inevitably lead to the conflict between revolution and production.

In this type of "revolution," all the past theories about the relationship between policy and the market, commodity and currency, and politics and economics, and explorations of the relationship between the superstructure and the economic base were mostly theoretical views coming from the perspective of fields such as history, science, culture, education, art, and management, all of which had been repeatedly denounced as anti-Party, anti-Socialist, and anti-Marxist "poisonous grass." At the same time, some Leftist theoretical perspectives started to develop. In late 1974, Mao Zedong's dialogue on the theory of the dictatorship of the proletariat, the Eight-Grade Wage System, the distribution of labor, and currency exchange rigidly followed some outdated statements of Marxism. Under the guise of "revolution," Jiang Qing, Zhang Chunqiao, and others exaggerated, modified, and introduced all sorts of Leftist fallacies that were devastating to production. They denied the decisive role productive forces played in production, and the role they ultimately played in determining the historical materialist superstructure, calling it "more productive forces." Many correct socialist principles, such as the development of productive forces and of a commodity economy, achieving a distribution of income based on performance, and learning foreign advanced technology, were all seen as revisionism and capitalism, and were thus criticized. In this way, under the conditions of socialism, the main motivations for people to engage in productive labor was not from material benefit, but from a spiritual, moral, and revolutionary zeal. It was endless class struggle, which was a departure from the basic principles of Marxism. As a result, the national economy went through a long period of serious structural and regional imbalances. The people's enthusiasm for production was low, there was a significant decline in economic efficiency, and the national economy was on the verge of crashing. The original hope that the baptism of revolution would achieve the "revolutionary thought of the people" and a "spiritual and material change" brought neither the brilliant flower of spiritual transformation nor the sweet fruit of material results. This was one key tragedy in the "revolution."

4. The Party Model Under the Theory of Continuing Revolution: The "Fifty Words" Party Program

According to the theory of continuing revolution, a large number of representatives of the bourgeoisie and counter-revolutionary revisionists began to infiltrate the

Party, the government, and the military, forming a bourgeois command center within the Party, having agents in various departments at the provincial, municipal, autonomous region, and central government levels. It was from this erroneous estimate that the Cultural Revolution was launched, with the object of seizing power over the Party committee at every level. Operating under the slogan of "revolution through taking control of the Party committee," the criticism of the "bourgeois reactionary line" had a great impact on the Party committees in certain central ministries and in government departments at the provincial, municipal, and autonomous region level, as well as in grassroots organizations, with the exception of the People's Liberation Army. Power was seized and most Party members were forced to cease their routine Party activities.

After October 1967, Mao Zedong again proposed the task of Party consolidation. At the Third Plenary Session of the Ninth Congress of the CPC, he stressed that the Party "actually need[ed] to be rebuilt" so that "every branch will reintegrate the masses in the reorganization." He said, "Party organization should be composed of advanced elements from the proletariat, and should be able to lead the vanguard of the proletariat and the revolutionary masses to fight class enemies." He called this the Party's "Fifty Words Program." This program took "fighting class enemies" as the Party's primary task, while leading the nation's economic, political, and cultural construction was not mentioned. The "class enemies" mentioned at the time were led mainly by Liu Shaoqi, who was seen as representative of the "bourgeois command" and its "agents" who were found in various places. By 1971, the Party congress had been held at the grassroots level to appoint new provincial Party committees on the level of province, municipality, or autonomous region.

The main purpose of this party reorganization was to "remove the old and take in the new," with emphasis on "absorbing those vibrant proletarian revolutionaries into the Party and advance class struggle." Under the guidance of such an idea, some of the real Party members who truly met the requirements were wrongly expelled from the Party or their routine Party activities were interrupted, while some new members were absorbed, even though some of them did not meet all the requirements. This movement in the Party did not give proper consideration to class struggle or the main internal conflicts within the country, but simply emphasized the two classes and the extreme gravity of the struggle between two paths, taking restoration and revisionism as the real dangers and requiring each Party member to arm their minds with continuing revolution under the dictatorship of the proletariat and erroneous Leftist theories to raise revolutionary consciousness. As a result, the Cultural Revolution saw a serious development of the personality cult, anarchism, and other similarly flawed ideas that led to erosion and damage of the Party that simply could not be resolved. The relationships between Party members, and between Party members and Party organizations were thrown into a very abnormal state. In this way, with the erroneous "Leftist" development in the understanding of socialist class struggle, the Party not only failed to complete the transition from revolutionary Party to ruling Party, but actually developed its own opposition in the Cultural Revolution.

5. The Way to Achieve an Ideal Society Under the Theory of Continuing Revolution: "Fighting, Criticizing, and Reforming"

The original meaning of "fighting, criticizing, and reforming" was "fighting to take power back from the leaders following the capitalist way, criticizing reactionary bourgeois academic authority and the ideology of the bourgeoisie and all the other exploitative classes, and reforming education, culture, and all superstructures not suited to the socialist economic base, in order to consolidate and develop the socialist system." In September 1968, when all the provincial revolutionary committees in the nation were set up, the *People's Daily* published an editorial announcing that the Cultural Revolution had moved into the "fighting, criticizing, and reforming" stage.

After the founding of New China, based on the understanding of what socialism was and how it could be established and developed according to China's national conditions at different periods in China's process of exploring the socialist road, Mao formulated some views, abandoned some ideas, and adhered to and developed some theories. In the "fighting, criticizing, and reforming" stage, he continued to base some of these changes on those ideas, persisting in or developing this basic understanding of socialist theory.

Throughout his long revolutionary career, Mao continued to enthusiastically look forward to a fair, level, affluent, and pure socialist society. There would be no obvious difference or division of labor in this society, and people could engage in both physical and mental labor. Everyone would hold lofty ideals and a high sense of morality, putting constant effort into transforming and improving themselves.

In this society, production departments, superstructures, and ideologies would all have strong reactionary elements, and all of these areas would constantly serve as innovative forces for the rapid development of the economy. Through uninterrupted class struggle and the development of production and science, the entire society would be empowered and the people able to live rich, happy lives. The fundamental feature of this society would be public ownership of property, because "public ownership is the root of prosperity." Once this singular socialist society had been realized through collective ownership, this would be a "source of strength," and the Party would lead in everything. In order to ensure that the Party did not degenerate, it would be necessary to carry out rectification of the entire Party through Cultural Revolution. The management organ of this society must be carried out on the principle of simplification and efficiency, reflecting the principles of the Paris Commune. As such, the management of the masses should be carried out by elected officials who could be removed at any time. These officials would only have the narrowest wage difference from ordinary workers, and they would often participate in a variety of manual labor tasks. Management authorities and their staff must be subjected to mass supervision, bureaucracy would be sternly opposed, and they would maintain close contact with the masses. The Cultural Revolution would aim to "to partially transform our national machine." Although this society would maintain commodity production and currency exchange, they must be supervised and kept to a minimum, since after all, these were products of the old society and, even under socialism, bourgeois and capitalist thought could still soil the will and continue producing a "new bourgeois class." Though this society could not help but retain a gap in distribution, this gap could not be allowed to expand, but must continually shrink. Only in this way could the spirit of purity and equality be maintained. This society must bring the masses of the people to live a rich life, but the ruling Party must be vigilant about this affluence, because a wealthy life would always kill a people's revolutionary will, and would even come at the price of moral degradation, while poverty and hardship would always cultivate a "pure moral life, serving as fertile soil for noble ideals." To varying degrees, these assumptions and pursuits were part of the activities of the "fighting, criticizing, and reforming" movement.

The "fighting, criticizing, and reforming" movement reflected Mao's concerted effort toward establishing a new type of socialism. In the "fighting, criticizing, and reforming" campaign, there was a strong pursuit of equality and fairness, with a "burst of the soul of revolution" driving the pursuit of pure morals, pure public ownership of property, and the purity of the class system. This was a response both to the drawbacks seen in the abuses of the Soviet model of socialism and to the unavoidable misdeeds in the process of worldwide modernization. According to Mao's vision, the "fighting, criticizing, and reforming" campaign was intended to end the Cultural Revolution by confirming its victory and consolidating its established pattern to restore normal order to the nation. However, because Leftist errors were concretized and systemized in various fields, which were highly utopian and damaging, in the "fighting, criticizing, and reforming" campaign, they not only harmed a large number of cadres and masses, but in many ways, constantly manufactured chaos.

In short, the theory of continuing revolution that came about in Mao's late years was an erroneous Leftist view of class struggle, and it was not in line with either Marxist-Leninist Thought or with the situation in China. It distorted both Marxism and the Chinese situation, and so led to a distorted combination of the two, resulting in numerous setbacks and mistakes. According to the theory of continuing revolution, there could be no sense of revolution, nor of social progress. It was not just "disrupting the enemy," but also causing oneself "a world of chaos" which can never result in "a world of order." History had proven that the Cultural Revolution was led by a group that was in error and who were utilized by a counter-revolutionary group to do serious damage to the Party, the state, and the people, causing civil strife for all ethnic groups. The long period of upheaval caused the Party, nation, and people to suffer the most severe setbacks since the founding of New China and instigated such serious losses as to bring the economy to the brink of collapse. During that decade, the loss to the national income hit about 50 billion *yuan*, and people's living standards declined. Party organization and state power were greatly weakened, a large number of cadres and people suffered brutal persecution, and democracy and the rule of law were trampled on. Scientific and cultural education were seriously damaged, and the gap between the nation's science and technology and that of the rest of the world was glaring. The fine tradition of the Party and the people's morality were, to a great extent, destroyed. Metaphysics were rampant and idealism prevailed. What was especially severe was the great damage done to the reputation of Marxism, weakening the people's faith in Marxist thought, resulting in extreme ideological confusion. It led to a serious political and social crisis.

IV

Resistance and Struggle: Relentless Exploration of the Localization of Marxism in China During the Cultural Revolution

During the Cultural Revolution, the Party made a serious mistake in terms of the overall guiding principle on the path to integrating Marxism into China, seriously frustrating the process of modernizing Marxism. Even so, there were a large number of Party members and cadres among the people who adhered to the truth of Marxism, resisting the Cultural Revolution and continuing to carry on a relentless exploration of integrating Marxism into China. During the chase, they led two waves of criticism of extreme Leftist thinking, implementing Party policy and rectification in all areas. In the years before and after 1972, Zhou Enlai led the criticism of the extreme left, and in 1975, Deng Xiaoping led the overall rectification. These two reorganization efforts restored the true face of Marxism and, to a certain extent, started correcting the errors of the Cultural Revolution and began a certain level of adjustment and reform of the rigid system, bringing China more in line with the developing knowledge of Marxism. Even though Mao himself had committed serious errors, even throughout the period of his errant thought, he repeatedly urged the entire Party to seriously study the writings of Marx, Engels, and Lenin, and he always believed that his own practice was in line with Marxism, particularly his efforts to consolidate the dictatorship of the proletariat. After the Third Plenary Session of the Eleventh Congress of the CPC, these explorations and efforts discovered the uniquely Chinese form of Marxism, in preparation for the second historic leap toward the realization of Chinese Marxism.

1. The Central Committee Leads the Resistance and Struggle Against Unrest at the Beginning of the Turmoil

When the Cultural Revolution had been launched, Liu Shaoqi, Zhou Enlai, Deng Xiaoping, and other key Party leaders maintained orderly production, preventing the chaos from continuing to expand. Their reaction to the violent mass movement was that they did "not understand, nor did they find it serious or effective." Regarding Mao's big character posters criticizing Nie Yuanzi and others, Liu Shaoqi said he "didn't see how it could be considered as significant as the Declaration of the Paris Commune." In a December speech, Zhou Enlai said, "the speed, depth, and breadth of the spread of the Cultural Revolution have gone well beyond what we expected. Every one of us, including me, had not sufficiently prepared our minds." They felt that there was a serious gap between what was then going on and their own understanding of Marxism.

At the end of 1966, regarding the question of how to carry out the Cultural Revolution in the industrial and mining sectors, Zhou Enlai and some other old Party comrades launched a fierce confrontation with the Central Committee Cultural Revolution Group in an effort to maintain both order in production and the basic principles of Marxism. From November to December 1966, a symposium was held for China's entire industrial transportation system. All of the participating comrades advocated that industrial and commercial enterprises be unified under the guidance of the Party. In order to properly handle the relationship between revolution and production, they said, production could not be stopped for revolution, and those at the meeting rejected the bill drafted by the Central Committee Cultural Revolution Group to launch in full scale the Cultural Revolution in the industrial and mining sectors. But those at the meeting were criticized and repressed by Lin Biao and Jiang Qing.

The Cultural Revolution triggered a complete seizure of power and numerous fights, causing Chen Yi, Xu Xiangqian, Nie Rongzhen, Ye Jianying, Li Xiannian, Tan Zhenlin, and other revolutionaries to become deeply worried. In early 1967, a fierce conflict broke out between them and the Central Committee Cultural Revolution Group. In a meeting at the Jingxi Hotel and Huiren Hall, they discussed whether the Party leadership was indispensable, whether veteran cadres' contributions were essential, whether the military should be stabilized, and other similar fundamental issues. They criticized Lin Biao and the Central Committee Cultural Revolution Group for the chaos they had caused in the Party and the military since the Cultural Revolution, denouncing the practice of destroying production in factories, rural areas, and the military. They thought the army was a pillar of the dictatorship of the proletariat, so if the army was in chaos, it would not be able to defend the country, nor would it be up to the task of blocking foreign invasion. They asked, if Shanghai had seized power and renamed itself "the Shanghai Commune" without discussing it with the Politburo, simply changing the name arbitrarily, then what could happen next? Could revolution be carried out without Party leadership? Without Party leadership, it would be up to the masses to liberate themselves and to educate themselves – which was just metaphysics. But this struggle was dismissed and suppressed as the "February Countercurrent."

These resistances and protests were against the misunderstandings of and dissatisfaction with the Cultural Revolution and some of its extreme practices. Although they did not reach their theoretical height, they still managed to make people reconsider and reflect on the theory and origin of the Cultural Revolution, leading to some independent thinking even during the period of strict confinement.

2. The Criticism of Extreme Leftist Thought Led by Zhou Enlai in 1972

After the Lin Biao incident, the evil fruit of the Cultural Revolution's opposition to the basic principles of Marxism objectively demonstrated the bankruptcy of the Cultural Revolution. The majority of the cadres and the masses gradually shook off the thinking behind the Cultural Revolution, and Mao grew more deeply dissatisfied with extreme Leftist ideology. Zhou Enlai took advantage of this favorable situation to lead the criticism of extreme Leftist thought, to speed up the work of adjustment, and to implement policies for cadres and intellectuals that would strive to restore the true face of Marxism. He led the rehabilitation of defeated Party members and leading cadres, restoring them to positions of leadership in fields such as the economy, science, and education. During the adjustment, Zhou pointed out that extreme Leftist thought was "empty, extremist, formalist, and a great deal of hot air shouted by the commanders of proletarian politics." Opposing the evil of the anarchist trend in economic work, Zhou and the leadership of the State Council put forward measures to rectify enterprises, trying to restore the damaged rules and regulations. By vigorously compressing the scale of infrastructure, streamlining the number of workers, and implementing other measures, he helped address the problem of the number of workers, the total wages for workers, and food sales greatly exceeding indicators, and reversed the decline of the national economy. In the countryside, the Party Central Committee issued instructions on distribution within the people's communes and reiterated the need to adhere to the principle of distribution according to work, denying the criticism that policies allowing a variety of businesses or sideline industries was a capitalist tendency. In scientific and educational work, Zhou wanted to see basic scientific and theoretical research taken up. He also grasped the implementation of the Party's cultural, national, united front, and other policies. Throughout this rectification, Zhou continually emphasized the necessity of business studies for revolution, and that improved quality, courage under attack, and proletarian politics all "hang on business."

Zhou Enlai led the critique of ultra Leftist thought, which demonstrated the continuity of the efforts many leading comrades required in early 1967 to correct the error of the Cultural Revolution. After nearly two years of adjustment and rectification, obvious improvements could be seen in all aspects of the work, and there were less extreme Leftist leanings. However, in Mao Zedong's view, criticism of extreme Leftist thinking was no different from denying the Cultural Revolution. He believed the main responsibility at the time was to oppose extreme Rightist thought, not extreme Leftism. In May 1973, during the CPC Central Committee Working Conference, Mao's instructions were conveyed that it was "not right to focus only on production, but not on the construction of superstructure or the ideological path." In this way, Zhou's efforts to remedy the extreme Leftism had to be discontinued.

3. The Overall Rectification Led by Deng Xiaoping in 1975

The long, continuously repeated Cultural Revolution led to an increasing sense of weariness in the people, so that they increasingly held doubts about the whole notion of a Cultural Revolution, though everyone held a general hope for economic improvement, social stability, and an improved life. Against this background, Deng Xiaoping brought order to the crisis by leading the drastic task of rectification, trying to reverse the wrong direction that had been taken to integrate Marxism into China and to restore the true face of Marxism.

In January 1975, the Fourth National People's Congress reaffirmed the four grand goals of modernization, hoping to once again turn the attention of the people to economic development and the cause of national revitalization as determined by Zhou Enlai and Deng Xiaoping, who served as the core of leaders in the State Council, laying the fundamental thinking and organization for the comprehensive work of rectification. From that time, Deng Xiaoping presided over the daily work of the State Council and the CPC Central Committee, beginning the drastic work of rectification. During this comprehensive rectification, Deng led the drafting of "A Number of Questions on the Acceleration of Industrial Development," "Outline of the Working Report from the Academy of Sciences," "A General Outline of the Work of the Entire Party and Nation," and other documents, held a series of professional meetings, and put forward a series of significant long-term ideological points of view. He repeatedly stressed that: 1) the Four Modernizations were the main concern, 2) it was necessary to establish a strong leadership team to resolutely fight factionalism and to establish the necessary rules and regulations, 3) unity and stability must be well managed and the socialist economy developed, 4) the rectification of the core was the rectification of the Party, and the Party had to be rectified at all levels of leadership to speed up the implementation of cadres, 5) the Four Modernizations must increase efforts to modernize agriculture, 6) science and technology were also forms of production, and science and technology personnel were workers, and 7) scientific research needed to progress to promote the advancement of production. During this time of rectification, Deng also suggested that the main issue at this point was "how to promote Mao Zedong Thought," and he reiterated that Lin Biao has caused division in Maoist teaching, a point obviously targeting the Gang of Four. Deng presided over the comprehensive rectification, putting forward an ideological point of view that both inherited and developed important ideas from Zhou Enlai's 1972 adjustment. This correction of the leadership and the extreme Leftist thought in the Party during the Cultural Revolution triggered another major struggle. The attempt at overall consolidation of some important issues aimed at clarifying some ideological theories and policies reversed in the Cultural Revolution, hence the beginning of rectification within a certain scope. The results of comprehensive reorganization once again proved the correctness of the path to integrating Marxism into China. On the other hand, the deepening of rectification would inevitably lead to a more systematic correction to the Cultural Revolution. This not only met with rabid opposition from the Gang of Four, but was completely intolerable to Mao. As a result, the comprehensive reorganization met the same fate as Zhou Enlai's criticism of extreme Leftism, and was ultimately interrupted. From one side, this reflected the great difficulty of adhering to the integration of Marxism into China under the guidance of Leftist thought. But the comprehensive rectification led cadres and the masses to gradually see who was in line with the direction of development and the voice of the people, what the true face of Marxism was, and what was the ultimate goal of the development of socialism. This laid a solid ideological foundation for the new historical movement of Reform and Opening Up, preparing the ground for the second historical leap toward Chinese Marxism. Deng later said, "In fact, we have attempted reform from 1974 to 1975. That reform is called by the name 'rectification,' and it emphasized that the economy had to come first so that order could be restored to production."

4. New Judgments of the International Situation and New Openness in Diplomacy

In the 1970s, the international situation again changed dramatically. Mao Zedong and Zhou Enlai made the bold, visionary decision to undertake diplomatic work to improve China's relations with the world around it so that China's foreign affairs could have a turn for the better. Among these, two key parts included recovering the legal seat of the People's Republic of China at the United Nations and easing relations with the United States.

With the rise of China's international status, many Asian, African, and other nations combined efforts with China and, on October 25, 1971, the Twenty-Sixth Session of the General Assembly adopted the resolution to restore the legal seat of the People's Republic of China at the United Nations. Subsequently, President Nixon visited China in February 1972, and after talks, he signed the Sino-US Joint Communiqué on February 28, marking the beginning of the process of normalizing relations between the two nations. The easing of Sino-US relations directly promoted improvement of Sino-Japan relations and led to China's peak period of establishing relations with many countries in Western Europe.

Against this backdrop of a newly opened diplomatic situation, China opened up foreign relations on the economic front as well. Zhou Enlai endured the pressure of the Jiang Qing faction's criticism that he "worshipped foreign things" as he sought to carry out trade and economic and technical exchange, importing many complete sets and much stand-alone equipment from overseas. Chen Yun, who assisted Zhou Enlai in his foreign trade efforts, conducted bold research and utilized capitalism, emphasizing that "the trend of dealing with capitalists has been set. If we do not study capitalism, we will suffer." He instructed foreign trade departments to make bold use of capitalist countries' capital, technology and equipment, and their methods of commodity exchange and futures market management. The economic recovery played a significant role in deepening the Party's understanding of the relationship between capitalism and socialism, and of deepening the Party's knowledge of contemporary characteristics of progress and trends in the world.

In the 1970s, China further developed friendly cooperation with the Third World countries in Asia, Africa, and Latin America. Through this process, Mao Zedong had gradually formed the "Three Worlds" theory. This was one of the more strategic developments in his thinking in his later years. This division highlighted the conflict between the Soviet Union and the US, two hegemonic states vying for world hegemony. He emphasized those countries in the Third World and the importance of joining them with the Second World nations and making use of the conflict between the two superpowers. If all the countries of the Third World would unite, it would become the most extensive united front in the world, and it would be capable of fighting for world peace. Although analysis of this theory shows that it did not meet the practical demands, it played a positive role in guiding China's diplomatic work, a doctrine to adhere to in the face of the hegemony of the superpowers and threats of war, and to strive to establish and develop friendly relations with Third World countries as well as other nations, including the normalization of Sino-US relations.

5. All Forms of Resistance and Protest from Party Members, Cadres, and the People During the Cultural Revolution

During the Cultural Revolution, the difficult work of protest done by Zhou Enlai, Deng Xiaoping, and other leaders at the upper levels echoed that of many Party veterans and ordinary Party members, workers, and peasants who also went through profound reflections on what happened during the Cultural Revolution. They resisted the Cultural Revolution's ideological trends in many different ways, making efforts to adhere to Chinese Marxism, to consolidate Marxism in China, and to continue to progress with wisdom and strength. Many frankly criticized the errors of Leftist extremism or thought calmly, or earnestly wrote down their understanding of the Party's experience in theoretical articles, while others put forward views and suggestions on important issues in the work of the Party or continued to earnestly declare the fine tradition of the Party to the masses. In fact, these things were all different ways to resist or protest the Cultural Revolution, the wrong means of integrating Marxism into China. For instance, after the September 13 Incident, Zhang Wentian wrote numerous contributions offering a more systematic discussion of the nature of socialism, the stages, the tasks, and basic laws of building socialism in China, and other issues. He emphasized that all work in a socialist society "is, in the final analysis, to significantly improve productivity and develop the socialist economy." He sharply criticized the Leftist argument that "spoke only of politics, fearing to speak of economics or of material interests," pointing out that "in short, no amount of politics can command" and that only a politics of good "economic performance" was truly acting on behalf of the proletariat and in the people's most basic interest, and only this sort of politics could mobilize millions of people to act. This once again demonstrated that it was an error to put the economy and politics in opposition, taking politics beyond the economy, or detaching politics from the economy. Those "politicians" who talked such high-sounding political theories but dared not mention the economy would have been better served "studying closely what the statement means that 'politics is the reflection of the economy,' which is expressed in Marxist truths."

He went on to say, "Of course, socialist revolution and the consolidation of the dictatorship of the proletariat are extremely important. But I ask, what is the goal of socialist revolution and the consolidation of the dictatorship of the proletariat? Is revolution for revolution's sake or dictatorship for dictatorship's sake? Certainly not. If we do not try to improve socialism, productivity, and the lives of the people, but are simply blindly obsessed with the statements of 'communism,' then the communist doctrine will be reduced to mere superstition. This would be an insult to the great cause of communism.

"Under the dictatorship of the proletariat, in the absence of war, whether the Party's political line is right or wrong, how correct the consolidation of the dictatorship of the proletariat is, how it has been consolidated – these are ultimately measured against the extent of the achievements in the construction of the socialist economy. If politics fails to mobilize and energize the masses, or to fuel and boost economic growth, no matter how good things look on the surface or how sweet they sound, in the end, it is only empty, and might even bring only disaster to the people and to national construction. Correct political leadership must be in proportion to the achievements of economic construction."

Regarding the Party's anti-tendency struggle, Zhang Wentian said in *The Party's Struggle to Be Correct*, "The Party's internal conflict is not just a conflict between the people, but a conflict between revolutionary comrades striving for the cause of communism," and, "Is it right to call those comrades within the Party who had opportunistic tendencies 'bourgeois agents within the Party'? Although the results of this tendency might be good for the bourgeoisie and not conducive to the proletariat, it does not mean comrades with this tendency are bourgeois agents within the Party.

"Regarding the dangers of right leaning and the need to struggle against the right, we now know more clearly that there is also a danger in left leaning, and we must fight against the left, which seems to be something that not many people understand. Some comrades think left is better than right, so they think it is good to lean left. If we ignore the changes in social conditions and the struggle between two extreme factions within the Party, it will be attributed to a struggle against right-wing thought, so an anti-right, extreme Leftist tendency is naturally encouraged and becomes a major danger under certain circumstances. In a left-leaning environment, the greatest danger is that we will continue to focus on the right, and we can call a thing Rightist, hurting our comrades in the process. This will cause serious consequences for the Party."

He went on to say, "Marxism-Leninism and Mao Zedong Thought are very cohesive, comprehensive, and scientific doctrines or systems of thought. They require comprehensive study to prevent one-dimensional understanding or taking things out of context." This was consistent with Deng Xiaoping's criticism of the "Two Whatevers."

Some Party theorists and thinkers also considered the issue of the future development of China. The renowned economist Sun Yifang was imprisoned in April 1968 because of his views promoting the commodity economy, the law of values, and other ideas. While in prison, he continued to study economics, and even took the opportunity to write more than thirty thousand words outlining the socialist economy.

The first person to put forward China's theory of a socialist economy under market conditions was the former head of the research department of economics at the Academy of Social Sciences, Gu Zhun. During the Cultural Revolution, he endured brutal persecution. It was during that time that he thought deeply about socialist theory.

In speaking of the Soviet model, he said, "Their economy is developing, but this is still an economic system based on preparation for war, and it is a very clumsy economic system offering all that it has for military supply (i.e., a Stalinist economic system). It is, to them, something like an ingrained habit difficult to get rid of, and is therefore mortally infected. Because of this, their economic system is essentially a system of waste and suffocation. All the new income driving economic growth is used to expand the military and basic industry, or to increase the amount of consumer funds, but never to keep up with increased wages."

He went on to say, "I think, in the foreseeable future, this uncomfortable system will move obliquely forward." But there would be some force "that ultimately overthrows this suffocating system." Twenty years later, drastic change came to the Soviet Union, proving to be the catastrophe Gu Zhun had predicted.

After the founding of New China, the socialist revolution, and the lessons learned in the Cultural Revolution, Gu Zhun considered and put forward a fundamental question, "What would happen when Nora left?" This was the question of how to build socialism after a successful socialist revolution, or how to achieve specific ideals after gaining the victory. That is, as was later said, "What is socialism and how do we achieve socialist construction?" In fact, this problem was the one Mao struggled with after the founding of New China, and it was a question of life and death that faced all socialist countries. The rare thing about Gu Zhun was that he not only raised the question so sharply, but also that, against such a broad ideological background, he provided new ideas to analyze and address the problem.

As Gu Zhun pointed out, those of his generation had gone through the baptism of "the wars and revolutions in the 1930s and the 1940s, some big dreams beyond the anti-Japan ideal and its resulting religious fervor." Then in the 1950s, they had been through the leaping revolutionary romanticism that "one day would have been like twenty years, and all the earth would have been won over," and the decade of chaos of the Cultural Revolution. This sort of experience made him suggest, "The revolution brought the victory we sought, but what happens when Nora leaves? I praise the revolutionary fervor. But the question still remains, where do we go from here?" What was the road to socialism? This question "can only be resolved empirically." He reminded, "Don't think all our issues have been resolved. Look at the issues soberly and we will know how much we have settled, what remains unsettled, and what has been overdone. We must seek the truth from facts, rather than dealing with objective reality through dogmatism. Soon, our nation will soar economically."

Based on his profound observation during the Cultural Revolution, Gu Zhun said, "I have conflicting feelings about the Spartan system. Egalitarianism, the spirit of struggle, and democratic collectivism – I've personally experienced this sort of life, and I have a deep understanding of how indispensable it is to defeat the oppressor in this sort of environment. However, Sparta's own history shows that an oligarchy and the harsh discipline required to maintain this long-term egalitarianism, a martial spirit, and collectivism will result in formalism and hypocrisy. Outwardly it appears dignified, but inwardly it is corrupt. There is beauty on the outside, but only corruption inside."

All these things Gu Zhun had pointed out were both problems encountered in socialist countries at the time and his analysis of those problems and the conclusions he drew from them. Along with those of Zhang Wentian, Sun Yifang, and others, these were a shining light of Chinese Marxism. During the ten years of turmoil, these pioneers endured the arduous quest, fearlessly pursuing the ideal. They left a heavy mark on contemporary Chinese Marxism, pushing Marxism to be fully integrated into China.

During the decade of turmoil, the majority of young people, students, intellectuals, workers, and peasants experienced a process of moving from frenzy, blind following, confusion and, ultimately, to awakening. This sort of awakening eventually led to the explosion of April 1976 that culminated in the "Tiananmen Incident" as a representative mass protest movement. This protest movement came when the Gang of Four sought to suppress the masses from attending Zhou Enlai's memorial service. The Gang of Four sought to pass the "criticism of Deng and the counterattack of the right" movement, toppling Deng as the representative of the older generation of revolutionaries who advocated the Four Modernizations. However, under the Party's long-term education of the masses, the practice of struggle had taught them to recognize right and wrong. In the protest movement, the people shouted, "Let those who castrated the Marxist-Leninist scholars go to hell!" This sort of protest movement took place against the backdrop of mourning for Zhou Enlai, but the main opposition was to the Gang of Four, and this proved a major breakthrough. In fact, the correct Party leadership, represented by Deng Xiaoping, kept comprehensive rectification as its main guiding principle. Even so, those protests were suppressed, but the national masses were now mobilized to smash the Jiang Qing faction and to promote the progress of the integration of Marxism into China as it embarked on a correct path.

Zhou Enlai and Deng Xiaoping, as representatives of a large number of Party veterans and cadres, carried out many forms of resistance and protest against the errors of the Cultural Revolution, becoming the guardians of Marxist truth as they sought to become pioneers of Reform and Opening Up. They were treated as "heretics" or "another class," and their ideas were called "revisionism," but within it was the essence of Marxism. The majority of workers, peasants, and intellectuals stuck to their posts and worked hard, even as Lin Biao and the Gang of Four incited them with the idea of "stop production; pursue revolution." No doubt these people laid the groundwork and gathered strength for toppling the Gang of Four, ending the chaos of the Cultural Revolution and setting the localization of Marxism in China back onto the correct path.

The Cultural Revolution was a total outbreak of extreme Leftist error and a serious misunderstanding of the process of integrating Marxism into China. As a counter example, it paved the way for the breaking of dogmatism and the obsession with empiricism, and hence providing a mental foundation and a great impetus for the second leap toward Chinese Marxism. In practice, the decade of the Cultural Revolution proved that the theory of continuing revolution was not a feasible guiding principle. The localization of Marxism in China had to be done in a correct way. The Leftist error and extreme Leftist thought were defeated in the Cultural Revolution, allowing it to become a cradle for new ideas and new paths to be pursued.

CHAPTER 10

The Great Ideological Liberation Movement and the Start of the Second Leap

The Cultural Revolution was carried out in the name of upholding and developing Marxism and consolidating the socialist system, but, in the most extreme way, it exposed the drawbacks of the political life of the Party and the state, damaged the reputation of Marxism, and deviated from the correct direction of the localization of Marxism in China. "The end of the Cultural Revolution has prompted people to think deeply about some basic issues concerning the development of socialism in China, such as, what is socialism and how to build it, what is Marxism and how to adhere to and develop it, how to develop China, which direction to go, where the masses and cadres are wandering, and why they are hesitating."

At the end of the Cultural Revolution, there were several roads before the Communist Party of China and the Chinese people. One was to continue to affirm the Cultural Revolution or the left-leaning errors of the past and correct the Cultural Revolution only within the framework of Mao Zedong's "three-percent error." At that time, most people did not accept this path on a psychological level. Another possible path was, by negating the Cultural Revolution, to negate Mao Zedong, the whole history of the Communist Party of China, and the socialist road, turning to the capitalist road. The Chinese people would not and could not agree to this road either. The third path was to sum up the lessons of the Cultural Revolution and, on the premise of adhering to the socialist orientation, to open up a new road for the development of socialism in China.

The serious lessons of the Cultural Revolution and the rectification of the chaos of the Cultural Revolution urgently needed to address and clarify a series of theoretical questions. Linked to China's development path and prospects, the localization of Marxism in China was also facing new situations and tasks. On the one hand, the end of the Cultural Revolution provided an opportunity to realize a great historical transformation, which would make it possible to break through the ideological imprisonment of dogmatism and re-embark on the correct path of the localization of Marxism in China. On the other hand, the change in the ideological field would not happen overnight. In particular, under the influence of left-leaning ideology and dogmatism over a long period, the Party had formed the idea that Leftism was better than Rightism, that the more Leftist one was, the more revolutionary, and that Leftism was a matter of method, while Rightism was a matter of position. These were deep-rooted concepts that could not be completely reversed in a short time. At that time, cadres and the masses strongly demanded that the mistakes of the Cultural Revolution be corrected, that the serious situation caused by the ten-year civil unrest be completely reversed, and that China rise again from the crisis. However, due to the limitations of the times, such urgent demands and aspirations were seriously hindered, and the work of the Party and the state was stagnating in its development. At that time, the policy of the "Two Whatevers" and the continued left-leaning policy, made it impossible to immediately start on the right track of the localization of Marxism after the end of the Cultural Revolution.

As mentioned earlier, the development and innovation of Marxism and the realization of the second leap in the localization of Marxism in China were meaningful only in a system that could be freely discussed and a fully developed socialist democracy. From the founding of New China to 1978, the reason this development and leap could not be realized was not the lack of talent or ability in theoretical thought, but the accumulation of practice (positive and negative experience and lessons), especially the lack of democracy as a result of the wrong expansion of the class struggle after 1957. To correct the orientation of Marxism, it was necessary to have a free democratic atmosphere for discussion within the Party. By carrying out an ideological emancipation campaign, the Party could break the bondage of deep-rooted dogmatism and rigid thought and allow ideological emancipation and democratic discussion to proceed in a proper direction. The old comrades in the Party, represented by Deng Xiaoping and others, fought resolutely against the erroneous ideas represented by the "Two Whatevers," triggering a huge ideological emancipation movement with discussion on the standard of truth as its main idea, creating the most fundamental conditions for correcting the orientation of the localization of Marxism and realizing a new era of history, and for the turning point and the new leap in the localization of Marxism in China. This ideological emancipation movement and the rectification of chaos in the ideological field were mainly achieved through several steps, including exposing and criticizing the Gang of Four and its erroneous theories, exposing their true face of falsifying Marxism and carrying out ideological imprisonment, and exposing the manifestations of the extreme Leftist line in all aspects and the harm it caused. Then, it was important to oppose the wrong ideas of the "Two Whatevers," to criticize its rigid attitude toward Marxism and its harmfulness, and put forward a scientific attitude and requirement for a complete and accurate understanding of Mao Zedong Thought. From there, it was necessary to initiate a major discussion on the issue of truth standards, promote the ideological emancipation movement of the entire Party and all the people, restore the ideological line of seeking truth from facts, and liberate the localization of Marxism from dogmatic texts. Finally, it was crucial to study new situations, solve new problems, formulate the policy of Reform and Opening Up and shift the focus of the Party's work, make a new step in the right direction for the localization of Marxism, and achieve new heights. The second leap had a good beginning.

After repeated contests in the earlier rounds, the localization of Marxism based on practice and standards had finally become an irresistible trend of the times, and the great turning point of history had finally been realized.

I

Moving Forward Hesitantly

1. The "Two Whatevers" and the Continuation of the Dogmatism of the Cultural Revolution

After the end of the Cultural Revolution, the Central Committee systematically published the evidence related to Wang Hongwen, Zhang Chunqiao, Jiang Qing, and Yao Wenyuan's counter-revolutionary groups and launched the struggle to expose and criticize the Gang of Four. However, it was impossible to shake off the influence of left-leaning errors in the guiding ideology quickly and thoroughly, and there were some restrictions on this struggle in the practical work, which imposed great limitations on clearing up the ultra-Leftist trend of thought advocated by the Gang of Four and its theoretical system. In spite of this, the masses and cadres, led by the older generation of revolutionaries inside the Party, still combined the exposition and criticism of the Gang of Four with the original and clean source of ideological theory, criticized the fallacy of the Gang of Four in forging and falsifying Marxism, initially clarified some theoretical and policy rights and wrongs, and improved the application of fundamental Marxist views to analyze major issues and began to restore the original outlook of Marxism on some major issues.

Among the criticisms of the Gang of Four, the most urgent problem to be solved was to eliminate the serious consequences of the ten-year turmoil as quickly as possible, to make the national economy, which was on the verge of collapse, recover rapidly, and to correct a large number of the injustices and wrongs caused by the Cultural Revolution. However, due to the limitations in understanding, for a period of time, the Party failed to fundamentally understand the problems of the Cultural Revolution, especially the relationship between the Cultural Revolution and Mao Zedong's errors in his later years. In this general pattern, although the Eleventh National Congress declared that the Cultural Revolution had ended and reiterated the fundamental task of building China into a modern socialist power in the 20th century, the revised Party Constitution still contained left-wing errors. On the one hand, the process of restoring the work of veteran cadres and redressing the wrongs and injustices in history began, but it was slow and faltering. Although the national economy began to emerge from the chaos, a new round of rash errors occurred, and some unrealistic high targets and slogans that were impossible to achieve were put forward. In July 1977, a State Council report said that "a new leap forward in the national economy is beginning."[1]

This situation arose mainly because of the limitation of the historical conditions at that time. On February 7, 1977, the *People's Daily*, *Red Flag Journal*, and the *PLA Daily* published an editorial entitled "Studying the Documents and Grasping the Guideline." While emphasizing the principle of "grasping the guideline to govern the nation," this editorial put forward the principle of the

"Two Whatevers," that is, "we firmly uphold whatever decisions Chairman Mao has made, and we unswervingly follow whatever instructions Chairman Mao has given." The editorial elevated the "Two Whatevers" as the "guideline" to govern the work of the entire Party and country.

The "Two Whatevers," which seemed to adhere to Mao Zedong Thought, defended Mao's mistakes in his later years and insistently held onto the dogmatism which had brought such serious disasters to the Chinese people, and fundamentally violated the basic principle of the localization of Marxism, which held that theory must be combined with, develop along with, and be tested by practice. For example, with the gradual development of the exposition and criticism of the Gang of Four and the further exposition of the dangers of the Cultural Revolution, the task of fundamentally clearing up the ultra-Leftist trend of thought of the Cultural Revolution soon emerged. In January 1977, theorists advocated criticism of Zhang Chunqiao's *On the Comprehensive Dictatorship of the Bourgeoisie* and Yao Wenyuan's *On the Social Basis of Lin Biao's Anti-Party Groups*. These two articles were representative works of the left-leaning theory in the late period of the Cultural Revolution, which collectively reflected the basic theory of the Cultural Revolution. The preliminary cleaning up of these two articles touched upon some fundamental problems of the left-leaning theory after the founding of New China. However, the leaders in charge of propaganda at that time believed that "these two articles were approved by the Central Committee and Chairman Mao, the great leader, and cannot be criticized."

Another example was that the incorrect theory of launching and guiding the Cultural Revolution was taken as the key content of studying and publicizing Volume 5 of the *Selected Works of Mao Zedong*, which was published on April 15, 1977. In the decision issued by the Central Committee to study this volume, the founding of the theory of "continuing revolution" was regarded as Mao Zedong's "greatest contribution to Marxism"[2] in the period of socialist revolution and construction. At that time, the leading comrades of the Central Committee published the article "Continuing the Revolution Under the Dictatorship of the Proletariat to the End." They upgraded the "theory of continuing revolution" to the basic thought that ran through Volume 5 of the *Selected Works of Mao Zedong* and regarded the toppling of the Gang of Four as another great victory of the Great Proletarian Cultural Revolution.[3]

A final example came in March 1977, when the Central Committee of the

Communist Party of China held a working meeting, stressing that it was the decision of Chairman Mao to criticize Deng Xiaoping and fight against the right-leaning approach of redressing previous cases, and that criticism was necessary. At the same time, it also proposed that Deng should be allowed to work at an appropriate time. On the one hand, the Tiananmen Incident was classified a counter-revolutionary event, but it was seen as acceptable for the masses to go to Tiananmen on the Qingming Festival (Tomb-sweeping Day) to express their condolences to Premier Zhou.[4] The various contradictory understandings reflected not only the preliminary development of great changes in history, but also an arduous transformation.

The "Two Whatevers" claimed to uphold Mao Zedong Thought, though they actually damaged and divided it. They violated the basic requirements of the continuous development of Marxism and the continuous promotion of the localization and modernization of Marxism in China. Even Mao himself did not regard his ideas as an unchangeable "theory." In the 1930s, when dogmatism prevailed and the whole Party suffered greatly, Mao made a famous assertion that "we should oppose doctrinairism" and that "no one has the right to speak without investigation," which made great contributions to the establishment of the ideological line of seeking truth from facts.

There was, therefore, no essential difference between the "Two Whatevers" and the statement that "every remark is truth and one prevails over all" that Lin Biao advocated the forged claim made by the Gang of Four that "we should always follow Chairman Mao's established policy." When history called for a great change, many people's hands and feet were still bound by invisible shackles. If the principle of "Two Whatevers" was followed, veteran comrades such as Deng Xiaoping and others could not be set free to work, and a large number of cases of injustice, falsehood, and wrongdoing could not be redressed. When the class struggle was still the guideline, the whole country would still be in utter silence and darkness, and the Party and the state would be unlikely to extricate themselves from the disaster of the Cultural Revolution. Theoretically speaking, if the "Two Whatevers" were followed, there would be no innovations in Marxism, Mao Zedong Thought could not develop, and the modernization of Marxism could not be realized.

There were subjective and objective reasons for putting forward and carrying out the "Two Whatevers." First of all, thoroughly eliminating the mistakes of the Cultural Revolution and safeguarding Mao Zedong's historical status and Mao Zedong Thought as the guiding ideology of the Party were not only sensitive political issues, but complex ideological and theoretical problems. In a long-term environment confined by rigid dogma, solving these problems required a certain amount of time to accumulate enlightened practice, but also required superb political wisdom. It would take some time for the cadres and the masses to understand that only by pointing out and correcting the mistakes made by Mao in launching the Cultural Revolution in his later years could the Party truly inherit the fine traditions of its predecessors under the banner of Mao Zedong and Mao Zedong Thought. Further, the influence of the left-leaning error was deep-rooted. The Party had been harmed for twenty years. Some Party habits became stubborn habitual forces. It was impossible to demand an instant change. In fact, dogmatic ways of thinking similar to those embodied in the Two Whatevers were a common and persistent illness in the post-World War II International Communist movement. Although there were a few attacks against the dogmatism regarding classical Marxist writers, the Stalinist model, and the leaders of respective countries, it was not only difficult to correct, but often occupied a dominant position. This was a very complicated problem that had ideological causes and deeper roots in the social system, cultural traditions, and other domains.

2. Putting Forward the Scientific Proposition of Accurately and Thoroughly Understanding Mao Zedong Thought

The proposition of the "Two Whatevers" and the continuation of the left-leaning principle in different fields to varying degrees triggered some discussion both inside and outside the Party. Many Party members expressed their disapproval of this attitude toward Mao Zedong Thought with the "Two Whatevers" and gradually began to ponder several questions, including what attitude the Party should adopt toward Mao Zedong Thought and Chairman Mao's instructions. After the publication of the editorial *Studying Documents and Grasping Guidelines*, Geng Biao, head of the Central Propaganda Department, pointed out, "If we publish this article, it means the Gang of Four has not been crushed. If we follow the "Two Whatevers" presented in this article, no work can be done."[5] On April 10, 1977, Deng Xiaoping wrote to Hua Guofeng and Ye Jianying a memo that was transferred to the Party Central Committee, proposing that "we must guide our Party, army, and people from generation to generation with accurate and complete Mao Zedong Thought."[6] It targeted the rigid attitude toward Mao Zedong Thought represented by the "Two Whatevers." On May 24, Deng once again criticized the "Two Whatevers," pointing out that "according to the 'Two Whatevers,' it is not reasonable to redress my case, nor to affirm the activities of the masses in Tian'anmen Square in 1976." Mao said that he himself had made mistakes. There was no such thing as everything a person said being right, or that person would be absolutely right. Rather, Mao Zedong Thought was an ideological system. Deng noted, "If we hope to uphold the banner, we should study and apply this ideological system."[7]

The so-called complete understanding of Mao Zedong Thought was to understand every principle of it from a concrete, historical, and connected point of view, and from its whole system, not from the individual words and phrases, and to distinguish the basic principles from the individual ones. In conclusion, to distinguish correct thoughts from certain mistakes was to distinguish Mao Zedong Thought as a guiding ideology from Mao's mistakes in his later years. It was wrong to either deny the scientific system and guiding role of Mao Zedong Thought because Mao made mistakes in his later years, or to avoid and ignore Mao's mistakes in his later years and their impact out of a desire to adhere to Mao Zedong Thought. The proposal of "the accurate and complete Mao Zedong Thought" reflected Deng Xiaoping's political courage and wisdom and theoretical courage and the urgent needs of the times, and it encouraged many cadres and theoretical workers to begin criticizing some important left-leaning theoretical viewpoints more directly and deeply. This made it increasingly difficult for the "Two Whatevers" to continue.

In July 1977, the Third Plenary Session of the Tenth Central Committee was held in Beijing. The conference did not mention the "Two Whatevers," but it still adhered to the theory of "continuing revolution under the dictatorship of the proletariat." The conference restored Deng Xiaoping's revoked leadership of the Central Party, the government, and the army.[8] In his speech after his comeback, Deng focused on how to adhere to Mao Zedong Thought. He emphasized once again the importance of having a complete and accurate understanding of Mao Zedong Thought and being skilled at studying, mastering, and applying the system of Mao Zedong Thought to guide all work. He pointed out that "only in this way can we keep from splitting and distorting Mao Zedong Thought and damaging it." He further pointed out that, of all the styles of work Mao had advocated, the mass line and seeking truth from facts were the two most fundamental things. He said, "For the present situation of our Party, I personally feel that the mass line and seeking truth from facts are particularly important."[9] Seeking truth from facts was the fine tradition and style of the Party and the basic principle of the localization of Marxism. However, during the Cultural Revolution, it was distorted and weakened to an unprecedented degree, resulting in rampant "fake, big, and empty" talk and dogmatism that pervaded the entire country. Deng Xiaoping's advocacy of seeking truth from facts directly targeted the Two Whatevers with great pertinence. It further profoundly revealed the essence of Mao Zedong Thought, resisted and weakened the influence of the Two Whatevers, and created favorable conditions for putting forward practical standards and the return of Marxism to the practical track in China.

The Eleventh National Congress of the Communist Party of China was held in Beijing in August 1977. The Congress put forward the idea that, as symbolized by the collapsing of the Gang of Four, the Cultural Revolution had come to an end. The Party's fundamental task in the new era was, then, to strive to build China into a great modern socialist power in the 20th century. However, the General Assembly still fully affirmed the Cultural Revolution, believing that "there will be many more revolutions of this political nature in the future," and described the theory of continuing revolution under the dictatorship of the proletariat as the most important achievement of contemporary Marxism. The Eleventh National Congress failed to undertake the historical task of correcting the mistakes of the Cultural Revolution and formulating correct lines and guidelines for the realization of historical turning points. This showed once again that it was a very arduous historical task to be completely liberated from the shackles of traditional ideas and dogmatism, correct the deep-rooted Leftist errors, and adjust the course of the localization of Marxism to the right track. The contradiction between progress and stagnation in the Eleventh National Congress reflected a general rule in the development of history. On the one hand, the trend of history was irreversible, but on the other, the progress of history was not smooth.

Around the time of the Eleventh National Congress of the Communist Party of China, the First Session of the Five National People's Congresses was held, and the CPPCC, democratic parties, and the Federation of Industry and Commerce resumed their activities. This was of great significance for improving socialist democracy and legal life, strengthening the cooperation between the CPC and the democratic parties, strengthening the people's democratic united front, and preparing a large number of cadre resources for ideological emancipation and rectifying chaos. These measures themselves clearly told people that the Cultural Revolution had to be negated.

At the same time, as a hard-hit area of the Cultural Revolution, the field of culture and education took the lead in rectifying the chaos. After Deng Xiaoping came back to work, he took the initiative to focus on science and technology education. He overthrew the "black-line dictatorship of literature and art" imposed by Lin Biao and Jiang Qing, as well as the "black-line dictatorship of education," emphasizing that in the seventeen years after the founding of New China, the dominant aspect of the scientific and educational front was the red-line, and that the vast majority of intellectuals in China voluntarily and consciously served socialism. He called for "respecting intellectual work and talent," and put forward scientific judgments such as "science and technology are productivity" and "intellectual workers serving socialism are part of the working people," which followed the correct views of the Party on the issue of intellectuals in 1956 and 1962, and reversed the Leftist policy toward intellectuals in more recent years. The majority of intellectuals were greatly encouraged, and various scientific research and academic activities, along with literary and artistic creation, gradually became active. The school examination system that had been canceled during the Cultural Revolution was restored, and colleges and universities across the country enrolled new students through the unified examination. Cultural and educational circles ushered in the atmosphere of early spring, becoming the field in which the disorder was first rectified and results achieved. These important measures gradually weakened the influence of traditional ideas and powerfully promoted the pace of ideological emancipation.

In short, after the end of the Cultural Revolution, great achievements were made in exposing and criticizing the crimes committed by Jiang Qing's Anti-Revolutionary Group. The rectification of the Party and state organizations at all levels and the partial redressing of wrongs, falsehoods, and errors began. Industrial and agricultural production recovered relatively quickly. Educational, scientific, and cultural work also began to get on the right track. However, the political and ideological chaos caused by the decade-long Cultural Revolution would not be easily eliminated in a short period. More importantly, the eradication of Leftist errors should not be confined to the clearance of the Cultural Revolution. It was imperative to rectify the chaos in the profound and extensive ideological field.

II

Discussion on the Criterion of Truth and the Preliminary Establishment of the Marxist Line of Thought

An accurate understanding of the general principles of Marxism and the establishment of the fundamental significance of practice for the development of Marxism (or "practice-based") were two basic conditions for the localization of Marxism in China. If "the complete and accurate formulation of Mao Zedong Thought" mainly referred to the understanding of theory itself, then the question of the criterion of truth went a step further, as it put forward the criterion of judging the right and wrong, which gradually went to the level of practice, restoring the authority of practice and shaking the foundation of dogmatism.

With the gradual development of all kinds of work, it was more obvious that in order to thoroughly clarify the ideological confusion caused by Lin Biao and the Gang of Four and correct the mistakes in the Cultural Revolution, it was first necessary to solve the important problem of how to correctly deal with Mao Zedong's instructions and decision-making. What exactly were the criteria for judging whether a history was right or wrong? This raised the fundamental question of the criterion of truth. Deng and other members of the older generation of revolutionaries repeatedly emphasized the need to accurately and completely understand Mao Zedong Thought and that seeking truth from facts was the essence of Mao Zedong Thought. In fact, after the overthrow of the Gang of Four, they further opened the gates of ideological emancipation, activated the democratic atmosphere inside and outside the Party, and provided the basis for seeking truth from facts. The cadres and theorists who tried to break away from the shackles of the "Two Whatevers" were greatly inspired and encouraged, triggering a debate on whether to adhere to the two ideological lines of "seeking truth from facts" or to the ideological lines of the "Two Whatevers." Some cadres and theorists who were at the forefront of the struggle against chaos raised this issue roughly at the same time, preparing and writing articles on it. Because they represented the correct direction of the development of Marxism, they were supported by some veteran cadres in the Party. With the support and promotion of the older generation of revolutionaries, the discussion on the standard of truth broke through many obstacles and flourished throughout the country.

1. Practice as the Sole Criterion for Testing Truth as a Marxist

In August 1977, under the organization and guidance of Hu Yaobang, the Central Party School set up an internal journal called *Theoretical Dynamics* for leading cadres and theoretical departments at or above the provincial and military levels to consult. It organized articles on some important frontier issues of Marxism-Leninism and Mao Zedong Thought, opening up a new active space to clarify the theoretical confusion that had existed for years.

At the end of 1977, according to Hu Yaobang's opinions, the Central Party School clearly stipulated two guiding principles for the study of the history of the Party. First, the basic principles of Marxism-Leninism and Mao Zedong Thought were to be fully and accurately applied, and second, practice should be the criterion for testing truth and distinguishing right from wrong in the Party's line. Inspired by these two principles, some students began to question some major events in the Cultural Revolution and the theory of continuing revolution. Some theorists began writing articles on the criteria for testing truth to clarify the ambiguous understanding of this issue. With the development of the situation, the question of judging the right and wrong line and of the ideological theory was gradually raised.

On March 26, 1978, the *People's Daily* published an ideological commentary entitled "There is Only One Standard." It clearly stated, "There is only one standard of truth, and that is social practice." After the publication of the article, more than twenty letters were received, most of which disagreed with the article's views, holding that Marxism-Leninism and Mao Zedong Thought were the criteria for testing truth. Given this, the editorial department of the newspaper decided to continue organizing articles to further clarify this issue.

On May 11, 1978, the front page of the *Guangming Daily* featured the article "Practice is the Sole Criterion for Testing Truth," which was reviewed and finalized by Hu Yaobang in his capacity as special commentator. This article emphasized that practice was not only the criterion for testing truth, but also the only criterion. There was only one criterion for testing truth, that is, the social practice of millions of people. The reason Marxism was called truth was the result of its long-term practice by millions of people. The article pointed out that the unity of theory and practice was a basic principle of Marxism. The theoretical treasury of Marxism was not a bunch of rigid doctrines. It required the constant addition of new viewpoints and conclusions in practice, and it needed to abandon some old viewpoints and conclusions that were no longer suitable for the new situation. To adhere to practice as the only criterion for testing truth was to adhere to Marxism. The article pointed out that at present, in theory and in practical work, many forbidden zones set up by the Gang of Four had not been completely broken down. Where there was a place beyond practice that regarded itself as an absolute forbidden zone, there would be no science, no real Marxism-Leninism, and no Mao Zedong Thought. Communists could not limit, cut, or tailor the infinitely rich, vivid real life with ready-made formulas. They should be brave enough to study the new problems raised in new practice. Only in this way could the Party develop a correct attitude toward Marxism. The article had a clear banner, which fundamentally negated the "Two Whatevers" and touched upon the problems of ideological rigidity, dogmatism, and personal worship that had prevailed for many years, with huge repercussions. The broad masses of Party members, cadres, and theoretical workers firmly supported the adherence to Marxism-Leninism and Mao Zedong Thought as a good thing which raised a major issue that touched the entire body.

At this time, on the basis of instructions from the leaders concerned, the Central Propaganda Department adopted the policy of "not expressing its position" and "not intervening in the discussion."[10] The leaders in charge of the propaganda work of the Central Committee also criticized this article on many occasions for targeting Mao's thought, criticizing comrades in charge of the newspapers that published this article as having no party spirit, and instructing the *Red Flag* to be cautious in its theory and keep a close watch of its publications. At that time, the Minister of the Central Propaganda Department also cautioned the leaders in charge of propaganda in various provinces, saying that the article "Practice is the Only Criterion for Testing Truth" could be discussed and disseminated in a small scope, that it should not become a final conclusion just because the *People's Daily* published it and the Xinhua News Agency issued it, and that it was important to be prudent and not follow every wind that blew. In this way, a sharp controversy concerning the divergence of principles concerning the Party's ideological line was entertained before the whole Party, bringing the ideological front to a crucial moment in the rectification after the chaos.

2. Restoring the Authority of Practice in the Discussion of the Criterion of Truth

When the discussion on the criterion of truth met with great pressure, a group of veteran comrades such as Deng Xiaoping, Ye Jianying, Chen Yun, and Li Xiannian expressed their support, which enabled the discussion to withstand the pressure and expand from ideological and theoretical circles to all walks of life in the Party, government, and army, thus becoming a major discussion with a broad mass base.

At that time, the army's political work conference was held in Beijing. At the meeting, it was emphasized that whatever Chairman Mao and Chairman Hua had said could not be changed. The divergence of opinions arising from the proposition of the criterion of truth aroused Deng Xiaoping's attention. On June 2, he delivered a speech at the conference, emphasizing his views on seeking truth from facts. He criticized some comrades who spoke of Mao Zedong Thought every day, but often forgot, abandoned, or even opposed the fundamental Marxist viewpoint and method of seeking truth from facts, proceeding from reality, and combining theory with practice. Moreover, some people believed that whoever stuck to seeking truth from facts was guilty of a heinous crime. In Deng's view, this issue was not a minor one, but a matter of how to treat Marxism-Leninism and Mao Zedong Thought. Opposing seeking truth from facts would result in something other than Marxism, Leninism, and Mao Zedong Thought, leaving only idealism and metaphysics as a guide, which would lead to the loss of work and the failure of the revolution. Deng called on all "to eliminate the poison of Lin Biao and the Gang of Four, rectify the chaos, break the spiritual shackles, and emancipate our minds."[III] This speech strongly refuted the insensible talk suggesting that adherence to the standard of practice was "cutting down flags," shocking those comrades whose thoughts were still in a rigid state and inspiring those who demanded emancipation of the mind and adherence to the standard of practice. The principle of seeking truth from facts and combining theory with practice would soon become a sharp weapon for emancipating the minds of the whole Party.

Emancipating the mind and seeking truth from facts had always been important "magic weapons" for the Party to maintain its vitality and a prerequisite for the continuous localization and modernization of Marxism. Emancipating the mind referred to breaking the shackles of customary forces and subjective prejudices, studying new situations, and solving new problems under the guidance of Marxism. To emancipate the mind was to bring the mind in line with reality, and the subjective with the objective, to oppose dogmatism, and to seek truth from facts. Only by emancipating the mind could the Party achieve the goal of seeking truth from facts, and only by seeking truth from facts could it achieve the true emancipation of the mind. After the founding of New China, the Party had several successful experiences in promoting socialist construction through ideological emancipation. Around the time of the Eighth National Congress, Mao put forward the policy of "taking the Soviet Union as a mirror, which was a good start, and produce positive results in independently exploring China's own road to building socialism." At the beginning of the 1960s, Mao called on the entire Party to vigorously investigate and study. The Party responded positively from top to bottom, and the people of the whole country worked hard, bringing about a turning point in all aspects of work and a correct or relatively correct development trend in the building of socialism. However, because of the influence of dogmatism, and especially the lack of democracy within the Party, the expansion of class struggle, and other left-leaning errors, emancipating the mind was either an unrealistic fantasy under the guidance of left-leaning thought (such as the Great Leap Forward and the people's commune movement, etc.), or it encountered tremendous difficulties or was even suffocated by new dogmatism. This may indicate that, on the whole, the time was not yet ripe for emancipating the mind, breaking through dogmatism, and putting Marxism in China on the right path. However, after the disaster of the Cultural Revolution and the continuous struggle between the two development tendencies within the Party, the conditions were finally ripe. Under the background of the gradual restoration and active democratic atmosphere inside and outside the Party, the principle of emancipating the mind and seeking truth from facts could be put into practice.

With the support of Deng Xiaoping and others, some newspapers and periodicals continued to organize discussion articles, and some units began to prepare seminars on the standard of truth. On June 24, with the support and instructions of Luo Ruiqing, Secretary-General of the Central Military Commission, the *PLA Newspaper* published an article entitled "A Basic Principle of Marxism" on the front page in the name of a special commentator, which systematically responded to the criticism for upholding the principle that practice was the sole criterion for testing truth. The article clearly pointed out that a thought could not prove itself, that theory was the guide of practice, and practice was the standard to test truth, which were two different issues and should not be confused. The idealism and metaphysics of Lin Biao and the Gang of Four were very prominent in their view of truth. Over a long period, they regarded truth as something that could be altered according to people's subjective thoughts, taking theory itself or the speech of authoritative persons or written documents as the criterion of judging truth and refusing to mention objective practice. Its harm was intense and severe, and almost everyone had a keen sense of it. Subsequently, several major newspapers in Beijing published and reproduced articles, strongly igniting the discussion of the standard of truth.

Deng Xiaoping closely watched the development of the discussion and guided the direction of the discussion with his superb political wisdom and powerful measures. On July 22, Deng Xiaoping, speaking with Hu Yaobang, said, "Practice is the sole criterion for testing truth." This article was Marxist. Arguments were unavoidable, and it was well argued, targeting the "Two Whatevers."[12] In September, he again explained how to emancipate the mind and uphold the banner. He pointed out that learning how to uphold the banner of Mao Zedong Thought was a major issue. The "Two Whatevers" did not aim to uphold this banner, and if they carried on, it would damage Mao Zedong Thought. The basic point of Mao Zedong Thought was to seek truth from facts, that is, to combine the general principles of Marxism-Leninism with the specific practice of the Chinese revolution. The essence of Mao Zedong Thought was to seek truth from facts.[13] Deng Xiaoping's proposition was clearly supported by Ye Jianying, Li Xiannian, and Tan Zhenlin, so that the discussion could continue in depth. During the discussion, it was pointed out that this issue was not only a fundamental theoretical issue, but also a practical one. The discussion of this issue concerned not only the Party's ideological and political lines, but also the future of the Party and the nation.

3. A New Ideological Liberation Movement and Removing Chaos

The discussion of the criterion of truth settled the issue of the Party's ideological line. It was a great ideological emancipation movement, and at the same time, it was a debate about how to treat Marxism. At the critical moment when the cause of socialism in China encountered difficulties and went astray, it broke the spiritual shackles of the "Two Whatevers" and proved with scientific theory and irrefutable facts that they were not only anti-Marxist, but also unworkable in practice, leading the people to restore and respect the authority of practice and making the idea that "practice is the only criterion for testing truth" more widely accepted. As Deng Xiaoping pointed out, "The debate on the criterion of truth is indeed an issue of an ideological line and of politics, and it concerns the future and destiny of the Party and the country."[14] He pointedly expounded the extreme importance of the ideological line. He said, "If a party, a country, or a nation does everything based on mere theory, its ideology will be rigid and superstition will prevail. It will not be able to move forward, its vitality will cease, and the party and the country will perish." He went on, "Only when our minds are emancipated can we correctly take Marxism-Leninism and Mao Zedong Thought as our guide, solve the problems left over from the past as well as a range of new problems, correctly reform the production relations and superstructure, which are incompatible with the rapid development of productivity, and determine, based on the actual situation of our country, the specific ways, policies, methods, and measures to realize the Four Modernizations."[15]

Extensive and in-depth discussions on the criterion of truth were conducted, and a general education of dialectical and historical materialism was carried out among the cadres and the masses, effectively promoting the general liquidation of Lin Biao's and the Gang of Four's false Marxist theory from the ideological and theoretical perspectives, along with the correction of Mao Zedong's errors in his later years, which paved the way for the Party to rectify wrongdoings, clear up the original source of trouble, and solve the remaining historical problems. From that time, the Party had gradually shaken off the impact of the "Two Whatevers" and dealt with various problems encountered in rectifying chaos based on facts. Organizational departments began to redress various unjust, false, and wrong cases and proposed that the Party should put an end to them regardless of the previous circumstances or authorities. Some industrial departments resolutely implemented the principle of distribution based on work and restored some previously criticized but effective practices. In rural work, some local leaders in Anhui, Sichuan, and other provinces began from the actual situation and boldly adjusted the rural policy, starting to try out the forms of contracted production and work to households, and gradually corrected some left-leaning practices in rural work over the years.

The in-depth discussion on the criterion of truth further encouraged many cadres and theorists to criticize some representative left-leaning theoretical viewpoints. After February 1977, the discussion of distribution based on work in economic theory circles deepened after the discussion on the issue of the criterion of truth was ushered in. The discussion focused on criticizing the fallacy of regarding distribution based on work as the economic basis for the emergence of bourgeois legal rights and developing production as "productivity-only theory." More importantly, the discussion delved further into how to embody the principle of distribution according to work in practice. On May 5, 1978, an article entitled "Implementing the Socialist Principle of Distribution According to Work" was published in the *People's Daily*, which was fully affirmed by Deng Xiaoping and Li Xiannian. This paper comprehensively demonstrated the socialist nature of distribution based on work, expounded various forms of labor remuneration distribution according to work, and cleared up theoretical errors and confusion on distribution based on work, which had aroused great repercussions in the theoretical circle.

In short, the discussion of the criterion of truth sharply raised the question of the attitude towards Marxism on the basis of returning the localization of Marxism to the standard of practice, which fundamentally corrected the orientation of the localization of Marxism, noting the importance of adhering to emancipating the mind, seeking truth from facts, proceeding from reality, and combining theory with practice. Only in this way could Marxism have vitality and the great practice of socialist construction in China have a clear direction. This discussion also strongly urged people to shake off dogmatism, emancipate their minds, boldly practice, dare to create, test truth, develop truth in practice, and constantly nurture new achievements in the localization of Marxism. History demonstrated that the transformation from the mistaken state to the new leap in the localization of Marxism had begun.

III

The New Starting Point of Socialism with Chinese Characteristics and the Beginning of the Second Historical Leap in the Localization of Marxism in China

1. Ideological Emancipation Promoting New Exploration

The rectification of the ideological line was the forerunner and premise of all rectification and Reform and Opening Up. "Only by emancipating the mind, adhering to seeking truth from facts, proceeding from reality, and integrating theory with practice can our socialist modernization drive go smoothly and the theories of our Party's Marxism-Leninism and Mao Zedong Thought develop smoothly."[16] In this sense, the discussion of the criterion of truth was also a prerequisite for the return of the localization of Marxism to the right path and the realization of the second historic leap.

The negation of the left-leaning thought with the focus on the discussion of opposing the "Two Whatevers" and of the criterion of truth strongly promoted a host of new explorations. This kind of exploration not only came from some correct practices before the Cultural Revolution, such as the Trust Test and the Agricultural Contract-to-Household Test, but also from the thinking that emerged after the setback of the Cultural Revolution. The new exploration not only negated the Cultural Revolution itself, but also began to reflect on the socialist construction mode in the first ten years after the Cultural Revolution. It was for this reason that the discussion had in essence, become an ideological emancipation movement that strongly called for great changes in the new period of socialism in China, an ideological emancipation movement that provided spiritual impetus, and a mode of thinking for the reform and development of the new period of socialism in China, and therefore an ideological emancipation movement that related to the overall political situation. It was for this reason that the discussion made sufficient ideological and theoretical preparations for the Third Plenary Session of the Eleventh Central Committee of the CPC, thus becoming a new historical starting point for the second leap in the localization of Marxism in China.

The new achievements in exploring socialist development brought about by ideological emancipation were manifold, covering many aspects, including the recognition of the external environment of socialist construction, the reflection on the experience and lessons learned from socialist construction in China, the contemplation of the policy of Reform and Opening Up, and the shift of the focus of work, as well as that of the major issues concerning the future development path of China.

2. Expanding World Communication and World Vision

Having an open mind and a global outlook were important conditions for realizing the localization of Marxism in China. Historically, the founding of the Communist Party of China was the product of the combination of the spread of Marxism-Leninism and the actual situation in the Chinese workers' movement. The spread of Marxism in China itself was the result of the open-mindedness at that time. The third milestone in the development of Marxism and the self-proclaimed "world revolutionary center" in the Cultural Revolution were precisely the time when the understanding of the outside world was very limited. After suffering the serious damage of the closed and rigid concept to the integration of Marxism into China, the whole Party opening up to the outside world, absorbing the positive results of the development of world civilization, drawing lessons from the successful practices of other socialist countries, and thus realizing the new development of the localization of Marxism became an urgent task. During the period before the Third Plenary Session of the Eleventh Central Committee, China's foreign exchanges increased rapidly, which enabled the Party to have a new understanding of the modernization process of the contemporary world and to have more reference points and a broader vision for socialist construction. In 1978, there were twenty visits by leaders above the Vice-Premier and Vice-Chairman level alone, and more than fifty countries were visited, including developing countries and developed capitalist countries. Among them, Deng Xiaoping's visit to Japan in October 1978 attracted the most attention. During his visit, Deng made a detailed understanding and investigation of Japan's modern enterprises and high-tech facilities with advanced international standards, expressing his strong desire to learn advanced foreign experience and technology and accelerate the pace of China's modernization.

In addition to these visits by the leaders of the Central Committee, various departments of the State Council, provinces, municipalities, and autonomous regions also organized delegations and visiting delegations during the year, focusing on the industrial, agricultural, and economic development of developed capitalist countries. Among them, the larger and higher-level delegation led by Vice Premier Gu Mu of the State Council visited five Western European countries. Before his departure, Deng Xiaoping specially talked to Gu Mu and asked him and the delegation to make a detailed investigation and study, emphasizing that they should learn from the advanced experience of capitalism. The delegation visited fifteen cities in five countries and had extensive contacts with government leaders and people from all walks of life. Such frequent and extensive visits not only attracted the attention of the Chinese people, but also made the world feel that China was moving toward the world with a new attitude.

Through the steady increase of foreign exchanges, the Party had a more direct and comprehensive understanding of the development and changes in the international situation and the development trend of the world economy. Accordingly, the Central Committee promptly made a series of important judgments and decisions.

On the one hand, it changed the old view that a "world war is imminent." In September 1977, when meeting with foreign guests, Deng Xiaoping said, "The international situation has changed greatly. Many old concepts and formulas can no longer reflect reality. Old strategic provisions in the past are not in line with reality. We need a peaceful environment."[17] That December, he put forward his judgment at the Plenary Meeting of the Central Military Commission that the outbreak of a world war might be delayed.[18] This judgment gradually became the consensus of the central leadership.

On the other hand, it was important to make a decision to seize a favorable opportunity and open up to the outside world. In many aspects of the exchanges, the Party and the government had a comprehensive understanding of the development and changes of the international situation and the economic development trend, and it made timely adjustments to its foreign economic policies. In September 1977, Deng said that the Party should not only learn from the world's most advanced science and technology, but also absorb the world's most advanced industrial management methods. In March 1978, Hua Guofeng also suggested that the introduction of advanced technology and equipment was an important measure for speeding up economic development. Deng said in 1975 that this was a major policy. The introduction also needed a long-term plan taking into account all aspects of development. On March 18, 1978, Deng pointed out in his speech to the National Science Congress that modern science and technology were undergoing a great revolution. To improve the level of science and technology in China, it was important to adhere to the principle of independence and self-reliance. However, any nation or country needed to learn the advantages of other ethnic groups or countries and learn the advanced science and technology of others. In 1978, the Central Committee set up a leading group on the introduction of new technologies to speed up the pace of this introduction.

Dogmatism and ideological rigidity were the products of closure and semi-closure. Once the Party established normal foreign contacts and a broad world outlook, they were still difficult to maintain. Opening the door and broadening China's horizons was not only the product of emancipating the mind, but also a greater impetus for emancipating the mind. Breaking through the shackles of closure not only enabled China to gain rich material results, but also enabled it to gain tremendous ideological results. After this step, the modernization of Marxism and the localization of Marxism in China also gained a more solid foundation.

3. A New Understanding of Socialism in the Planning of Reform and Opening Up and the Shift of Work Focus

After the discussion of the criterion of truth opened the door to ideological emancipation, the Party began to rethink how to build socialism in China. In 1978, the policy of Reform and Opening Up and the shift of the focus of work began to brew. Eventually, before and after the Third Plenary Session of the Eleventh Central Committee, the door of the second leap in the localization of Marxism in China was opened.

In view of the low level of economic management in China at that time, the Central Committee put forward the idea of reforming China's economic management system. Deng Xiaoping clearly pointed out, "After introducing advanced technology and equipment, we must manage the economy according to the international advanced management methods, and advanced quotas, that is, according to economic laws. In a word, we should revolutionize, not improve or mend."[19] In June 1978, Hua Guofeng pointed out that many aspects of China's superstructure and production relations were not perfect, and many links in its political and economic systems were flawed. These were incompatible with the requirements of realizing the Four Modernizations and hindered the development of productivity. Therefore, it was important to have the courage to resolutely and properly reform the parts of the superstructure and production relations that were not compatible with the development of productivity.

From July 6 to September 9, at a meeting held by the State Council, more than sixty heads of relevant departments put forward suggestions on reforming the economic management system and actively introducing advanced foreign technology and funds on the basis of earnestly summarizing the experiences and lessons learned since the founding of New China. In his concluding speech, Li Xiannian pointed out that the realization of the Four Modernizations was a great revolution that fundamentally changed the backward situation of China's economy and technology. This revolution would not only dramatically change the backward productivity at that time, but also inevitably change the relations of production in many ways, change the superstructure, and change the management mode of industrial and agricultural enterprises and the state. The management of industrial and agricultural enterprises should change people's ways of acting and thinking so as to adapt them to the needs of the modern economy. Therefore, in the work of economic leadership, it was important to resolutely eliminate the old frame of adhering to administrative levels and methods rather than paying attention to economic accounting, economic effects, and economic responsibilities, break the narrow horizon of small production, change the management methods of handicraft industry and the small-scale peasant economy, and even the feudal *yamen* style, and grasp the basis of leading and managing modern large-scale industrial and agricultural production. In order to carry out reform and deployment in accordance with the new requirements, the National Planning Conference, held from September 24 to October 22, also pointed out that economic work must undergo three changes. One was to shift attention to production struggle and technological revolution. Another was to shift from a bureaucratic management system and methods to scientific management in accordance with economic laws. And the last was to shift from a closed or semi-closed state to an open policy of actively introducing foreign funds and advanced technology and boldly entering the international market.

In September 1978, when the appeal for reform inside and outside the Party became increasingly stronger with the ongoing discussion of the criterion of truth, Deng Xiaoping inspected the three northeastern provinces and launched an important ideological campaign to develop productivity through emancipating the mind and reforming and opening up. In his speech, he pointed out, "The key to the problem before us now is to seek truth from facts, integrate theory with practice, and proceed from the actual situation. This is a political, ideological, and realistic issue that will enable us to realize the Four Modernizations… There are many conditions for us to realize the Four Modernizations now. Comrade Mao Zedong did not have them when he was alive, but now we have them… If the Central Committee does not think and make up its mind in accordance with the present conditions, many problems will not be raised and addressed… Every day the world changes, new things keep appearing, and new problems continually arise. We can't shut our doors and stay behind them forever without thinking."[20] He emphasized, "Marxism believes that the ultimate goal is to develop productivity. We are too poor and too backward to be honest with the people. We must now develop productivity and improve people's living conditions… If socialism intends to show its superiority, how can it be done as it is now, and if it has been so poor for more than twenty years, why should we have socialism? We should advocate and educate all cadres to think independently, so that we can boldly reform unreasonable things."[21] As soon as Deng's discussion on inspecting the Northeast came out, it sparked tremendous discussions among the cadres. After a period of deliberation, the policy of Reform and Opening Up became the consensus of the majority of the Party, creating conditions for opening up a new path of development in China.

With the deepening of the ideological emancipation movement and the advancement of various tasks, the Party had constantly broken through the "class struggle-oriented thinking pattern" and the "criticism and critique of the Gang of Four" restrictions, which had prompted the discussion of the shift of work focus to be put on the agenda. In March 1977, the National Planning Conference focused on "the confusion of ideas created by the Gang of Four in the economic field, emphasizing that enterprises should give priority to production and that all work should serve production." Subsequently, in the national discussion on distribution according to work, some comrades criticized the Gang of Four's criticism of "productivity-oriented theory" by citing Lenin's and Mao's relevant statements, especially emphasizing the extreme importance of developing productivity after the proletariat seized power.

Shortly after Deng Xiaoping was reinstated, he began to think about how to break through the problem of "shifting the focus of the Party's work with class struggle as the guiding principle." On August 23, 1977, he pointed out at the Military Commission Symposium, "For the time being, our guiding principle is to expose and criticize the struggle of the Gang of Four. We must carry this struggle to the end, but there must also be a time limit."[22] With the gradual deepening of the rectification of chaos on all fronts, the Party's thinking on China's development path and the formulation of the policy of Reform and Opening Up also showed that economic construction was increasingly becoming the focus of attention for the whole Party. In this context, Deng promptly raised the issue of shifting the focus of the Party's work. In his speech on inspecting Northeast China in September 1978, he clearly pointed out that "through campaigns, the main task is to improve the team and style of work. It will take half a year to do it well. Campaigns cannot be carried out for too long, or we will be tired of doing it." On October 11, in his speech to the Ninth National Congress of China's Trade Unions, he made it clearer that the struggle against the Gang of Four had won a decisive victory throughout the country. "We have been able to start new combat tasks on the basis of this victory,"[23] and this new combat task was to be substantially changed. To change the backward productivity and the backward productive relations and superstructure was to realize the Four Modernizations.

Deng's opinions soon reached consensus in the central leadership, thus preparing more sufficient conditions for making the decision to shift the focus of the Party's work and realizing a historic turning point for the Party and the country.

4. A New Starting Point for the Second Leap in the Localization of Marxism

After the end of the Cultural Revolution and another two years of hesitation and various preparations, the conditions for shifting the focus of the work of the Party and the state had basically matured. The Third Plenary Session of the Eleventh Central Committee, held at the end of 1978, completed this great turning point of historical significance.

The Third Plenary Session of the Eleventh Central Committee, as a new starting point of Reform and Opening Up and socialist modernization, was recorded in the history books. At the same time, it had also been recorded in the history books because it had corrected the direction of the development of Marxism. Therefore, it had become a new starting point for the development of Marxism in China, a new starting point for the second leap in the localization of Marxism in China, and a new starting point for the latest achievement of the localization of Marxism in China – the theory of socialism with Chinese characteristics.

From November 10 to December 15, 1978, the Central Committee held a working conference in Beijing. On December 13, Deng delivered a speech entitled "Emancipating the Mind, Seeking Truth from Facts, Uniting, and Looking Forward" at the closing meeting. He warned the entire Party, "If we do not carry out reform anymore, our cause of modernization and socialism will be buried." With the promotion of the older generation of revolutionaries and the joint efforts of the overwhelming majority of comrades participating in the conference, the 36-day Central Working Conference finally broke the shackles of the Two Whatevers and held a meeting intended for discussion of economic work to prepare for the overall rectification of disorder and the opening up of an innovative situation. Deng's speech became the theme of the Third Plenary Session of the Eleventh Central Committee.

After full preparation for the Central Working Conference, the Third Plenary Session of the Eleventh Central Committee of the Communist Party of China was held in Beijing from December 18–22, 1978. The plenary broke through the serious shackles of the long-term Leftist mistakes, criticized the principle of the Two Whatevers, and clearly pointed out that the scientific system of Mao Zedong Thought must be completely and accurately grasped. The plenary highly appraised the discussion on the criterion of truth, re-established the ideological, political, and organizational lines of Marxism, and made a decision. It determined to shift the focus of the Party's and the state's work to socialist modernization and carry out the strategic policy of Reform and Opening Up. The Plenary Session solemnly pointed out that the lofty task of the Central Committee on the theoretical front was to lead and educate the entire Party and all the people of the country to understand Mao's great achievements historically and scientifically, to master the scientific system of Mao Zedong Thought completely and accurately, and to present the general principles of Marxism-Leninism and Mao Zedong

Thought with socialism. The concrete practice of the construction of modernization was to be combined and developed under new historical conditions.[24] This was the restoration of the basic principles of the localization of Marxism, and it would certainly open a new road for the localization of Marxism.

In this way, the Third Plenary Session of the Eleventh Central Committee ended two years after the collapse of the Gang of Four, halting the Party's indecision, its misunderstanding, and its hesitation in the localization of Marxism in China, marking one of the major turning points in the history of the Party and the development of the localization of Marxism in China after the founding of New China. As Deng Xiaoping noted, "Our real turning point is the Third Plenary Session of the Eleventh Central Committee, which was held at the end of 1978. The Third Plenary Session of the Central Committee formulated new programs, guidelines, and policies, as well as new ideological, political, and organizational lines."[25]

As the main report of this plenary session, Deng Xiaoping's speech "Emancipating the Mind, Seeking Truth from Facts, and Looking Forward Together" was renamed "After the End of the Cultural Revolution: China's major historical juncture, breaking through the shackles of the Two Whatevers, opening up a new road in the new era, and creating a new theory of socialism with Chinese characteristics."[26]

The so-called new period was one that took the Third Plenary Session of the Eleventh Central Committee as a new historical starting point, Reform and Opening Up as a distinct feature, and the overall socialist modernization construction as its central task. It was also a new period that initiated the second historic leap in the localization of Marxism in China.

The so-called new path was to inherit all the correct and comparatively correct experiences accumulated by the Party in leading socialist construction on the basis of the great achievements made in building socialism since the founding of New China, correct the long-term left-leaning mistakes from the past, face new situations, and solve new problems, thus opening up socialism with Chinese characteristics. The path was also a new way to promote a new leap in the localization of Marxism in China.

The so-called new theory was to adhere to, develop, and inherit Mao Zedong Thought, correct Mao's mistakes in his later years, combine Marxism-Leninism with contemporary Chinese reality and characteristics of the times, and develop it in the practice of Reform and Opening Up and socialist modernization. It was the theory of socialism with Chinese characteristics held by contemporary Chinese Marxism, a brand new achievement of the second leap in the localization of Marxism in China.

After the Third Plenary Session of the Eleventh Central Committee, the CPC adhered to the Marxist ideological line and continuously promoted the localization and modernization of Marxism. Historic changes took place before the eyes of the Chinese people, socialist China, and the CPC. These changes were inseparable from the ideological emancipation campaign carried out more than two years before the Third Plenary Session of the Eleventh Central Committee, as well as the efforts to rectify the chaos after the Cultural Revolution. These two years were the period of change from hesitation to a great historical turning point, the period for making direct preparations and full gestation for realizing the localization of Marxism, and the period for the localization of Marxism to be systematically put on the right track and avoid major divergences. In the previous two years, through the criticism of and struggle against the "Two Whatevers," the scientific attitude of understanding Mao Zedong Thought completely and accurately was made clear, and the ideological foundation was laid for breaking the dogmatism and rigid attitude toward Mao Zedong Thought. Through the discussion of the criterion of truth, it was clear that the basic theory of Marxism, including Mao Zedong Thought, had a test criterion problem. This standard was social practice, and practice was colorful and constantly changing, and theory itself accordingly needed to develop continuously.

In order to realize this turning point of history, Deng became the core of the Party's leadership and prepared the basis of leadership and the cadres' grassroots level and organization by putting an end to the wrongdoings and errors and speeding up the process of reinstating veteran cadres, even by the Third Plenary Session of the Eleventh Central Committee. In this process, with his rich revolutionary experience and outstanding leadership, Deng showed great political courage and wisdom, along with great theoretical courage and depth, and became the pioneer and founder of the theory of socialism with Chinese characteristics, realizing a new leap in the localization of Marxism in China and closely linking this contemporary Chinese Marxism to his own name.

Through the heated discussion of major theoretical issues and the struggle against left-leaning ideas in various fields, the recovery and development of intra-

Party democracy were promoted. During this period of time, the atmosphere of democracy and free discussion was relatively strong. Different opinions could be expressed and different ideas collided with each other. Deng emphasized that "democracy is an important condition for emancipating the mind."[27] The ideological emancipation movement initiated by the question of the criterion of truth had gradually broken its spiritual shackles and ideological autocracy, broken the influence of dogmatism and personal worship, awakened the democratic consciousness of the cadres and masses, and made independent thinking a trend of the times. Many issues were gradually clarified after full discussion, which provided favorable conditions to develop and innovate Marxism.

Through the promotion of all aspects of the rectification of the chaos and the breakthrough of the left-leaning policy and mutual promotion with the ideological liberation movement, an irresistible trend was formed, the process of the historical turn was accelerated, various preparations were made for putting the localization of Marxism onto the right track, and a broad mass foundation had been laid.

By studying new situations and solving new problems, new theoretical achievements were bred. Deng Xiaoping once said at the 1978 Army Political Work Conference, "If we just copy some of the past documents word for word, we won't be able to solve any problems at all, let alone do so in a proper way."[28] He also said, "The world changes every day and new things and problems keep emerging, so we can't close the door and stay behind it forever without thinking." He went on, "There are many conditions for us to realize the Four Modernizations, which Mao Zedong did not have when he was alive, but we now have." The process of the localization of Marxism was a process of combining the basic principles of Marxism with the actual situation in contemporary China and the characteristics of the times. Facing the changing situations at home and abroad, it was important not to turn a blind eye or a deaf ear to them. The only correct way was to study new situations and solve new problems. It was this keen observation and the ability to discover and solve new problems that made the liberation of the mind possible and brought about this turning point of history. It was also possible to sum up new experiences, make new generalizations, push theory forward, and fuel a new leap in the localization of Marxism in China.

NOTES

Chapter 1

1. "Walking along the Road of Socialism with Chinese Characteristics." October 25, 1987. See *Selection of Important Documents since the Thirteenth National Congress, Vol. 1*. People's Publishing House, 1991. p. 56.
2. "Deng Xiaoping Theory and the Center for Important Thoughts of the Three Represents in Beijing." *Collected Works on the Localization of Marxism*. Hong Qi Publishing House, 2006. p. 5.
3. The important links of the new economic policy were emphasizing the development of the commodity economy, substituting commodity trade for product distribution, allowing various economic components to exist, building socialism with the achievements of capitalist civilization, and so on. After 1921, Lenin emphasized that the more backward the country, the longer the transitional period.
4. Documentation Research Office of the Central Committee of the Communist Party of China, ed. *Liu Shaoqi's Manuscripts After the Founding of the People's Republic of China, Volume 4*. Central Documentation Publishing House, 2005. p. 536.
5. Hu Sheng, ed. *Seventy Years of the Communist Party of China*. Party History Publishing House of the Communist Party of China, 1991. p. 438.
6. Mao Zedong. Speech at the Expanded Central Working Conference." January 30, 1962. *Collected Works of Mao Zedong, Vol. 8*. People's Publishing House, 1999. p. 305.
7. *Collected Works of Mao Zedong, Volume 6*. People's Publishing House, 1999. p. 301.
8. Mao Zedong. "Two Talks on Agricultural Mutual Cooperatives." October and November 1953.
9. Bo Yibo. *Review of Several Major Decisions and Events, Vol. 1*. Party School Press of the CPC Central Committee, 1991. p. 351.
10. *Biography of Mao Zedong (1949–1976) Vol. 1*. Central Literature Publishing House, 2003. p. 267.

11. Propaganda Department of the Central Committee of the Communist Party of China. *Outline of Study and Propaganda on the Party's General Line in the Transitional Period.* Edited by the Documentation Research Office of the Central Committee of the Communist Party of China. *Selection and Edition of Important Documents after the Founding of the People's Republic, Volume 4.* Central Documentation Publishing House, 1993. p. 697.
12. Lin Yunhui. "Historical Orientation in 1953." *Research on the History of the Communist Party of China*, No. 5, 2000.
13. Wu Lengxi. *Ten Years Debate, Vol. 1.* Central Documents Publishing House, 1999. p. 23.
14. Hu Sheng, ed. *Seventy Years of the Communist Party of China.* Party History Publishing House of the Communist Party of China, 1991. p. 438.
15. *Mao Zedong Anthology, Volume 7.* People's Publishing House, 1999. p. 369.
16. Deng Xiaoping said, "The Great Leap Forward and the Great Cultural Revolution are not problems of using other countries' models." *Selected Works of Deng Xiaoping, Volume 3.* People's Publishing House, 1993. p. 237.
17. Document Editorial Committee of the Central Committee of the Communist Party of China. *Selected Readings of Mao Zedong's Works, Volume 2.* People's Publishing House, 1986. p. 829.
18. In terms of the degree of social development in China at that time, it was more difficult to understand the reform tasks that only appeared urgent and could be put forward to a certain extent in the course of socialist development. That is to say, there was a greater likelihood of regarding them as capitalism and revisionism.
19. Bo Yibo. *Review of Several Major Decisions and Events, Vol. 2.* Party School Press of the CPC Central Committee, 1933. p. 901.
20. *Selected Works of Deng Xiaoping, Volume 3.* People's Publishing House, 1993. p. 272.
21. Documentation Research Department of the Central Committee of the Communist Party of China, ed. *Deng Xiaoping Chronicle (1975–1997) Part 2.* Central Documentation Publishing House, 2004. p. 1242.
22. Joe Urban. *European Communism.* Xinhua Publishing House, 1980. p. 9.
23. This was pointed out by the General Secretary of the Italian Communist Party, Togliatti, in his speech the day after the end of the 20th CPSU Congress. See Bernardo Wally. *The Origin of Communism in Europe.* China Social Science Press, 1983. p. 148.
24. It is necessary to distinguish the Stalinist model from the Soviet model after 1956. Although there are many similarities between the two, the latter, ultimately, has some elements of reform.
25. Documentation Research Room of the Central Committee of the Communist Party of China. *Mao Zedong's Manuscripts after the Founding of the People's Republic, Volume 4.* Central Documentation Publishing House, 1990. p. 45–46.
26. In February 1957, the Prime Minister of the Polish Council of Ministers, Piotr Jaroszewicz, addressed the training course for propagandists of the Polish Party Central Committee. Quoted from *Comments Ten Years Later.* CPC Party History Information

Publishing House, 1987. p. 267.
27. *Selected Works of Marx and Engels, Volume 4*. People's Publishing House, 1995. p. 337.
28. Many scholars in China and abroad also call it Marxist modernization.
29. Lu Zhenyang. "Investigation of Several Issues in the History of the Interpretation of the Sinicization of Marxism." Beijing Research Center of Deng Xiaoping Theory and Important Thoughts of Three Represents, ed. *Collection of Studies on the Sinicization of Marxism.* Hong Qi Publishing House, 2006. p. 25.
30. Maurice Meisner. *Rethinking Marxist Criticism of Capitalism.* Yu Keping, ed. *Marxist Ambiguity in the Age of Globalization.* Central Compilation and Publishing House, 1998. p. 195.
31. Ibid.
32. *The Complete Works of Lenin, Vol. 34.* People's Publishing House, 1985. p. 466.
33. Mitchell Blovi's report to the Chinese Academy of Social Sciences on June 27, 2006.
34. Friedrich Jameson. *Cultural Logic of Late Capitalism.* Zhan Mingxin, trans. Sanlian Bookstore, 1997. p. 19.
35. Zhang Yixing. "The Enlightenment and Reference of Western Marxist Trend of Thought." *Marxism and Reality*, No. 4, 1995.
36. Friedrich Jameson. *Cultural Logic of Late Capitalism.* Zhan Mingxin, trans. Sanlian Bookstore, 1997. p. 19.
37. For example, there is Marxism as Lenin understands it or Marxism as Stalin understands it, and so on. An important point of view in hermeneutics is that we should not only recognize the historicity of the author, but also the historicity of the reader.
38. Mao Zedong. Speech at the National Conference on Propaganda of the Communist Party of China, 12 March 1957.
39. *Selected Works of Deng Xiaoping, Volume 3.* People's Publishing House, 1993. p. 291.
40. *Selected Works of Deng Xiaoping, Volume 3.* People's Publishing House, 1993. p. 291–292.
41. *Works of Mao Zedong, Volume 8.* People's Publishing House, 1999. p. 299.

Chapter 2

1. Mao Zedong. *On New Democracy.* See *Selected Works of Mao Zedong, Volume 2.* People's Publishing House, 1991. p. 669.
2. Ibid, p. 678.
3. Ibid, p. 672.
4. Mao Zedong. *On New Democracy.* See *Selected Works of Mao Zedong, Volume 2.* People's Publishing House, 1991. p. 675.
5. Ibid.
6. Mao Zedong. *On New Democracy.* See *Selected Works of Mao Zedong, Vol. 2.* People's Publishing House, 1952. p. 613.

7. Yu Guangyuan. *From New Democratic Socialism to the Primary Stage of Socialism.* People's Publishing House, 1996. p. 28–29.
8. *Selected Works of Mao Zedong, Volume 3.* People's Publishing House, 1991. p. 1056.
9. Mao Zedong. *On the United Government.* See *Selected Works of Mao Zedong, Volume 3.* People's Publishing House, 1991. p. 1060.
10. *Liberation Daily,* May 26, 1944.
11. Mao Zedong. To Qin Bangxian (31 August 1944). See *Selected Letters from Mao Zedong.* People's Publishing House, 1983. p. 238–239.
12. *Mao Zedong Anthology, Volume 3.* People's Publishing House, 1996. p. 275.
13. Mao Zedong. *On the United Government.* See *Selected Works of Mao Zedong, Volume 3.* People's Publishing House, 1991. p. 1060.
14. Ibid, p. 1061.
15. Ibid, p. 1082.
16. *Liu Shaoqi on New China's Economic Construction.* Central Document Publishing House, 1993. p. 1.
17. *Selected Works of Mao Zedong, Volume 4.* People's Publishing House, 1991. p. 1347.
18. *Mao Zedong Anthology, Volume 5.* People's Publishing House, 1996. p. 135.
19. Ibid, p. 139.
20. *Mao Zedong Anthology, Volume 5.* People's Publishing House, 1996. p. 146.
21. *Liu Shaoqi on New China's Economic Construction.* Central Document Publishing House, 1993. p. 3.
22. Ibid.
23. Ibid.
24. Ibid, p. 2.
25. *Liu Shaoqi on New China's Economic Construction.* Central Document Publishing House, 1993. p. 5, 7.
26. Ibid, p. 6.
27. Ibid, p. 10–13.
28. Ibid, p. 10–13.
29. Ibid, p. 14.
30. Yu Guangyuan. *From New Democratic Society Theory to Primary Stage of Socialism.* People's Publishing House, 1996. p. 48.
31. *Selected Works of Zhang Wentian.* People's Publishing House, 1985. p. 397.
32. Ibid, p. 407.
33. Ibid, p. 408.
34. Ibid, p. 415–416.
35. *Liu Shaoqi on New China's Economic Construction.* Central Literature Publishing House, 1993. p. 30.
36. Ibid.
37. Ibid, p. 42.
38. Ibid, p. 33.

39. Ibid, p. 46.
40. *Liu Shaoqi on New China's Economic Construction*. Central Literature Publishing House, 1993. p. 47.
41. Ibid, p. 48.
42. *Selected Works of Mao Zedong, Volume 4*. People's Publishing House, 1991. p. 1427.
43. Ibid, p. 1430.
44. *Selected Works of Mao Zedong, Volume 4*. People's Publishing House, 1991. p. 1431.
45. Ibid, p. 1430.
46. *Selected Works of Mao Zedong Volume 4*. People's Publishing House, 1991. p. 1431.
47. Ibid, p. 1432.
48. Ibid, p. 1428.
49. Ibid, p. 1432.
50. Hu Sheng. *From the May 4th Movement to the Establishment of the People's Republic*. Social Science Literature Publishing House, 2001. p. 51.
51. *Selected Works of Ren Bishi*. People's Publishing House, 1987. p. 478–479.
52. See the Anniversary of Li Li's 300th Birthday. CPC Party History Publishing House, 1999. p. 122–123.
53. *Selected Works of Mao Zedong, Volume 4*. People's Publishing House, 1991. p. 1474.
54. Ibid, p. 1476.
55. Ibid, p. 1478.
56. Ibid, p. 1479.
57. Bo Yibo. *Review of Several Major Decisions and Events Part 1*. Publishing House of the Party School of the Central Committee of the Communist Party of China, 1911. p. 50–51.
58. *Liu Shaoqi on New China's Economic Construction*. Central Documents Publishing House, 1993. p. 77–78.
59. Ibid, p. 81.
60. Ibid, p. 47.
61. Ibid, p. 48.
62. Ibid.
63. *Liu Shaoqi on New China's Economic Construction*. Central Literature Publishing House, 1993. p. 91.
64. Ibid, p. 107.
65. Ibid, p. 105.
66. *Liu Shaoqi on New China's Economic Construction*. Central Literature Publishing House, 1993. p. 146.
67. Ibid, p. 145.
68. Ibid, p. 147.
69. Hu Sheng. *From the May 4th Movement to the Establishment of the People's Republic*. Social Sciences Literature Press, 2001. Chapter 2: "Two Theories on New Democracy," p. 50.
70. Hu Sheng. *From the May 4th Movement to the Establishment of the People's Republic*. Social Sciences Literature Press, 2001. p. 52.

346 NOTES

71. *Liu Shaoqi on New China's Economic Construction.* Central Documents Publishing House, 1993. p. 50.
72. *Selected Works of Mao Zedong, Volume 1.* People's Publishing House, 1991. p. 276.
73. *Selected Works of Mao Zedong, Volume 4.* People's Publishing House, 1991. p. 1480.
74. *Liu Shaoqi's Manuscripts After the Founding of the People's Republic, Volume 1.* Central Documents Publishing House, 2005. p. 6.
75. *Chronicle of Liu Shaoqi (1898–1969).* Central Literature Publishing House, 1996. p. 222.
76. *Mao Zedong Anthology, Volume 5.* People's Publishing House, 1996. p. 141.
77. *Selected Works of Mao Zedong, Volume 4.* People's Publishing House, 1991. p. 1433.
78. *The History of the Communist Party of China, Volume 2 (Part 1).* The Party History Publishing House of the Communist Party of China, 2011. p. 12–14.
79. *Selection of Important Documents after the Founding of the People's Republic, Volume 1.* Central Documents Publishing House, 1992. p. 15–16.
80. *Selected Documents of the Central Committee of the Communist Party of China, Volume 1.* Party School Press of the Central Committee of the Communist Party of China, 1982. p. 78.
81. *Selected Documents of the Central Committee of the Communist Party of China, Volume 15.* Party School Press of the Central Committee of the Communist Party of China, 1982. p. 116.
82. *People's Daily,* October 10, 1947.
83. *Selected Works of Zhou Enlai's United Front.* People's Publishing House, 1984. p. 139–140.
84. *Selected Works of Zhou Enlai, Volume 1.* People's Publishing House, 1980. p. 368.

CHAPTER 3

1. *The Chronicle of Zhou Enlai (1949–1976), Part 1.* Central Literature Publishing House, 1997. p. 32.
2. *Selected Works of Zhou Enlai's United Front.* People's Publishing House, 1984. p. 168–170.
3. *Mao Zedong's Manuscripts after the founding of the People's Republic Vol. 1.* Central Documents Publishing House, 1987. p. 292–294.
4. Bo Yibo. *Review of Several Major Decisions and Events, Vol. 1.* Party School Press of the Central Committee of the Communist Party of China, 1991. p. 98–99.
5. Ibid, p. 99.
6. *Mao Zedong Anthology, Volume 6.* People's Publishing House, 1999. p. 61–62.
7. *Mao Zedong Anthology, Volume 6.* People's Publishing House, 1999. p. 71.
8. Ibid, p. 73–76.
9. *Selection of Important Documents since the Founding of the People's Republic, Volume 1.* Central Documents Publishing House, 1992. p. 323.
10. *Mao Zedong Anthology, Volume 6.* People's Publishing House, 1999. p. 47–48.

11. At the meeting, some held the view that the situation was different in different parts of the country. It was suggested that in areas with very little land, it would be impossible to solve the minimum living conditions of most poor peasants and peasants without expropriating land for rent by rich peasants, and that there should be some flexibility in policy implementation.
12. *Liu Shaoqi on New China's Economic Construction.* Central Document Publishing House, 1993. p. 158–159.
13. *Liu Shaoqi on New China's Economic Construction.* Central Document Publishing House, 1993. People's Publishing House, 1985. p.166.
14. *Selected Works of Liu Shaoqi, Volume 2.* People's Publishing House, 1985. p. 50.
15. *Liu Shaoqi's Manuscripts after the Founding of the People's Republic, Volume 1.* Central Documents Publishing House, 2005. p. 398–399.
16. *Liu Shaoqi on New China's Economic Construction.* Central Document Publishing House, 1993. p. 152–154.
17. Ibid, p. 154–155.
18. Bo Yibo. *Review of Several Major Decisions and Events, Part 1.* Party School Press of the Central Committee of the Communist Party of China, 1991. p. 185.
19. Compilation of Important Documents on Agricultural Cooperativeness (1949–1957). Central Party School Press, 1981. p. 35–36.
20. Bo Yibo. *Review of Several Major Decisions and Events, Part 1.* Party School Press of the Central Committee of the Communist Party of China, 1991. p. 187.
21. *Liu Shaoqi on New China's Economic Construction.* Central Documents Publishing House, 1993. p. 183–184.
22. Ibid, p. 192.
23. *Liu Shaoqi on New China's Economic Construction.* Central Documents Publishing House, 1993. p. 219.
24. Bo Yibo. *Review of Several Major Decisions and Events, Volume 1.* Party School Press of the Central Committee of the Communist Party of China, 1991. p. 203–205.
25. *Mao Zedong Anthology, Volume 6.* Central Documents Publishing House, 1999. p. 4.
26. *Selected Works of Liu Shaoqi, Volume 2.* People's Publishing House, 1985. p. 60.
27. *General Situation and Documents of All Previous National United Front Work Conferences.* Archives Publishing House, 1988. p. 6.
28. *Selected Works of Zhou Enlai's United Front.* People's Publishing House, 1984. p. 171–172, 179.
29. Ibid, p. 203.
30. *Selected Works of Zhou Enlai's United Front.* People's Publishing House, 1984. p. 192–194.
31. *Selected Works of Zhou Enlai's United Front.* People's Publishing House, 1984. p. 182–186.
32. *Selected Works of Liu Shaoqi, Volume 2.* People's Publishing House, 1985. p. 82–83.
33. *Selected Works of Liu Shaoqi, Volume 2.* People's Publishing House, 1985. p. 92–93.
34. Ibid.
35. Ibid, p. 94.

36. *Liu Shaoqi on New China's Economic Construction*. Central Documents Publishing House, 1993. p. 182.
37. Ibid, p. 214.
38. *Liu Shaoqi on New China's Economic Construction*. Central Literature Publishing House, 1993. p. 206–207.
39. *Selected Works of Zhou Enlai's United Front*. People's Publishing House, 1984. p. 235.
40. *Selected Works of Liu Shaoqi, Volume 2*. People's Publishing House, 1985. p. 62.
41. *Liu Shaoqi on the Construction of New China*. Central Documents Publishing House, 1993. p. 197.
42. *Selected Works of Mao Zedong, Volume 4*. People's Publishing House, 1991. p. 1433.
43. *Selected Works of Liu Shaoqi, Volume 1*. People's Publishing House, 1981. p. 427.
44. *Selected Works of Mao Zedong, Volume 4*. People's Publishing House, 1991. p. 1429.
45. *Selected Works of Liu Shaoqi, Volume 1*. People's Publishing House, 1981. p. 426.
46. *Liu Shaoqi's Manuscripts after the founding of the People's Republic, Volume 1*. Central Documents Publishing House, 2005. p. 6–7.
47. *Mao Zedong's Manuscripts After the Founding of the People's Republic of China, Volume 1*. Central Documents Publishing House, 1987. p. 292.

CHAPTER 4

1. *Liu Shaoqi Anthology, Volume 2*. People's Publishing House, 1985. p. 1–5.
2. *Mao Zedong Anthology, Volume 6*. People's Publishing House, 1999. p. 329.
3. *Biography of Li Fuchun*. Central Literature Publishing House, 2002. p. 421.
4. *Biography of Mao Zedong (1949–1976), Volume 1*. Central Literature Publishing House, 2003. p. 273.
5. *Mao Zedong's Manuscripts after the Founding of the People's Republic of China, Volume 3*. Central Literature Publishing House, 1987. p. 361–362.
6. *Mao Zedong Anthology, Volume 6*. People's Publishing House, 1999. p. 231.
7. *Liu Shaoqi's Manuscripts after the Founding of the People's Republic of China, Volume 4*. Central Documents Publishing House, 2005. p. 533–534.
8. *Mao Zedong's Manuscripts after the Founding of the People's Republic, Volume 4*. Central Documents Publishing House, 1990. p. 251.
9. *Selection and Compilation of Important Documents since the Founding of the People's Republic, Volume 4*. Central Documents Publishing House, 1993. p. 700–701.
10. *Selected Works of Zhou Enlai's United Front*. People's Publishing House, 1984. p. 255.
11. *Mao Zedong Collection of Literature, Volume 6*. People's Publishing House, 1999. p. 432.
12. See *Mao Zedong's Manuscripts after the Founding of the People's Republic of China, Volume 4*. Central Literature Publishing House, 1990. p. 251.
13. *Mao Zedong Anthology, Volume 6*. People's Publishing House, 1999. p. 301, 305.

14. "Mao Zedong: A Debate on Agricultural Cooperation and Current Class Struggle (October 11, 1955)." See *Selected Works of Mao Zedong, Volume 5*. People's Publishing House, 1977. p. 198–199.
15. *Selected Works of Zhou Enlai, Volume 2*. People's Publishing House, 1984. p. 105.
16. *Selection and Compilation of Important Documents after the Founding of the People's Republic of China, Volume 4*. Central Documents Publishing House, 1993. p. 702.
17. *Mao Zedong Collection of Literature, Volume 6*. People's Publishing House, 1999. p. 432.
18. Mao Zedong. *On the People's Democratic Dictatorship*. June 1949.
19. *Mao Zedong Anthology, Volume 6*. People's Publishing House, 1999. p. 49.
20. Ibid, p. 71.
21. *Mao Zedong's Anthology, Volume 6*. People's Publishing House, 1999. p. 264.
22. Liu Shaoqi. Speech at the Third Anniversary Conference of the Sino-Soviet Treaty of Friendship, Alliance, and Mutual Assistance in Beijing. See *Xinhua Monthly News* No. 3, 1953.
23. Liu Shaoqi. Report on the Draft Constitution of the People's Republic of China (September 15, 1954). See *Selected Works of Liu Shaoqi, Volume 2*. People's Publishing House, 1985. p. 155.
24. *Selection and Compilation of Important Documents after the Founding of the People's Republic, Volume 4*. Central Documents Publishing House, 1993. p. 141.
25. Mao Zedong. *Summary of Ten Years. Mao Zedong's Manuscripts after the Founding of the People's Republic of China, Volume 9*. Central Literature Publishing House, 1992. p. 213.
26. *Biography of Mao Zedong (1949–1976), Volume 1*. Central Literature Publishing House, 2003. p. 791.
27. *Mao Zedong Anthology, Volume 8*. People's Publishing House, 1999. p. 305.
28. *Biography of Mao Zedong (1949–1976), Volume 1*. Central Literature Publishing House, 2003. p. 530.
29. Engels. *Farmers in France and Germany*. See *Selected Works of Marx and Engels, Volume 4*. People's Publishing House, 1972. p. 310.
30. Mao Zedong. Report on the Second Plenary Session of the Seventh Central Committee of the Communist Party of China (March 5, 1949). See *Selected Works of Mao Zedong, Volume 4*. People's Publishing House, 1991. p. 1432.
31. *Selected Works of Marx and Engels, Volume 4*. People's Publishing House, 1972. p. 314–315.
32. Mao Zedong. On the National Capitalist Economy (July 1953). See *Mao Zedong's Collection of Literature, Volume 6*. People's Publishing House, 1999. p. 282.
33. Mao Zedong. The Only Way to Reform Capitalist Industry and Commerce (September 7, 1953). See *Mao Zedong Anthology, Volume 6*. People's Publishing House, 1999. p. 291.
34. In addition to wages, private enterprises have four parts of income distribution: income tax 5%, welfare 15%, provident fund 30%, and management dividend 20.5%.
35. Liu Shaoqi. *Political Report at the Eighth National Congress of the Communist Party of China (September 15, 1956)*. Central Documents Publishing House, 1994. p. 84.
36. Ibid, p. 55.

Chapter 5

1. *The Complete Works of Lenin, Volume 34*. People's Publishing House, 1985. p. 281.
2. *Mao Zedong Anthology, Volume 7*. People's Publishing House, 1999. p. 127.
3. Wu Lengxi. *Recalling Chairman Mao*. Xinhua Publishing House, 1995. p. 4 and 6.
4. *Mao Zedong Anthology, Volume 7*. People's Publishing House, 1999. p. 64.
5. *Selected Works of Mao Zedong, Volume 5*. People's Publishing House, 1977. p. 320–321.
6. *Chronicle of Liu Shaoqi (1898–1969), Volume 2*. Central Literature Publishing House, 1996. p. 371.
7. *Zhou Enlai Chronicle (1949–1976), Volume 1*. Central Documents Publishing House, 1997. p. 621.
8. *Selected Economic Essays of Zhou Enlai*. Central Documents Publishing House, 1993. p. 257.
9. *Selected Works of Deng Xiaoping, Volume 1*. People's Publishing House, 1994. p. 258–259.
10. *Mao Zedong's Criticism and Revision of the Draft Historical Experiences of Several Proletarian Dictatorships*. April 2 and 4, 1956.
11. *Mao Zedong Anthology, Volume 7*. People's Publishing House, 1999. p. 44.
12. Ibid, p. 23.
13. Ibid, p. 42.
14. *Selection of Important Documents after the Founding of the People's Republic, Volume 9*. Central Documents Publishing House, 1994. p. 315–316.
15. *Mao Zedong Anthology, Volume 7*. People's Publishing House, 1999. p. 25.
16. Mao Zedong. "On the Correct Handling of Contradictions among the People." See *Selected Works of Mao Zedong, Volume 5*. People's Publishing House, 1977.
17. *Selected Works of Zhou Enlai, Volume 2*. People's Publishing House, 1984. p. 232.
18. Mao Zedong. *On the Ten Relations*. See *Mao Zedong Anthology, Volume 7*. People's Publishing House, 1999. p. 23–42.
19. *Selected Works of Chen Yun, Volume 3*. People's Publishing House, 1995. p. 13.
20. *Selection of Important Documents after the Founding of the People's Republic, Volume 10*. Central Documents Publishing House, 1994. p. 164–165.
21. *Chronicle of Liu Shaoqi (1898–1969)*. Central Literature Publishing House, 1996. p. 399.
22. Ibid.
23. *Biography of Mao Zedong (1949–1976), Volume 1*. Central Literature Publishing House, 2003. p. 482.
24. *Mao Zedong Anthology, Volume 7*. People's Publishing House, 1999. p. 35.
25. *Selection of Important Documents after the Founding of the People's Republic, Volume 6*. Central Documents Publishing House, 1992. p. 143.
26. *Selected Works of Zhou Enlai, Volume 2*. People's Publishing House, 1984. p. 207.
27. *Selected Works of Dong Biwu*. People's Publishing House, 1985. p. 419–420.
28. *Selected Works of Zhou Enlai, Volume 2*. People's Publishing House, 1984. p. 181.
29. *Selection of Important Documents after the Founding of the People's Republic, Volume 8.*

Central Documents Publishing House, 1994. p. 133–134.
30. *History of the Communist Party of China, Volume 2 (1949–1978)*. CPC Party History Publishing House, 2011. p. 386.
31. *Mao Zedong Anthology, Volume 7*. People's Publishing House, 1999. p. 278.
32. *Mao Zedong Anthology, Volume 7*. People's Publishing House, 1999. p. 33.
33. Ibid, p. 227.
34. *Selected Works of Liu Shaoqi, Volume 2*. People's Publishing House, 1985. p. 251.
35. *Selection of Important Documents after the Founding of the People's Republic, Volume 9*. Central Documents Publishing House, 1994. p. 319.
36. Ibid, p. 105.
37. *Mao Zedong Anthology, Volume 7*. People's Publishing House, 1999. p. 89.
38. *Selected Works of Deng Xiaoping, Volume 1*. People's Publishing House, 1994. p. 218.
39. *The Complete Works of Lenin, Volume 60*. People's Publishing House, 1990. p. 281–282.
40. *Selected Works of Stalin, Volume 2*. People's Publishing House, 1979. p. 445, 449.
41. Ibid, p. 577.
42. *Liu Shaoqi on New China's Economic Construction*. Central Documents Publishing House, 1993. p. 187.
43. *Mao Zedong Anthology, Volume 7*. People's Publishing House, 1999. p. 44.
44. *Selected Letters of Mao Zedong*. People's Publishing House, 1983. p. 514–515.
45. Mao Zedong's Speech at the Meeting of Party Secretaries of Provinces, Municipalities, and Autonomous Regions, January 27, 1957.
46. Record of Mao Zedong's Speech at the Second Plenary Session of the Eighth Central Committee of the Communist Party of China, November 15, 1956.
47. Mao Zedong's Speech at the Meeting of Party Secretaries of Provinces, Municipalities, and Autonomous Regions, January 27, 1957.
48. *Mao Zedong Anthology, Volume 7*. People's Publishing House, 1999. p. 213–215.

Chapter 6

1. See Mao Zedong's Speech at the Second Plenary Session of the Eighth Central Committee of the Communist Party of China.
2. Ibid.
3. *Mao Zedong Anthology, Volume 7*. People's Publishing House, 1999. p. 249.
4. Ibid, p. 275.
5. *Mao Zedong Anthology, Volume 7*. People's Publishing House, 1999. p. 274.
6. *Mao Zedong Anthology, Volume 7*. People's Publishing House, 1999. p. 291.
7. *Mao Zedong Anthology, Volume 7*. People's Publishing House, 1999. p. 285.
8. *Selection of Important Documents after the Founding of the People's Republic, Volume 10*. Central Documents Publishing House, 1994. p. 250.
9. *Selected Works of Liu Shaoqi, Volume 2*. People's Publishing House, 1985. p. 303–305.

10. *Mao Zedong's Manuscripts after the Founding of the People's Republic of China, Volume 6.* Central Documents Publishing House, 1992. p. 543.
11. *Mao Zedong's Manuscripts after the Founding of the People's Republic of China, Volume 6.* Central Documents Publishing House, 1992. p. 497.
12. Ibid, p. 491.
13. Ibid, p. 548.
14. *Mao Zedong's Manuscripts after the Founding of the People's Republic of China, Volume 6.* Central Documents Publishing House, 1992. p. 245.
15. *Mao Zedong Anthology, Volume 7.* People's Publishing House, 1999. p. 164.
16. *Selection of Important Documents after the Founding of the People's Republic of China, Volume 10.* Central Documents Publishing House, 1992. p. 606–607.
17. *Selection of Important Documents after the Founding of the People's Republic of China, Volume 11.* Central Documents Publishing House, 1992. p. 288.
18. *Mao Zedong's Manuscripts after the founding of the People's Republic, Volume 7.* Central Documents Publishing House, 1992. p. 51.
19. Bo Yibo. *Review of Several Major Decisions and Events, Part 2.* People's Publishing House, 1997. p. 756–757.
20. Bo Yibo. *Review of Several Major Decisions and Events, Part 2.* Party School Press of the CPC Central Committee, 1993. p. 732–733.
21. Important Instructions of the Great Leader Chairman Mao on Visiting the Eighth Fourth Team of Xushui County, August 1958.
22. *Selection of Important Documents after the Founding of the People's Republic, Volume 11.* Central Documents Publishing House, 1995. p. 447.
23. *Selection of Important Documents after the Founding of the People's Republic, Volume 11.* Central Documents Publishing House, 1995. p. 450.
24. *Selected Works of Deng Xiaoping, Volume 3.* People's Publishing House, 1993. p. 63.

Chapter 7

1. The meeting was held from February 27 to March 5, 1959.
2. *Biography of Mao Zedong (949–1976), Volume 1.* Central Literature Publishing House, 2003. p.511.
3. *People's Daily,* March 7, 1953.
4. Mao Zedong. "On the Ten Major Relations." *Mao Zedong Anthology, Volume 7.* People's Publishing House, 1999. p. 23–42.
5. Mao Zedong. "Summary of Ten Years." *Mao Zedong's Manuscripts after the founding of the People's Republic, Volume 9.* Central Documents Publishing House, 1992. p. 213.
6. *Biography of Mao Zedong (949–1976), Part 1.* Central Literature Publishing House, 2003. p. 817.
7. Bo Yibo. *Review of Several Major Decisions and Events, Volume 2.* Party School Press of

the Central Committee of the Communist Party of China, 1993. p. 734.
8. Bo Yibo. *Review of Several Major Decisions and Events, Volume 2.* Party School Press of the Central Committee of the Communist Party of China, 1993. p. 767.
9. *Biography of Mao Zedong (1949–1976), Volume 1.* Central Literature Publishing House, 2003. p. 838.
10. Ibid, p. 839.
11. *Selection of Important Documents after the Founding of the People's Republic, Volume 11.* Central Documents Publishing House, 1995. p. 450.
12. *Biography of Mao Zedong (1949–1976), Volume 2.* Central Documents Publishing House, 2003. p. 890–891.
13. *Mao Zedong's Manuscripts after the Founding of the People's Republic, Volume 7.* Central Documents Publishing House, 1992. p. 510–511.
14. Refer to the first three chapters on the nature of economic rules under the socialist system, the production of commodities under the socialist system, and the law of value under the socialist system in Stalin's "Comments on Economic Issues Relating to the Symposium of November 1951," in *Socialist Economic Issues of the Soviet Union.*
15. *Mao Zedong Anthology, Volume 7.* People's Publishing House, 1999. p. 435.
16. *Mao Zedong's Reading Commentaries and Talks on Socialist Political Economy.* Edited by the Society of National History of the People's Republic of China. p. 25.
17. *Mao Zedong Anthology, Volume 7.* People's Publishing House, 1999. p. 436.
18. *Biography of Mao Zedong (1949–1976).* Central Documents Publishing House, 2003. p. 894.
19. *Mao Zedong Anthology, Volume 7.* People's Publishing House, 1999. p. 439.
20. *Mao Zedong's Manuscripts after the Founding of the People's Republic, Volume 7.* Central Documents Publishing House, 1999. p. 525.
21. Ibid, p. 638.
22. *Mao Zedong's Manuscripts after the founding of the People's Republic, Volume 7.* Central Documents Publishing House, 1992. p. 504, 513–521.
23. Ibid, p. 664.
24. *Mao Zedong's Reading Commentaries and Talks on Socialist Political Economy.* Edited by the Society of National History of the People's Republic of China. p. 40.
25. *The Textbook on the Soviet Union's Political Economy* is divided into two volumes: the first is the capitalist section, and the second is the socialist section. The first edition was published in 1954. It is the first textbook in the world that contained a socialist political economy and a theoretical summary of the traditional socialist economic model. The third edition of the book was published in 1958.
26. Mao Zedong's speech at the Wuchang Conference (November 21, 1958).
27. *Biography of Mao Zedong (1949–1976), Volume 2.* Central Documents Publishing House, 2003. p. 961.
28. *Mao Zedong's Manuscripts after the founding of the People's Republic of China, Volume 8.* Central Documents Publishing House, 1993. p. 331.

29. Ibid, p. 446.
30. *Mao Zedong's Reading Commentaries and Talks on Socialist Political Economy, Volume 2.* Edited by the Chinese Society of National History of the People's Republic of China, 1998. p. 919.
31. *Mao Zedong's Reading Commentaries and Talks on Socialist Political Economy.* Edited by the Society of National History of the People's Republic of China. p. 835, 836, 799.
32. Speech by Comrade Liu Shaoqi at the Political Economy (Socialist Part) Reading Conference. See *Teaching References for the History of the Communist Party of China, Volume 23.* 1986. p. 192.
33. Ibid, p. 189.
34. Ibid, p. 193.
35. *Biography of Mao Zedong (1949–1976), Volume 1.* Central Literature Publishing House, 2003. p. 792, 540.
36. *Mao Zedong Anthology, Volume 8.* People's Publishing House, 1999. p. 289.
37. Before the mid-1930s, the Comintern was a highly centralized organization. Its relationship with the parties of different countries was that of leading and being led, commanding and being commanded. The resolutions and instructions of the Comintern were to be obeyed, and there was not much democracy to speak of.
38. *Biography of Mao Zedong (1949–1976), Volume 2.* Central Documents Publishing House, 2003. p. 941.
39. *Mao Zedong's Manuscripts after the Founding of the People's Republic of China, Volume 8.* Central Documents Publishing House, 1993. p. 237.
40. *Selected Works of Liu Shaoqi, Volume 2.* People's Publishing House, 1985. p. 374.
41. Ibid, p. 485.
42. *Selected Works of Chen Yun, Volume 3.* People's Publishing House, 1986. p. 187.
43. Communist style, exaggeration style, command style, cadre's special style, and blind command style
44. Luo Rongqu. *Sequel to the New Theory of Modernization.* Peking University Press, 1997. p. 122.
45. Hobsbawm. *The Age of Revolution.* Jiangsu People's Publishing House, 1999. p. 407–409.

Chapter 8

1. *Seventy Years of the Communist Party of China.* Party History Publishing House, 1991. p. 361.
2. *Mao Zedong and His Secretary Tian Jiaying (updated edition).* Edited by Dong Bian, et al. Central Documents Publishing House, 1996. p. 174.
3. *Mao Zedong's Manuscripts after the Founding of the People's Republic of China, Volume 9.* Central Documents Publishing House, 1996. p. 215–216.

4. The Directive of the Central Committee of the Communist Party of China on the Complete Correction of the Five Surges Problem. November 15, 1960. See *Selection of Important Documents after the Founding of the People's Republic, Volume 13*. p. 693.
5. Ibid.
6. *Chronicle of Liu Shaoqi (1898–1969)*. Central Literature Publishing House, 1996. p. 519.
7. *Mao Zedong's Manuscripts after the Founding of the People's Republic of China, Volume 9*. Central Documents Publishing House, 1996. p. 566.
8. The Five Determinations were to determine product plan and production scale, to determine personnel and institutions, to determine consumption quotas and supply sources of major raw materials, to determine capital and liquidity funds, and to determine collaborative relationships.
9. The Five Guarantees were to guarantee the variety, quality, and quantity of products, to guarantee not exceeding the total amount of work and transportation, to guarantee the completion of the cost plan, to guarantee the completion of promised profits, and to guarantee the service life of major equipment.
10. Instructions of the Central Committee of the Communist Party of China on Socialist Education in Rural Areas, November 13, 1961. See *Selection of Important Documents after the Founding of the People's Republic, Volume 14*. p. 767.
11. *Mao Zedong and His Secretary, Tian Jiaying*. Central Literature Publishing House, 1989. p. 67.
12. *Collection of Deng Zihui's Works*. People's Publishing House, 1996. p. 598–599.
13. *Chen Yun and New China's Economic Construction*. Central Documents Publishing House, 1991. p. 168.
14. *Biography of Chen Yun, Volume 2*. Central Literature Publishing House, 2005. p. 1321.
15. *Chronicle of Liu Shaoqi (1898–1969)*. Central Literature Publishing House, 1996. p. 549.
16. Clean up the accounts, clean up the warehouse, clean up the property, clean up the work hours.
17. Oppose corruption and waste, speculation, extravagance and waste, decentralization, and bureaucracy.

CHAPTER 9

1. Lin Biao. "Long Live the Victory of the People's War: Commemorating the 20th Anniversary of the Chinese People's War of Resistance Against Japanese Aggression." *People's Daily*. September 3, 1969.
2. "Political Reports of the Ninth CPC National Congress." *People's Daily*. April 28, 1969.
3. Kang Sheng adopted this statement when he presided over the revision of the Party Constitution, pointing out, "At this historic stage, there will always be class, contradictions, and class struggle." He included the word "always."

4. According to Hu Qiaomu, Mao himself later raised objections to this formulation, disagreeing with the idea of the third milestone. See *Hu Qiaomu on the History of the CPC*. People's Publishing House, 1999. p. 34.
5. *People's Daily, Red Flag*, and *Liberation Army Daily* editorial. "Long Live the Dictatorship of the Proletariat: Commemorating the 100th Anniversary of the Paris Commune." March 18, 1917.
6. "Following the Path Opened by the Socialist October Revolution." *People's Daily*. November 6, 1967.
7. *Compiled Works of the Ninth National Congress of the CPC*. People's Publishing House, 1969. p. 21.
8. *Writings of Mao Zedong, Volume 2*. Central Literature Publishing House, 2003 edition. p. 1713–1714.
9. Ibid.
10. *Red Flag*. Issue 4. 1975.

Chapter 10

1. Quoted in "Seventy Years of the Communist Party of China," by the Party History Research Office of the Central Committee of the Communist Party of China. The Party History Publishing House of the Communist Party of China, 1991. p. 523.
2. *People's Daily*, April 15, 1977.
3. *People's Daily*, May 1, 1977.
4. Edited by the Documentation Research Office of the Central Committee of the Communist Party of China. *The Chronicle of Deng Xiaoping (1975–1997), Volume 1*. Central Documentation Publishing House, 2004. p. 156.
5. Wang Hongmou and Su Pinduan. *Journey of Reform and Opening Up*. Henan People's Publishing House, 2001. p. 21.
6. *Selected Works of Deng Xiaoping, Volume 2*. People's Publishing House, 1994. p. 39.
7. Ibid.
8. Members of the Central Committee, the Politburo, the Standing Committee of the Politburo, the Vice-Chairman of the Central Committee of the CPC, the Vice-Chairman of the Military Commission of the Central Committee, the Vice-Premier of the State Council, and the Chief of the General Staff of the People's Liberation Army.
9. *Selected Works of Deng Xiaoping, Volume 2*. People's Publishing House, 1994. p. 42, 45.
10. The Research Office of Party History of the Central Committee of the Communist Party of China. *Seventy Years of the Communist Party of China*. Party History Publishing House of the Communist Party of China, 1991. p. 420.
11. *Selected Works of Deng Xiaoping, Volume 2*. People's Publishing House, 1994. p. 119.
12. Edited by the Documentation Research Department of the Central Committee of the Communist Party of China. *Annals of Deng Xiaoping Thought (1975–1997), Volume 1*.

Central Documentation Publishing House, 1998. p. 72–73.
13. *Selected Works of Deng Xiaoping, Volume 2*. People's Publishing House, 1994. p. 126.
14. *Selected Works of Deng Xiaoping, Volume 2*. People's Publishing House, 1994. p. 143.
15. Ibid, p. 141, 143.
16. *Selected Works of Deng Xiaoping, Volume 2*. People's Publishing House, 1994. p. 143.
17. Edited by the Documentation Research Office of the Central Committee of the Communist Party of China. *The Chronicle of Deng Xiaoping (1975–1997), Volume 1*. Central Documentation Publishing House, 2004. p. 200.
18. Ibid, p. 251.
19. *Selected Works of Deng Xiaoping, Volume 2*. People's Publishing House, 1994. p. 129–130.
20. Edited by the Documentation Research Department of the Central Committee of the Communist Party of China. *Annals of Deng Xiaoping Thought (1975–1997), Volume 1*. Central Documentation Publishing House, 1998. p. 79.
21. Ibid, p. 80, 81, and 83.
22. Edited by the Documentation Research Department of the Central Committee of the Communist Party of China. *The Chronicle of Deng Xiaoping (1975–1997), Volume 1*. Central Documentation Publishing House, 2004. p. 187.
23. *Selected Works of Deng Xiaoping, Volume 2*. People's Publishing House, 1994. p. 135.
24. *Selection of Important Documents since the Third Plenary Session of the Central Committee, Volume 1*. People's Publishing House, 1982. p. 12–13.
25. Deng Xiaoping's talk with the Chairman of the Communist Party of Australia (Mali-Lenin) on November 6, 1983.
26. *Selection of Important Documents since the Fifteenth National Congress, Volume 1*. People's Publishing House, 2000. p. 10.
27. *Selected Works of Deng Xiaoping, Volume 2*. People's Publishing House, 1994. p. 144.
28. *Selected Works of Deng Xiaoping, Volume 2*. People's Publishing House, 1994. p. 119.

INDEX

A

A Mao Zedong Anthology **Vol. 1**: 493
"A Single Spark Can Start a Prairie Fire" **Vol. 1**: 179, 181, 331, 411
AB League **Vol. 3**: 102
Abe Awang Jinmei **Vol. 3**: 119
Abolition Party **Vol. 3**: 102
"Absorbing a Large Number of Intellectuals" **Vol. 1**: 210
Accelerating the Training and Education of Young Cadres **Vol. 3**: 457, 459
Accelerating the Progress of Science and Technology **Vol. 3**: 398
Active Military Officers Law **Vol. 3**: 436
advanced socialist culture with Chinese characteristics **Vol. 3**: 386, 387, 388, 389, 391, 394, 466, 474, 476, 487, 514, 525, 546
African Union **Vol. 3**: 216
agrarian revolution (Agrarian Revolutionary War) **Vol. 1**: 43, 65, 80, 95, 105, 110, 130, 136, 137, 143, 144, 151, 163, 165, 167, 168, 172, 174, 175, 176, 179, 182, 183, 188, 254, 277, 279, 284, 288, 296, 298, 311, 326, 329, 331, 334, 336, 341, 344, 350, 361, 371, 379, 382, 385, 389, 393, 405, 420, 434, 459, 467, 481, 486, 525, 531, 533; **Vol. 2**: 49
Agreement on Trade in Goods Vol 3: 518
Agriculture, Sixty Articles of **Vol. 2**: 235, 236, 238, 254, 255
agricultural cooperatives **Vol. 2**: 71, 73, 75, 76, 108, 113, 118, 122, 123, 124, 125, 126, 182, 188, 192, 193, 194, 236

Air Force Engineering University Vol 3: 434
Ali Hassan Mwinyi **Vol. 3**: 264, 265
All-China Federation of Industry and Commerce Vol 3: 242
All-China Federation of Trade Unions **Vol. 1**: 126; **Vol. 2**: 40
All-China Women's Federation Vol 3: 312
Allied Army of the World Socialist Revolutionary Front **Vol. 1**: 110, 112, 118
Allied League **Vol. 1**: 62
American Association in Taiwan Vol 3: 213
An Overview of Social Issues **Vol. 1**: 9
An Ziwen **Vol. 2**: 67; **Vol. 3**: 72
Anguo County **Vol. 2**: 204
Anhui Province **Vol. 1**: 79, 171, 352; **Vol. 2**: 328; **Vol. 3**: 102, 103, 106, 155, 318, 384
Anti-Encirclement **Vol. 1**: 82, 157, 158, 159, 183, 194, 319, 334, 341
anti-Japan base (anti-Japanese base area) **Vol. 1**: 66, 73, 108, 198, 199, 200, 201, 202, 203, 210, 231, 241, 262, 318, 334, 336, 493, 530; **Vol. 2**: 32, 46, 269, 308
Anti-Japanese Guerrilla War **Vol. 1**: 184, 198, 298, 311, 329
Anti-Japanese National United Front **Vol. 1**: 66, 68, 69, 79, 80, 81, 108, 200, 201, 204, 228, 229, 230, 232, 233, 234, 235, 236, 237, 238, 239, 240, 241, 243, 249, 280, 289, 300, 400, 514, 515, 542; **Vol. 3**: 106
Anti-Japanese Salvation **Vol. 1**: 199
anti-landlord class **Vol. 1**: 50

anti-Leftism movement **Vol. 2**: 203, 220
anti-Marxist **Vol. 1**: 164; **Vol. 2**: 177, 290, 294, 327
anti-Party **Vol. 2**: 280, 294, 315; **Vol. 3**: 23, 76, 91, 100, 101, 102, 323
anti-rash advance (anti-rash progress) **Vol. 2**: 188, 189, 190, 207, 246, 255
Anti-Revolt Campaign **Vol. 3**: 102, 103
anti-revolutionary group **Vol. 1**: 49, 52, 283; **Vol. 2**: 320; **Vol. 3**: 100, 103, 105, 170
Anti-Rightist Movement **Vol. 1**: 58; **Vol. 2**: 152, 173, 174, 178, 180, 182, 183, 184, 186, 188, 190, 191, 192, 207, 220, 222, 230, 231, 239, 241, 242, 245, 246, 251, 253, 254, 255, 257, 258, 274; **Vol. 3**: 83, 84, 85, 88, 90, 93
anti-Socialist Vol 2: 294; **Vol. 3**: 91, 323
anti-war movement **Vol. 1**: 260, 274; **Vol. 2**: 263
April 5th Movement (*see* Tiananmen Incident) **Vol. 2**: 309, 316; **Vol. 3**: 9, 10, 11, 12, 15, 53, 54
Arkhipov, Ivan **Vol. 3**: 219
Armed Division of Workers and Peasants **Vol. 1**: 164, 166, 169, 170, 172, 173, 174, 175, 176, 178, 180, 188
armed revolution **Vol. 1**: 143, 283, 284, 361
armed struggle (theory or doctrine) **Vol. 1**: 36, 37, 43, 45, 55, 78, 83, 91, 102, 149, 171, 173, 174, 175, 176, 184, 187, 273, 274, 275, 276, 277, 278, 279, 282, 283, 284, 285, 286, 287, 331, 333, 336, 337, 361, 364, 366, 368, 372, 491; **Vol. 2**: 135, 292; **Vol. 3**: 72, 106
arming the masses **Vol. 1**: 210, 305
ASEAN and Chinese Leaders' Meeting **Vol. 3**: 518
Asia-Africa Summit **Vol. 3**: 517–518
Asian Cooperation Dialogue **Vol. 3**: 518
Association for Cross-Strait Relations **Vol. 3**: 414
Association for Relations Across the Taiwan Straits (ARATS) **Vol. 3**: 414
Audio-Visual Products Management Regulations **Vol. 3**: 394
Audit Office **Vol. 3**: 278
August defeat **Vol. 1**: 170, 173
August 7th Meeting **Vol. 1**: 43, 44, 46, 47, 48, 51, 53, 55, 57, 151, 154, 166, 167, 169, 277, 364, 420, 421
Autumn Harvest Riots **Vol. 1**: 151, 154, 167, 168, 174, 189, 306, 315, 323, 324, 361

B
Basic Law of the Hong Kong Special Administration Region **Vol. 3**: 236, 266
bad elements **Vol. 1**: 423; **Vol. 2**: 167; **Vol. 3**: 113, 126, 145, 146, 147, 309
Bai Chongxi **Vol. 1**: 234
Baiwan Village **Vol. 3**: 199
Bakunin, Mikhail **Vol. 1**: 6, 396
Bakuninists **Vol. 1**: 396, 430
balanced development **Vol. 1**: 62; **Vol. 3**: 285, 301, 302, 303, 305, 306, 307, 309, 310, 362, 486
Bao'an County **Vol. 3**: 277
Bao Huiceng **Vol. 1**: 19
Baoding **Vol. 2**: 204; **Vol. 3**: 313
Basel Conference **Vol. 1**: 396
Basic Program for the Rectification of the Party **Vol. 1**: 512
Basic Views and Policies on Religious Issues in the Socialist Period of China **Vol. 3**: 116, 127
Battle of Guangzhou **Vol. 1**: 36
Battle of Pingjin **Vol. 1**: 354
Bebel, August **Vol. 1**: 430
Becker, Johann Philipp **Vol. 1**: 430
Beidaihe **Vol. 2**: 191
Beidaihe Working Conference (Beidaihe Work Conference) **Vol. 2**: 195, 196, 212, 256, 257
Beijing **Vol. 1**: 3, 14–19, 61, 92, 162, 214, 256, 267, 275, 376, 510; **Vol. 2**: 61, 78, 205, 233, 243, 318, 319, 324, 326, 336; **Vol. 3**: 11, 12, 23, 24, 30, 31, 35, 43, 52, 53, 59, 72, 75–79, 99, 112, 123, 138, 139, 142, 143, 147, 173, 178–180, 199, 200, 210, 218, 219, 221, 227, 234, 236, 237, 263, 280, 305, 317, 318, 322, 323, 325, 372, 408, 414, 416, 417, 450, 455, 458, 462, 470, 472, 482, 513, 524, 536, 542
Beijing Coup **Vol. 1**: 92, 214
Beijing Communist Party Organization **Vol. 1**: 18

Beijing Daily **Vol. 3**: 11
Beijing Military Region **Vol. 3**: 76, 77
Beijing Normal University **Vol. 1**: 18; **Vol. 3**: 317
Beijing-Qinhuangdao Railway **Vol. 3**: 210
Beijing Treaty **Vol. 3**: 234, 416
Beijing University (*see* Peking University)
Beiping Way **Vol. 1**: 356
Beiyang government **Vol. 1**: 267
Beiyang Warlords (*see also* Northern Warlords) **Vol. 1**: 136
Bengbu **Vol. 1**: 354
Bertram, James **Vol. 1**: 231, 316
Big Bang Theory **Vol. 2**: 285
Big Character Poster **Vol. 2**: 182, 300; **Vol. 3**: 78, 79
Blowe, Mitchell **Vol. 2**: 18
Bo Yibo **Vol. 1**: 500; **Vol. 2**: 42, 238; **Vol. 3**: 53, 74, 81, 189, 283
Bo Yibo Group **Vol. 3**: 54
Bohai Sea **Vol. 3**: 210
Bolshevik **Vol. 1**: 59, 358
Bolshevik Party **Vol. 1**: 38, 358, 366, 367, 370, 375, 377, 382, 398, 400, 430, 458, 459; **Vol. 2**: 54, 118, 122, 137, 209, 210, 213, 217
Borodin, Mikhail **Vol. 1**: 40
bourgeois law **Vol. 2**: 268
bourgeoisie (bourgeois) **Vol. 1**: 5, 7, 9, 13, 25–32, 34, 35, 37, 41, 44, 46–47, 51–57, 60, 62, 63, 70–76, 80–81, 87, 92–94, 96–98, 100–118, 120–129, 131, 134, 138–146, 150, 172, 181, 185–186, 195, 199 200, 210, 213 219, 221–226, 230, 233–234, 237–244, 246, 253, 258, 261–263, 269–272, 277–278, 283, 292–293, 295, 298–299, 301, 308–310, 322, 329, 358, 360, 362–365, 370–375, 377–378, 381–384, 421, 427–428, 447, 466–468, 487, 495, 502–503, 507, 509, 513, 514, 516–519, 521–524, 526, 528, 530, 533–535, 540–544, 546; **Vol. 2**: 4, 10, 17, 26–29, 31–34, 36–37, 39, 41–43, 45–47, 49–50, 59–64, 69–70, 79–80, 83, 91–95, 103–105, 109, 116, 125–129, 136, 170, 181, 183–186, 191, 197, 201–202, 212, 241, 251, 257, 259, 265, 268–271, 273, 275, 279–291, 293–297, 307, 315, 328; **Vol. 3**: 22–24, 27, 54, 81, 88, 113, 160, 247, 255, 304, 315–316, 318, 323
bourgeois civil rights revolution **Vol. 1**: 51, 52, 53, 54, 103, 105
bourgeois republic **Vol. 1**: 71, 106, 467, 517
bourgeois revolution **Vol. 1**: 5, 28, 52, 107, 118, 121, 122, 123, 134, 301, 466
Branch Office **Vol. 1**: 503; **Vol. 3**: 143
Brezhnev, Leonid **Vol. 2**: 264, 287, 289; **Vol. 3**: 217
bribery **Vol. 2**: 104; **Vol. 3**: 294, 298, 299, 304, 309, 321
British colonial rule (Hong Kong) **Vol. 3**: 234, 416
Buddhist temples (in Han areas) **Vol. 3**: 127
Bukharin, Nikola Ivanovic **Vol. 1**: 153; **Vol. 2**: 164
Bureau of Religious Affairs (Religious Affairs Bureau) **Vol. 3**: 127
bureaucracy **Vol. 1**: 136, 203, 380, 383, 414, 430, 431, 432, 440, 458, 473; **Vol. 2**: 104, 138, 153, 160–161, 163, 167, 175–182, 297; **Vol. 3**: 47, 57, 146, 271, 281, 284, 372
bureaucratic capitalism **Vol. 1**: 88, 130–131, 133, 138, 245–247, 253, 262–263, 265, 268, 283, 287, 350, 467, 520, 525–534; **Vol. 2**: 26, 37, 87; **Vol. 3**: 148, 252
Bush, George H. W. **Vol. 3**: 215
Bush, George W. **Vol. 3**: 519
Business Group of the United Front Work Conference **Vol. 2**: 92
Business Performance Management Regulations **Vol. 3**: 394

C

Cadre Censorship Bureau **Vol. 3**: 17
Cadre Education **Vol. 3**: 449
cadre retirement system **Vol. 3**: 288
Cadre Route **Vol. 3**: 13
cadre system **Vol. 3**: 185, 286–287, 291, 458, 460
Cai Chang **Vol. 3**: 288
Cai Hesen **Vol. 1**: 16, 17, 29, 30, 49, 52, 53, 92, 102, 167, 219, 399, 400, 507
Cai Tingkai **Vol. 1**: 233, 264
Cai Xitao **Vol. 3**: 30

Cai Yuanpei **Vol. 1**: 14, 233
Cao Diqiu **Vol. 3**: 75
Cao Juren **Vol. 3**: 227
Caolanzi Prison **Vol. 3**: 74
capitalism **Vol. 1**: 3, 5, 6, 7, 8, 10, 12, 13, 20, 26, 30, 31, 39, 53, 54, 76, 88, 94–98, 102–105, 107, 108, 109, 111, 112, 113, 116, 117, 118, 130, 131, 133, 138, 139, 140, 145, 146, 161, 186, 216, 245, 246, 247, 253, 262, 263, 265, 268, 277, 283, 285, 287, 350, 358, 377, 397, 466, 467, 487, 488, 496, 510, 518, 520, 522, 524, 526, 528, 529, 530, 533–538, 543; **Vol. 2**: 4–6, 14, 17–19, 26, 28–35, 37, 39, 41, 43–47, 51–52, 58–59, 61–62, 67, 70, 74, 83, 91, 94–95, 103, 107–108, 111, 113–116, 118, 120, 124–128, 131, 135–137, 151–152, 185, 201, 203, 214, 218–219, 234, 257–259, 267, 272–275, 277–281, 283, 286–288, 290–292, 294, 304–305, 331; **Vol. 3**: 21–22, 27, 46, 56, 93, 146, 148, 233, 235, 241, 246–247, 249, 252, 268, 304, 309, 316, 328, 333, 345–348, 382, 487
capitulationism **Vol. 1**: 232, 240, 280
Carter, Jimmy **Vol. 3**: 145, 213–214
cat theory (Deng Xiaoping) **Vol. 2**: 249, 255
Caudine Forks of capitalism **Vol. 2**: 135
Central Action Committee **Vol. 1**: 61
Central Advisory Committee **Vol. 3**: 67, 180, 186, 188–189, 242, 244–245, 269, 290, 311, 410, 450, 453, 464
Central Bureau **Vol. 1**: 20; Vol 2: 64, 73, 77, 233, 234; **Vol. 3**: 67
Central Bureau of the Shaanxi-Gansu-Ningxia Border Region **Vol. 1**: 199
Central Committee Vol 1: 20, 25, 36, 38, 39, 40, 43–46, 48, 50, 51, 55–59, 63, 66, 67, 71, 75, 79, 83, 86, 87, 88, 92, 94, 103, 104, 105, 150–161, 163–169, 176, 178, 181, 183, 189, 199, 203, 204, 205, 207, 210, 211, 222, 226–238, 240, 244, 245, 248, 249, 250, 251–254, 257, 259, 260, 261, 263, 264, 265, 271, 275, 276, 279, 283, 299, 304, 305, 306, 309, 311, 313, 318, 324, 337, 351, 354, 355, 362, 366, 367, 369, 370, 382, 386, 387, 395, 398, 400, 401, 403, 405, 411, 415, 419, 421, 424, 425, 426, 427, 434, 437, 459, 482, 485, 486, 492–496, 499, 500, 501, 503, 504, 505, 510, 511, 532, 537, 538; **Vol. 2**: 3, 5, 9, 11, 16, 22, 29, 32–33, 35–40, 42, 44–45, 49–52, 56–65, 71–79, 81–87, 89, 91–93, 95, 97–99, 101, 103–105, 107, 109–110, 113–114, 116–119, 122–123, 132, 142, 144–145, 148–152, 154–158, 161, 168, 174–181, 183–185, 188–189, 192–193, 195, 199–200, 202–203, 205–207, 209–210, 214–215, 222, 226, 231–238, 240–241, 243–245, 247–252, 254, 256–258, 260, 272, 277, 290, 299–302, 313, 315, 318, 323, 329–332, 334–338; **Vol. 3**: 3, 6, 9–13, 16–17, 34, 37–38, 40, 46, 48, 51–55, 57, 59–83, 85, 87–99, 101–117, 119–129, 131, 135–139, 141–142, 144–145, 147–163, 165–168, 170–171, 173–180, 182–183, 186, 188–189, 192–193, 196, 198–203, 205, 207, 217, 219, 221, 225–227, 232, 234–235, 240–242, 244–249, 252–255, 257–260, 263, 265–266, 268–270, 273–274, 279–281, 283, 286–295, 297–299, 302, 305–327, 334–335, 337–338, 343, 345–348, 350, 352–355, 357–358, 363–364, 368–370, 373–374, 376–377, 379–384, 386, 390–391, 393–394, 397–405, 407–413, 416, 419, 421, 427, 429, 432, 440, 443, 446–450, 452–470, 479, 481–483, 488, 491, 493–497, 499–502, 506–517, 519–521, 523–526, 531–532, 536, 538, 542, 544–545, 550–551
Central Committee for Ethnic Affairs Vol 2: 250
Central Disciplinary Inspection Commission (Central Commission for Discipline Inspection) **Vol. 3**: 60, 62, 77, 80, 93, 180, 186, 188–189, 242, 244–245, 294, 296, 311, 320–321, 410, 450, 453, 462–465, 467, 483, 524
Central Economic Work Conference **Vol. 3**: 512
Central Leading Group **Vol. 2**: 199; **Vol. 3**: 352, 387, 398, 446
Central Military Commission **Vol. 1**: 59, 61, 238, 239, 313, 314, 346, 351, 355; Vol 2: 326, 331; **Vol. 3**: 10, 42, 73, 75, 189, 203, 282, 307, 429–432, 434, 437–439, 516–517
Central Organizational Department **Vol. 2**: 67; **Vol. 3**: 14–17, 54, 66–68, 70–72, 77, 79, 81, 84–86, 89–90, 93–99, 101, 103–104, 106–108, 111, 114–117, 245, 278–279, 296, 311, 373, 410, 450–454, 460, 464, 471
Central Party School **Vol. 1**: 391; **Vol. 2**: 30,

322; **Vol. 3**: 14, 35–36, 90, 154, 269, 348, 358, 449–450, 472, 502
Central People's Government **Vol. 1**: 268; **Vol. 2**: 77–78, 80; **Vol. 3**: 103, 273
Central Plains **Vol. 1**: 59, 351, 352, 505; **Vol. 3**: 107–108
Central Political Report **Vol. 1**: 39
Central Political System Reform Seminar Group **Vol. 3**: 269–270
Central Project Group **Vol. 3**: 71
Central Provisional Politburo Vol 1: 48, 167
Central Secretariat **Vol. 1**: 238, 482; **Vol. 2**: 154, 251; **Vol. 3**: 99, 115, 117, 218, 235, 269, 273, 311–312
Central Soviet Area **Vol. 1**: 157, 341; **Vol. 3**: 15, 102
Central Soviet Government **Vol. 1**: 61
Central Special Task Force **Vol. 3**: 54, 70, 100
Central Steering Committee for Party Consolidation **Vol. 3**: 281–283
Central Task Force **Vol. 3**: 72, 81
Central United Front Department (Ministry) **Vol. 2**: 80; **Vol. 3**: 89–90, 111, 113, 126
Central Working Conference **Vol. 2**: 103, 237–238, 240, 243, 257, 259, 336; **Vol. 3**: 11–12, 48, 52, 54, 59–61, 73, 93, 100, 123, 135, 138, 259, 286, 305
centralism **Vol. 1**: 190, 359, 365, 368, 369, 379, 387, 394, 395, 397–403, 408–419, 427, 450, 452, 474, 475, 488, 499, 509, 515, 518, 523; **Vol. 2**: 26, 48, 49, 159, 160, 169, 190, 221–222, 243–244, 246; **Vol. 3**: 57–58, 62, 136, 150, 161, 163, 172, 176–177, 184–185, 190, 281, 370
Chairman of the General Committee **Vol. 1**: 395
Chaling County **Vol. 1**: 189
Changchun **Vol. 1**: 353; **Vol. 3**: 115
Changsha **Vol. 1**: 16, 19, 25, 58, 61, 151, 152, 168, 174, 376; **Vol. 2**: 233
Changxindian Railway Vol 1: 14
Chen Boda Vol 1: 483; **Vol. 2**: 194, 204, 278; **Vol. 3**: 73–75, 77, 79
Chen Chi **Vol. 3**: 30, 74
Chen Duxiu **Vol. 1**: 4, 7, 8, 12, 14, 15, 17–20, 29, 33–34, 38–41, 44, 46–47, 92–93, 101–102, 121–122, 125, 218–219, 227–228, 230, 277, 371, 378, 399, 411, 420, 545
Chen Geng **Vol. 1**: 352
Chen Gongbo **Vol. 1**: 19
Chen Gongpei Vol 1: 19
Chen Jingrun **Vol. 3**: 30
Chen Jiongming **Vol. 1**: 24, 274
Chen Jitang **Vol. 1**: 234
Chen Lifu **Vol. 1**: 246, 531
Chen Mingshu **Vol. 1**: 233
Chen Muhua **Vol. 3**: 189
Chen Pixian **Vol. 3**: 189
Chen Qiyou **Vol. 1**: 264
Chen Shaomin **Vol. 3**: 107–108
Chen Shui-bian **Vol. 3**: 419
Chen Tanqiu **Vol. 1**: 19
Chen Wangdao **Vol. 1**: 18
Chen Yeping **Vol. 3**: 71
Chen Yi **Vol. 1**: 172, 327, 351, 352, 484; **Vol. 2**: 156, 251, 300; **Vol. 3**: 73
Chen Yun Vol 1: 195, 424, 426, 427, 464, 476, 477; **Vol. 2**: 62, 150, 188, 246–249, 304, 324; **Vol. 3**: 11, 14–15, 33–34, 49, 53, 56, 62, 167, 179, 186–189, 193, 200, 245–246, 285, 289, 344
Chen Zaidao **Vol. 3**: 62, 72
Chendai Town **Vol. 3**: 320
Chiang Ching-kuo **Vol. 1**: 271; **Vol. 3**: 413
Chiang Kai-shek **Vol. 1**: 38, 42, 66, 69–70, 85–88, 93–94, 131, 163, 217–218, 221–222, 226, 234, 236, 245–248, 250, 253, 256, 258, 263, 269, 271, 276, 281, 284, 290, 292, 328, 346, 350, 353, 494, 531, 533; **Vol. 3**: 145, 225–228, 252
China Agenda for the 21st Century **Vol. 3**: 250, 424
China Buddhist College **Vol. 3**: 127
China Catholic Theological and Philosophical College **Vol. 3**: 127
China Christian Nanjing Jinling Union Theological College **Vol. 3**: 127
China Democratic League **Vol. 1**: 264
China Human Rights Alliance (China Human Rights League) **Vol. 3**: 142
China Human Rights League (*see* China Human Rights Alliance) **Vol. 3**: 143
China Islamic Economics College **Vol. 3**: 127

China News **Vol. 1**: 10
China Petrochemical Group Corporation **Vol. 3**: 405
China Petroleum and Natural Gas Corporation **Vol. 3**: 405
China Taoist College **Vol. 3**: 127
China Tibetan Language Department Senior Buddhist College **Vol. 3**: 127
China-Africa Cooperation Forum **Vol. 3**: 518
China-ASEAN Comprehensive Economic Cooperation Framework Agreement **Vol. 3**: 518
China-ASEAN Strategic Partnership for Peace and Prosperity Action Plan **Vol. 3**: 518
China-ASEAN Summit **Vol. 3**: 425
China-Russia border **Vol. 3**: 519
China-Russia Joint Declaration on International Order in the 21st Century **Vol. 3**: 517
China-Russia Summit **Vol. 3**: 517
China-Russia Tokk Exchange **Vol. 3**: 519
Chinese Academy of Sciences **Vol. 2**: 156, 215; **Vol. 3**: 23
Chinese Academy of Social Sciences **Vol. 3**: 26, 41, 43, 193, 195, 311, 438
Chinese Association of Science and Technology **Vol. 3**: 43
Chinese Buddhist Association **Vol. 3**: 127
Chinese Catholic Patriotic Congress **Vol. 3**: 127
Chinese Christian Three-Self Patriotic Movement Committee **Vol. 3**: 127
Chinese Culture **Vol. 1**: 21, 76, 209, 540, 544–547, 550; **Vol. 2**: 254; **Vol. 3**: 415, 471, 511
Chinese Customs Commission **Vol. 3**: 200, 288, 290
Chinese Federation of Trade Unions **Vol. 1**: 15
Chinese Foreign Ministry **Vol. 3**: 215, 218
Chinese Industry Association **Vol. 1**: 15
Chinese KMT Democratic Promotion Meeting **Vol. 1**: 264
Chinese Land Law **Vol. 1**: 250–251, 255, 532
Chinese Marxism **Vol. 1**: 485–486, 488–491; **Vol. 2**: 261, 267, 273, 299, 304–305, 309–310, 338; **Vol. 3**: 7, 359, 546

Chinese Marxist Workers' Movement **Vol. 1**: 15
Chinese Muslim pilgrimage group **Vol. 3**: 128
Chinese National Liberation Action Committee **Vol. 1**: 233
Chinese National Salvation Congress **Vol. 1**: 264
Chinese Peasants **Vol. 1**: 33, 102, 287, 525
Chinese People's Political Consultative Conference **Vol. 1**: 87, 244, 511, 523; **Vol. 2**: 4, 25, 48, 50
Chinese Red Army **Vol. 1**: 153; **Vol. 3**: 15
Chinese Revolution **Vol. 1**: 23, 25, 27, 29–32, 36–37, 43–45, 47, 49–56, 58–60, 62–63, 65–66, 69, 72–79, 81–84, 86, 91, 93–97, 99–107, 109–110, 112–118, 128–131, 133–134, 136–137, 139–147, 150–153, 157, 159, 161, 163–164, 166, 172–173, 176, 178–182, 184–186, 188, 213, 222, 230, 237, 244, 246, 257, 263, 273, 275–276, 278–287, 292, 299, 308–310, 329–331, 339, 341, 360, 363, 367–368, 371, 379, 385, 388, 390–393, 407, 420, 422, 431, 439–441, 443–445, 448, 452, 466, 468–471, 474, 486–487, 489–494, 504, 507–509, 517, 521–523, 528, 531, 533, 540, 542, 544, 546; **Vol. 2**: 24, 27–29, 32, 35, 38–40, 52, 90, 98, 114, 143–144, 210, 326; **Vol. 3**: 40, 132, 150, 162, 164, 169, 248, 317
Chinese Soviet **Vol. 1**: 160, 191, 194; **Vol. 3**: 105
Chinese Taoist Association **Vol. 3**: 127
Chinese Workers' and Peasants' Red Army **Vol. 1**: 178, 470
Chinese Workers' Movement **Vol. 1**: 16–17, 360, 370, 376, 470; **Vol. 2**: 330
Chinese Youth **Vol. 3**: 11
Chinese Zhi Gong Party **Vol. 1**: 264
Chongqing **Vol. 1**: 152, 167, 281
City-centered Theory **Vol. 1**: 149–151, 153–154, 157, 159–161, 163–164, 166
Civil Morality Construction **Vol. 3**: 391
Civil Servants Law **Vol. 3**: 460, 541
class analysis **Vol. 1**: 33, 80, 103, 121–123, 125
class struggle **Vol. 1**: 8, 10–11, 20, 24, 27–28, 32, 100, 129, 198, 218–219, 236–237, 277, 288–290, 293, 308, 385, 425; **Vol. 2**: 8, 10, 13–14, 47, 65, 103, 136, 138, 167–168, 170, 173–174, 178, 180, 182–187, 189, 207, 219, 221, 224, 226, 245,

256–259, 265, 270–278, 281, 285–286, 292–298, 312, 316, 325, 335; **Vol. 3**: 4, 51, 55, 60, 66, 93, 130, 135, 140–141, 161, 170, 173, 191, 254, 283, 332, 525, 531

class war **Vol. 1**: 59, 159

Classical Marxist Writers **Vol. 2**: 19, 69, 113, 121, 134, 165, 200, 254, 273, 317; **Vol. 3**: 34

Clausewitz, Carl **Vol. 1**: 289

clearing up historical problems **Vol. 3**: 66

clique **Vol. 1**: 235, 242, 248, 271–272, 281; **Vol. 2**: 289–290; **Vol. 3**: 73, 124

Cold War **Vol. 2**: 101, 120, 131, 225; **Vol. 3**: 426–427, 429, 437

collectivization **Vol. 1**: 498, 512, 531, 537–538; **Vol. 2**: 31, 71, 73, 75–76, 85, 99, 115, 120–125, 138, 193, 195, 209

college entrance examination **Vol. 3**: 9, 17–20

Combating Serious Criminal Activities in the Economic Field **Vol. 3**: 306, 319–320

Comintern (*see also* Communist International) **Vol. 1**: 18–20, 25, 38, 40, 42–44, 47, 49, 51–56, 58, 62–63, 65–66, 68, 92, 94, 103–104, 106, 150, 152–154, 157, 164, 169, 178, 214–215, 217–219, 221–228, 232, 362–363, 371, 482, 486, 507–508

Commerce, Forty Articles of **Vol. 2**: 237

Commission for Economic Reform (*see also* State Economic Reform Office) **Vol. 3**: 194

commodity economy **Vol. 1**: 96, 162, 537–538; **Vol. 2**: 6, 8–10, 15, 20, 35–36, 44, 120–121, 137–138, 218, 224, 226, 267–268, 271, 291, 294, 307; **Vol. 3**: 21–22, 192–196, 198–201, 241, 243–244, 249–251, 283, 294, 302, 323, 335–337, 345, 365, 447

Common Program **Vol. 1**: 87, 268, 511, 523, 538–539; **Vol. 2**: 4–5, 25–26, 48, 50–58, 60, 62, 72, 78, 80–82, 89, 99, 103–104, 114, 116, 141

Communications Secretary **Vol. 1**: 395

Communist Alliance **Vol. 1**: 357, 394–396

Communist International (*see also* Comintern) **Vol. 1**: 17, 25, 121

Communist International East Asia Secretariat **Vol. 1**: 17

Communist League **Vol. 1**: 397

Communist Manifesto **Vol. 1**: 79, 97, 374, 458

Communist morality **Vol. 2**: 160

Communist Organization **Vol. 1**: 18

Communist Party of Beijing **Vol. 1**: 18, 406

Communist Party of China (*see also* CPC) **Vol. 1**: 13–14, 18–20, 23–30, 33, 35, 49, 57, 64–65, 73, 75, 78, 89, 93, 97, 103, 107, 114, 123, 129–130, 132, 139, 141–142, 146, 149, 153–154, 215, 224, 229–230, 232, 235, 237, 256, 284, 309, 339, 359, 363, 367, 369, 376, 382, 400–401, 410–411, 419, 466, 468–469, 491, 499, 512, 528; **Vol. 2**: 3, 5, 7, 13, 16, 21, 25, 27, 32, 41, 45, 52–53, 56, 61, 66, 73–74, 84, 86, 89, 97–99, 109, 118, 123, 140, 142, 148, 158, 166, 168, 170, 183, 186, 194–195, 210, 217, 229, 231, 233, 237, 249, 266, 274, 292, 311, 316, 319, 330, 336; **Vol. 3**: 3, 6, 12, 33, 37, 44, 45, 53, 59–61, 63, 65–66, 73, 75, 77–79, 89, 91, 94–95, 99, 102–106, 109–110, 112, 115–117, 119–125, 127–133, 138, 146, 148, 151, 154, 158–159, 161–163, 169, 172–174, 176, 179–182, 186, 194–196, 198, 200, 203, 207, 216, 221, 225–228, 230–231, 239–240, 242, 247–249, 251–255, 258, 260, 262, 265–266, 273, 279–281, 287–289, 291–295, 297–299, 303, 306, 311–316, 318, 320–322, 324–327, 334–338, 340, 343, 345–346, 350, 353, 355, 357, 359–361, 363–364, 366–368, 370–373, 375, 377, 379, 382–384, 388–389, 391, 393–394, 398, 400–401, 411, 413, 415–416, 419, 422, 427–429, 434, 440, 444, 446–447, 450, 457, 459, 461, 466–467, 470, 474–476, 480, 482–483, 490, 521, 523–527, 531–533, 536, 542, 544, 546, 550

Communist Party Political Consultative Conference (*see also* CPPCC) **Vol. 1**: 266, 406

Communist Surge **Vol. 2**: 236

Communist Youth League **Vol. 1**: 40, 61, 314

Comrades Union of the Three People's Principles (Nationalism, Democracy, the People's Livelihood) **Vol. 1**: 264

"Conflict Theory" **Vol. 1**: 389–391

Conference on Educational Work **Vol. 3**: 82, 102

Confucianism **Vol. 1**: 4, 16

Congress of Chinese Literature and Arts Workers **Vol. 3**: 198

Constitution of the People's Republic of China **Vol. 2**: 117; **Vol. 3**: 122, 231, 287, 377, 475

Construction of Socialist Spiritual Civilization **Vol. 2**: 116; **Vol. 3**: 249, 308, 313–314, 368, 383–384

construction of the People's Army **Vol. 1**: 82, 299; **Vol. 2**: 116; **Vol. 3**: 308

contracted production **Vol. 2**: 202, 248, 328

contradiction **Vol. 1**: 118, 367, 412, 437, 516; **Vol. 2**: 14–15, 33, 36, 39–40, 45, 84, 91–92, 94, 102–103, 105–106, 111, 124, 128–129, 139, 146–147, 157, 164–170, 174, 178, 185–186, 218–219, 226, 236, 245, 256, 258–259, 319; **Vol. 3**: 27, 85, 130, 171, 191, 199, 251, 259, 292, 328–329, 344, 346, 362, 430, 433, 491, 494

Contradictions **Vol. 1**: 66, 68, 118, 228; **Vol. 2**: 165

corruption **Vol. 1**: 197, 358; **Vol. 2**: 104, 309; **Vol. 3**: 293–295, 297, 299, 307–309, 319, 323, 325, 331, 447–448, 454, 460–462, 464–467, 474, 531, 536, 546, 549

counter-revolutionaries **Vol. 1**: 124, 143, 193, 284, 514; **Vol. 2**: 57, 167, 252; **Vol. 3**: 104–105, 113, 115

counter-revolutionary **Vol. 1**: 31, 43, 74, 85–87, 112, 122, 127, 160, 181, 192, 214, 250, 268, 272, 275–276, 279, 284, 291, 298, 320, 340, 355, 378, 474, 494, 514; **Vol. 2**: 111, 136, 284–285, 294, 298, 314, 316; **Vol. 3**: 72, 77, 86, 161, 163, 285

countryside Vol 1: 56, 83, 115, 128, 136, 140, 144, 150–151, 154–155, 157, 160–162, 164, 166, 169, 171, 174–175, 178–180, 182, 184–185, 187, 189, 330–331, 334–335, 360–361, 373, 377–378, 420, 495–497, 499, 502, 508, 527, 533; **Vol. 2**: 30, 32, 38, 41, 65–66, 69, 72, 87, 102, 111, 124, 175, 189, 193–194, 196, 206, 248, 259, 301; **Vol. 3**: 4–6, 148, 250, 282–283, 378, 450, 509, 528, 542–545

County People's Congress **Vol. 1**: 515

CPC **Vol. 1**: 20–21, 24–28, 32–45, 47, 49–58, 61, 63, 66–72, 75, 77–79, 82–87, 89, 91–95, 99–101, 103–106, 108–110, 115–116, 118–121, 123, 125–126, 129–134, 139, 141–143, 145–146, 149–158, 160–161, 163–167, 169, 172, 174, 177–178, 183–184, 186–189, 191–192, 198–203, 208–211, 213–245, 247–273, 275, 277–279, 281–282, 284–285, 287–288, 291–294, 299, 301, 304–311, 313–314, 316, 318, 324, 327, 331–333, 337, 351, 354–355, 360–373, 376–379, 381–382, 384, 386–389, 391–393, 399, 401, 403, 405–408, 410, 414–415, 419–425, 428–429, 431–442, 444–456, 458–463, 465–479, 481–482, 484–486, 489, 491–493, 495–497, 499–501, 503–505, 507–510, 512, 515–517, 519–524, 526, 528, 531–532, 534–539, 541–543, 545; **Vol. 2**: 11, 16, 20–22, 26, 28, 30, 32, 40, 48–49, 52–54, 57, 62, 64, 78–81, 90, 99, 105, 109, 117, 130, 133, 135, 140–143, 145, 152–153, 155, 157–162, 170, 173, 176, 202, 210, 220, 222, 249, 264, 267, 274–277, 279, 291–292, 295, 299, 302, 320, 329, 338; **Vol. 3**: 3–7, 10–13, 15, 46, 52, 59, 63, 70, 74, 76–78, 80–84, 86, 91–93, 98, 100, 103, 105–106, 109, 113–114, 126, 128, 132–133, 136, 139, 141, 146–147, 150, 157, 161–163, 168, 174, 177–178, 180, 189, 191, 199, 225–226, 232, 234, 239–240, 242, 247–248, 253, 255, 257, 275, 280, 290, 298–299, 301, 305, 307, 324, 329, 334, 341, 348, 350, 352, 360, 363, 365, 370, 372–373, 375, 381, 390, 394, 397, 415, 417, 419–421, 432, 438, 443–444, 446–447, 449–450, 454, 457, 459, 461, 465–466, 474, 479–484, 486, 488, 494, 509–510, 513, 515, 517–518, 520–521, 526, 528, 550

CPPCC (*see also* Communist Party Political Consultative Conference) **Vol. 1**: 266–268, 272, 511; **Vol. 2**: 48, 55–56, 62, 64, 111, 117, 154, 249, 319; **Vol. 3**: 129, 133, 136, 269, 374, 450, 454

criterion of truth **Vol. 2**: 11, 23, 321, 324, 327–329, 332, 334, 336, 338–339; **Vol. 3**: 32, 35, 37, 40–41, 43–45, 58, 135, 140, 152–154, 157–158, 162

criticism **Vol. 1**: 5, 13, 41, 61, 79, 102, 154, 160, 265, 322, 364, 374, 380, 385–387, 391, 398, 408, 425, 427–428, 430, 432, 437, 439, 446–456, 463, 471, 479–480, 502, 504, 534, 546; **Vol. 2**: 10–11, 23, 62, 73, 76, 139, 141, 143, 156–157, 162–163, 167, 176–177, 179, 182, 184, 202, 207, 219, 225, 242, 244, 246, 255–256, 259, 268–269, 272, 275, 283–287, 291, 295, 299, 301–304, 307, 314–316, 326, 334, 338; **Vol. 3**: 27, 33, 101, 144, 194–196, 280–281, 284, 455–456

Critique of the Gotha Program **Vol. 2**: 90

Crook, Isabel **Vol. 3**: 117
cross-century development **Vol. 3**: 5, 384, 397, 403, 412
cultural construction **Vol. 1**: 82–83, 135, 189, 197, 208–211, 373, 548; **Vol. 2**: 158, 295; **Vol. 3**: 120, 123, 191, 364, 366, 387–388, 393, 395, 503–504, 511, 528, 534
Cultural Revolution **Vol. 1**: 76, 528, 541–544, 548, 550; **Vol. 2**: 10–11, 14, 23, 155, 174, 187, 191, 221, 230, 236, 252, 260–262, 267, 269–270, 272, 274–280, 282–285, 287, 291–293, 295–303, 305–317, 319–322, 325, 329–330, 335, 337–338; **Vol. 3**: 9–10, 12, 14–16, 18–20, 29–33, 35, 37, 42, 44–45, 53–54, 56, 61–63, 69–70, 73–74, 76–88, 92–93, 96, 98, 100–101, 105, 108–110, 114, 117–118, 122–123, 126, 128, 132, 136, 140–142, 159–160, 162–163, 166–168, 170–171, 187, 203, 228, 253, 283–285, 525, 530
Cultural System **Vol. 2**: 156; **Vol. 3**: 251, 389, 393, 511

D

Dabie Mountains **Vol. 1**: 352
Dachen Island **Vol. 3**: 226
Dadan Island **Vol. 3**: 228
Dalai Lama **Vol. 3**: 123–124
Dalian **Vol. 1**: 493; **Vol. 3**: 112, 410
Daqing **Vol. 2**: 269; **Vol. 3**: 21–22
Daqing Oilfield **Vol. 2**: 269
Das Kapital **Vol. 1**: 10; **Vol. 3**: 353
Dazhai **Vol. 3**: 21–22
decentralization **Vol. 2**: 102, 125, 149–150; **Vol. 3**: 271, 352, 356, 445
Decision on the China Issue **Vol. 1**: 152
Declaration of the Second National Congress of the CPC **Vol. 1**: 120, 215
democracy **Vol. 1**: 4–5, 8, 29, 65, 67, 69, 71, 73, 75–79, 81, 83, 85, 87, 89, 99, 101, 106–112, 114, 117, 131, 146, 190, 192, 199–200, 209, 216, 224, 232, 237, 241–242, 244–245, 258, 264, 266, 268, 272, 281, 298, 312, 317, 321–322, 365, 395–396, 398, 401–403, 409–413, 425, 449–450, 467–468, 482, 487, 491, 500–502, 509, 513, 515–516, 518–520, 522–523, 525, 528, 531, 534–537, 539, 542–544, 546, 548; **Vol. 2**: 4, 8, 10, 13, 25–34, 37, 40–42, 45, 47–49, 51–53, 56–59, 62–63, 65, 69–70, 72, 76–79, 81–83, 86–91, 95, 98–99, 104–105, 111–112, 114, 116–117, 119, 121, 130, 136, 141, 152–154, 159, 163, 169, 176, 179, 183, 185–186, 207–209, 221–222, 226, 232, 241, 245–246, 250, 274, 291, 298, 312, 320, 325, 339; **Vol. 3**: 31, 48, 56–58, 62, 129, 136–138, 140–147, 150, 152, 155, 161, 177, 182, 184, 191, 241, 252, 257–258, 269, 272, 305, 314, 316, 318, 364, 367, 369–372, 376–381, 385, 449, 452–453, 458, 460, 484–485, 509–510, 528, 532, 534, 545
Democratic Alliance **Vol. 1**: 224, 527, 535; **Vol. 2**: 30, 49
democratic centralism **Vol. 1**: 190, 359, 365, 368–369, 379, 387, 394–395, 398–403, 408–419, 427, 450, 452, 474–475, 488, 499, 509, 515, 518, 523, 527, 535; **Vol. 2**: 26, 48–49, 159–160, 190, 221–222, 243–244, 246; **Vol. 3**: 57–58, 62, 150, 161, 163, 172, 176–177, 184–185, 190, 281, 370
Democratic Management in Rural Areas **Vol. 1**: 527, 535; **Vol. 3**: 377
democratic parties (other) **Vol. 1**: 87, 120, 224, 256, 262–269, 271–272, 516, 527, 535; **Vol. 2**: 49, 53, 61, 79–81, 127, 129, 152–153, 170, 179, 249–250, 319–320; **Vol. 3**: 128–133, 168, 180, 242, 245, 372–375, 454
Democratic Republic **Vol. 1**: 27, 72, 76, 100, 109–110, 117, 236, 491, 509, 513, 515, 517, 521, 527, 529, 535–536; **Vol. 2**: 28–29, 49
democratic system within the Party **Vol. 1**: 527, 535; **Vol. 3**: 452
Democratic United Front **Vol. 1**: 29, 87–88, 213, 244–245, 254, 256, 259, 261–262, 264, 268–269, 271, 527, 535; **Vol. 2**: 53, 79–80, 87, 153, 170, 320
Deng Enming **Vol. 1**: 19
Deng Liqun **Vol. 3**: 25, 125, 189, 193, 195, 199–200
Deng Xiaoping **Vol. 1**: 158, 200, 351, 352, 410, 485, 500; **Vol. 2**: 9, 11, 18, 21, 23, 142, 153, 160–163, 166, 197, 233, 237–238, 240, 245, 248–249, 251, 254–255, 299, 302–305, 307, 309–310, 312, 316–321, 324–328, 330–332, 334–339; **Vol. 3**: 4–5, 7, 9–11, 14–15, 18, 20, 24–26, 28, 34, 39–40, 45–47, 49–51, 57–60,

62–63, 74, 88, 90, 94, 110, 123, 125, 129, 132–133, 136–138, 140, 144–152, 157, 159, 162–163, 165–168, 178–181, 186, 188–189, 193, 195, 199–200, 202, 205–208, 210–211, 213, 215, 217–219, 221, 225, 229, 231–233, 235–237, 240–242, 245–246, 255, 258–266, 268–269, 286–291, 301, 304–311, 315–319, 323–338, 340, 344–349, 351, 354, 357–364, 366, 368–372, 380, 382, 385, 390, 392–393, 398–401, 406, 415, 427, 430, 440, 446–449, 468, 472–476, 479, 481, 483–484, 492, 500, 502, 504, 514, 524–526, 533, 550–551

Deng Xiaoping Chronology **Vol. 3**: 137

Deng Xiaoping Theory **Vol. 3**: 5, 7, 63, 301, 326, 357–360, 368, 448, 468, 472–476, 483–484, 500, 504, 514, 524–526, 533, 550–551

Deng Xiaoping's Selected Works **Vol. 3**: 372, 448–449

Deng Yingchao **Vol. 3**: 62, 179, 188–189, 288

Deng Zhongxia **Vol. 1**: 14–15, 17, 29, 35, 102, 123–127, 139, 274

Deng Zihui **Vol. 1**: 497; **Vol. 2**: 166, 248

Deng's Six Articles **Vol. 3**: 232

Department of Theory of the Ministry of Publicity and Propaganda **Vol. 2**: 104

Developing Civilized and Courteous Activities **Vol. 3**: 367

Diaoyu Islands **Vol. 3**: 212

dialectical materialism **Vol. 1**: 64, 83, 294–295, 302, 326, 367, 388, 438; **Vol. 2**: 164, 232; **Vol. 3**: 41, 154, 156, 158, 168, 505

dictatorship of the proletariat **Vol. 1**: 13, 27–28, 34, 53–54, 60, 78, 89, 100, 103, 108, 190–191, 194, 227, 458, 507, 513, 519–520; **Vol. 2**: 49–50, 92, 135, 219, 262, 277–282, 290, 294, 296, 299–300, 306, 315, 318–319; **Vol. 3**: 21, 23, 49, 51, 140–142, 145, 147, 149–150, 283, 329

Ding Guangen **Vol. 3**: 245

Ding Guangxun **Vol. 3**: 127

Dingxi County **Vol. 3**: 277

diplomatic guidelines **Vol. 3**: 203

Discipline Commission (provincial or municipal) **Vol. 3**: 164, 200, 288, 294, 298–299, 318, 321–322, 460, 464–465, 467

Dispute Settlement Mechanism Agreement **Vol. 3**: 518

distribution **Vol. 1**: 13, 174, 199, 251, 420, 525, 532; **Vol. 2**: 4, 8, 107, 126, 128, 135, 141, 201, 205, 219, 236, 238, 268, 270, 280, 287, 294, 297, 301, 328, 334; **Vol. 3**: 14, 21–28, 37, 150, 194–195, 201, 249, 292, 329, 337, 349, 351, 355, 365–367, 394, 401, 473–474, 480, 489, 492, 496, 507, 510, 529, 531, 533, 541, 543, 548

District People's Congress **Vol. 1**: 515

doctrinairism **Vol. 1**: 366, 389

dogmatism (dogmatist) **Vol. 1**: 61, 65, 68, 157, 183, 188, 366–367, 391, 437, 441, 463, 485, 491, 546; **Vol. 2**: 8, 11, 13, 15, 17–18, 20, 23, 50, 120, 134, 139–143, 145, 156, 176–177, 184, 197, 204, 209–213, 220, 225, 273–274, 309–310, 312–313, 315–317, 319, 321, 323, 325, 328, 332, 338–339; **Vol. 3**: 332

Dong Biwu **Vol. 1**: 19, 38, 257; **Vol. 2**: 153

Dong Fureng **Vol. 3**: 199

Dong Yingbin **Vol. 1**: 234

Dong Zhentang **Vol. 3**: 104

Dong Zhiyong **Vol. 3**: 299

Double Hundred policy **Vol. 3**: 390

Draft Law of the People's Republic of China **Vol. 3**: 275

Duanjin **Vol. 1**: 191

E

East China Bureau **Vol. 2**: 249

Eastern Europe **Vol. 1**: 522; **Vol. 2**: 15, 40, 46, 50, 133; **Vol. 3**: 247, 323, 326

Economic and Technical Cooperation Agreement for the Construction and Reconstruction of Industrial Projects in China **Vol. 3**: 219

Economic Center of the State Council **Vol. 3**: 194

economic construction **Vol. 1**: 105, 193–197, 204–205, 292–294, 404, 505, 519, 526–528, 538–539; **Vol. 2**: 5–8, 26, 35, 38, 44, 46, 51, 78, 82, 84, 91, 94, 98–99, 101, 118, 120, 122, 131–132, 136, 138, 147–148, 174, 181, 186–188, 190, 192, 197, 202, 205, 211, 245, 268, 270, 306, 335; **Vol. 3**: 4, 21,

45, 47, 61, 148, 150, 161, 170–172, 174, 181–182, 191, 202–203, 207, 225, 243, 251–252, 254–256, 261, 266, 280, 293, 301, 309–310, 314, 318, 328, 334, 336, 339, 364, 386, 399, 408, 412, 433, 435, 484, 501, 503, 525, 531, 535, 545, 547

Economic Research **Vol. 3**: 24, 26, 192

economic system reform **Vol. 3**: 193, 198, 201–202, 241, 268, 313, 334–335, 344–346, 348–352, 354, 367, 378, 428, 488–489

Economic, Trade, and Science and Technology Commission **Vol. 3**: 219

Editorial Department of Philosophical Research **Vol. 3**: 43

egoism **Vol. 2**: 282–284

Eight-Character Principle **Vol. 3**: 132

Eight Conditions for the Standard of Communist Party Members **Vol. 2**: 86

Eight Major Routes **Vol. 2**: 74, 181, 185

Eight-Grade Wage System **Vol. 2**: 294

Eight-Nation Alliance **Vol. 1**: 3

Eighth Five-Year Plan **Vol. 3**: 212, 337, 364, 481

Eighth National Congress of the Communist Party of China **Vol. 2**: 7, 13, 183, 194; **Vol. 3**: 253

Eighth Political Report **Vol. 2**: 183

Eighth Route Army **Vol. 1**: 69, 202, 231, 241, 285–286, 305, 308–309, 311, 336–337, 342, 344

Eleventh Five-Year Plan **Vol. 3**: 177, 503, 508, 530, 550

Eleventh National Congress of the Communist Party of China **Vol. 3**: 3, 177, 530

emancipating the mind **Vol. 1**: 470; **Vol. 2**: 8, 21, 140, 209, 211, 226, 325, 328–329, 332, 334, 339; **Vol. 3**: 35, 57, 60, 68–69, 90, 153–155, 158, 173, 243, 333, 336, 343, 359, 472, 525, 549

Engels, Friedrich **Vol. 1**: 7, 97, 163, 188, 224, 357, 364, 374–375, 381, 384, 393–397, 429–432, 434, 443, 445, 447, 451, 458, 492–493; **Vol. 2**: 12, 53, 113, 125, 135–137, 164, 209, 211–212, 215, 280, 299; **Vol. 3**: 41, 481

Enlightenment Society **Vol. 3**: 143

Enlightenment (Western Enlightenment) **Vol. 1**: 5, 545, 547; **Vol. 3**: 143

equalitarianism **Vol. 2**: 77, 201, 235, 238; **Vol. 3**: 365

Erdan Island **Vol. 3**: 228

ethnic groups (ethnic minorities) **Vol. 1**: 201–202, 228, 258, 266, 268, 289, 298, 449, 466, 516, 545; **Vol. 2**: 22, 53–55, 81–82, 135, 152, 157–158, 250, 298, 332; **Vol. 3**: 119–123, 126, 130, 131, 133, 137, 177, 179, 229, 231, 240, 242, 358, 367, 372, 482, 527, 530, 550

ethnic policy **Vol. 2**: 55; **Vol. 3**: 116, 118–122, 125

ethnic relations **Vol. 2**: 55, 157; **Vol. 3**: 120–122, 125, 130

etiquette system **Vol. 1**: 317

European Capitalist Society **Vol. 1**: 161

European proletarian revolution **Vol. 1**: 161

Exchange and Payment Agreement **Vol. 3**: 219

Executive Committee **Vol. 1**: 33, 35, 38–39, 51, 54, 103–104, 152–153, 190–191, 215–217, 221, 226–227, 232, 275, 363; **Vol. 3**: 105, 537

extremism **Vol. 2**: 305

F

fake party **Vol. 3**: 79

fall of Shanghai **Vol. 1**: 308

Fallaci, Oriana **Vol. 3**: 163, 289

Fan Hongjie **Vol. 1**: 17

Fang Fang **Vol. 1**: 257

Fang Jisheng **Vol. 3**: 32

Fang Lingxuan **Vol. 3**: 32

Fang Lizhi **Vol. 3**: 316, 318

Fang Yi **Vol. 3**: 42, 189

Fang Zhenwu **Vol. 1**: 233

Fang Zhimin **Vol. 1**: 175, 178

February Countercurrent **Vol. 3**: 54, 76

February 7th Movement **Vol. 1**: 36

February Revolution **Vol. 1**: 28, 89

Federal Republic of China **Vol. 2**: 54

Federation of China **Vol. 2**: 54

Federation of Industry and Commerce **Vol. 2**: 127, 319; **Vol. 3**: 242

Feng faction: **Vol. 1**: 215

Feng Wenbin **Vol. 3**: 154

Feng Yuxiang **Vol. 1**: 214, 234, 248

Fenghua **Vol. 3**: 227

Fengtian warlords **Vol. 1**: 214
feudalism **Vol. 1**: 28, 37, 45, 52, 60, 62, 72–74, 88, 92, 94, 96, 98–100, 107, 114, 119–120, 130–131, 133–137, 140, 145, 246–247, 263, 268, 278, 280, 283, 285, 287, 316, 329, 331, 350, 466–468, 487, 509, 520, 525, 530, 535, 540–541, 543; **Vol. 2**: 26, 31, 37, 53, 83, 91, 93, 111, 116, 286; **Vol. 3**: 57, 148, 252, 309
Fifth Anti-Encirclement Campaign **Vol. 1**: 82, 158–159, 194
Fifteenth National Congress of the Communist Party of China **Vol. 3**: 359, 361, 363, 368, 371, 388, 400, 408, 419, 434
Fighting, Criticizing, and Reforming **Vol. 1**: 296
Fighting Egoism and Repudiating Revisionism **Vol. 2**: 283
Figueiredo, João **Vol. 3**: 264
Finance and Economic Commission **Vol. 2**: 37
Financial and Trade Economy **Vol. 3**: 193
First Congress of the Chinese Socialist Youth League **Vol. 1**: 25
First Five-Year Plan **Vol. 2**: 98, 101–102, 106, 131–132, 148–149, 188, 190; **Vol. 3**: 160, 482
First International **Vol. 1**: 357, 395
First National Congress of the Communist Party of China **Vol. 1**: 19, 29, 419
First National Labor Conference **Vol. 1**: 25
First Resolution of the Communist Party of China **Vol. 1**: 20
First World War (*see also* World War I) **Vol. 1**: 4; **Vol. 2**: 54
Five Always **Vol. 3**: 468
Five Coordinations **Vol. 3**: 495, 505
Five Determinations **Vol. 2**: 238
Five Emphases and Four Beauties **Vol. 3**: 312
Five Emphases, Four Beauties, and Three Loves **Vol. 3**: 313
Five Guarantees **Vol. 2**: 238
Five Oppositions Campaign **Vol. 2**: 94, 103–105, 109, 259, 292; **Vol. 3**: 93
Five Principles of Peaceful Co-existence **Vol. 3**: 206–208, 221, 426–427
Five Surges **Vol. 2**: 230, 232

Five-Year Plan **Vol. 1**: 498, 511; **Vol. 2**: 98, 101–102, 106, 114, 117–119, 124, 131–132, 147–149, 183, 188–190, 209, 260–261; **Vol. 3**: 160, 183, 212, 254, 261–262, 265, 286, 313, 337, 364, 381, 384, 399, 401–402, 481–482, 503, 508, 550–551
focus of work **Vol. 1**: 155; **Vol. 2**: 136, 145, 185, 330, 332; **Vol. 3**: 49, 51–55, 60–61, 254
Foreign Experts **Vol. 3**: 116–118
Foreign Language Bureau **Vol. 3**: 117
Foreign Language Institute **Vol. 3**: 117
Foreign Liaison Department **Vol. 3**: 82
Former Businessmen **Vol. 3**: 113–114
Four Adherences **Vol. 3**: 155
Four Basic Principles **Vol. 3**: 4, 136, 144, 148–152, 154–155, 162, 241, 243, 252, 254–256, 259, 281, 305, 310, 314, 318, 323–324, 336, 339, 525, 546–547
Four Cardinal Principles **Vol. 3**: 135, 484
Four Clean-ups **Vol. 2**: 259, 269; **Vol. 3**: 93–96
Four Clean-ups Movement **Vol. 2**: 269; **Vol. 3**: 93–96
Four Clearance Movement **Vol. 2**: 221
Four Little Dragons **Vol. 3**: 331
Four Modernizations **Vol. 2**: 03, 309, 327, 333–335, 339; **Vol. 3**: 28, 47, 49, 51, 53, 58, 64, 70, 115, 129–130, 136–137, 140, 145, 147–149, 154, 158, 175, 229, 258–261, 263, 267, 286–287, 290–292, 307, 309, 311, 319, 398, 458
Four Nevers **Vol. 3**: 520
Four Obediences **Vol. 3**: 453
Four Purifications Movement **Vol. 3**: 83, 85, 92
Four Subordinations **Vol. 1**: 410–411, 417
Fourth Army **Vol. 1**: 69, 202, 241, 285–286, 299, 307, 311, 323, 336–337; **Vol. 3**: 106–107
Fourth National Congress of the Communist Party of China **Vol. 1**: 30–34, 101–102, 125–126, 128, 139, 218, 220, 225–226, 400, 507; **Vol. 2**: 277, 302
Fourteen Articles for Scientific Research **Vol. 2**: 285
Fourteen Articles of Science **Vol. 2**: 240, 254
free market **Vol. 2**: 151, 287
French Revolution **Vol. 1**: 105, 165
Front Line Committee **Vol. 1**: 307

Fu Chongbi **Vol. 3**: 75–76
Fu Zuoyi **Vol. 1**: 234
Fujian Front Force **Vol. 3**: 228
Fujian Province **Vol. 1**: 299; **Vol. 3**: 96, 298, 313, 320–321
Further Development of the Western Region **Vol. 1**: 263; **Vol. 3**: 337, 508

G

Gang of Four **Vol. 2**: 303, 309–310, 313–317, 319, 321, 323–324, 326, 334–335, 337; **Vol. 3**: 9–14, 17, 20–23, 28–29, 32–34, 36, 40, 47, 49–52, 54, 60, 65, 72–73, 75–77, 79, 81, 83, 85, 88, 92–93, 100–101, 110, 118, 121, 126, 128, 130, 147–151, 154, 156, 159, 161, 163–164, 170, 175, 187
Gansu Province **Vol. 3**: 277
Gao Gang **Vol. 3**: 101
Gao Shanquan **Vol. 3**: 199
Gao Shuxun **Vol. 1**: 248
Gaozhou City **Vol. 3**: 456
General Administration of Civil Aviation of China **Vol. 3**: 539–540
General Administration of Customs **Vol. 3**: 278
General Administration of Radio and Television **Vol. 3**: 455
General Assembly **Vol. 1**: 19–20, 153, 202, 221, 232, 369–370, 387, 395, 403, 421, 504; **Vol. 2**: 148, 160, 212, 243, 245, 304, 319; **Vol. 3**: 139–141, 179–180, 182, 185–188, 190, 220, 224, 240, 244, 360, 473, 521, 524, 551
General German Workers' Association **Vol. 1**: 430
general line of the new democratic revolution **Vol. 1**: 143
General Political Department (PLA) **Vol. 3**: 82, 106, 156, 306, 432
General Secretary **Vol. 1**: 395; **Vol. 3**: 6, 78, 123, 189, 207, 211, 219, 221, 245, 324, 497, 516, 526, 545
Geng Biao **Vol. 2**: 317
German Democrats **Vol. 1**: 224
German Social Democratic Labor Party **Vol. 1**: 357
"going global" **Vol. 3**: 402

Gong Yuzhi **Vol. 2**: 3; **Vol. 3**: 199
Gorbachev, Mikhail **Vol. 3**: 219–221
Gotha Program **Vol. 1**: 430; **Vol. 2**: 90
governance **Vol. 1**: 119, 208, 439; **Vol. 2**: 292; **Vol. 3**: 4–5, 234, 241, 301–302, 325, 366, 440, 449, 465, 503, 511–513, 516, 534, 546
Government of the Ningkang County Workers, Peasants, and Soldiers **Vol. 1**: 136, 189, 202, 255
Government of the Workers and Peasants of Chaling County **Vol. 1**: 136, 189, 202
Government of the Workers, Peasants, and Soldiers of Suichuan County **Vol. 1**: 136, 189, 202, 255
Government of the Yongxin and Lianhua County Workers, Peasants, and Soldiers **Vol. 1**: 136, 189, 202, 255
Government Work Report **Vol. 1**: 136, 202; **Vol. 3**: 254, 262
Gramsci, Antonio **Vol. 2**: 18
Grasping Revolution and Promoting Production
grasping with both hands ("two handed grasp") **Vol. 3**: 302, 304, 309, 331, 364, 382
grassroots autonomy **Vol. 1**: 36 **Vol. 3**: 376
Great Hall of the People **Vol. 3**: 148, 239, 242
Great Harmony World **Vol. 3**: 533
Great Ideological Liberation Movement **Vol. 2**: 311
Great Leap Forward **Vol. 2**: 8–9, 130, 185, 187–193, 197, 199–200, 203–204, 206, 208–209, 211–216, 218–222, 226, 230–232, 234, 237–244, 246, 250, 253–254, 267–268, 270, 273, 276, 293, 325; **Vol. 3**: 332
Great Proletarian Cultural Revolution (*see* Cultural Revolution)
Great Revolution **Vol. 1**: 29, 42–47, 52, 58, 65, 79, 82, 112, 137, 145, 149–150, 152, 154, 163, 167, 172, 176, 180–181, 185, 189, 217, 222, 228, 234, 249, 278, 284, 361, 377–378, 419–420, 488, 494, 504, 508; **Vol. 2**: 170, 332–333; **Vol. 3**: 49, 51, 359, 546
Gu Bai **Vol. 1**: 158
Gu Mu **Vol. 2**: 331; **Vol. 3**: 46, 189

Gu Zhenfu **Vol. 3**: 414, 419
Gu Zhun **Vol. 2**: 307–309
Guangdong Province **Vol. 1**: 33; **Vol. 3**: 277, 322, 331, 456, 468, 500
Guangdong Province Second Peasant Congress **Vol. 1**: 33
Guangdong Provincial Committee **Vol. 3**: 322
Guangming Daily **Vol. 2**: 322; **Vol. 3**: 12, 24, 35–36, 53
Guangxi Province **Vol. 1**: 234; **Vol. 3**: 80, 96, 106, 125, 284, 455
Guangxi Student Army **Vol. 3**: 106
Guangzhou **Vol. 1**: 16, 18–19, 24, 36, 51, 61, 151, 165, 214, 353; **Vol. 2**: 235, 251, 254; **Vol. 3**: 143, 468–469
Guangzhou Conference **Vol. 2**: 254
Guangzhou National Government **Vol. 1**: 214
Guangzhou Uprising **Vol. 1**: 151, 165
guerrilla forces **Vol. 1**: 331, 333
guerrilla war **Vol. 1**: 83, 152, 169, 184, 198, 231, 298, 311, 329, 333, 373, 383
Gui Shifu **Vol. 3**: 199
guiding ideology **Vol. 1**: 3, 5, 7, 9, 11, 13, 15, 17, 19, 21, 23, 25, 27, 29, 31, 33, 35, 37, 39, 41, 43, 45–47, 49, 51, 53, 55, 57–59, 61, 63, 84, 157, 199, 205, 313, 370, 376, 384, 469, 485, 491; **Vol. 2**: 82, 125, 144, 157, 161, 171, 179–180, 203, 209, 229, 246, 255, 260, 277, 293, 314, 317–318; **Vol. 3**: 3, 6–7, 20, 51–53, 55, 59, 61, 63, 67, 95, 118, 141, 152, 158, 163, 169, 171–172, 174, 181, 283, 313, 334, 360, 365, 384–385, 387, 389, 443, 465, 468, 473–476, 492, 501, 512, 514, 526, 533, 550
Guidong County **Vol. 1**: 323
Guiyang City **Vol. 3**: 94
Guizhou Province **Vol. 1**: 323; **Vol. 3**: 78–79, 94–96
Guo Fan **Vol. 1**: 405
Guo Hongtao **Vol. 3**: 105
Guo Junyu **Vol. 1**: 17
Guo Moruo **Vol. 1**: 264
Gutian Congress **Vol. 1**: 178
Gutian Meeting **Vol. 1**: 289, 304, 307, 316, 321, 364, 366, 382, 400, 410

H
Ha'erbin (Harbin) **Vol. 1**: 16: **Vol. 3**: 277–278
Hai Rui **Vol. 2**: 222
Hainan Island **Vol. 3**: 226, 320–321
Han **Vol. 1**: 201; **Vol. 2**: 55, 81, 157; **Vol. 3**: 11, 62, 120–121, 124–125, 127, 189
Han Tianshi **Vol. 3**: 189
Han Zhixiong **Vol. 3**: 11
Handan **Vol. 2**: 204
Handicrafts, Thirty-five Articles of **Vol. 2**: 236
handicraft workers **Vol. 1**: 128, 292, 525, 539; **Vol. 2**: 62, 125
Handling Cases before the Cultural Revolution **Vol. 2**: 152; **Vol. 3**: 87
Hangzhou **Vol. 1**: 260, 355
Hankou **Vol. 1**: 18, 34, 40, 42–43, 166–167, 222
Hankou Special Meeting **Vol. 1**: 222
Hao Jianxiu **Vol. 3**: 189
Harmonious Socialist Society **Vol. 3**: 466, 514, 523, 525, 530–535
harmonious world **Vol. 3**: 516–518, 548
Hartling, Paul **Vol. 2**: 280; **Vol. 3**: 22
He Changgong **Vol. 3**: 288
He Kaifeng **Vol. 1**: 492
He Long **Vol. 1**: 178; **Vol. 3**: 81
He Mengxiong **Vol. 1**: 17
He Shuheng **Vol. 1**: 19
He Xiangning **Vol. 1**: 264
He Zhigui **Vol. 3**: 299
Heath, Edward **Vol. 3**: 139, 235
Hebei Province **Vol. 3**: 277
Hegel, Georg Wilhelm Friedrich **Vol. 1**: 374
hegemony **Vol. 2**: 263, 305; **Vol. 3**: 160, 181–182, 184, 203–207, 327, 421, 426, 437
Heilongjiang Province **Vol. 3**: 122, 299
Henan Province **Vol. 2**: 204; **Vol. 3**: 90, 277
Higher Education, Sixty Articles of **Vol. 2**: 240, 254
historical idealism **Vol. 1**: 92, 456
historical materialism **Vol. 1**: 7–11, 92, 302, 326, 374, 435–436, 444, 456–457, 461, 546; **Vol. 2**: 135, 164, 327; **Vol. 3**: 50, 84, 168, 329, 332–333, 506
History and Class Consciousness **Vol. 2**: 17

History of the Communist Party of China **Vol. 2**: 118
Hong Kong **Vol. 1**: 25, 34, 36, 228; **Vol. 2**: 42; **Vol. 3**: 56, 132, 134, 182, 216, 227, 231–237, 260, 266, 416–417, 420, 519–520
Hong Kong Business Group **Vol. 3**: 233
Hope Project **Vol. 3**: 383–384
"How Can the Party Last?" (article) **Vol. 1**: 193, 365
Howe, Jeffrey **Vol. 3**: 263
Hu Fuming **Vol. 3**: 35
Hu Jintao **Vol. 3**: 6, 439, 455, 458–459, 465, 499–503, 510, 512, 515–521, 523–524, 526, 532, 545
Hu Jiwei **Vol. 3**: 12, 42, 139
Hu Qiaomu **Vol. 1**: 483; **Vol. 3**: 22, 25, 28, 48, 62–63, 72, 139, 145, 165, 178, 185, 189
Hu Qili **Vol. 3**: 189, 245
Hu Sheng **Vol. 2**: 40, 229; **Vol. 3**: 139
Hu Shih **Vol. 1**: 10–11, 14, 24
Hu Yaobang **Vol. 2**: 322, 326; **Vol. 3**: 12–17, 33, 35, 38, 62–63, 67, 71, 96, 107, 111, 123–125, 133, 136–140, 145, 165, 177–179, 182, 186, 189, 199–200, 206–207, 211, 218, 245, 317, 323
Hu Zhaopei **Vol. 3**: 193
Hu Zongnan **Vol. 1**: 352
Hua County **Vol. 3**: 277
Hua Gang **Vol. 1**: 483
Hua Guofeng **Vol. 2**: 317, 324, 331, 333; **Vol. 3**: 10–12, 22, 40, 52, 54, 57, 59, 63, 136, 138, 171, 179, 203, 289
Hua Luogeng **Vol. 3**: 30
Huadong Field Army Corps **Vol. 1**: 351
Huaibei Base **Vol. 3**: 106
Huaihai **Vol. 1**: 327–328, 342, 352–355
Huainan Base **Vol. 3**: 106
Huairen Hall **Vol. 3**: 380
Huang Baitao Corps **Vol. 1**: 354
Huang Chao **Vol. 1**: 332
Huang Hua **Vol. 3**: 217
Huang Huoqing **Vol. 3**: 62
Huang Kecheng **Vol. 3**: 62, 81, 91, 164, 189, 288
Huang Lingshuang **Vol. 1**: 12
Huang Rikui **Vol. 1**: 17

Huang Zhen **Vol. 3**: 104, 139
Huang Zhongyue **Vol. 3**: 104–105
Huangpu Student Army **Vol. 1**: 274
Hubei Province **Vol. 1**: 43; **Vol. 2**: 109; **Vol. 3**: 85
Hubei Provincial Party Committee **Vol. 3**: 72–73, 108
Hume, David **Vol. 3**: 41
Hunan Peasant Movement **Vol. 1**: 331, 389
Hunan Province **Vol. 1**: 38, 169, 323; **Vol. 2**: 233
Hunan Provincial Party Committee **Vol. 1**: 151, 169, 174
Hunan-Guangdong-Guangxi Border War **Vol. 1**: 59
Hundred Days Reform Movement **Vol. 1**: 540
Hungarian Incident **Vol. 2**: 181
Huxi **Vol. 3**: 84, 105–106

I

ideological and cultural education **Vol. 2**: 82
ideological construction **Vol. 1**: 364, 373–376, 378–382, 384, 388, 400, 422, 427; **Vol. 3**: 432, 448
ideological emancipation **Vol. 2**: 11–12, 142, 186, 222, 312–313, 320–321, 325, 327, 329–330, 332, 334, 338–339; **Vol. 3**: 24, 32, 44–45, 69, 118, 136, 154–155
Ideological Liberation Movement **Vol. 2**: 311, 339
ideological line **Vol. 1**: 63–64, 66, 366–367, 378–379, 388–391, 393, 427, 438, 548; **Vol. 2**: 5, 11, 203, 232–235, 313, 316, 324, 327, 329, 338; **Vol. 3**: 34, 55, 58, 60, 69, 135, 153–158, 254, 472
imperialism **Vol. 1**: 3–4, 13, 24–27, 30–31, 34, 37, 44, 51–54, 56, 60–62, 66, 72–74, 87–88, 92–95, 98–100, 105, 107–108, 111–115, 119–123, 125–127, 130–131, 133–137, 140, 145, 160, 173, 187, 238, 243, 245–247, 253, 263, 268, 272, 275, 280, 283, 285, 287, 289, 292, 326, 329, 331, 350–351, 358, 375, 377, 397, 400, 434, 466–468, 487, 509, 514, 517, 519–520, 525–526, 530, 535, 540–541, 543–545; **Vol. 2**: 16, 18, 26, 31, 33, 37, 40–41, 53, 55, 60–61, 83, 91, 116, 136, 262–266, 274, 285, 288; **Vol. 3**: 145, 148, 172, 182, 226, 234, 252, 332, 416

Indies Social Democratic Alliance **Vol. 1**: 224
industrialization **Vol. 1**: 251, 497–498, 519, 533; **Vol. 2**: 5–6, 31, 64–65, 73, 76–78, 85–86, 88, 100–102, 104–105, 107–110, 112–115, 117–120, 122, 130–131, 137–138, 141, 146–150, 183, 187, 209–210, 218, 223, 225; **Vol. 3**: 253, 485, 490, 499, 529, 543
Industry, Seventy Articles of **Vol. 2**: 238–239, 254
Information Engineering College **Vol. 3**: 434
Information Work Office **Vol. 3**: 539
informationization **Vol. 3**: 437, 439
initial stage of capitalism **Vol. 1**: 475
Inner Mongolia **Vol. 1**: 202; **Vol. 3**: 15, 116, 122, 125, 277, 455
Institute of Philosophy **Vol. 3**: 43
institution building **Vol. 3**: 279
institutional reform program **Vol. 3**: 276, 538
Instructions on Land Issues (May 4th Instructions) **Vol. 1**: 249, 532
integrating Marxism into China **Vol. 1**: 77, 489, 491, 550; **Vol. 2**: 27, 273, 299, 303, 306, 310; **Vol. 3**: 550
intellectuals **Vol. 1**: 5, 7, 11–12, 14–16, 20, 46, 57, 72, 76, 113–114, 117, 128, 144, 198, 210, 215, 241, 253–254, 262–263, 288, 293, 367, 383, 399, 471, 488, 495, 499, 501, 513; **Vol. 2**: 61–62, 80–81, 130, 154–155, 157, 177, 179, 239, 241–243, 250–251, 254, 259, 263–264, 270, 288, 291, 301, 309–310, 320; **Vol. 3**: 18, 20, 30, 88, 110–112, 129–131, 145, 185, 242, 308, 317, 339, 372
International Law Commission **Vol. 3**: 224
International Monetary Fund **Vol. 3**: 224
International General Committee **Vol. 1**: 396
International Labor Day Commemorative Event **Vol. 1**: 15
International Workers' Association **Vol. 1**: 395–396
intra-Party struggle **Vol. 1**: 490; **Vol. 3**: 141
Iskra **Vol. 1**: 399
Islamic Union **Vol. 1**: 224

J

James Soong **Vol. 3**: 521
Jameson, Friedrich **Vol. 2**: 18–19
January Revolution **Vol. 3**: 66, 75
Japan **Vol. 1**: 9, 18–19, 30, 73, 75, 81, 229–230, 233–240, 242–243, 290, 297, 376, 400, 514, 532; **Vol. 2**: 263–264, 330; **Vol. 3**: 46, 106, 210–212, 228–229, 241, 347, 419, 423–425
Japanese imperialism **Vol. 1**: 61, 66, 73, 80, 98–99, 160, 238, 243, 289, 326, 400, 526, 530
Ji Dengkui **Vol. 3**: 70, 104
Ji Pengfei **Vol. 3**: 104
Jia Shuang **Vol. 3**: 299
Jiang Qing **Vol. 2**: 292, 294, 300, 304, 310, 313, 320; **Vol. 3**: 75–77, 79, 86, 170, 187, 285
Jiang Qing Anti-Revolutionary Group **Vol. 3**: 170
Jiang Zemin **Vol. 2**: 21; **Vol. 3**: 6, 245, 324–326, 338, 348–349, 351–352, 358–360, 364–365, 368–371, 375, 378–380, 383, 387–388, 390–392, 397, 401–402, 408, 410, 415, 417, 419, 421, 423–424, 426–427, 429–431, 433–435, 438, 444, 446–447, 454, 456, 458–459, 462, 468–472, 484, 526
Jiangshan Island **Vol. 3**: 226
Jiangsu Province **Vol. 1**: 352; **Vol. 3**: 53, 87, 105, 141, 263
Jiangxi Province **Vol. 1**: 38, 41, 178, 299; **Vol. 3**: 91
Jiangxi Provincial Political Committee **Vol. 1**: 38
Jiao Ren **Vol. 3**: 414
Jicheng County **Vol. 3**: 277
Jilin Province **Vol. 3**: 39, 122
Jin-Cha-Ji Territorial Doctrine **Vol. 3**: 76–77
Jinan **Vol. 1**: 19; **Vol. 3**: 38
Jinchaji **Vol. 1**: 202, 211, 493
Jinchaji Daily **Vol. 1**: 493
Jinggangshan (Jinggangshan Revolutionary Base) **Vol. 1**: 105, 168–170, 173–174, 189, 191, 306, 315, 317, 319, 323, 331, 336, 345, 361, 365, 382, 404
Jingxi Hotel **Vol. 2**: 300
Jinjiang Region **Vol. 3**: 298, 320–321
Jinjiluyu Central Bureau **Vol. 1**: 493
Jinmen Islands **Vol. 3**: 228

Jinsui Cadres Meeting **Vol. 1**: 533
Jinzhai County **Vol. 3**: 384
Jinzhou **Vol. 1**: 353–354
Joint Commission **Vol. 1**: 395
Joint Statement of the People's Republic of China and the Government of Portugal on Macao **Vol. 3**: 237
joint-stock enterprises **Vol. 3**: 406
July 1st Speech (Jiang Zemin) **Vol. 3**: 115, 471

K

Kang Sheng **Vol. 2**: 279; **Vol. 3**: 54, 73, 77, 79, 100–101
Kant, Immanuel **Vol. 3**: 41
Khrushchev **Vol. 2**: 143, 256, 264, 289; **Vol. 3**: 163, 247
KMT Legislative Body **Vol. 1**: 258, 260
KMT Revolutionary Committee **Vol. 1**: 258, 264
KMT ruling clique **Vol. 1**: 258, 271, 281
Kong Xiangxi (H H Kung) **Vol. 1**: 246
Korean War **Vol. 2**: 84–85, 99; **Vol. 3**: 226
Kosygin **Vol. 2**: 287, 289
Kowloon **Vol. 3**: 234, 416
Kropotkin, Peter **Vol. 1**: 6
Kung, H H (*see* Kong Xiangxi)
Kuomintang (*see also* Nationalist Party) **Vol. 1**: 24, 26, 29, 32–33, 35, 41, 48–49, 66, 69, 85, 102, 115, 123, 126, 136, 153, 192, 197, 215, 223, 235, 239, 248, 254, 257, 261, 467; **Vol. 2**: 37, 43, 49–50, 57, 60–61, 91–93, 116; **Vol. 3**: 79, 104, 107, 130–131, 226–228, 230, 232, 413, 419, 521
Kuomintang New Army **Vol. 1**: 33, 136
Kuybyshev, Valerian **Vol. 2**: 118

L

labor market **Vol. 3**: 354
labor-based distribution **Vol. 3**: 21, 23–27, 37
Lakeside Prefectural Committee **Vol. 3**: 105
Lan Gongwu **Vol. 1**: 11
land ownership **Vol. 1**: 51–52, 136–137, 143, 162, 523, 527, 532–533; **Vol. 2**: 26, 63–65, 123
Land Reform **Vol. 1**: 87, 250–256, 263, 271, 370, 439, 531–533; **Vol. 2**: 39, 57, 61, 63–67, 69, 71, 73–77, 87, 92, 94, 98, 102, 107, 111, 116; **Vol. 3**: 166
landlord class **Vol. 1**: 37, 52–54, 56, 75, 87, 93, 98, 129, 131, 135–138, 171, 185, 200, 246, 249–252, 271, 280, 288, 293, 371, 468, 528, 531–533; **Vol. 2**: 61, 64, 105, 286
landlords **Vol. 1**: 33, 46, 74–75, 80–81, 122, 129, 136–138, 143–145, 201, 237–238, 240, 249–255, 271, 278, 336, 377, 427, 467, 530, 532–533; **Vol. 2**: 64, 136, 257; **Vol. 3**: 112–113
Law of the Unity of Opposites **Vol. 2**: 168, 281; **Vol. 3**: 236
leadership of the CPC **Vol. 1**: 42, 87, 108, 115, 142, 172, 174, 178, 186, 198, 200, 229, 262, 264–265, 267, 272, 307, 310, 313, 368, 414, 466–467, 469, 521; **Vol. 2**: 152–153; **Vol. 3**: 257, 270, 483, 486
leadership system **Vol. 1**: 368–369, 415, 418; **Vol. 2**: 161, 186, 223, 230; **Vol. 3**: 3, 188, 241, 244, 268, 270, 337, 371, 449, 454, 513–514
League membership **Vol. 3**: 92
Lee Teng-hui **Vol. 3**: 418–419
Left-Wing Corps **Vol. 1**: 310
leftism **Vol. 2**: 138, 175, 200, 202–204, 206–208, 213, 216, 230–231, 234, 247, 252–253, 262, 302–303, 312; **Vol. 3**: 155
Leftist bias **Vol. 1**: 252, 254, 372; **Vol. 2**: 64
Leftist errors (*see also* Leftist mistakes) **Vol. 1**: 47, 58, 63, 251, 285, 378; **Vol. 2**: 10, 42, 95, 250, 258, 260, 277, 298, 319, 321; **Vol. 3**: 28, 31, 62–63, 66, 98, 126, 131, 135, 159, 162, 164, 171
Leftist mistakes (*see also* Leftist errors) **Vol. 1**: 55, 534; **Vol. 2**: 8, 10, 59, 175, 239, 246, 336; **Vol. 3**: 92, 174, 185, 250, 252, 334
Leftist tendencies **Vol. 1**: 105, 370; **Vol. 2**: 62, 74; **Vol. 3**: 283
Legislative Adjustment Bill **Vol. 3**: 213
Legislative Law Lecture **Vol. 3**: 380
Lenin, Vladimir **Vol. 1**: 6, 25, 149–150, 163, 188, 289, 291, 358–359, 364, 375–376, 379, 381, 384, 393–394, 397–399, 411, 430–432, 434, 443, 445, 447, 458–459, 492–493, 520; **Vol. 2**: 16, 18–19, 45, 54, 66, 118–119, 121, 126–127, 136–137, 140, 164, 181, 209, 211–212, 215, 266, 274, 280, 299;

Vol. 3: 28, 39, 147, 246, 332, 512
let a hundred flowers bloom and a hundred schools of thought contend **Vol. 2**: 156–157, 178, 183, 241; **Vol. 3**: 365, 390
Letter to Taiwan **Vol. 3**: 228
"letting in" and "reaching out" **Vol. 3**: 402–403
Li Chang **Vol. 3**: 189, 311
Li Da **Vol. 1**: 9, 12, 18–20; **Vol. 3**: 104
Li Dazhao **Vol. 1**: 7–8, 10–12, 14, 16–19, 21, 29, 33, 102, 127, 399, 545, 547
Li Dingming **Vol. 1**: 202
Li Fuchun **Vol. 1**: 38; **Vol. 2**: 101, 156, 238; **Vol. 3**: 73
Li Hanjun **Vol. 1**: 9–10, 18–20
Li Honglin **Vol. 3**: 139
Li Jiantong **Vol. 3**: 100
Li Jingquan **Vol. 3**: 94, 288
Li Jishen **Vol. 1**: 248, 264
Li Jun **Vol. 1**: 17
Li Kenong **Vol. 1**: 234
Li Lisan **Vol. 1**: 52, 58–62, 105, 157, 285; **Vol. 2**: 40, 166; **Vol. 3**: 72
Li Peng **Vol. 3**: 221, 245, 275
Li Ruihuan **Vol. 3**: 245
Li Shangyin (Tang Dynasty poet) **Vol. 3**: 187
Li Siguang **Vol. 3**: 30
Li Tieying **Vol. 3**: 245
Li Weihan **Vol. 1**: 95; **Vol. 3**: 189
Li Xiannian **Vol. 2**: 300, 324, 326, 328, 333; **Vol. 3**: 11, 40, 48–49, 73, 179, 188–189, 200, 215, 246, 289
Li Ximing **Vol. 3**: 245
Li Zhangda **Vol. 1**: 264
Li Zicheng **Vol. 1**: 332
Li Zongren **Vol. 1**: 234
Liang Qichao **Vol. 1**: 5, 7
Liaoning Province **Vol. 3**: 122, 141
Liao Chengzhi **Vol. 3**: 189
Liao Jili **Vol. 3**: 198
Liao Zhongkai **Vol. 1**: 7
Liaoshen **Vol. 1**: 327–328, 342, 352–355
Liberation **Vol. 1**: 27–28, 37, 53, 76, 85–88, 105, 111, 113, 130, 132, 135–137, 142, 188, 203, 210, 224, 233, 244–245, 247–248, 255, 258, 261–263, 265, 267, 269–271, 278, 281, 284–286, 300, 305–306, 309, 311–313, 317, 320–321, 324, 327–329, 334, 337–338, 342, 344, 346–347, 350–351, 353, 355, 372, 383, 388, 403, 410, 421, 433, 466–467, 470, 475, 477, 484, 486, 491, 494, 500, 516, 522, 531, 534–535; **Vol. 2**: 32, 41–42, 49, 53–54, 99, 141, 252, 263, 272, 278–280, 295, 311, 327, 339; **Vol. 3**: 23, 29, 41, 65, 82, 97, 106, 109, 114, 137, 148, 153, 162, 169, 178, 225–229, 240, 244, 309, 327, 358, 433, 435, 487, 496, 517
Liberation Army Daily **Vol. 2**: 278–279; **Vol. 3**: 41, 137
Lien Chan **Vol. 3**: 521
Lihuang Municipal Committee **Vol. 3**: 106
Lin Biao **Vol. 1**: 179; **Vol. 2**: 269, 280, 300–301, 303, 310, 316, 320–321, 324, 326; **Vol. 3**: 40, 60, 72–77, 79, 83, 85–86, 93, 100–101, 121, 126, 130, 147–148, 150, 154, 156, 159, 161, 163–164, 170, 175, 187, 285
Lin Feng **Vol. 3**: 72
Lin Jianqing **Vol. 3**: 139, 199
Lin Zuhan **Vol. 1**: 38
lingering historical issues (post Cultural Revolution) **Vol. 3**: 53, 55, 82–88, 103
linking theory and practice **Vol. 1**: 423, 436, 440, 445, 471
Lisan Road **Vol. 1**: 157
literature and art **Vol. 1**: 198, 210, 300, 549; **Vol. 2**: 240, 242, 254, 259; **Vol. 3**: 32, 304–305, 315, 393
Literature and Art, Ten Articles of **Vol. 2**: 240
Literature and Art, Eight Articles of **Vol. 2**: 240, 254
Liu Binyan **Vol. 3**: 316, 318
Liu Bocheng **Vol. 1**: 347, 351; **Vol. 2**: 249; **Vol. 3**: 288
Liu Changsheng **Vol. 1**: 257
Liu Demin **Vol. 3**: 299
Liu Guoguang **Vol. 3**: 195
Liu Jingfan **Vol. 3**: 100
Liu Lantao **Vol. 3**: 72
Liu Renjing **Vol. 1**: 17, 19, 21
Liu Shaoqi **Vol. 1**: 34, 102, 249, 360, 367, 369, 381, 402, 410, 412, 425, 438, 460, 471, 475,

484, 489–490, 493, 496, 510–512, 522; **Vol. 2**: 33–34, 36, 42–44, 46–48, 50, 59, 64, 67–69, 72–74, 76, 78, 82–83, 85–86, 89, 91, 99–100, 109, 116–117, 129, 142, 147, 151, 153, 158–159, 165, 178, 188, 193–194, 212, 216, 219, 222, 233, 243, 247–248, 254, 257, 295, 299–300; **Vol. 3**: 15, 66, 77–78, 81
Liu Shaoqi Memorial Conference **Vol. 3**: 78
Liu Wenhui **Vol. 1**: 234
Liu Xiang **Vol. 1**: 234
Liu Xiao **Vol. 1**: 257, 259
Liu Xinwu **Vol. 3**: 30
Liu Zhidan **Vol. 3**: 66, 100–101
local nationalism **Vol. 2**: 149, 157; **Vol. 3**: 121
local religious organizations **Vol. 2**: 149; **Vol. 3**: 126
localization of Marxism **Vol. 1**: 481, 484; **Vol. 2**: 3–5, 8, 10–11, 13, 16–17, 20–25, 27–28, 41, 54, 57, 89–90, 95, 120, 125–126, 132–134, 145–146, 158, 163–164, 168, 170–171, 173–174, 182, 186, 191–192, 197, 200, 203, 206–208, 220–223, 225–227, 230–232, 234, 238, 245, 252–254, 258, 260–261, 299, 310–313, 315, 319, 321, 328–330, 332, 335–339; **Vol. 3**: 3, 6–7, 169, 335, 341, 376, 395, 417, 443, 461, 525, 527, 546, 550
localized Marxism **Vol. 1**: 444; **Vol. 2**: 170
Lominadze, Vissarion **Vol. 1**: 43, 56–58
Long March **Vol. 1**: 159–160, 286, 311, 341, 504; **Vol. 3**: 37, 104, 140, 154, 513
Long Yun **Vol. 1**: 234
Longhai Line **Vol. 1**: 352
Lu Dingyi **Vol. 1**: 483; **Vol. 2**: 193; **Vol. 3**: 72, 81
Lu Ping **Vol. 3**: 78–79
Luanchuan **Vol. 1**: 323
Lukács, György **Vol. 2**: 18
Luo Ronghuan **Vol. 3**: 105
Luo Ruiqing **Vol. 2**: 326; **Vol. 3**: 42, 76, 81
Luo Yinong **Vol. 1**: 276
Luo Yunguang **Vol. 3**: 299
Luo Zhanglong **Vol. 1**: 17
Luojing Mountains (Luojing Mountain Rage) **Vol. 1**: 169, 171
Lushan Conference **Vol. 2**: 175, 186, 191, 208, 216–217, 219–222, 226–227, 229–231, 255; **Vol. 3**: 91, 164
Lushan Preparatory Conference **Vol. 2**: 200
Lutai **Vol. 1**: 354
Luxemburg, Rosa **Vol. 2**: 18
Luyu District **Vol. 1**: 351

M

Ma Bufang **Vol. 1**: 356
Ma Guorui **Vol. 3**: 189
Ma Hong **Vol. 3**: 28
Ma Hongkui **Vol. 1**: 356
Ma Mingfang **Vol. 3**: 15
Ma Mingshan **Vol. 3**: 299
Ma Wanqi **Vol. 3**: 237
Ma Xulun **Vol. 1**: 264
Macao **Vol. 3**: 132, 134, 182, 231–234, 237, 416–417, 420
MacLehose, Barry **Vol. 3**: 234
macro-control (of the economy) **Vol. 3**: 302, 347, 349–351, 354–356, 365–366, 480, 491–492, 495–496, 505, 507, 538–539, 541
mandatory planning **Vol. 3**: 191
Malenkov, Georgy **Vol. 2**: 118
Malthusian theory **Vol. 1**: 8
Malyn, **Vol. 1**: 19
Manabendra Nath Roy **Vol. 1**: 222
Manchu **Vol. 1**: 201
Mao Zedong **Vol. 1**: 16, 19, 29–31, 33, 46, 51–53, 57, 66–79, 81–86, 89, 91–92, 95, 99, 102, 105–117, 127, 129–133, 139–141, 143, 146–147, 150, 158–161, 164, 166–176, 178–199, 203–210, 216, 228–249, 252–258, 262, 264, 266, 269–271, 273, 276–286, 288–292, 294–302, 304–308, 310–313, 315–324, 326–350, 353–356, 361–363, 365–369, 377, 379–382, 384–389, 391–401, 403–411, 416, 423–424, 426–428, 431–438, 440, 443–445, 448, 452–454, 459, 461–464, 469–470, 472, 474, 476, 478–479, 481–497, 499–501, 503–549; **Vol. 2**: 5–8, 11, 13–14, 16, 18, 20, 22–24, 27–32, 34, 37–41, 43, 47, 49, 51–53, 55, 59–65, 74–77, 79–82, 84–85, 88, 91–93, 97, 99–101, 103–105, 109–111, 114–117, 119–120, 122–123, 126–127, 130, 132, 134, 141, 143–144, 146–157, 161, 163, 166–170, 174–181,

184–191, 193–194, 196–197, 199–217, 220–222, 227, 231–235, 238, 244–245, 254, 256–259, 262, 265–267, 269–280, 282–283, 286, 291–292, 294–296, 299, 301–305, 307–308, 311, 313–319, 321–327, 329, 334, 336–339; **Vol. 3**: 10, 22–23, 33–40, 42, 58, 60, 62–63, 66, 73, 79, 93, 104, 126, 128, 132, 135–136, 140, 142–151, 154, 157, 161–170, 173, 180, 184, 204, 226–227, 234, 247–248, 252, 259, 280, 285, 315, 325, 327, 332, 337, 340, 358–360, 364–365, 385, 393, 416, 444, 472–476, 483, 500, 504, 513–514, 525–527, 533

Mao Zedong Thought **Vol. 1**: 81, 83–85, 183, 188, 279, 312–313, 363, 382, 394, 424, 459, 469–470, 479, 481–495, 497, 499, 501, 503, 505, 507, 509, 511, 513, 515, 517, 519, 521, 523, 525, 527, 529, 531, 533, 535, 537, 539, 541, 543, 545, 547, 549; **Vol. 2**: 13, 22, 82, 88, 143, 161, 170, 262, 272–273, 278, 282–283, 286, 303, 307, 313, 315–319, 321–324, 326–327, 329, 336–338; **Vol. 3**: 33–37, 39–40, 42, 58, 60, 62–63, 126, 128, 140, 142–145, 147, 149–151, 154, 157, 161–169, 173, 180, 184, 280, 325, 337, 340, 359–360, 365, 385, 393, 472–476, 483, 500, 504, 514, 525–527, 533

Maoism/Maoist **Vol. 1**: 483, 492; **Vol. 2**: 264, 303

Maoming City **Vol. 3**: 468

Mari Incident **Vol. 1**: 166

Marin (Jakob Rudnick, Comintern leader) **Vol. 1**: 215, 224

market economy **Vol. 1**: 54, 507; **Vol. 2**: 4, 13, 15, 23, 152, 196, 222, 225–226, 291; **Vol. 3**: 6, 195, 200, 328–329, 344–354, 357, 362, 366, 371, 379–382, 385–386, 391, 393, 404–405, 410, 432, 436, 444–447, 454, 461, 467, 480, 488–489, 492–497, 507, 513–514, 525, 540, 543, 545, 547

market regulation **Vol. 2**: 14, 288; **Vol. 3**: 191–197, 199, 344–348, 350, 365, 488

Marx, Karl **Vol. 1**: 7–8, 97, 163, 188, 224, 357, 364, 374–376, 381, 384, 392, 394–397, 429–431, 434, 443, 445, 447, 456, 458, 493; **Vol. 2**: 12, 19, 53, 90, 113, 119, 125, 127, 135–137, 144, 164, 209–212, 215, 266, 280, 299; **Vol. 3**: 39, 332

Marxism **Vol. 1**: 3, 5–19, 21, 23, 27, 29, 37, 63, 65, 67–71, 77, 79, 81, 92, 102, 134, 141, 149–151, 163–164, 302, 308, 311, 358–359, 367, 374–375, 381, 385, 389–393, 405–407, 420, 431, 433–435, 437, 440–442, 444, 446, 448, 451, 456–457, 464, 473, 481–486, 488–491, 496, 502, 509, 535, 541, 546, 550; **Vol. 2**: 3–28, 30, 39, 41, 47, 50, 54, 56–57, 66, 73, 77, 82, 87–90, 94–95, 104, 113, 120, 125–126, 130–134, 136, 139–140, 142–146, 148, 156–158, 163–164, 168, 170–171, 173–174, 177, 182, 186–188, 191–192, 195, 197, 200, 202–204, 206–210, 215–216, 219–227, 230–232, 234, 238, 245, 252–254, 258, 260–262, 264–268, 271–274, 276–278, 282, 284, 290–291, 294, 298–306, 309–316, 319, 321–325, 327–330, 332, 335–339 **Vol. 3**: 3, 6–7, 28, 36–37, 39, 41, 63, 110, 169, 181, 185, 191–192, 202, 233, 243, 250–251, 315–317, 329, 332–335, 338, 340–341, 346, 357, 359–360, 368, 376, 388–389, 395, 397, 403, 417, 443, 461, 468, 475–477, 487, 495, 497, 504–505, 514, 525, 527, 530, 535, 546, 549–550

Marxism with Chinese characteristics **Vol. 1**: 6, 481; **Vol. 3**: 334

Marxism-Leninism (*see also* Marxist-Leninist Thought) **Vol. 1**: 26, 63, 65, 67–68, 79, 82–84, 89, 99, 106, 116, 128, 130, 144, 150, 164, 188, 218, 276, 311–313, 357, 359–360, 363, 371, 373, 376, 379–384, 387, 392, 405–406, 424–425, 439, 441, 459, 468–470, 479, 482–486, 490–492, 502, 517; **Vol. 2**: 8, 14, 21, 28, 54, 82–83, 128, 143–144, 162, 210, 233, 244, 283, 286, 322–324, 326–327, 329–330, 336–337; **Vol. 3**: 33–35, 37, 39–40, 58, 60, 62, 126, 128, 140, 143, 145–147, 149–151, 154, 157, 169, 184, 280, 325, 340, 359–360, 365, 385, 393, 472–474, 476, 500, 504, 514, 526–527, 533

Marxist Economic Theory **Vol. 1**: 7, 9; **Vol. 3**: 20, 488, 493

Marxist epistemology **Vol. 1**: 409, 444, 463; **Vol. 3**: 41, 137, 452

Marxist line **Vol. 2**: 321; **Vol. 3**: 241

Marxist line of thought **Vol. 2**: 321

Marxist-Leninist Thought (*see also* Marxism-Leninism) **Vol. 1**: 24, 65; **Vol. 2**: 262, 265, 272, 277–279, 281, 298; **Vol. 3**: 483, 504

Marxist Research Society of Peking University **Vol. 1**: 17

Marxist Studies **Vol. 1**: 7, 20

Masayoshi Ōhira **Vol. 3**: 210, 260
mass historical view **Vol. 1**: 41, 456–458
mass line **Vol. 1**: 41, 326, 366, 380, 409, 459–461, 463, 470–471, 474–475, 488; **Vol. 2**: 161, 219, 243, 246, 319; **Vol. 3**: 16, 72, 155, 163, 169, 177, 296, 452, 457–458
mass movement **Vol. 1**: 39, 41–42, 220, 228, 231, 259, 285; **Vol. 2**: 190, 193, 299; **Vol. 3**: 12, 50, 52, 60, 93
masses (peasant masses) **Vol. 1**: 9, 13–15, 24, 33, 35, 37–38, 42–44, 48, 52–53, 58–59, 73, 75, 85–86, 95, 108–109, 124, 130–131, 133, 143, 150, 156, 168, 171, 173–177, 179–181, 183–185, 187, 190–194, 198, 200–201, 207, 209–212, 218, 226, 237, 241–242, 247, 249, 251–252, 254–256, 258–261, 267, 270, 277–278, 284–287, 293, 300–307, 310–312, 315, 317, 320–321, 326, 328–329, 332–335, 337–338, 358, 363, 366–367, 372, 374, 376–377, 380, 384, 387, 389, 393, 396, 402, 404–409, 412–413, 415, 417, 419–420, 424, 426–428, 430, 432, 435–436, 439, 444, 449–450, 456–465, 469–475, 477–480, 484, 487, 502, 506, 518, 548–549; **Vol. 2**: 9, 65, 67, 78, 80, 84, 104, 124, 129, 159–163, 175–176, 179, 181, 188, 190–192, 206, 218–219, 224, 234–236, 241, 244–245, 249, 252, 261, 269, 276, 286, 292, 295, 297–298, 301, 303, 305–306, 309, 311–312, 314, 316–318, 323, 327, 339; **Vol. 3**: 10, 12–13, 15, 19, 38, 53–54, 58, 69, 72–75, 77, 81, 83, 85, 102, 106, 109, 113–114, 121–122, 126, 142–143, 146–147, 150, 157–158, 161, 177, 184–185, 202, 252–253, 257, 271–272, 281–282, 284–285, 291, 308–309, 323, 338–339, 362, 367, 377–378, 380, 382, 386, 388, 393, 418, 445, 447, 451, 453, 456–459, 471, 476, 531, 547
material stimulus **Vol. 2**: 31 **Vol. 3**: 183
May Day **Vol. 1**: 16
May 7 Instructions **Vol. 2**: 269–272
May 16 Notice **Vol. 2**: 270
May Instructions **Vol. 1**: 223
May 4th Movement (May Fourth Movement) **Vol. 1**: 5, 7, 12, 14, 19, 36, 72, 81, 110, 114–116, 139, 259, 267, 363, 376, 508, 541–542, 546–547; **Vol. 3**: 31
May 19th Movement **Vol. 1**: 108

May 30th Movement **Vol. 1**: 29–34, 36, 274
May 4th Instructions **Vol. 1**: 250–251, 254
Mazu **Vol. 3**: 228
McNamara, Robert **Vol. 3**: 205
means of production **Vol. 1**: 6, 12, 162; **Vol. 2**: 6, 65, 112, 115, 118–119, 122, 124–128, 133, 135–136, 138, 141, 147, 165, 181, 185, 196, 216, 218, 223, 281; **Vol. 3**: 149, 193–195, 250, 355, 365
Meeting of Theoretical Work **Vol. 1**: 215, 265; **Vol. 3**: 137–139, 141
Meng Zi **Vol. 1**: 305
Mengcheng **Vol. 1**: 354
Mensheviks **Vol. 1**: 398; **Vol. 2**: 54
militant communism **Vol. 2**: 268, 271
Military and Civilian Congress of the Jinchaji Border Region **Vol. 1**: 211
Military Commission Symposium **Vol. 2**: 335
Military Committee **Vol. 1**: 172
Military Dialectics **Vol. 1**: 288
military drills (Taiwan) **Vol. 3**: 418
Military Facilities Protection Law **Vol. 3**: 436
Military Movement Resolution **Vol. 1**: 275
military reform **Vol. 3**: 429, 431, 438–439, 516
Military Region **Vol. 1**: 503 **Vol. 3**: 43, 50, 73, 76–77
military revolution with Chinese characteristics **Vol. 3**: 429
Military Service Law **Vol. 3**: 436
Min Xing **Vol. 1**: 6
Ming Pao Daily **Vol. 3**: 233
Ministry of Central Organizations **Vol. 3**: 97, 99
Ministry of Civil Affairs **Vol. 3**: 89–90, 103, 378
Ministry of Communications Vol 3: 539–540
Ministry of Construction Vol 3: 539–540
Ministry of Culture **Vol. 3**: 39, 82, 312
Ministry of Culture (Japan) **Vol. 3**: 212
Ministry of Economy and Trade **Vol. 3**: 322
Ministry of Education **Vol. 2**: 240; **Vol. 3**: 18–19, 67, 312, 455
Ministry of Environmental Protection **Vol. 3**: 540
Ministry of Finance **Vol. 3**: 455, 538–539
Ministry of Foreign Affairs **Vol. 3**: 217
Ministry of Health **Vol. 3**: 312, 540

Ministry of Housing and Urban-Rural Construction **Vol. 3**: 540
Ministry of Human Resources and Social Security **Vol. 3**: 540
Ministry of Information Industry **Vol. 3**: 539
Ministry of Land and Resources **Vol. 3**: 455
Ministry of National Defense **Vol. 3**: 91
Ministry of Organizations and Personnel of the Central Committee **Vol. 3**: 279
Ministry of Personnel **Vol. 3**: 277, 279, 540
Ministry of Propaganda **Vol. 2**: 104, 156, 240; **Vol. 3**: 37–38, 312, 384, 471
Ministry of Public Security **Vol. 2**: 104, 215; **Vol. 3**: 67, 89–90, 117, 312
Ministry of Publicity **Vol. 3**: 138, 312
Ministry of Railways **Vol. 3**: 87, 298–299, 539
Ministry of the Machinery Industry **Vol. 3**: 47
Ministry of Transportation **Vol. 3**: 539
minority ethnic groups **Vol. 2**: 157; **Vol. 3**: 121
moderately well-off society (moderately prosperous society) **Vol. 3**: 4, 260, 263, 266, 347, 479–488, 491, 495, 497, 501, 506–507, 523–524, 527–531, 533–534, 542, 545, 551
modern enterprise system **Vol. 1**: 24; **Vol. 3**: 351–353, 404–406, 410–412, 451, 494
modernization **Vol. 1**: 35–137, 463, 538; **Vol. 2**: 12, 15–17, 19–20, 23, 71, 76, 113, 130, 139–140, 181–182, 197, 210, 213, 216–217, 220–221, 225, 227, 253, 260–263, 267–268, 271–272, 284, 298, 302, 316, 325, 329–330, 332, 336–338; **Vol. 3**: 3–5, 7, 46–47, 49–52, 55, 57–63, 118, 130, 133, 136–137, 148–149, 151, 171–175, 177, 179–182, 185–186, 190, 192, 202, 205, 207, 210, 223, 225, 239–240, 243–245, 251, 254–260, 262–263, 266–268, 270, 279–280, 286–287, 290, 299, 303, 305, 307, 309–312, 314–315, 318–319, 322, 324, 326, 333–334, 336–337, 339–341, 343, 345, 348, 350, 357–360, 362–364, 366, 369, 373, 383–384, 387, 390, 392, 397–401, 403, 423, 434, 436–437, 441, 443, 446, 473, 475–476, 479, 482–488, 494, 498–500, 502, 505, 508–509, 516, 523–526, 531, 535–536, 543–544, 547, 549–550
modernization of Marxism **Vol. 2**: 12, 15–17, 19–20, 23, 113, 139–140, 182, 210, 216, 220–221, 227, 253, 267–268, 316, 325, 332, 338

Molotov, Vyacheslav **Vol. 2**: 118
Mongolia **Vol. 1**: 61, 202; **Vol. 3**: 15, 116, 122, 125, 201, 218–220, 222, 277, 455
Montargis Conference **Vol. 1**: 17
Mopping-Up Operation **Vol. 1**: 69
Moral Education **Vol. 3**: 383, 466
Moscow Conference **Vol. 2**: 189
multi-ethnic **Vol. 2**: 54–55; **Vol. 3**: 97, 172
multi-party **Vol. 1**: 209, 262, 264–265, 268; **Vol. 2**: 7, 52–54, 79, 152–153; **Vol. 3**: 272, 316, 365, 367, 372–373, 375–376, 510
Mutual Aid Organizations **Vol. 1**: 206; **Vol. 2**: 73, 76
Mutual Assistance Groups **Vol. 2**: 123
My View of Marxism (Li Dazhao article) **Vol. 1**: 7

N

Nakasone Yasuhiro **Vol. 3**: 211, 263
Nanchang **Vol. 1**: 57, 61, 168, 176
Nanchang Uprising **Vol. 1**: 57, 168
Nanjing **Vol. 1**: 18, 34, 61, 93, 156, 231, 235, 249, 256, 260, 354–355; **Vol. 3**: 35, 127, 234, 414, 416
Nanjing Peace Talks **Vol. 1**: 256
Nanjing Treaty **Vol. 3**: 234, 416
Nanning Conference **Vol. 2**: 185
National Army **Vol. 1**: 40, 214–215
national bourgeoisie **Vol. 1**: 27, 31–32, 37, 51–52, 56, 70, 74, 80, 87, 106, 114–115, 127, 138, 143, 145, 213, 216–218, 233–234, 237–238, 240, 242, 244, 253, 258, 261–263, 270–271, 283, 310, 468, 495, 517–519, 523, 540; **Vol. 2**: 4, 26–27, 41–44, 46, 49–50, 59–61, 63–64, 69, 80, 92–93, 103–105, 116, 126–129, 170, 202
national capitalism **Vol. 1**: 98, 138–139, 377, 534
National Civil Service Bureau **Vol. 3**: 540
National Civilization and Politeness Month **Vol. 3**: 312
national conditions **Vol. 1**: 25, 27–28, 66, 81, 91, 94, 130, 133, 140, 150, 161, 163–164, 175, 179–180, 186, 224, 298, 361, 376, 379, 392–393, 432, 508, 519–520; **Vol. 2**: 6–7, 11, 13, 19, 27, 39–40, 46–47, 54, 59, 66, 69, 87, 89, 93, 116, 129–130, 139–140, 144–146, 154, 166, 173, 187, 204, 206–207, 213, 234, 238, 246, 260, 264,

266–267, 296; **Vol. 3**: 170–171, 174, 241, 243, 246–248, 252, 257, 259, 266, 336, 351, 361, 369, 371, 397–399, 421, 488, 525–527, 544
National Conference on Education **Vol. 3**: 37
National Conference on Scientific and Technological Work **Vol. 3**: 264
National Congress of Workers, Peasants, and Soldiers **Vol. 1**: 191, 255; **Vol. 3**: 112
National Cultural System Reform Work Conference **Vol. 3**: 511
National Defense Law **Vol. 3**: 436
National Development and Reform Commission **Vol. 3**: 538–539
National Economic Plan **Vol. 3**: 61
National Energy Leading Group **Vol. 3**: 539
National Ethnic Work Conference **Vol. 2**: 250
National Ethnic Work Plan **Vol. 2**: 158
National Federation of Literature and Arts **Vol. 2**: 240
National Federation of Trade Unions **Vol. 3**: 311, 450
National General Assembly **Vol. 1**: 19
national independence **Vol. 1**: 173, 466, 470
National People's Congress **Vol. 1**: 268, 515; **Vol. 2**: 26, 48, 53, 153, 249, 251, 260, 277, 302; **Vol. 3**: 24, 56–57, 118–119, 123, 198, 217, 224, 226, 228, 230–232, 236, 254, 261–262, 269, 271, 274–275, 287, 299, 319–320, 349–350, 373, 376–377, 380–381, 384, 399, 402, 413, 436, 439, 475, 482, 500, 503, 509, 517, 536, 551
National Planning Conference **Vol. 2**: 333–334; **Vol. 3**: 48
national religious groups **Vol. 3**: 126
national reunification **Vol. 3**: 413, 438
National Revolutionary Groups of the Far East **Vol. 1**: 92
National Riot Plan **Vol. 1**: 61
national salvation **Vol. 1**: 13, 233, 264, 282
National Salvation Times **Vol. 1**: 233
National Science and Technology Commission **Vol. 2**: 240; **Vol. 3**: 42
National Science Congress **Vol. 2**: 332; **Vol. 3**: 20, 45, 110
National Security Bureau **Vol. 3**: 104
National Socialist Party **Vol. 1**: 69

National Statistical Bureau **Vol. 3**: 278
National Symposium on Ethnic Work **Vol. 2**: 250
National United Front Conference **Vol. 2**: 59, 250
National United Front Work Conference **Vol. 2**: 79, 250; **Vol. 3**: 129–131, 133, 375
national unity **Vol. 2**: 157, 250; **Vol. 3**: 119–122, 124, 126, 336, 401
National University of Defense Science and Technology **Vol. 3**: 434
National Workers, Peasants, and Soldiers Congress **Vol. 1**: 105, 191, 255; **Vol. 3**: 112
Nationalism, Democracy, the People's Livelihood **Vol. 1**: 264, 518
Nationalist Party (*see also* Kuomintang) **Vol. 1**: 41, 93, 109, 266
nationalities (*see also* ethnic groups) **Vol. 1**: 523; **Vol. 2**: 26, 157, 249; **Vol. 3**: 314
nationalization of industry **Vol. 2**: 72, 85
nationalization of Marxism **Vol. 2**: 225
Naval Engineering University **Vol. 3**: 434
Navy **Vol. 3**: 156–157, 226
new capitalism **Vol. 2**: 45, 335; **Vol. 3**: 394, 508
New China **Vol. 1**: 72–73, 76, 79, 81, 85–86, 132, 210, 263, 265, 306, 369, 424, 439, 466–467, 494, 498, 510–511, 517; **Vol. 2**: 4, 11–12, 16, 20, 22, 24, 26, 32, 39, 41, 44–45, 48, 52–53, 55–56, 58–59, 61–63, 65–66, 70, 80, 82–83, 87–95, 97–101, 103, 108–111, 114–116, 119, 122, 126, 129, 132, 140, 146, 148, 155, 156, 165, 180, 187, 203, 226, 231, 238, 253, 261, 284–285, 293, 296, 298, 308, 312, 315, 320, 325, 333, 335, 337; **Vol. 3**: 6, 15–16, 18, 47, 60, 80, 84, 92, 96, 98, 102–103, 109, 114–115, 119, 126, 128, 130, 141, 145–146, 148, 155, 158–162, 164–168, 170–171, 174, 203, 208, 225, 234, 240, 248, 252, 256, 270, 274, 316, 358, 363, 373, 387, 394, 404, 416, 427, 484, 498, 508, 512–513, 530, 545
New Citizen Study Society **Vol. 1**: 17; **Vol. 2**: 45, 335; **Vol. 3**: 394, 508
New Constitutional Referendum **Vol. 2**: 45, 335; **Vol. 3**: 394, 508, 521
New Cultural Movement **Vol. 1**: 4–5, 8, 10, 541, 546, 548

New Democracy **Vol. 1**: 65, 67, 69, 71, 73, 75–79, 81, 83, 85, 87, 89, 99, 106–108, 110, 112, 117, 131, 146, 199, 209, 268, 467–468, 482, 487, 491, 509, 513, 515, 520, 522–523, 525, 528, 531, 534, 536–537, 539, 542–544, 546, 548; **Vol. 2**: 4, 13, 25, 27–34, 37, 40–42, 47, 49, 51–52, 56–59, 62–63, 65, 69–70, 72, 76–78, 81–83, 86–91, 95, 98–99, 104–105, 111–112, 114, 116–117, 119, 121, 141, 208–209, 274; **Vol. 3**: 252, 364

New Democracy National Founding Program **Vol. 2**: 95

New Democracy Program **Vol. 2**: 4, 57, 63, 69, 81, 87, 117

New Democratic Outline for the Founding of the People's Republic **Vol. 1**: 527, 535; **Vol. 2**: 4

New Democratic Revolution **Vol. 1**: 23, 25, 27, 29, 31, 33, 35, 37, 39, 41, 43, 45, 47, 49, 51, 53, 55, 57, 59, 61, 63, 71–73, 75, 78, 84–85, 89, 91, 93, 95, 97, 99, 101, 103, 105, 107–111, 113, 115–119, 121, 123, 125–127, 129–133, 135, 137–141, 143–147, 188, 199, 245–247, 263, 266, 268, 301, 370, 372, 421–422, 448, 460, 467–470, 487, 494, 508, 511–512, 521, 523, 527–529, 531, 534–536, 543, 548; **Vol. 2**: 3–4, 11, 27–29, 38–39, 41, 48, 53, 56, 63, 69, 72, 87, 89, 94, 98–99, 110, 114, 117, 126, 129, 143–144; **Vol. 3**: 180, 247, 252, 358

New Democratic Revolutionary Theory **Vol. 1**: 130, 507, 512, 527, 535; **Vol. 2**: 25, 32

New Democratic Socialization Theory **Vol. 1**: 527, 535; **Vol. 2**: 25

New Democratic Sociology **Vol. 1**: 527, 535; **Vol. 2**: 27, 41

New Democratic Theory **Vol. 1**: 73, 81–82, 85, 89, 107, 109, 130, 198, 495, 507, 523, 527–528, 535; **Vol. 2**: 4, 70, 93, 105, 117

new deployment of rural reform **Vol. 3**: 536

New Fourth Army **Vol. 1**: 69, 202, 241, 285–286, 311, 336–337; **Vol. 3**: 106–107

New Great Project **Vol. 3**: 443–444, 447–448, 474, 476, 484

New Historical Period **Vol. 3**: 18, 120, 130–131, 170, 182, 191, 254, 311, 457, 525

New Long March **Vol. 3**: 37, 140, 154

New Right (KMT) **Vol. 1**: 41, 93, 216, 221, 226

New Territories (Hong Kong) **Vol. 3**: 234, 416

New Youth (Youth Magazine) **Vol. 1**: 4, 7–8, 12, 16

Ni Zhengyu **Vol. 3**: 224

Ni Zhifu **Vol. 3**: 189

Nie Rongzhen **Vol. 2**: 156, 240, 300; **Vol. 3**: 33, 73, 76, 179, 188–189, 288

Nie Yuanzi **Vol. 2**: 300; **Vol. 3**: 78

Nikolsky, Vladimir **Vol. 1**: 19

Ningdu Uprising **Vol. 3**: 104

Ningxia Province **Vol. 1**: 76, 160, 199, 201, 203–204, 206–209, 211, 530; **Vol. 2**: 30, 323; **Vol. 3**: 122, 125, 455

Ningxiang County **Vol. 2**: 233

Ninth Five-Year Plan **Vol. 3**: 380, 384, 399, 401, 481

Ninth National Congress of the Communist Party of China **Vol. 3**: 179, 380

non-Party democrats **Vol. 2**: 81, 179, 249 **Vol. 3**: 133

non-public enterprises **Vol. 3**: 452

Nong'an County Committee **Vol. 3**: 115

North China Bureau **Vol. 2**: 71–72, 74, 76

North China Finance and Economic Commission **Vol. 2**: 37

North China University **Vol. 1**: 492

North China Territorial Doctrine **Vol. 3**: 76–77

North Korean Denuclearization Target Document **Vol. 3**: 519

Northeast Army **Vol. 1**: 234

Northeast Group **Vol. 3**: 53

Northeast Military Work Committee **Vol. 1**: 234

Northern Expedition **Vol. 1**: 24, 37–38, 40, 110, 150, 171, 221, 226–227, 267, 273, 275, 277, 279, 283–284, 371, 467; **Vol. 3**: 227

Northern War **Vol. 3**: 71

Northern Warlords (*see also* Beiyang Warlords) **Vol. 1**: 137, 150, 226, 467

Northwest Bureau **Vol. 1**: 310; **Vol. 3**: 101–102

Northwest Field Army **Vol. 1**: 356, 532

Northwest United University **Vol. 3**: 97

Northwestern High-level Conference **Vol. 1**:

205
Nuclear Power Management of the National Defense Science, Technology, and Industry Commission **Vol. 2**: 304; **Vol. 3**: 176, 211, 539
Nyers, Rezsö **Vol. 3**: 197

O

October Revolution **Vol. 1**: 6–7, 28, 30, 60, 89, 92, 108, 110–113, 150, 154, 162, 164–165, 182, 188, 227, 274, 276, 363, 370, 430, 432, 458, 542; **Vol. 2**: 14, 121, 126, 136, 142, 278; **Vol. 3**: 146
Office of Institutional Reform **Vol. 3**: 277
old cadres **Vol. 3**: 187, 286, 290
Ombudsman **Vol. 3**: 407
On Contradiction **Vol. 1**: 367, 437; **Vol. 2**: 80, 188; **Vol. 3**: 5, 206, 226, 282, 514
"On Investigation" (*see also* "Opposing Doctrines") **Vol. 2**: 233
On New Democracy **Vol. 1**: 491; **Vol. 2**: 27–30, 37, 45, 49, 86, 141
On Practice **Vol. 1**: 367, 437, 443; **Vol. 2**: 136, 174, 211, 233, 313; **Vol. 3**: 332
On Ten Relations **Vol. 2**: 7, 148, 150, 210
On the Correct Handling of Contradictions Among the People **Vol. 1**: 178; **Vol. 2**: 7, 168
On the Party **Vol. 1**: 117, 178, 249, 391, 402; **Vol. 2**: 144, 161, 180, 221, 295; **Vol. 3**: 34, 52, 88
On the People's Democratic Dictatorship **Vol. 1**: 89, 178, 249; **Vol. 2**: 116, 144
"On the People's Democratic Dictatorship" (article) **Vol. 2**: 49
On the Ten Relations **Vol. 1**: 178, 249
"On the United Government" **Vol. 2**: 30, 37, 45
one center, two basic points **Vol. 1**: 349; **Vol. 3**: 227
one country, two systems **Vol. 1**: 349; **Vol. 3**: 227
Open Rural Affairs **Vol. 3**: 377
Opium War **Vol. 1**: 3, 50, 96, 110, 114, 133, 517, 540; **Vol. 3**: 234, 416
opportunism **Vol. 1**: 44, 57, 120, 122, 145, 277, 296, 311, 358, 378, 389, 391, 474; **Vol. 2**: 38, 177, 235, 256; **Vol. 3**: 92, 160
"Opposing Doctrines" ("On Investigation") **Vol. 2**: 233

"Opposing Doctrinairism" (article) **Vol. 1**: 478
Organic Law of the CPPCC **Vol. 1**: 267–268
organization **Vol. 1**: 8, 12–13, 17–20, 45, 56, 68, 78, 80, 88, 140, 142, 144, 184, 187, 190, 208, 210–211, 219–220, 222, 225–226, 228, 233, 241, 255, 258–259, 261, 265–268, 271, 282–283, 285, 290, 304, 307–308, 310, 314, 321, 324, 333, 336, 343, 359, 361, 363–370, 372, 374, 376–377, 379–383, 385, 388, 394–396, 399–400, 402–404, 409–410, 413–415, 417–419, 421–422, 424–425, 427–428, 432, 434, 438–440, 460–461, 471, 488, 495, 513, 523, 531; **Vol. 2**: 49, 78, 116, 159–160, 192–193, 195–196, 223, 288, 292, 295, 298, 302, 322, 338; **Vol. 3**: 15, 17, 71, 79, 91, 93–94, 104, 106, 109, 112, 114, 181–182, 186, 271, 280–282, 296–297, 307, 354, 357, 377, 406, 414, 424, 427–429, 433, 448, 450–452, 465, 532
Organization Newsletter **Vol. 3**: 17, 94
Organizational Communications **Vol. 3**: 90, 447
organizational construction **Vol. 1**: 364–365, 368–369, 379, 394, 403, 408, 419, 428; **Vol. 3**: 280, 447–448, 450, 452
Organizational Work Conference **Vol. 1**: 512; **Vol. 2**: 86; **Vol. 3**: 447
orthodoxy **Vol. 1**: 164; **Vol. 2**: 23, 138
Outline of Vision for 2010 **Vol. 3**: 384
overseas Chinese **Vol. 1**: 228, 258, 261, 266, 268, 516; **Vol. 2**: 53, 250; **Vol. 3**: 67, 132, 134, 182
Overseas Chinese Daily **Vol. 3**: 233
Overseas Chinese Office **Vol. 3**: 67
Overseas Economic Cooperation Fund **Vol. 3**: 210

P

Palace of Hell **Vol. 3**: 82
Pan Hannian **Vol. 3**: 80–81, 98
Pan Keming **Vol. 3**: 299
Paris Commune Uprising **Vol. 1**: 358
Paris Coordination Commission **Vol. 3**: 217
Party Charter **Vol. 1**: 8, 362, 406; **Vol. 2**: 292; **Vol. 3**: 281
Party Committee System **Vol. 1**: 403, 410–411, 503
Party constitution **Vol. 1**: 84, 382, 402, 410–411,

424, 452, 455, 460, 486, 488, 500; **Vol. 2**: 159–162, 244, 314; **Vol. 3**: 151, 177–178, 181, 184–186, 188, 190, 287, 340, 360, 453, 467, 474–475, 526
Party construction **Vol. 1**: 75, 285, 367–368, 372, 376, 432; **Vol. 3**: 451–452
Party discipline **Vol. 1**: 405–406, 411, 424; **Vol. 2**: 160; **Vol. 3**: 62, 280, 298, 320–322, 464–465
Party Group **Vol. 1**: 307; **Vol. 2**: 240; **Vol. 3**: 43, 66, 87, 99, 108, 117, 121, 299, 321
Party leadership **Vol. 1**: 43, 88, 165, 230, 243, 275, 308, 313, 368–369, 404, 408, 422, 429, 439, 466, 469, 471, 478; **Vol. 2**: 180, 276, 288, 300–301, 309; **Vol. 3**: 47, 360, 514
Party Life **Vol. 1**: 200, 365, 413, 418, 420, 427, 440, 450–451, 455, 479
Party membership **Vol. 1**: 57, 364, 419–420, 422–424, 512; **Vol. 2**: 69; **Vol. 3**: 85, 97, 105–108, 188, 287
party organization **Vol. 1**: 18–20, 68, 78, 220, 228, 258, 361–365, 368, 370, 377, 381, 385, 394–395, 400, 403, 409, 413, 421–422, 432, 438, 471; **Vol. 2**: 223, 288, 292, 298; **Vol. 3**: 79
Party spirit **Vol. 1**: 70, 380, 411, 416–417, 423, 432, 436–438, 443–444, 449, 451
party-building **Vol. 1**: 46, 284–285, 357, 359–379, 381, 383, 385, 387, 389, 391, 393–395, 397, 399–401, 403, 405, 407, 409–411, 413, 415, 417, 419, 421–423, 425, 427–429, 431, 433–435, 437, 439, 441, 443, 445, 447–451, 453, 455, 457–461, 463, 465, 467, 469, 471, 473, 475, 477, 479, 488, 491, 497, 500, 504–505; **Vol. 2**: 162–163
Party's absolute leadership of the military **Vol. 1**: 306, 311–313
Party's basic line **Vol. 1**: 404; **Vol. 3**: 4, 152, 174, 239, 243–244, 253–257, 303, 325, 328, 332, 358, 361, 363, 366, 368, 385, 398, 432, 447, 453, 458, 514, 533
Pastoral Work, Forty Articles of **Vol. 2**: 250
Patriotic Education **Vol. 3**: 383
peaceful evolution **Vol. 3**: 323, 332, 447
peaceful reunification **Vol. 3**: 225, 228–230, 232, 340, 414–415, 420, 438, 516, 520–521, 546
peasant class (*see also* peasantry) **Vol. 1**: 33, 72, 109, 113, 127, 129, 141, 143, 185, 253, 283, 288, 310, 330; **Vol. 2**: 41, 49, 80, 83
peasant movements **Vol. 1**: 50, 171
peasant party **Vol. 1**: 153, 361–362; **Vol. 2**: 67, 69–70
peasant revolution **Vol. 1**: 33, 44–45, 47, 49–50, 52, 54, 58, 62, 143, 152, 287, 331
peasant self-defense force **Vol. 1**: 153
peasantry (*see also* peasant class) **Vol. 1**: 33–34, 50, 53–54, 63, 120–123, 125, 127–129, 140–141, 143–144, 163, 168, 191, 194, 196–197, 219, 227, 241, 246, 252–253, 279–280, 282, 309, 330, 362, 371, 378, 420–421, 471, 487, 491, 501, 507–508, 512, 517, 519, 523, 526–528, 532
peasants' allied force **Vol. 1**: 164
Peking Girl's High School **Vol. 1**: 8
Peking People's Art Theatre **Vol. 3**: 32
Peking University (Beijing University) **Vol. 1**: 8, 10, 14–15, 17, 258; **Vol. 3**: 23, 78–79, 434
Peking University Civilians Lecture Group **Vol. 1**: 14
Peng Dehuai **Vol. 2**: 217, 275; **Vol. 3**: 15, 53–54, 81, 91, 93, 101–102
Peng Gongda **Vol. 1**: 57
Peng Peiyun **Vol. 3**: 78–79
Peng Shuzhi **Vol. 1**: 124–125
Peng Zemin **Vol. 1**: 264
Peng Zhen **Vol. 3**: 72, 81, 179, 188–189, 211
Peng, Gao, and Xi Anti-Party Group **Vol. 3**: 101–102
Penghu **Vol. 3**: 228
People's Bank of China **Vol. 3**: 354, 538–539
People's Commune Movement **Vol. 2**: 9, 130, 192, 195–197, 199–200, 204, 206, 211–213, 218, 221–222, 231, 239, 246, 267, 270, 273, 325
People's Congress **Vol. 1**: 190, 192, 268, 509, 515; **Vol. 2**: 7, 26, 48, 50, 53, 77–78, 141, 153, 221, 243, 246–247, 249–254, 256–257, 260, 277, 302; **Vol. 3**: 24, 56–57, 118–119, 123, 198, 217, 224, 226, 228, 230–232, 236, 254, 261–262, 269, 271–272, 274–275, 287, 299, 319–320, 349–350, 365, 367, 373, 376–377, 380–381, 384, 402, 413, 436, 439, 454, 475, 482, 500, 503, 509–510, 517, 536, 551

People's Court (provincial or municipal) **Vol. 3**: 321

People's Daily **Vol. 1**: 7; **Vol. 2**: 117, 143, 166, 179, 188–189, 272, 278–280, 296, 314, 322–323, 328; **Vol. 3**: 12–13, 17, 19, 21, 24, 26, 28, 30, 32, 35–38, 40–42, 53, 79, 137, 153, 165, 195, 217, 318, 373, 394

people's democratic dictatorship **Vol. 1**: 85, 89, 146, 261, 268, 282, 468, 510, 513, 516–521, 523; **Vol. 2**: 7, 25, 32, 41, 48–51, 79–80, 87, 92, 116, 153; **Vol. 3**: 250, 316, 318, 337, 365, 367, 440

People's Democratic United Front **Vol. 1**: 87–88, 244–245, 254, 256, 261–262, 264, 268–269, 271; **Vol. 2**: 53, 79–80, 87, 153, 170, 320

People's Liberation Army (PLA) **Vol. 1**: 86, 188, 247, 258, 261, 281, 286, 305, 309, 311, 313, 342, 494, 500, 516; **Vol. 2**: 53–54, 272, 295; **Vol. 3**: 41, 82, 137, 153, 169, 178, 225–226, 228–229, 433, 435, 517

People's Liberation War **Vol. 1**: 86, 188

People's Literature **Vol. 3**: 30

People's Republic **Vol. 1**: 88, 268, 284–285, 421, 467, 508, 517, 520, 523, 534, 539; **Vol. 2**: 4–5, 25–26, 39, 48, 51–55, 57, 63, 69, 76–77, 79, 82, 86–87, 89–90, 110–111, 117–118, 165, 183, 209, 233, 240, 304; **Vol. 3**: 4, 44, 77, 87, 97, 108, 111, 119, 122, 131, 140, 144, 158–159, 161–163, 165, 167–169, 172, 213–215, 224, 228–229, 233–237, 248, 252–253, 263, 275, 287, 310–311, 333, 335, 345, 376–378, 402, 413, 416–417, 460, 475, 498, 519, 541, 551

People's Republic of China **Vol. 1**: 88, 268, 284–285, 421, 517, 520, 523, 539; **Vol. 2**: 25–26, 39, 48, 51–53, 55, 57, 63, 77, 79, 86, 89–90, 110–111, 118, 165, 183, 233, 240, 304; **Vol. 3**: 4, 44, 77, 87, 97, 108, 111, 119, 122, 140, 144, 158–159, 162–163, 165, 169, 172, 213–215, 224, 228–229, 233–237, 248, 252–253, 263, 275, 287, 310, 345, 376–378, 402, 413, 416–417, 460, 475, 498, 519, 541, 551

People's Self-Defense Force **Vol. 1**: 333–334

personnel system **Vol. 3**: 269, 271, 277, 279, 295, 460

Petőfi Club **Vol. 2**: 259

Pingjiang **Vol. 1**: 61

Pingjin **Vol. 1**: 328, 342, 352–355

Pioneer **Vol. 1**: 13, 16; **Vol. 2**: 338

PLA (*see also* People's Liberation Army) **Vol. 1**: 86–89, 188, 248, 254, 256, 265–266, 268, 280, 285, 290, 298, 306, 315, 317–319, 324–325, 328, 350, 353, 505; **Vol. 2**: 314, 326; **Vol. 3**: 36, 42, 73, 156, 158, 176, 228, 281, 306, 429, 433–434, 436, 438–440

planned economy **Vol. 1**: 202; **Vol. 2**: 13–15, 17, 20, 36, 105–106, 108, 119, 130, 132, 151–152, 174, 186, 223–226, 287–288; **Vol. 3**: 21, 191–192, 194–196, 199–201, 328–329, 335, 344–348, 352, 357, 365, 461, 480, 540, 545

police **Vol. 1**: 260–261, 519; **Vol. 3**: 435, 464

Policies for Foreign Experts and Allies **Vol. 2**: 113; **Vol. 3**: 117

Policy of Intelligence Workers **Vol. 1**: 195

Politburo **Vol. 1**: 42, 45, 48, 51, 55–59, 79, 103–104, 154, 167, 199, 222, 229, 231–232, 240, 400, 482, 495, 501, 503, 511, 516; **Vol. 2**: 32, 51, 60, 63, 85, 105, 110, 143, 156, 166, 188, 191, 214, 240, 247, 257, 300; **Vol. 3**: 10, 12, 16, 38, 52, 54, 59, 62, 71, 73, 91, 138, 165, 168, 175–179, 189, 200, 218, 232, 245–246, 259, 268–270, 273, 286, 306, 309, 319, 323–325, 331, 380, 409, 455–456, 465, 509, 513, 515

political boundary issues **Vol. 3**: 518

political consultation **Vol. 1**: 87, 264; **Vol. 2**: 7, 52–54, 79, 152; **Vol. 3**: 272, 365, 367, 372–373, 375, 510

political line **Vol. 1**: 63–64, 285, 365, 367, 378, 403–404, 433, 470, 482; **Vol. 2**: 306; **Vol. 3**: 4, 13, 28, 53, 157–158, 285, 331, 457

political strike **Vol. 1**: 153

political struggle (*see also* struggle) **Vol. 1**: 35, 115, 122, 259–260, 263, 290; **Vol. 2**: 138, 190, 242, 281

political system reform **Vol. 3**: 244, 255, 268–270, 273, 275, 316–317, 369–372, 376, 380, 547

Political Weekly **Vol. 1**: 103

Polytechnic University **Vol. 3**: 434

populism **Vol. 1**: 55–56, 535; **Vol. 2**: 30, 39

popularization of Marxism **Vol. 3**: 7

Practical Theory **Vol. 1**: 66, 68, 183, 389–391
practice is the sole criterion for testing truth **Vol. 3**: 157
pre-Qin scholars **Vol. 3**: 31
primary stage of socialism **Vol. 2**: 133; **Vol. 3**: 152, 239, 241, 243, 245, 249–252, 254–258, 266, 268, 270, 303, 325, 335, 338, 354, 358, 360–363, 366–368, 493–494, 526, 544
Printing Industry Management Regulations **Vol. 3**: 394
private sector **Vol. 3**: 451
production **Vol. 1**: 4–6, 8, 12, 29, 44, 53, 123, 127, 131–132, 162, 174, 184, 192–193, 196–197, 203–208, 246–247, 255, 270–271, 282, 293–294, 302, 304–306, 312, 328, 335, 361, 383, 393, 457, 468, 473, 496–500, 502, 505–506, 519, 524, 526–527, 529–530, 533, 535–536; **Vol. 2**: 4, 6, 9, 15, 26, 28, 30–31, 33–35, 39–40, 42–44, 51, 57–58, 60, 62, 64–69, 72, 74–76, 84, 87–88, 91, 94, 100, 102–103, 105–108, 112–115, 118–119, 121–128, 131–133, 135–139, 141, 146–148, 150–151, 154–155, 164–165, 168–169, 181, 183, 185, 187, 189–190, 192–193, 195–197, 200–203, 205, 207, 214, 216–219, 222–223, 235–239, 243, 247–250, 253–257, 260–261, 267, 269–271, 281, 284, 286–288, 293–294, 297, 299–300, 302–304, 310, 320, 327–328, 333–334; **Vol. 3**: 3, 10, 21–22, 25–27, 48–51, 55, 61, 64, 72, 75, 142, 149, 171, 183, 192–195, 197–198, 200–201, 209, 250–251, 253, 256, 260, 262, 275, 304, 309, 325, 329, 344, 349, 352–353, 355–356, 365, 394, 406–407, 433, 435, 480, 489, 493, 498, 503, 507, 509, 511, 531–532, 542–544
program of action **Vol. 1**: 246, 543; **Vol. 2**: 48; **Vol. 3**: 244, 343
proletarian (*see also* proletariat) **Vol. 1**: 12, 17, 21, 28, 30, 35, 37, 39, 53, 63, 75, 100, 102, 104, 107–108, 110–114, 116–118, 123, 126–128, 140–142, 149, 153–154, 161, 163–164, 178, 185–186, 188, 194, 213, 217–220, 225, 229, 271, 275–277, 284–285, 288, 299, 301, 306–310, 321, 326, 331, 357–364, 370, 372, 374–378, 380–382, 384–385, 388, 392, 394, 396–399, 406, 421–423, 426, 429, 434, 437, 440, 442–445, 447, 457–458, 461, 472, 474, 479, 487, 507–508, 514, 516, 520, 526, 541–542, 544–545; **Vol. 2**: 18, 20, 27, 33–34, 36, 50–51, 118, 135–136, 139, 143, 152, 166, 208, 262, 274–276, 278–279, 282, 295, 301–302, 315; **Vol. 3**: 77–78, 101, 119, 137, 146, 160–161, 169, 240, 242, 245–246, 316
proletarian dictatorship **Vol. 1**: 12, 363, 514; **Vol. 2**: 34, 50–51, 118, 136, 143, 152, 166; **Vol. 3**: 137, 146
proletarian organization **Vol. 1**: 308, 399
proletariat (*see also* proletarian) **Vol. 1**: 4, 13, 19–20, 26–30, 32, 34–35, 50, 53–54, 57, 60, 63, 72–78, 89, 92, 94, 100–106, 108–118, 122–125, 127–131, 138–146, 149–150, 152, 154, 162–163, 171, 173, 175–176, 180, 190–191, 194, 196–197, 199, 213–215, 217–218, 220–222, 224–225, 227, 230–231, 241, 243, 252, 255, 263, 267, 269, 276–279, 282–284, 286–287, 298, 301, 308–310, 330–331, 357–359, 362, 364–365, 371–372, 374–378, 381, 383, 394, 397, 405, 417, 419–422, 425, 429–431, 433–435, 438, 443–444, 447, 449, 457–458, 466–468, 470–471, 478–479, 487, 490, 497, 504, 507, 509, 513, 515–517, 519–524, 530–531, 534–536, 538, 541–544, 547; **Vol. 2**: 25, 27–28, 31–37, 43–47, 49–51, 53–54, 91–92, 103, 125–126, 135–136, 184–185, 219, 257, 262, 272–273, 275, 277–283, 288, 290, 294–296, 299–300, 306–307, 315, 318–319, 335; **Vol. 3**: 21, 23, 49, 51, 58, 140–142, 145, 147, 149–150, 161, 252, 283, 329
propaganda **Vol. 1**: 7–8, 25, 36, 40, 48, 69, 75, 128, 144, 163, 191, 210–211, 220, 222, 248, 286, 319, 376, 404, 464, 492, 537, 543–544; **Vol. 2**: 6, 56, 72, 82, 85, 104, 110, 115, 117, 135, 156–157, 176–177, 179, 184, 240, 289, 315, 317, 323; **Vol. 3**: 37–39, 55, 63, 68, 82, 89–90, 121–122, 138, 140–142, 144, 154, 158, 312, 316, 325, 373, 383–384, 393, 470–471
Propaganda Outline **Vol. 2**: 6, 110, 115
Protection of Taiwanese Compatriots' Investment **Vol. 3**: 413
Protection of the Rights of Party Members **Vol. 3**: 453, 466
Proudhon, Pierre-Joseph **Vol. 1**: 6

Provincial Civil Affairs Department **Vol. 3**: 108
Provincial Military Control Council **Vol. 3**: 96
Provincial People's Congress **Vol. 1**: 515
Provincial Reform Commission **Vol. 3**: 96
Provincial Reform Committee **Vol. 3**: 72–73
public ownership **Vol. 2**: 6, 8, 14, 103, 106, 108, 114, 118, 120, 124, 130, 141, 165, 193, 195–196, 200–202, 205, 213–214, 219, 223, 237, 297–298; **Vol. 3**: 21, 146, 150, 193–195, 200–202, 249–251, 279, 329, 335, 337, 345, 349–350, 352, 365–366, 410, 473, 489, 491, 493–494, 496, 507, 511
Public Welfare Culture Reform **Vol. 3**: 511
Publicity (Propaganda) Committee **Vol. 1**: 20, 131
Publishing Management Regulations **Vol. 3**: 394
Pudong **Vol. 3**: 4, 354
Pudong District **Vol. 3**: 4

Q
Qi Qi **Vol. 3**: 192
Qian Qichen **Vol. 3**: 220
Qian Ying **Vol. 1**: 257; **Vol. 3**: 72
Qiao Shi **Vol. 3**: 189, 245
Qiliying **Vol. 2**: 204
Qin Jiwei **Vol. 3**: 189, 245
Qing Dynasty (Qing court) **Vol. 1**: 133, 135, 267, 514
Qingdao **Vol. 1**: 34; **Vol. 3**: 277, 410
Qinghai Province **Vol. 3**: 125, 502
Qingming Festival (see Tomb-Sweeping Day)
Qinhuangdao Port **Vol. 3**: 210
Qionglai County **Vol. 3**: 277
Qu Qiubai **Vol. 1**: 29–30, 34, 36, 43, 52–53, 55–56, 58, 102, 105, 126–127, 139, 167, 274; **Vol. 3**: 81
Quanzhou City **Vol. 3**: 320

R
radicalism **Vol. 2**: 262, 264
Radio and Television Management Regulations **Vol. 3**: 394
re-education **Vol. 3**: 121–122
re-employment of laid-off workers **Vol. 3**: 408

reactionary **Vol. 1**: 24, 26, 37, 41, 44, 56, 60, 62, 77, 85–89, 127, 135–136, 138, 149, 163, 172, 181, 197, 216, 242, 245–250, 258, 260, 265, 268–270, 272, 274, 276, 280–282, 288, 291–293, 301, 312, 320–321, 329, 339, 350, 355, 401, 420, 467, 495, 500, 505, 519–520, 528, 533, 535, 540–541; **Vol. 2**: 49, 104, 257, 264, 275, 283, 286, 289–291, 295–297; Vol 3: 22, 151, 226, 228, 304
Reagan, Ronald **Vol. 3**: 215–216
rectification **Vol. 1**: 54, 83–84, 210, 282, 366–370, 380, 385–389, 391, 394, 402, 410, 421, 423, 425, 427–428, 433–434, 437–440, 448, 484–486, 492, 512; **Vol. 2**: 167, 175–182, 184–185, 188–189, 192, 199, 203, 207–209, 211, 213, 215, 220–221, 226–227, 230, 235, 237, 246, 297, 299, 302–303, 309, 312–313, 320, 324, 329, 335–336, 339; **Vol. 3**: 4–5, 10, 19, 65–66, 78, 81, 84, 88, 90, 93–94, 100, 118, 139, 152, 155, 158–159, 175, 183, 186, 280, 282–284, 301–302, 325, 334, 454–457, 515
Rectification Movement **Vol. 1**: 83–84, 210, 282, 367–368, 380, 385–389, 391, 394, 402, 410, 421, 425, 433–434, 437, 439, 448, 484–486; **Vol. 2**: 175–182, 184–185, 189; **Vol. 3**: 155, 457
Red Army **Vol. 1**: 59–62, 66, 153, 156–161, 164, 168–172, 174–176, 178–181, 183, 185, 193, 229–231, 233–236, 279, 285–286, 288, 296, 299–300, 304–305, 307, 311, 316–317, 319, 321, 323, 331–332, 334, 336, 341, 350, 361, 364–367, 382, 420, 459; **Vol. 3**: 15, 104–105, 432
Red Army University **Vol. 1**: 288
Red Flag **Vol. 1**: 59, 170, 176, 279; **Vol. 2**: 190, 194, 278–279, 314, 323; **Vol. 3**: 33, 38, 40, 55, 79–80, 137
Red Flag Party **Vol. 3**: 79–80
Red Guards **Vol. 1**: 175, 332, 334, 336
Red regime **Vol. 1**: 53, 170–173, 179–180, 182, 292, 331, 365
redeployment **Vol. 3**: 124
Reform and Opening Up **Vol. 2**: 22–23, 249, 304, 310, 313, 329–330, 332, 334–338; **Vol. 3**: 3–5, 7, 9, 18, 32, 44–45, 48–49, 51–52, 56, 61, 123, 129, 132–133, 181, 192, 225, 241–243, 251–252, 254–256, 279, 292, 297, 301–306, 310,

313, 318, 323–324, 326–328, 330–337, 341, 343, 348, 350, 352–353, 355, 357–359, 364, 369, 379, 381, 384, 387, 391, 397, 402, 408, 416, 422, 427, 435, 437, 444, 446–447, 454, 461, 475, 480, 482, 484, 488, 497–498, 501–502, 506, 513, 524–526, 531, 534, 536, 541, 545–547, 549–551

Reform Group of the Financial and Economic Committee **Vol. 3**: 193

Reform Movement of 1888 **Vol. 1**: 140

Reform Movement of 1898 **Vol. 1**: 110

reform of the cultural system **Vol. 2**: 20; **Vol. 3**: 389, 393, 511

rejuvenating the nation **Vol. 3**: 398

Religious Affairs Bureau (*see also* Bureau of Religious Affairs) **Vol. 3**: 126, 128

Religious Policy **Vol. 3**: 116, 122, 126, 128

Removing Chaos **Vol. 2**: 327

Ren Bishi **Vol. 1**: 254, 484, 497–498, 501–502, 504–505; **Vol. 2**: 40

Ren Wanding **Vol. 3**: 142

Ren Zhuoxuan (*see* Ye Qing) **Vol. 1**: 70

Republic of China **Vol. 1**: 4, 24, 88, 114, 268, 284–285, 421, 517, 520, 523, 539; **Vol. 2**: 25–26, 39, 48, 51–53, 55, 57, 63, 77, 79, 86, 89–90, 110–111, 118, 165, 183, 233, 240, 304; **Vol. 3**: 4, 44, 77, 87, 97, 108, 111, 119, 122, 140, 144, 158–159, 162–163, 165, 169, 172, 213–215, 224, 228–229, 231, 233–237, 248, 252–253, 263, 275, 287, 310, 345, 376–378, 402, 413, 416–417, 460, 475, 498, 519, 541, 551

Republic of China in Taiwan **Vol. 3**: 233

Republic of Workers and Farmers **Vol. 1**: 508

Resolution of the Central Committee of the Communist Party of China on Some Historical Issues of the Party Since the Founding of the People's Republic of China **Vol. 3**: 3

Resolution on Land Issues **Vol. 1**: 49

Resolution on Relations between the KMT and the CPC **Vol. 1**: 215

Resolution on Several Historical Issues **Vol. 1**: 387, 485; **Vol. 3**: 102, 131, 163, 165, 168, 311, 335

Resolution on the Party's Organizational Issues **Vol. 1**: 45

Resolution on the Relationship between the Communist Party of China and the Kuomintang **Vol. 1**: 35

Resolution on the United Workers and Peasants **Vol. 1**: 32

Restructuring Party **Vol. 3**: 102

revisionism **Vol. 1**: 358; **Vol. 2**: 14, 184, 219, 253, 256, 259, 265–266, 268, 273, 279–280, 282–283, 287–291, 294–295; **Vol. 3**: 27, 161

Revolutionary Army of Workers and Peasants **Vol. 1**: 140, 315

Revolutionary Base Area **Vol. 1**: 36, 82, 140, 174, 176, 189, 329

revolutionary bourgeoisie **Vol. 1**: 101, 121, 140

revolutionary path (se also revolutionary road) **Vol. 1**: 37, 49, 140, 149, 151, 153, 155, 157, 159–161, 163, 165–167, 169, 171, 173, 175, 177–179, 181–183, 185, 187, 189, 191, 193, 195, 197, 199, 201, 203, 205, 207, 209, 211, 361, 379, 389, 466, 470

revolutionary practice **Vol. 1**: 23, 25, 29, 37, 81–82, 140–141, 151, 163, 169, 188, 273, 406, 428, 443–446, 463, 484, 508; **Vol. 2**: 262; **Vol. 3**: 37, 41–42

revolutionary road (*see also* revolutionary path) **Vol. 1**: 140, 149, 163, 176, 178; **Vol. 2**: 5

revolutionary struggle **Vol. 1**: 23, 25, 29, 37, 45, 47, 50–51, 54, 56, 62, 78, 92, 130, 140, 142, 149, 151, 155, 157, 161, 176, 182, 186, 190, 192, 198, 271, 277, 283, 285–286, 300, 308, 312–313, 330, 357, 362–363, 372, 376, 397, 399, 403, 419, 423, 425, 431, 440, 442, 444, 456–457, 464, 466–467, 469, 472–473, 490, 521, 531; **Vol. 2**: 53, 136, 268; **Vol. 3**: 62, 101, 115

Revolutionary United Front **Vol. 1**: 29, 93, 140–141, 218, 227, 235, 244, 268, 372

rich peasant (*see also* wealthy peasant) **Vol. 1**: 536; **Vol. 2**: 63, 65–66, 68–69, 125; **Vol. 3**: 113

right opportunists **Vol. 3**: 66, 87

Right-Wing Correction Office **Vol. 3**: 90

rightism **Vol. 2**: 183, 230, 312

Rightist deviation **Vol. 3**: 91, 93

Rightist errors **Vol. 1**: 46, 58, 232, 391, 401, 550; **Vol. 3**: 252

rightist labels **Vol. 3**: 87
Rightist tendencies **Vol. 3**: 241
riot **Vol. 1**: 48, 61, 151, 156, 165, 167–169, 179, 237, 276, 334
Rogachev, Igor **Vol. 3**: 219
Ruan Ming **Vol. 3**: 139
rule of law **Vol. 2**: 163, 269, 298; **Vol. 3**: 58, 137, 146, 379–381, 436, 499, 510, 514, 520, 532–534
ruling party **Vol. 1**: 285, 308, 370, 430, 458, 465, 504–505; **Vol. 2**: 158–159, 161–163, 183, 185, 190, 296–297; **Vol. 3**: 241, 243, 280, 336, 446, 472, 512–514
Rural People's Commune Work Regulations **Vol. 2**: 9, 235; **Vol. 3**: 52, 60, 112
Rural People's Commune Work Regulations (60 Agricultural Articles) **Vol. 2**: 9
rural policy **Vol. 2**: 63, 235, 328
rural reform **Vol. 3**: 61, 262, 335, 509–510, 523, 536, 542–545
rural revolutionary base **Vol. 1**: 82–83, 157–158, 164, 174–176, 195, 329, 364, 471
Rural Socialist Education Movement **Vol. 3**: 93
rural system **Vol. 3**: 544
rural to urban (transfer) **Vol. 1**: 370, 494–495, 497, 499
rural work **Vol. 1**: 83, 155, 255, 495; **Vol. 2**: 189, 328; **Vol. 3**: 543–544
Russell, Bertrand **Vol. 1**: 18
Russian Bolshevik Party **Vol. 1**: 358
Russian Revolution **Vol. 1**: 56, 113, 149, 152, 379; **Vol. 2**: 54, 137
Russian Social Democratic Labor Party **Vol. 1**: 397–398

S

SACO **Vol. 3**: 109
Sancatsu Mushakoji **Vol. 1**: 6
Sanming City **Vol. 3**: 313
Sanwan Reorganization **Vol. 1**: 315
SARS **Vol. 3**: 500–502
scar literature **Vol. 3**: 31
School of Marxism **Vol. 2**: 73
science education **Vol. 3**: 29
Science, Fourteen Articles of **Vol. 2**: 240, 254

scientific evaluation **Vol. 3**: 135, 159
Scientific View of Development **Vol. 3**: 479, 494, 497, 500–507, 512, 514, 523, 533, 550–551
Second Civil Revolutionary War **Vol. 2**: 46
second combination **Vol. 2**: 7, 14, 143, 145
Second Expanded Plenary Session of the Central Executive Committee **Vol. 1**: 39
Second Leap **Vol. 2**: 3, 9, 11–13, 16–17, 20–23, 133–134, 182, 222, 225–226, 310–313, 329, 332, 335–336, 338; **Vol. 3**: 359, 490
Second National Conference of Workers and Peasants **Vol. 1**: 195
Second National Congress of the Chinese Soviet Workers, Peasants, and Soldiers **Vol. 1**: 191, 255; **Vol. 3**: 112
Second National Congress of the Communist Party of China **Vol. 1**: 26–28
Second National Labor Conference **Vol. 1**: 32, 126
Second National Workers, Peasants, and Soldiers Congress **Vol. 1**: 105, 255; **Vol. 3**: 112
Second Revolutionary Civil War **Vol. 1**: 296; **Vol. 3**: 103
Second World War (*see also* World War II) **Vol. 1**: 113; **Vol. 2**: 19, 46, 138, 187, 263–264, 269; **Vol. 3**: 46
Secondary Education, Fifty Articles of **Vol. 2**: 240
Secretariat in Irkutsk **Vol. 1**: 19
seeking truth from facts **Vol. 1**: 294, 379, 388–391, 424, 453–454, 463, 474, 546; **Vol. 2**: 5, 11, 21, 203, 233–234, 243, 245–246, 313, 316, 319, 321, 324–325, 328–329, 336–337; **Vol. 3**: 20, 33–35, 39, 51, 55, 57–58, 60–61, 63, 67, 69, 74, 83–84, 86, 89, 97, 108, 135, 150, 155, 165, 169, 173, 243, 332–333, 336, 338, 344, 359, 393, 472, 525, 549
Selected Works of Mao Zedong **Vol. 1**: 73, 79, 493–494; **Vol. 2**: 29, 315
self-criticism **Vol. 1**: 322, 364, 385–387, 426–428, 430, 432, 436–437, 446–456, 463, 469, 471, 477, 502, 504; **Vol. 2**: 162, 167, 176, 179, 244–246, 249, 283; **Vol. 3**: 55, 57, 280–281, 284, 455–456
semi-colonial, semi-feudal society **Vol. 1**: 3, 50,

72, 91, 96, 99, 110, 115, 133, 173, 376, 392, 431, 509–510, 521, 525, 540
semi-socialist economy **Vol. 2**: 26, 33, 51
separation of Party and government **Vol. 1**: 191; **Vol. 3**: 269–270, 273, 275
September 13 Incident **Vol. 2**: 122, 306
September Letter **Vol. 1**: 178; **Vol. 2**: 122
serving the people wholeheartedly **Vol. 1**: 299–300, 302, 325, 465, 470; **Vol. 3**: 281, 308, 447–448, 459
Seven Thousand People's Congress (*see also* 7,000 People's Congress) **Vol. 2**: 221
Seventh National Congress of the Communist Party of China **Vol. 1**: 410
Seventh Plenum of the Executive Committee of the Comintern **Vol. 1**: 38
Seventh Regiment **Vol. 1**: 354
Seventeenth National Congress of the Communist Party of China **Vol. 3**: 524, 527, 546
Seventh Five-Year Plan **Vol. 3**: 183, 261, 265, 313
Shaanxi Province **Vol. 1**: 324; **Vol. 3**: 101–102
Shaanxi-Gansu-Ningxia Border Region **Vol. 1**: 76, 199, 201, 203–204, 206–209, 211; **Vol. 2**: 30
Shandong Province **Vol. 3**: 38, 84, 88, 450
Shanghai **Vol. 1**: 4, 6, 11, 15–19, 24–26, 34, 56, 58, 61, 155–157, 162, 167, 223, 256, 259–261, 276, 308, 355, 376, 525; **Vol. 2**: 43, 77, 151, 178, 200, 202, 204, 206, 300; **Vol. 3**: 4, 11, 31–32, 49, 66, 74–75, 141, 143, 147, 263, 318, 324, 327, 347, 354, 405–406, 414, 428
Shanghai Association **Vol. 3**: 414
Shanghai Baoshan Iron and Steel Works **Vol. 3**: 49
Shanghai Bureau **Vol. 1**: 259–261
Shanghai Commune **Vol. 2**: 300
Shanghai Communist Party **Vol. 1**: 18
Shanghai Conference **Vol. 2**: 200, 202, 206
Shanghai General League Strike **Vol. 1**: 61
Shanghai Municipal Committee **Vol. 3**: 75
Shanghai Party Organization **Vol. 1**: 18
Shanghai People's Commune **Vol. 3**: 74–75
Shanghai Stock Exchange **Vol. 3**: 406
Shanghai Xinbao Steel Group Company **Vol. 3**: 405
Shangyu County **Vol. 3**: 277
Shanxi Province **Vol. 1**: 160, 202, 234, 249, 251; **Vol. 2**: 71–76, 85, 108, 122; **Vol. 3**: 277
Shanxi Provincial Party Committee **Vol. 2**: 72–73, 76
Shao Lizi **Vol. 1**: 18
Shao Piaoping **Vol. 1**: 10
Shapiro, Sidney **Vol. 3**: 117
Shatian Village **Vol. 1**: 323
Shen Chong **Vol. 1**: 258
Shen Chong Incident **Vol. 1**: 258
Shen Junru **Vol. 1**: 233, 264
Shen Xuanlu **Vol. 1**: 18
Shen Yanbing **Vol. 1**: 18
Shenyang **Vol. 1**: 353; **Vol. 3**: 50
Shenzhen **Vol. 3**: 277–278, 327–328, 349, 354, 406, 468
Shenzhen Stock Exchange **Vol. 3**: 406
Shi Cuntong **Vol. 1**: 18–19
Shi Yousan **Vol. 1**: 239
Shijiazhuang **Vol. 2**: 204
Shijiusuo Port **Vol. 3**: 210
Shu Tong **Vol. 3**: 14
Shuai Mengqi **Vol. 3**: 72
Sichuan Province **Vol. 1**: 234; **Vol. 2**: 233, 249, 328; **Vol. 3**: 66, 79, 103, 109, 154, 277
Sinicization of Marxism (*see also* integrating Marxism into China) **Vol. 2**: 17
Sino-American Civil Aviation Agreement **Vol. 3**: 213
Sino-American Cooperative Organization (SACO) Prison **Vol. 3**: 109
Sino-American Maritime Transport Agreement **Vol. 3**: 213
Sino-American Textile Agreement **Vol. 3**: 213
Sino-British Joint Statement **Vol. 3**: 236
Sino-foreign joint ventures **Vol. 3**: 293
Sino-French War **Vol. 1**: 110
Sino-Japan relations **Vol. 2**: 304
Sino-Japanese Joint Declaration **Vol. 3**: 424
Sino-Japanese Joint Statement **Vol. 3**: 211
Sino-Japanese relations **Vol. 3**: 210–212, 424–425

Sino-Japanese Treaty of Peace and Friendship **Vol. 3**: 211
Sino-Japanese War **Vol. 1**: 4, 110
Sino-Soviet relations **Vol. 2**: 265; **Vol. 3**: 203, 206, 217–218, 221
Sino-Soviet Treaty of Friendship, Alliance, and Mutual Assistance **Vol. 3**: 217
Sino-US Joint Communiqué **Vol. 2**: 304
Sino-US relations **Vol. 2**: 304–305; **Vol. 3**: 206–207, 213, 215, 217, 423
Sixth Anti-Encirclement Campaign **Vol. 1**: 157
Sixteen-Character Principle **Vol. 3**: 133, 465
Sixteenth National Congress of Communist Party of China **Vol. 3**: 498
Sixth Five-Year Plan **Vol. 3**: 183, 261–262
social class **Vol. 1**: 119, 397, 513, 515; **Vol. 3**: 130, 141, 308, 504
Social Democratic Party **Vol. 1**: 111, 371, 397; **Vol. 3**: 102, 308, 504
Socialism **Vol. 1**: 6–10, 12–13, 16, 18, 24–25, 27, 30–31, 50, 54–56, 70, 75–76, 85, 89, 103–108, 111–114, 116–118, 144, 146, 196, 221, 301, 359, 394, 417, 458, 467–468, 498, 507–512, 517, 519–522, 526, 528, 534–538, 543–544; **Vol. 2**: 4–6, 9, 13–15, 17–20, 22, 27–30, 33, 37, 39–41, 43, 45–47, 50, 52, 56, 58–59, 61–62, 70, 72–73, 76, 80, 83, 85–86, 88–91, 94–95, 97–99, 101–103, 105–121, 123–126, 128–139, 142–145, 151–152, 154–155, 158, 164, 169–170, 173–174, 176, 180–182, 184–185, 187–188, 190, 192–193, 195–197, 199–200, 202, 205, 211–214, 216–219, 223, 226, 229–231, 234–236, 242, 245, 253–255, 257–259, 261–262, 264, 266–272, 274–275, 280–281, 284–285, 291, 294, 296–298, 304–306, 308, 311, 320, 325, 327, 329, 332, 334, 336–338; **Vol. 3**: 4–7, 27–28, 36, 58, 91, 93, 110, 115, 129–135, 141–143, 146–147, 150–152, 159, 170–171, 173–174, 181, 184–185, 189, 191–192, 195, 202, 233, 235, 239, 241, 243–258, 266–268, 270, 283, 286, 301, 303, 309, 312, 314–315, 318, 325–340, 343–348, 350–351, 354, 357–369, 371, 380, 382–383, 385–391, 393, 397, 400, 440, 447–448, 458–459, 468, 472–473, 475–476, 482–484, 486–487, 493–494, 504, 511, 513,

523–527, 530–531, 533–535, 540, 544–547, 549–551
socialism with Chinese characteristics **Vol. 1**: 509; **Vol. 2**: 13, 130, 329, 336–338; **Vol. 3**: 4–7, 134, 142, 152, 173–174, 181, 185, 189, 243–244, 246, 255, 257, 268, 286, 301, 303, 314, 318, 325–327, 331, 333–338, 340, 350–351, 357–360, 362, 364–366, 368–369, 371, 380, 382–383, 385–391, 393, 397, 400, 447–448, 459, 468, 472, 475–476, 483–484, 486, 504, 513, 523–527, 531, 533–535, 545–547, 549–551
socialist commodity economy **Vol. 2**: 9; **Vol. 3**: 22, 77, 192, 201, 241, 249, 302, 335
socialist commodity production **Vol. 2**: 15; **Vol. 3**: 21–22
socialist construction **Vol. 1**: 145, 458–459; **Vol. 2**: 5, 7–8, 13, 15, 22–23, 110, 116, 118–120, 128, 134, 136–138, 141, 145–148, 154–155, 158–159, 165–166, 170, 173, 185, 187–188, 190, 192, 195, 197, 201, 209–210, 212, 214, 217, 221, 225, 244, 268, 270–271, 273, 291–292, 308, 325, 328–330, 337; **Vol. 3**: 20, 27, 61, 63, 77, 123, 126, 142, 159, 171–172, 180–181, 184, 188–189, 191, 218, 253, 335–336, 339, 360, 443, 476, 505, 530, 534–535
Socialist Education Movement (*see also* Four Clean-ups) **Vol. 2**: 258, 269, 275, 292; **Vol. 3**: 93
socialist market economic system **Vol. 3**: 5–6, 63, 77, 202, 334, 343, 348–353, 355–357, 366, 370, 379, 384, 409–411, 447, 465–466, 474, 480–481, 484–486, 488–489, 491–496, 499, 501, 507–508, 528, 534
socialist model **Vol. 2**: 12–13, 21, 23, 87, 121, 139–141, 170, 195, 215, 253, 255–256, 271
Socialist Reform **Vol. 2**: 10–11, 13–15, 23, 138–140, 145, 174, 181, 186, 221, 255, 268; **Vol. 3**: 5, 334, 358
Socialist Youth League **Vol. 1**: 25, 214
Some Historical Issues **Vol. 2**: 6; **Vol. 3**: 4, 158–159, 165, 172, 248, 345
Song Baoqi **Vol. 3**: 30
Song Jiaoren **Vol. 1**: 7
Song of the Heart **Vol. 3**: 32
Song Ping **Vol. 3**: 245

Song Qingling **Vol. 1**: 233
Song Renqiong **Vol. 3**: 62, 68, 81, 189
Song Shuo **Vol. 3**: 78–79
Song Zheyuan **Vol. 1**: 234
Song Ziwen (TV Soong) **Vol. 1**: 246
Songjiang County **Vol. 2**: 77
Soong, TV (*see* Song Ziwen)
South Beijing Riot **Vol. 1**: 61
South China Sea **Vol. 3**: 425
Southern Anhui Incident **Vol. 1**: 79
Southern Expedition **Vol. 3**: 71
Southern Talks (Deng Xiaoping) **Vol. 3**: 327–328, 333, 338, 347, 362, 366
sovereignty (Hong Kong) **Vol. 1**: 524; **Vol. 3**: 203, 212, 231, 235–237, 416–417, 421, 426, 519
soviet **Vol. 1**: 7, 43, 48, 51, 53–54, 59, 61, 63, 66, 79, 84, 109, 113, 149–150, 153, 155, 157–160, 164–165, 180, 189, 191–192, 194–197, 224, 227, 230, 232, 304, 341, 351, 432, 458–459, 482, 484, 486, 507–508, 511, 513–514, 528; **Vol. 2**: 5–8, 12–15, 18–21, 23, 27, 40, 44–46, 50, 54–55, 59, 66, 76, 87, 89, 91, 94–95, 97, 102, 105–106, 108–109, 113, 116–122, 124–125, 129–134, 136–145, 147–153, 156, 159–160, 163, 165–166, 173, 184, 187–189, 191–192, 200, 209–211, 213–220, 231, 238, 252–253, 255, 258, 262, 264–268, 271, 274, 287–291, 298, 305, 308, 325; **Vol. 3**: 15, 38, 47, 84, 102–105, 163, 193, 203–206, 208–209, 213, 217–221, 246–247, 326, 347, 423, 437, 512
Soviet Communist Party **Vol. 1**: 51; **Vol. 2**: 12, 44, 50, 109, 124, 139, 141, 143, 163, 166, 184, 209–210, 213, 288–290; **Vol. 3**: 221, 247, 512
Soviet Government of the Workers, Peasants, and Soldiers **Vol. 1**: 189, 255; **Vol. 3**: 112
Soviet Revisionist Group **Vol. 2**: 288–291
Soviet Union **Vol. 1**: 7, 53–54, 66, 84, 109, 113, 149, 180, 232, 511, 513–514; **Vol. 2**: 5–8, 12–15, 20, 23, 40, 45–46, 50, 54, 59, 66, 89, 91, 102, 106, 108, 113, 116–120, 122, 124, 130–134, 137–144, 148–153, 156, 159–160, 165–166, 173, 191–192, 200, 209–211, 213–214, 216–218, 220, 252–253, 255, 265, 287–290, 305, 308, 325; **Vol. 3**: 47, 104, 193, 203–204, 206, 208–209, 213, 217–221, 246–247, 326, 347, 423, 437

Special Article on the Development of Hong Kong Border Sites **Vol. 3**: 234, 416
Special Case Office **Vol. 3**: 71
Special Committee **Vol. 1**: 172, 174; **Vol. 3**: 373
Speech at Chun Qu Zhai (Liu Shaoqi) **Vol. 3**: 10
Speech at the Yan'an Forum on Literature and Art **Vol. 1**: 300; **Vol. 3**: 10
Stalin, Joseph **Vol. 1**: 51, 94, 113, 227, 283, 364, 371, 381, 384, 393, 430–431, 434, 443, 492–493, 507; **Vol. 2**: 6, 18, 91, 109, 118–119, 121–122, 137, 139, 141, 143, 164–165, 209–212, 214–215, 218, 265, 290; **Vol. 3**: 21, 247
Standing Committee **Vol. 1**: 43, 167, 276, 395; **Vol. 2**: 111, 115, 153, 247, 257; **Vol. 3**: 11–12, 38–39, 50, 53–54, 56–57, 62, 75, 119, 137–138, 156–157, 160, 178–180, 189, 217, 226, 228, 230, 245, 269, 273–274, 298–299, 309, 319–321, 324, 331, 373, 376–377, 381, 413, 431, 455–456, 509, 515
State Bureau of Defense Science, Technology, and Industry **Vol. 2**: 304; **Vol. 3**: 176, 211, 539
State Bureau of Foreign Experts **Vol. 3**: 117
State Civil Aviation Administration **Vol. 3**: 539
State Commission for Reform of Sports and Physical Education **Vol. 3**: 450
State Construction Commission **Vol. 3**: 127
State Council **Vol. 2**: 80, 82–83, 152, 156, 188, 245, 249, 301–302, 314, 331, 333; **Vol. 3**: 10, 21–22, 24–25, 28, 40, 46–48, 51–52, 56, 67, 71, 74, 103, 121–122, 125, 127–128, 160, 193–194, 196, 198, 215, 221, 259, 269, 271, 273–274, 276–278, 289–290, 293–294, 297–299, 306, 313, 318–319, 322, 344, 350, 353–355, 373–374, 377, 380–381, 398–399, 406–410, 413, 419, 436, 461–463, 465, 467, 482, 506, 508–509, 511, 519, 536, 538–539
State Economic Commission **Vol. 3**: 322
State Economic Reform Office (Commission for Economic Reform) **Vol. 3**: 194
State Environmental Protection Administration **Vol. 3**: 540
State Environmental Protection Bureau **Vol. 3**: 278

State Food and Drug Administration **Vol. 3**: 540
State General Administration of Labor **Vol. 3**: 23–24
State Personnel Department **Vol. 3**: 278
State Planning Commission **Vol. 2**: 237; **Vol. 3**: 23–24, 196–197, 262, 346
state power **Vol. 1**: 13, 131, 138, 188, 246, 458, 513, 517–518, 520, 522–523, 538; **Vol. 2**: 26, 34, 41, 48–50, 121–122, 196, 223, 292–293, 298
State Tax Administration **Vol. 3**: 278
state-owned enterprises **Vol. 1**: 195, 496; **Vol. 2**: 238–239; **Vol. 3**: 196–197, 349, 351–353, 378, 402–412, 450–451, 460, 464, 489–490, 494, 496
Stirner, Max **Vol. 1**: 6
Straits Exchange Foundation (SEF) **Vol. 3**: 414–415, 419
Strategic military policy in a high-tech environment **Vol. 1**: 182, 341–342; **Vol. 3**: 429
"Strategy for Opposing Japanese Imperialism" **Vol. 1**: 229
strike **Vol. 1**: 25, 36, 47, 58, 61–62, 124, 153, 156, 185, 187, 192, 243, 258, 261, 278, 280; **Vol. 2**: 175; **Vol. 3**: 127, 142, 304
struggle **Vol. 1**: 8, 10–11, 13–15, 20–21, 23–25, 27–37, 41–43, 45–48, 50–52, 54–56, 58–60, 62, 66–68, 70, 78, 80, 82–83, 86, 88–89, 91–92, 100–103, 105–106, 109, 112–113, 115, 119, 122, 125, 129–130, 133–135, 139, 141–142, 144, 146, 149–151, 155, 157–159, 161, 164–166, 169–171, 173–177, 180, 182, 184–187, 189–190, 192, 198, 210, 212, 218–219, 221, 223–224, 230, 232, 234, 236–245, 247–249, 252–254, 257–261, 263, 265, 269, 271, 273–279, 281–291, 293–295, 297, 299–305, 307–309, 311–313, 315, 317, 319–321, 323, 325, 327, 329–333, 335–339, 341, 343, 345, 347, 349, 351–353, 355–359, 361–369, 371–372, 376, 382, 384–386, 388, 391, 394, 396–399, 401, 403, 406, 408, 412, 419, 421, 423, 425–426, 431, 440, 442, 444, 451, 454–458, 461, 464, 466–467, 469–473, 476, 479, 483, 486, 489–491, 501, 504, 509, 512, 521, 525–528, 531, 538, 540–541, 545; **Vol. 2**: 6, 8, 10, 13–14, 20, 28, 33–34, 36–37, 42–43, 45, 47, 49, 53, 59–61, 65, 91–93, 99, 103, 105, 116, 128–129, 135–136, 138, 153, 161–163, 167–168, 170, 173–174, 178–180, 182–187, 189–191, 207, 219, 221, 224, 226, 230–231, 234, 241–242, 244–247, 251–252, 254–259, 265, 268–279, 281, 285–286, 292–299, 301, 303, 307, 309, 312, 314, 316, 321, 325, 333, 335, 338; **Vol. 3**: 4, 11, 17, 32–33, 40, 48, 51, 55, 60, 62–63, 66, 72–73, 80, 85, 88–93, 96, 99, 101, 106, 115, 120–121, 130, 135, 140–141, 143, 152, 160–161, 170, 173, 191, 205, 207, 228, 253–254, 257–258, 261, 264, 283, 299, 307, 311, 319, 323, 332, 362, 368, 390, 415, 418, 429, 431–432, 437–440, 454, 460–461, 464–465, 483, 516, 520, 525, 527, 530–531, 548
Struggle, Criticism, and Reform Campaign **Vol. 1**: 425, 450; **Vol. 2**: 272
Stuart, John Leighton **Vol. 1**: 281
Su Hua **Vol. 1**: 50
Su Jin **Vol. 3**: 104
Su Shuyang **Vol. 3**: 32
Su Yu **Vol. 1**: 327, 351
Su Zhaozheng **Vol. 1**: 39
Sun Yat-sen **Vol. 1**: 3, 7, 24, 93, 111, 126, 224–225; **Vol. 3**: 358
Sun Yifang **Vol. 2**: 9, 307, 309
Sunzi **Vol. 1**: 296
superstructure **Vol. 1**: 131, 137, 468; **Vol. 2**: 4, 70, 81, 113–114, 164, 167–169, 189, 239, 245, 253, 281–283, 293–294, 302, 327, 333, 335; **Vol. 3**: 27, 49–50, 57, 64, 191, 250, 256, 329–330, 498, 503, 543, 547
Supreme State Conference **Vol. 2**: 179, 249
sustainable development **Vol. 3**: 372, 398–400, 485, 490, 496, 501, 503, 505, 542
Suzhou **Vol. 1**: 260
Symposium of the Secretary of Culture and Education **Vol. 3**: 37
Symposium on Implementing the Cadre Policy **Vol. 3**: 84

T
Taiping Heavenly Kingdom **Vol. 1**: 133
Taiping Rebellion **Vol. 1**: 110

Taiwan **Vol. 1**: 228, 534; **Vol. 2**: 55, 61; **Vol. 3**: 56, 132, 181, 206–207, 213–217, 225–234, 413–416, 418–420, 520–522

Taiwan Relations Act **Vol. 3**: 206, 214–215

Taiwan Strait **Vol. 3**: 225–226, 229–230, 413–415, 420

Taiwan Strait Exchange foundation **Vol. 3**: 414

Taiwan's Legal Independence **Vol. 3**: 521

Taiwanese independence **Vol. 3**: 438

Taiyue Corps **Vol. 1**: 352

Taking and managing the cities **Vol. 1**: 453

Tan Pingshan **Vol. 1**: 19, 38–39, 57, 226, 264

Tan Zhenlin **Vol. 1**: 189; **Vol. 2**: 300, 326; **Vol. 3**: 40, 72–73, 81, 189

Tang Aoqing **Vol. 3**: 30

Tang Sheng-chih **Vol. 1**: 38

Tang Shubei **Vol. 3**: 414

Tanggu **Vol. 1**: 354

Tangshan **Vol. 1**: 16, 354; **Vol. 3**: 50

Tangxian County **Vol. 2**: 204

Tao Xingzhi **Vol. 1**: 233

Tao Xisheng **Vol. 1**: 94–95

Tao Zhu **Vol. 1**: 483; **Vol. 3**: 15, 53–54, 72, 81

Taoist temples (in Han areas) **Vol. 3**: 127

Ten Combinations **Vol. 3**: 546, 549

Ten Military Principles **Vol. 1**: 86

Ten-Year Summary (Mao Zedong) **Vol. 2**: 130

Tenth Five-Year Plan **Vol. 3**: 401–402, 482, 508

testing truth **Vol. 2**: 21, 233, 322–323, 326; **Vol. 3**: 20, 35–36, 38–42, 44, 58, 60, 137–138, 153–157, 243, 336, 338

Thatcher, Margaret **Vol. 3**: 231, 235

Thaw Society **Vol. 3**: 143

The Chinese Peasant **Vol. 1**: 33

The Chinese Revolution and the Communist Party of China **Vol. 1**: 7, 20, 34, 37, 50–51, 63, 71, 73–75, 79, 97, 100–101, 103, 107, 114, 122–123, 125, 133, 142, 146, 155, 159, 176, 178, 185, 204, 237, 247, 251, 264, 269, 307, 313, 321, 334, 352, 369, 372, 375–376, 384–385, 387, 400, 410, 412, 427, 436, 442, 444, 454, 474, 483, 499, 508, 514–515, 532, 534, 545; **Vol. 2**: 10, 14, 17, 20, 27, 32, 49, 53, 55, 65, 74, 89–90, 142, 144, 147, 155, 160, 165, 169, 201, 214, 224, 237, 246, 268, 294, 314–315, 327; **Vol. 3**: 4, 11–12, 18, 21, 32, 62–63, 73, 75, 88, 99, 127–128, 139, 149, 168, 170, 195, 200, 208, 213–214, 224, 236, 247, 252–253, 259, 265–266, 270, 278, 283, 317, 327, 330, 355, 371, 375, 411, 427, 431, 433, 448, 466, 499–500, 502, 515, 517

The Communist Manifesto **Vol. 1**: 79, 97, 374, 458; **Vol. 3**: 527

The First Program of the Communist Party of China **Vol. 1**: 20

The History of the Communist Party of the Soviet Union (Bolshevik) **Vol. 2**: 118, 122

the masses **Vol. 1**: 7, 9, 14–15, 20, 24, 34–35, 37, 42, 44, 48, 50–53, 58–59, 63, 71, 73–75, 79, 85–86, 95, 100–101, 108–109, 114, 122, 125, 130–131, 133, 142, 150, 155–156, 159, 168, 171, 173–179, 181, 183, 185, 187, 190–194, 198, 200–201, 204, 207, 210–212, 218, 226, 237, 241–242, 247, 251, 254–255, 258–261, 264, 269–270, 277, 286, 293, 301–307, 310–311, 313, 315, 317, 320–321, 326, 328, 332–335, 337–338, 352, 358, 363, 366, 369, 372, 375–377, 380, 384–385, 387, 389, 393, 396, 400, 402, 404–406, 409–410, 412–413, 415, 417, 419, 424, 426–428, 430, 432, 435–436, 439, 442, 444, 449–450, 454, 456–465, 469–475, 477–480, 483–484, 487, 499, 502, 506, 508, 514–515, 532, 534, 545, 548–549; **Vol. 2**: 9–10, 14, 17, 20, 32, 49, 53, 55, 65, 67, 74, 78, 84, 89–90, 104, 142, 144, 147, 155, 159–163, 165, 169, 175–176, 179, 181, 191, 201, 206, 214, 218–219, 224, 234–237, 241, 244–246, 249, 252, 261, 268–269, 276, 286, 292, 294–295, 297, 301, 303, 305–306, 309, 311–312, 314–318, 327; **Vol. 3**: 4, 10–13, 15, 18–19, 21, 32, 53–54, 58, 62–63, 69, 72–73, 75, 77, 81, 83, 85, 88, 99, 106, 109, 113–114, 121–122, 127–128, 139, 142–143, 146–147, 149–150, 158, 161, 168, 170, 177, 184–185, 195, 200, 202, 208, 213–214, 224, 236, 247, 252–253, 259, 265–266, 270, 272, 278, 281, 283–285, 291, 308–309, 317, 323, 327, 330, 338, 355, 367, 371, 375, 377–378, 393, 411, 427, 431, 433, 447–448, 451, 453, 456–459, 466, 476, 499–500, 502, 515, 517, 531, 547

"The Scars" **Vol. 3**: 31

The Socialist Economic Problems of the Soviet Union **Vol. 2**: 139, 165, 209–211, 213–214, 216, 218
"The United Government" (article) **Vol. 1**: 487
The Weekly Review **Vol. 1**: 18
Theoretical Dynamics **Vol. 2**: 322; **Vol. 3**: 36, 340
Theoretical Education of Cadres **Vol. 2**: 118; **Vol. 3**: 340
theoretical work **Vol. 1**: 37, 72, 78; **Vol. 3**: 137–145, 149, 152, 159, 310, 340
Theory of Continuing Revolution (permanent revolution) **Vol. 1**: 359, 362; **Vol. 2**: 277–279, 281–283, 291, 293–294, 296, 298, 310, 319, 322; **Vol. 3**: 170, 493
theory of descent **Vol. 1**: 359, 362; **Vol. 3**: 493
Third Beijing People's Congress **Vol. 2**: 78
Third Five-Year Plan **Vol. 3**: 254
Third Party **Vol. 1**: 233; **Vol. 3**: 102
Third World **Vol. 2**: 263–264, 305; **Vol. 3**: 128, 206, 260, 268, 426
Thirteenth National Congress of the Communist Party of China **Vol. 2**: 3; **Vol. 3**: 112, 151, 239, 241–242, 249, 266, 273, 289, 303, 327, 335–336, 361, 372, 455
Three Advocates **Vol. 3**: 454–457, 468
Three Great Transformations **Vol. 2**: 266
Three Guarantees **Vol. 3**: 490
Three Major Disciplines and Eight Codes of Behavior **Vol. 1**: 322
Three Major Tasks **Vol. 1**: 245, 298, 304, 306, 312, 318; **Vol. 2**: 125; **Vol. 3**: 181, 207
Three Orientations **Vol. 3**: 390
Three People's Principles **Vol. 1**: 69–71, 77, 106, 109, 264, 529; **Vol. 3**: 227
Three Principles **Vol. 1**: 8, 223, 243, 280, 315–316, 320, 425, 427, 515; **Vol. 3**: 211, 427
Three Represents **Vol. 3**: 6–7, 388, 432, 443, 468–477, 479, 483–484, 487, 462, 500, 502, 504, 514–515, 524–526, 533, 551
Three Rules for Discipline and Eight Points for Attention (*see* Three Major Disciplines and Eight Codes of Behavior) **Vol. 1**: 312
Tian Jiaying **Vol. 2**: 204, 231
Tian Jiyun **Vol. 3**: 245
Tian Zengpei **Vol. 3**: 219
Tiananmen Incident (April 5th Movement) **Vol. 2**: 316; **Vol. 3**: 9–12, 15, 53–54
Tiananmen Poetry **Vol. 3**: 11
Tiananmen Square **Vol. 3**: 11–12, 142, 323
Tianjin **Vol. 1**: 18, 34, 256, 353–354, 356; **Vol. 2**: 42–44, 59, 70, 204–205; **Vol. 3**: 50, 143, 157, 451
Tianjin speech (Liu Shaoqi) **Vol. 2**: 43–44, 59, 70
Tianjin Way **Vol. 1**: 356
Tibet **Vol. 2**: 55, 61, 201; **Vol. 3**: 116, 123–125, 127, 226
Tomb-Sweeping Day **Vol. 2**: 316; **Vol. 3**: 11, 54
Tong Dalin **Vol. 3**: 139, 199
Tong Dizhou **Vol. 3**: 30
Top Documents **Vol. 3**: 338
Torui Huko **Vol. 3**: 241
Touring Europe (Liang Qichao article) **Vol. 1**: 5
Township People's Congress **Vol. 1**: 515
Trade Union **Vol. 1**: 219; **Vol. 3**: 49
Training and Selection of Excellent Young Cadres **Vol. 3**: 459
transition to socialism **Vol. 1**: 105, 512; **Vol. 2**: 5, 30, 37, 56, 59, 70, 76, 85–86, 89–90, 95, 97–99, 102–103, 105–113, 115–117, 120–121, 124–125, 136
tribalism **Vol. 2**: 157
Trotsky Doctrine Incident **Vol. 3**: 105–106
Trotskyists **Vol. 1**: 95, 116; **Vol. 3**: 84, 105, 106
Tsinghua University **Vol. 3**: 317, 434
Turati, Filippo **Vol. 1**: 430
Twelfth Five-Year Plan **Vol. 3**: 550–551
Twelfth National Congress of the Communist Party of China **Vol. 3**: 133, 174, 180, 182, 194–195, 248, 254, 262, 280, 287, 312, 345
Two Directions **Vol. 1**: 61
"Two Step" System **Vol. 1**: 103
Two Theories **Vol. 1**: 389, 391; **Vol. 2**: 25
Two Whatevers **Vol. 2**: 317, 319, 336–337; **Vol. 3**: 55, 173

U

Ulanhu **Vol. 3**: 189

ultra-Leftist **Vol. 2**: 10, 314–315; **Vol. 3**: 30, 79, 92, 150, 156, 175
UN Human Rights Commission **Vol. 3**: 426
Underground Party Organizations **Vol. 3**: 80, 97
UNFPA **Vol. 3**: 225
UNICEF **Vol. 3**: 225
United Front **Vol. 1**: 27, 29, 33, 40–41, 43, 49–51, 66, 71, 74–75, 78–83, 87–88, 93, 108–109, 123, 137, 141–142, 198–201, 204, 210, 213–221, 223, 225, 227–241, 243–247, 249, 251–269, 271, 280, 283, 289, 300, 309, 368, 371–372, 400, 425, 469, 483, 487–488, 491, 511, 514–516, 526–527, 539, 542, 547; **Vol. 2**: 30, 49, 53–54, 59, 62, 64, 79–81, 87, 92, 129–130, 153–154, 157–158, 170, 239, 249–250, 302, 305, 320; **Vol. 3**: 67, 80, 82, 89–90, 106, 111, 113, 118–122, 126, 128–134, 204, 339, 360, 373, 375, 469
United Front Ministry **Vol. 2**: 80, 249; **Vol. 3**: 126
United Front Work Conference **Vol. 1**: 511; **Vol. 2**: 79, 92, 250; **Vol. 3**: 129–131, 133, 217, 375, 469
United Nations **Vol. 2**: 304; **Vol. 3**: 220–221, 224–225, 426–427, 518–519, 521
United States Navy **Vol. 3**: 226
university enrollment **Vol. 3**: 17
Unjust and False Cases **Vol. 3**: 12–17, 61, 66, 68–70, 82–85, 92, 95, 100, 110, 114, 118, 175
Unjust, False, and Wrong Charges **Vol. 3**: 66, 85
urban center **Vol. 1**: 60, 158, 161
Urban Residents' Committee **Vol. 1**: 60
urban work **Vol. 1**: 60, 83, 154, 156, 158, 165–166, 186–187, 494–498; **Vol. 2**: 42, 58–59; **Vol. 3**: 451
US-Taiwan Joint Defense Treaty **Vol. 3**: 214
utopian **Vol. 2**: 69, 73, 76, 193, 196, 212, 284, 298; **Vol. 3**: 329, 533

V
vanguard of the proletariat **Vol. 1**: 308, 419, 421, 429, 431, 433–435, 438, 458, 466, 470–471; **Vol. 2**: 295

Vietnam War **Vol. 2**: 263; **Vol. 3**: 203
Villagers' Committee **Vol. 3**: 377
Voitinsky, Grigori **Vol. 1**: 17–18, 40

W
Wall of Democracy **Vol. 1**: 310; **Vol. 3**: 142–143, 145, 147
Wallace, Mike **Vol. 3**: 288
Wan Li **Vol. 3**: 124–125, 189, 245, 320
Wang Bingnan **Vol. 1**: 234
Wang Congwu **Vol. 3**: 189, 288
Wang Daohan **Vol. 3**: 414, 419
Wang Dongxing **Vol. 3**: 10–11, 23, 26, 37–38, 63, 70
Wang Feng **Vol. 1**: 234
Wang Guangmei **Vol. 3**: 72
Wang Heshou **Vol. 3**: 62, 189
Wang Hongwen **Vol. 2**: 313
Wang Jiaxiang **Vol. 1**: 238, 482, 484; **Vol. 2**: 252
Wang Jingwei **Vol. 1**: 38, 115, 217–218, 222, 239
Wang Jinmei **Vol. 1**: 19
Wang Ming **Vol. 1**: 65–67, 105, 157, 159, 195, 232, 280, 285, 401, 408, 420, 482
Wang Minglu **Vol. 1**: 62
Wang Ninzhi **Vol. 3**: 199
Wang Renzhong **Vol. 3**: 15, 62, 72, 81, 289
Wang Ruowang **Vol. 3**: 316, 318
Wang Shao'ao **Vol. 1**: 264
Wang Xuewen **Vol. 3**: 192
Wang Xuren **Vol. 3**: 105
Wang Yitang **Vol. 1**: 239
Wang Youping **Vol. 3**: 104
Wang Zhen **Vol. 3**: 11, 49, 62, 189, 289
Wang Zhuo **Vol. 3**: 197–198
Wang-Gu Talks **Vol. 3**: 414, 418
War Against Japanese Aggression **Vol. 1**: 130, 297–298, 549
war of aggression **Vol. 1**: 135, 290, 297–298, 400, 549; **Vol. 3**: 204
War of Liberation **Vol. 1**: 85, 87–88, 130, 136–137, 188, 244–245, 248, 255, 262–263, 265, 267, 269, 271, 284–285, 297–298, 305, 311, 317, 320–321, 324, 328–329, 334, 337–338, 342, 344, 346–347, 350–351, 355, 372, 388, 403, 410, 421, 433, 467,

477, 494, 531, 534, 549; **Vol. 2**: 32, 41, 49; **Vol. 3**: 240
War of Resistance Against Japanese Aggression **Vol. 1**: 66–67, 69–70, 72, 79–85, 106, 108, 110, 115, 130–131, 135, 137, 183–184, 186, 198, 200, 202, 204–206, 209–211, 228–229, 231, 240–242, 244, 246–247, 249, 253, 261–262, 267, 279–282, 284–285, 289–290, 297–298, 300, 305, 308, 311, 319, 321, 326, 334, 337, 341, 344, 368, 371, 385, 401–402, 421, 433, 439, 459, 466–467, 486, 493, 500, 526, 528, 532–533, 535, 539, 549; **Vol. 2**: 29, 38, 49, 97, 99, 271; **Vol. 3**: 227, 247, 286
War of Resistance Against US Aggression and Aid to North Korea (*see* Korean War) **Vol. 2**: 99
warlord bureaucrats **Vol. 1**: 26, 98, 135
warlords **Vol. 1**: 4–5, 23–27, 30–32, 34, 36, 40, 56, 92, 100, 105, 120–122, 124–125, 127, 134–137, 150, 171, 173, 185, 214, 216, 226, 274–275, 278, 292–293, 467, 533
Wayaobao Meeting **Vol. 1**: 160, 508
wealthy peasant (*see also* rich peasant) **Vol. 1**: 54, 62, 129, 138, 144, 201, 250–255, 270, 529–532; **Vol. 3**: 112
Wei Guofan **Vol. 3**: 299
Wei Guoqing **Vol. 3**: 137, 189
Wei Jingsheng **Vol. 3**: 143
Wen Jiabao **Vol. 3**: 245, 502, 518
Wenhui Newspaper **Vol. 3**: 31
West Lake Conference **Vol. 1**: 224
Western Enlightenment **Vol. 1**: 5
Western Marxism **Vol. 2**: 18
Westernization **Vol. 3**: 241, 249, 365
Whampoa Military Academy **Vol. 1**: 40
White Area **Vol. 1**: 82–83, 89, 257
White regime **Vol. 1**: 170–171, 173, 332
White Terror **Vol. 1**: 47, 411; **Vol. 3**: 97
wholeheartedly serve the people **Vol. 1**: 447, 460–461
Work and Mutual Aid Group **Vol. 1**: 14
Work of Mixed and Diaspora Ethnic Minorities **Vol. 3**: 121
work style (Party style) **Vol. 1**: 367–368, 380, 388, 428–434, 436–440, 446, 455–456, 462, 471, 478, 488, 505; **Vol. 2**: 180; **Vol. 3**: 111, 444, 461
Workers and Peasants League (Workers' and Peasants' Alliance) **Vol. 1**: 33, 195, 249, 470, 548
Workers and Peasants' Revolutionary Army **Vol. 1**: 548
Workers' Picket Corps **Vol. 1**: 36, 470
working class (*see also* proletariat) Vol 1: 9, 15, 17, 20, 32–34, 36, 45, 53, 72, 74, 87–89, 100, 115, 117, 120–125, 127, 131, 139, 141, 149, 154, 162, 185, 195, 219, 263, 268–269, 271, 276, 300, 321, 357, 360, 371, 373–378, 394, 420–421, 431, 433, 458, 461, 471, 495–497, 499, 501, 504, 517, 519, 538, 543; **Vol. 2**: 17, 30, 39, 41–43, 48–50, 53, 58, 83–84, 87, 91–92, 94, 105, 113, 119, 121, 126–127, 129, 136, 155, 159, 165, 170, 177, 183; **Vol. 3**: 20, 110, 129–130, 185, 337, 365, 367, 412, 440, 451, 468, 474
World Bank **Vol. 3**: 205, 224
World Federation of Taiwan Fellow Citizens **Vol. 3**: 419
World Multi-polarization and the Establishment of a New International Order **Vol. 3**: 424
World Trade Organization (WTO) **Vol. 3**: 357, 427
World War I (*see also* First World War) **Vol. 1**: 4–6, 108, 542
World War II (*see also* Second World War) **Vol. 1**: 117; **Vol. 2**: 113, 274; **Vol. 3**: 138
Worldwide Proletarian Socialist Revolution **Vol. 1**: 113, 544
Wu Bangguo **Vol. 3**: 409
Wu Guozhen **Vol. 1**: 260
Wu Jiang **Vol. 3**: 139
Wu Jichang **Vol. 3**: 30
Wu Lengxi **Vol. 2**: 204; **Vol. 3**: 139
Wu Peifu **Vol. 1**: 214
Wu Yuzhang **Vol. 1**: 257, 492
Wu Zhonghua **Vol. 3**: 30
Wuchang **Vol. 2**: 199, 205–206, 215; **Vol. 3**: 327
Wuchang Conference **Vol. 2**: 199, 206, 215
Wuhan **Vol. 1**: 19, 58, 60–61, 69, 155–156, 223,

355, 376; **Vol. 2**: 214; **Vol. 3**: 72–73, 112, 143, 277, 410
Wuhan Kuomintang government **Vol. 1**: 223
Wuhan-Changsha Railway **Vol. 1**: 61
Wuhan Military Region Party Committee **Vol. 3**: 73

X

Xi Maozhao **Vol. 3**: 109
Xi Zhongxun **Vol. 3**: 62, 72, 81, 100–102, 189
Xi'an **Vol. 1**: 235–236, 282; **Vol. 3**: 101–102, 401, 410
Xi'an Incident **Vol. 1**: 235–236, 282
Xiamen University **Vol. 3**: 193
Xiao Chunu **Vol. 1**: 102
Xiao Jinguang **Vol. 3**: 288
Xibaipo **Vol. 2**: 32
Xidan Wall of Democracy **Vol. 3**: 142–143
Xie Fuzhi **Vol. 3**: 54
Xie Huimin **Vol. 3**: 30
Xie Minggan **Vol. 3**: 199
Xie Weijun **Vol. 1**: 158
Xie Xide **Vol. 3**: 30
Xikou **Vol. 3**: 227
Xin Douyin **Vol. 1**: 276
Xinhai Revolution **Vol. 1**: 3–4
Xinhua Gate **Vol. 3**: 143
Xinhua News Agency **Vol. 2**: 323; **Vol. 3**: 12, 36, 38, 53, 109, 113, 117, 276
Xinjiang **Vol. 1**: 356; **Vol. 2**: 55; **Vol. 3**: 15, 116, 122, 125
Xinmin Congbao **Vol. 1**: 7
Xinxiang **Vol. 2**: 204
Xishan Conference **Vol. 1**: 225
Xiuwu **Vol. 2**: 204
Xu Chi **Vol. 3**: 29
Xu Jun **Vol. 3**: 299
Xu Kexiang **Vol. 1**: 276
Xu Qian **Vol. 3**: 179, 288
Xu Qianfu **Vol. 3**: 189
Xu Qianqian **Vol. 3**: 33, 73, 76, 188–189
Xu Shiyou **Vol. 3**: 189
Xu Xiangqian **Vol. 2**: 300
Xue Muqiao **Vol. 3**: 193, 195

Xushui County **Vol. 2**: 204
Xuzhou **Vol. 1**: 354

Y

Yagodin, Gennadiy **Vol. 2**: 290
Yan Xishan **Vol. 1**: 234
Yan'an **Vol. 1**: 71–73, 76, 106, 116, 199, 210, 230, 232, 240, 281, 300, 366–369, 380, 386–387, 389, 391, 393, 400, 402, 410, 412, 421, 426, 433–434, 437, 439, 448, 482, 484–485, 539, 548; **Vol. 2**: 176–177; **Vol. 3**: 79–80, 104, 155, 457
Yan'an Cadre Conference **Vol. 1**: 281
Yan'an Cadre Trial Campaign **Vol. 3**: 79
Yan'an Rectification Movement **Vol. 1**: 367–368, 380, 386–387, 389, 391, 402, 410, 421, 433–434, 437, 439, 448, 484–485; **Vol. 2**: 176; **Vol. 3**: 155, 457
Yan'an Senior Cadre Conference **Vol. 1**: 199
Yang Anan **Vol. 1**: 9
Yang Dezhi **Vol. 3**: 189
Yang Hucheng **Vol. 1**: 234; **Vol. 3**: 79
Yang Jingren **Vol. 3**: 119
Yang Liyu **Vol. 3**: 232
Yang Mingzhai **Vol. 1**: 18
Yang Qixian **Vol. 3**: 193, 199, 201
Yang Rudai **Vol. 3**: 245
Yang Shangkun **Vol. 3**: 54, 81, 189, 221, 245
Yang Xiguang **Vol. 3**: 12, 35
Yang Yong **Vol. 3**: 189
Yang Zhong **Vol. 3**: 299
Yang, Yu, and Fu **Vol. 3**: 66
Yangtze River **Vol. 1**: 51, 221, 249, 355, 534; **Vol. 2**: 63; **Vol. 3**: 263
Yanshi Railway **Vol. 3**: 210
Yantai **Vol. 3**: 88
Yao Wenyuan **Vol. 2**: 278, 280; **Vol. 3**: 23, 74–75, 100
Yao Yilin **Vol. 3**: 49, 63, 189, 245
Yasukuni Shrine **Vol. 3**: 212
Ye Jianying **Vol. 1**: 231; **Vol. 2**: 300, 317, 324; **Vol. 3**: 11, 14, 57, 73, 104, 137–138, 158, 160–161, 165, 179, 186, 188–189, 230–231, 248, 288, 310, 363, 415
Ye Qing **Vol. 1**: 70, 77

Yellow River **Vol. 1**: 351–352
Yeltsin, Boris **Vol. 3**: 424
Yichang **Vol. 3**: 85
Yokohama Ohira **Vol. 3**: 212
Yongcheng County **Vol. 3**: 90
young and middle-aged cadres **Vol. 3**: 187, 286–287, 290–291
Young Pioneers **Vol. 1**: 334
Youth Magazine (New Youth) **Vol. 1**: 4
Yu Guangyuan **Vol. 3**: 24–25, 28, 139, 199
Yu Lijin **Vol. 3**: 75–76
Yu Muming **Vol. 3**: 521
Yu Qiuli **Vol. 3**: 189
Yu Xiusong **Vol. 1**: 18
Yuan Mu **Vol. 3**: 199
Yuan Shikai **Vol. 1**: 4, 134
Yuan Xuezu **Vol. 3**: 104
Yuanping County **Vol. 3**: 277
Yugoslavian nationalists **Vol. 1**: 113
Yulin **Vol. 1**: 352
Yun Daiying **Vol. 1**: 21, 29, 102, 274, 464
Yunnan Province **Vol. 1**: 160, 176–177, 234; **Vol. 3**: 79, 96–97, 116, 125
Yuquan Mountain **Vol. 3**: 199
Yusui Soviet Area **Vol. 1**: 351

Z

Zedong School for Young Cadres **Vol. 1**: 279; **Vol. 2**: 336
Zeng Qinghong **Vol. 3**: 502
Zeng Tao **Vol. 3**: 12
Zeng Zhi **Vol. 1**: 79
Zenko Suzuki **Vol. 3**: 210
Zhang Bojun **Vol. 1**: 233, 264
Zhang Chunqiao **Vol. 2**: 280, 294, 313; **Vol. 3**: 23, 74–75
Zhang Dongsun **Vol. 1**: 11–12
Zhang Guangdou **Vol. 3**: 30
Zhang Guotao **Vol. 1**: 14, 17–20, 502; **Vol. 3**: 33
Zhang Jieqing **Vol. 3**: 72
Zhang Luping **Vol. 3**: 109
Zhang Naiqi **Vol. 1**: 233
Zhang Pinghua **Vol. 3**: 39
Zhang Ruxin **Vol. 1**: 483

Zhang Shenfu **Vol. 1**: 18–19
Zhang Shizhao **Vol. 3**: 227
Zhang Tingfa **Vol. 3**: 189
Zhang Wentian **Vol. 1**: 50, 68, 71, 95, 195, 230–231, 367, 537–538; **Vol. 2**: 9, 35–36, 306–307, 309; **Vol. 3**: 81, 91
Zhang Xueliang **Vol. 1**: 234
Zhang Zhen **Vol. 3**: 431
Zhang Zhiyi **Vol. 3**: 107
Zhang Zhizhong **Vol. 1**: 249
Zhang Zuolin **Vol. 1**: 214
Zhangqiu **Vol. 3**: 450
Zhao Bosheng **Vol. 3**: 104
Zhao Cangbi **Vol. 3**: 71
Zhao Puchu **Vol. 3**: 127
Zhao Shiyan **Vol. 1**: 19, 276
Zhao Yimin **Vol. 3**: 72
Zhao Ziyang **Vol. 3**: 179, 189, 199–200, 210–211, 215, 221, 224, 240, 242, 245, 324
Zhejiang Province **Vol. 1**: 177–178, 420; **Vol. 2**: 204, 233; **Vol. 3**: 53, 79, 263, 277, 455
Zheng Bijian **Vol. 3**: 199
Zheng Boke **Vol. 3**: 96
Zheng Shaowen **Vol. 3**: 107
Zheng Weisan **Vol. 3**: 107–108
Zheng Zhenduo **Vol. 1**: 5
Zhengding County **Vol. 2**: 204
Zhengzhou Conference **Vol. 2**: 199–202, 204–206, 213–214, 226, 230–231, 236
Zhengzhou Railway Administration **Vol. 3**: 298
Zhongnanhai **Vol. 3**: 143, 196, 199, 380
Zhongshan Warship Incident **Vol. 1**: 221, 226–227
Zhou Enlai **Vol. 1**: 19, 29, 35–36, 57, 71, 102, 178, 181, 231, 234, 257, 259–260, 262, 274, 276, 307, 382, 399, 410, 434, 464, 485, 493, 511; **Vol. 2**: 11, 53, 55–56, 59, 79–80, 82, 86, 92, 111, 115, 142, 147–151, 153–154, 156, 188, 193, 207, 212, 216, 233–234, 237, 245, 249, 251, 254, 260, 299–302, 304–305, 309–310; **Vol. 3**: 11, 32, 74, 226–227, 254
Zhou Fuhai **Vol. 1**: 19
Zhou Hui **Vol. 3**: 62
Zhou Yang **Vol. 3**: 139

Zhu De **Vol. 1**: 175, 231, 234, 238, 288, 299, 304, 328, 334, 338, 461–462, 484, 493, 499; **Vol. 2**: 233, 246; **Vol. 3**: 74
Zhu Muzhi **Vol. 3**: 139
Zhu Wushan **Vol. 1**: 17
Zhu Xuefan **Vol. 1**: 245
Zhu Zhixin **Vol. 1**: 7
Zhuang Autonomous Region **Vol. 3**: 284
Zhuhai **Vol. 3**: 327
Zhuo Jiong **Vol. 3**: 193
Zhuozi Mountain **Vol. 3**: 277
Zong Fu **Vol. 3**: 11
Zong Fuxian **Vol. 3**: 32
Zou Taofen **Vol. 1**: 233
Zunyi Conference (Zunyi Meeting) **Vol. 1**: 63, 84, 159, 182, 285, 311, 364, 366, 379, 421, 482, 485; **Vol. 3**: 285

Numbers

17th Route Army **Vol. 1**: 234
1911 Revolution **Vol. 1**: 25, 33, 92, 134; **Vol. 3**: 234, 358, 416
26th Route Army **Vol. 3**: 104
3-3 System **Vol. 1**: 199–200, 262
57th Army **Vol. 1**: 234
61 traitors (61 People's Case) **Vol. 3**: 74
7/20 Incident **Vol. 3**: 72–73
7,000 People's Congress (*see* Seven Thousand People's Congress) **Vol. 2**: 243, 246–247, 249–254, 256–257

ABOUT THE AUTHOR

ZHENG QIAN was born in 1949 in Beijing. He is a researcher, former director of the No. 2 Research Department of the Party History Research Office of the CPC Central Committee, director of the Chinese Communist Party Literature Research Association, and an expert entitled to the special government allowances granted by the State Council. Long engaged in the study of the history of the CPC and the People's Republic of China, he is the chief author and chief editor of *The History of the Communist Party of China* (Volume II) and has participated in the compilation of *Resolutions on Several Historical Issues of the Party since the founding of the People's Republic of China*. His publications include *Research on Mao Zedong Thought in the Socialist Period*, *From the Cultural Revolution to Reform*, *"Revolutionized" Education: Educational Revolution in the Cultural Revolution*, *History of the People's Republic of China*, *Development History of the Guiding Thought of the Communist Party of China*, *China in Mao Zedong Era*, and *Mao Zedong and Deng Xiaoping*, as well as multiple papers.

ABOUT THE TRANSLATORS

SUN LI is a professor of English Literature, Language, and Translation at Shanghai International Studies University, where she has taught since 1992. Her work includes translation, editing, and teaching. She has been involved in numerous translations of academic and literary writing, and has been a part of the editorial team for the The Cambridge History of American Literature and The New Century Multi-functional English-Chinese Dictionary. Her most recent translation projects include translation of A New Way Forward for Tibet (National University of Singapore Press) and editing the Chinese translation of Journey to the Beginning of the World (Rapscallion Press).

SHELLY BRYANT divides her year between Shanghai and Singapore, working as a poet, writer, and translator. She is the author of nine volumes of poetry (Alban Lake and Math Paper Press), a pair of travel guides for the cities of Suzhou and Shanghai (Urbanatomy), a book on classical Chinese gardens (Hong Kong University Press), and a short story collection (Epigram Books). She has translated work from the Chinese for Penguin Books, Epigram Publishing, the National Library Board in Singapore, Giramondo Publishing, HSRC, and Rinchen Books, and edited poetry anthologies for Alban Lake and Celestial Books. Shelly's poetry has appeared in journals, magazines, and websites around the world, as well as in several art exhibitions. Her translation of Sheng Keyi's Northern Girls was long-listed for the Man Asian Literary Prize in 2012, and her translation of You Jin's In Time, Out of Place was shortlisted for the Singapore Literature Prize in 2016. Shelly received a Distinguished Alumna Award from Oklahoma Christian University of Science and Arts in 2017.